Call and Response

Call and Response

Biblical Foundations of a Theology of Evangelism

Walter Klaiber

Translated by
Howard Perry-Trauthig
and
James A. Dwyer

Nashville
Abingdon Press

CALL AND RESPONSE:
BIBLICAL FOUNDATIONS OF A THEOLOGY OF EVANGELISM

Originally published as *Ruf und Antwort: Biblische Grundlagen einer Theologie der Evangelisation*, copyright © 1990 by Christliches Verlagshaus GmbH, Stuttgart, and Neukirchener Verlag, Neukirchen-Vluyn, Germany.

English translation copyright © 1997 by Abingdon Press.

Library of Congress Cataloging-in-Publication Data

Klaiber, Walter.
    [Ruf und Antwort. English.]
    Call and response: biblical foundations of a theology of evangelism /
Walter Klaiber: translated by Howard Perry-Trauthig and James A. Dwyer
       p. cm.
    Includes bibliographical references and indexes.
    ISBN 0-687-04602-5 (alk. paper)
    1. Evangelistic work.   I. Title.
BV3793.K4313   1997
266´.001—DC21   97-20335
                                                       CIP

Unless otherwise noted, all Scripture quotations are from the New Revised Standard Version Bible, copyright © 1989 by the Division of Christian Education of the National Council of the Churches of Christ in the USA. Used by permission.

Scripture quotations marked RSV are from the Revised Standard Version of the Bible, copyright © 1946, 1952, 1971 by the Division of Christian Education of the National Council of the Churches of Christ in the USA. Used by permission.

Scripture quotations marked NJB are from *The New Jerusalem Bible*, copyright © 1985, 1990 by Darton, Longman & Todd, Ltd., and Doubleday, a division of Bantam Doubleday Dell Publishing Group, Inc. Used by permission.

This book is printed on recycled, acid-free, elemental-chlorine–free paper.

97 98 99 000 01 02 03 04 05 06—10 9 8 7 6 5 4 3 2 1

MANUFACTURED IN THE UNITED STATES OF AMERICA

CONTENTS

13.43/

98715

Foreword to the English Edition

This book intends to serve the cause of mutual understanding and reconciliation. The understanding I have in mind is that between evangelistic proclamation and theological reflection; the reconciliation I mean is that between the task of proclaiming the gospel to humankind in the clearest and most unambiguous manner and the necessity, shared with those people in the synagogue of Berea, to return to examine the Scriptures with new precision and a critical view to ascertain "whether these things were so" (Acts 17:11).

Perhaps for this very reason, some will perceive this book as a challenge to their own thinking. Questions from exegetical and systematic theological studies will find thorough and careful treatment. A plenitude of secondary literature—primarily from German-language sources—will be discussed and quoted. But the opinions of those who exert themselves for the sake of the gospel will also find thorough presentation—regardless of whether they can be classified as more evangelical, more charismatic, "mainstream," or even fundamentalist in their orientation. Even aspects of sociological and psychological studies of the phenomena related to evangelization will be included in our purview. For some, the one side or the other would perhaps be fully sufficient. But the point is to bring divergent views into conversation with one another, to understand one another, and—if somehow possible—to come to a reconciliation of differing viewpoints.

Above all, the task before us is that of making the gospel accessible to people of today. It is my hope that this book may provide foundational work for this task. It is intended to present the content of the message which has been given us in God's gospel in as clear a way as possible and in as careful a way as necessary. I am very pleased that recent exegetical and theological studies make it possible to do this in such a way as to answer the questions of what we may, and what we must, say to people today about the gospel.

Since the publication of the original German edition of this book, discussions about evangelization have continued, especially in theological studies in the United States. I have gratefully added a number of notes to the translation referring to recent publications, and hope that the translation of this book may contribute to these discussions.

9

Although the process of translation of this book has taken a relatively long time, I believe that its theme and content remain of immediate concern and relevance. I would like to express my thanks to the two translators, Howard Perry-Trauthig and James Dwyer, for their work. The editorial staff of Abingdon Press helped make a readable book out of the original manuscript, and a number of others contributed to the book's development. Thanks are due especially to my friend, Professor Geoffrey Wainwright of Duke University, for his help in finding the English originals or translations from my originally German sources, and to my son, Christoph, and my secretary, Barbara Schicker, for their help in creating the index and in tending to the many small details that are so necessary for such a book.

To my thanks to God, I add my petition that this book may offer help and encouragement to the many who ask how we can and should hand on the gospel of Jesus Christ today.

Walter Klaiber

Foreword to the German Edition

Almost everyone is talking about evangelism. Whoever observes the continuing secularization and "de-churching" of the previously Christian Western world, whoever sees the many people in our society who in spite of external affluence are insecure and die spiritually as a result, whoever suffers because of the indifference of many of his or her peers towards the gospel, simply must consider how the good news of Jesus Christ can be lived and proclaimed so that it might become a helping and saving message for people in our time. The dream of a Christian society is over. Today we must steadfastly strive to convince every single individual to be able to lead him or her to faith.

At a time of decreasing membership in most churches and Christian groups, many see in evangelism simply the question of the survival of the existing institutions. "Evangelize or perish!" was a much quoted slogan of the evangelism movement.[1] That of course led to a conflict of motivations. For is the foundation and goal of missionary activity the salvation of the neighbor or the continued existence of one's own group? Or are they not alternatives at all? In 1 Corinthians 9:22ff. after the sentence, "I have become all things to all men, that I might by all means save some. . . ." Paul oddly adds a second sentence, "I do it all for the sake of the gospel, that I may share in its blessings."

If we take the latter statement seriously, then evangelism is not only a rescue operation for people who would otherwise be lost, and under no circumstances only membership recruitment for a certain institution, but also above all a question of spiritual survival for Christianity itself. For only the active transmission of the gospel in the horizon of worldwide missionary activity preserves for Christianity the connection to the cycle of divine life which circulates in interaction between a proclamation, which again and again crosses boundaries, and the wonder of faith.

But how *evangel-like* (German: *evangelisch*) is evangelism?[2] Not everyone asks so pointedly, but for many Protestants this is the decisive question. Does not conventional evangelism have more to do with law than with gospel? Further questions follow: How *biblical* is evangelism? Do biblical texts or themes and experiences or indeed the person or the personal trustworthiness of the evangelist play the decisive role? And above all, how *pastoral* is evangelism? Is the call to decision helpful and compassionate, or does it make people uncertain because it focuses their attention on what they have to do by themselves?[3]

Sometimes we encounter people who describe themselves as "evangelism-injured" because they feel themselves manipulated or overpowered by an evangelistic preaching that they consider too legalistic, too threatening or too pushy. Are such experiences unavoidable side effects of invasive methods of preaching, and what conclusions for their use are to be drawn from such experiences? Are they symptoms presented as an excuse for the fundamental refusal of the claim of the word of God and therefore the responsibility of those who put them forward as pretexts? Do they rest upon technical mistakes of overzealous evangelists, and are they therefore avoidable by a preaching practice that is formed in a manner theologically more compatible with the gospel? Or must we pursue entirely different forms of missionary speech and activity of the church in which elements like the call to decision or repentance have to be given up in favor of an unobtrusive presence of a life for others?

The necessity and the questionable nature of evangelism confront one another directly, and this demands thorough theological reflection. What are the biblical bases of evangelism? Can heeding these help us to evangelize in an *evangel-like* (German: *evangelisch*) manner, i.e. in accordance with the gospel? Must we not conversely also learn something from sociological and psychological investigations of conversion sermons and conversion to avoid preaching *de facto* law despite verbal faithfulness to the biblical gospel because we exercise psychological force?

The critical accompaniment of the theologian should offer such reflections to those who evangelize. But it is even more important to me to persuade those who regard evangelism skeptically to orient themselves by the fundamental biblical commission, and not to form their opinion on the basis of some problematic isolated examples. I would like to encourage them, on the basis of the gospel, to participate or to support in an original way in the tasks of evangelistic preaching.

To this end I have collected and revised material and thoughts which arose in the preparation of a series of seminars during my work as professor of New Testament at the Theological Seminary of the United Methodist Church in Reutlingen, Germany. Originally I planned to pursue the dialog with the literature in practical and systematic theology very much more extensively. But since new responsibilities let it appear doubtful that there will be enough time for that task in the coming years, I would like here at least to present for discussion important biblical principles of a theology of evangelism.

As a gesture of thanks, I would like to dedicate this book to the colleagues and students of the Theological Seminary of The United Methodist Church in Reutlingen who worked with me on these questions in interdisciplinary seminars.

Chapter 1

The Meanings and Meaning of "Evangelism"

What does evangelism mean? A brief survey of theologians and non-theologians would show us quite clearly that the word evangelism is used with a wide variety of meanings. A host of variants ranging from a general term for all missionary activity to an expression for a certain kind of pietistic-evangelical event comes to mind. Thus it is necessary to specify what we mean by "evangelism" in this investigation.

The Understanding of Evangelism in History

Cynics maintain that a German-language academic investigation must begin with either the history of the object under investigation or a definition of terms. If we want to provide a suitable foundation for a systematic-theological treatment of evangelism, we must consider both, for as Heinrich Rendtorff establishes, "The current usual pregnant sense of the term evangelism arises from its history."[1] Oddly enough the only thorough, historical investigation of the term is to be found in Anglo-Saxon theology, while the German-language accounts of the history of evangelism offer practically no information about the historical use of the term.

David B. Barrett has presented a careful analysis of the term's use since New Testament times in his booklet, *Evangelize! A Historical Survey of the Concept.*[2] In the modern period this work considers primarily (but not exclusively) the Anglo-Saxon world where the existence of the two concepts "evangelization" and "evangelism" and the very varied history of their relationship greatly complicates the matter.[3] Barrett has found a thoroughgoing tension in the English language use of the entire spectrum of terms: "To evangelize" means either (1) "to preach, bring, tell, proclaim, announce or declare (the Gospel [Latin and German: *evangelium*]), whether people accept it or not, whether they are then won or converted by that activity or not, although this is the intent"; or (2) "not just to proclaim, but to actually win and convert people to the Christian faith."[4] The first meaning corresponds to the language use of the New Testament and is used by exegetes,

15

Christian lexicographers, and missiologists; the second meaning is used by practitioners of evangelism, non-theological dictionaries, and the majority of Christians.[5]

On the other hand, the distinction between "evangelism" as activity in one's own country and in the church and "mission" as preaching of the gospel in non-Christian countries scarcely plays a role in the Anglo-Saxon world. The few examples of this which Barrett cites are partially influenced by the German language use. In particular the word "evangelism," but also to some degree the word "evangelization," has often been used in the English language literature since the beginnings of the twentieth century as practically synonymous with "mission."

Only a thorough study of the sources could answer the question since when the term evangelization in the German-speaking world has been common in the language of the church. The etymological and historical dictionaries of the German language are silent in reference to this term. Paulus Scharpff prefaces his *Geschichte der Evangelisation* with a detailed definition of what he wants to include in his understanding of "evangelism." Its most important, distinguishing elements are (1) the testimony of "humankind's being lost without Christ" and of "the saving love of God in Christ which should be brought to every individual," and (2) the preaching of "the objective, central biblical truths, which could lead to personal faith in Christ," "the goal of being born again in the power of the Holy Spirit working in the evangelistic word," the preaching of salvation in Christ "in a subjectively exaggerated, conscience awakening manner," and "an attacking, winning call to God, which invites the individual to recognize the given hour, to repent, to decide and to turn him- or herself over to Christ."[6] This kind of evangelism has existed since the rise of Pietism. "It is directed mainly at nominal Christians, followers of a traditional, conventional Christianity, above all at unchurched, secular persons who have broken away from church and religion, in general at all persons called Christian who have no personal experience with Christ." But regarding the history of the term, Scharpff restricts himself to the one-sentence comment that "In contrast to 'mission' in heathen lands, one denotes the preaching of the gospel in Christian lands since the latter half of the previous century as 'evangelization.'"[7]

Among German-language authors, only Heinrich Rendtorff has dealt extensively with the various nuances in meaning of the term evangelism in its history. His presentation is, however, not semantically oriented; rather it describes the assorted understandings of evangelism from the perspective of their *content*. He first characterizes *"pietistic" evangelism*: "It is the offering of the gospel as salvation in Jesus Christ to humanity in the world; its goal is a personal decision in revival and conversion and the gathering of the converted in the church as the body of Christ."[7]

Rendtorff distinguishes from this the form of evangelism which is influenced by the *Anglo-Saxon* branch; this derives from the Methodist movement under George Whitefield and John Wesley, was further developed by evangelistic preachers like Charles G. Finney and Dwight L. Moody, and from the middle of the nineteenth century was practiced more and more in Germany as well.[8] In summarizing he describes it thus: Evangelism "is the individual charismatically gifted evangelist's sermon of conversion addressed to the masses. Its characteristics, which go beyond the usual churchly sermon, are, among other things: fearlessness in the choice of means; the spiritual resolution in the delivery of the proclamation; the passionate conviction of the evangelist himself; intensive prayer; plain, contemporary language; personal counseling."[9]

Rendtorff places in relation to that the *"Volksmission"* of the church which has its roots in the work of J. H. Wichern (1808–1881):

> The goal of the "Volksmission" is the same as that of evangelism: revival and conversion. But the sponsor of it is the church in its missionary responsibility for the world. The object is the individual who is to be saved from his lost state, but not in isolation: he is to be led into the church in order to live in it as a living member. And the church is to be awakened and prepared for its missionary service to the world.[10]

After World War II evangelism as understood by the *ecumenical movement* came to the forefront. In the first part of this century this definition was strongly influenced by the person and work of John Mott, and after 1945 became *the* expression for the missionary task of the church in general, not least thanks to the influence of the Dutch missiologist Johannes Christiaan Hoekendijk.[11] In this respect, Rendtorff cites the following summarizing definition:

> [Evangelism] is the participation of the entire Christian community in Christ's mission in the world; every single aspect of the life and doings of the church has evangelistic meaning: Through preaching, brotherhood, and service the church must make the gospel visible in the actual life of the community. The laity stand on the front, and they are served by the bearers of the office whose task is to arm the people of God for its mission.[12]

The missiologist David J. Bosch[13] has described no less than twelve different positions which arise from the assorted combinations of the terms mission and evangelism in the current discussion; the articulated position on social responsibility is, of course, an additional distinguishing aspect. At the same time this indicates that, proceeding from biblical evidence which very pointedly speaks of the preaching of the gospel for the poor, the subject of "evangelism among the poor" has captivated extraordinary attention and led to controversial positions in the last twenty years.[14]

Since Vatican II a renewed missionary conception appeared in the Roman Catholic Church. The papal encyclical *Evangelii nuntiandi* by Pope Paul VI "On Evangelism in the Modern World"[15] unfolds an impressive outline of the whole missionary responsibility of the church. In the center stands a view of the church as an "evangelized and evangelizing community" which "through continual conversion and renewal evangelizes itself in order to evangelize the world credibly."[16]

The term "evangelization" has no notable history in Roman-Catholic theology and is generally understood in the sense of "complete Christianization."[17] But even in the Roman-Catholic sphere voices are more and more loudly to be heard which consider the special connection of the biblical term "evangelizing" with the poor constituitive and demand appropriate consequences.[18]

Beyond the fundamental meaning that evangelism in any particular form always describes the missionary dimension of the preaching and activity of the church, the term historically carries the following particular connotations:

(1) In content and form evangelistic preaching aims to lead its hearers to a clear personal decision of faith. This use with reference to persons is so clear in general language usage that some dictionaries only list "evangelize" as a transitive verb with the meaning "to bring someone home to the gospel, to convert someone to the gospel."[19]

(2) In some areas, especially German-speaking areas, evangelism means the re-evangelism of those alienated from the church. In that context the missionary aspect, which has as its target group those who have become superficially, or at least inwardly, estranged from the church, can stand more strongly in the foreground. But a revival aspect can also be included which aims at those who support the church and on the basis of baptism, confirmation and more or less regular church attendance consider themselves Christians but lack a clear inner certainty of belief.

The distinction between mission as mission to "heathens" and evangelism as missionary preaching among Christians or those who live in areas formed by the Christian tradition is also to be found in systematic theologians such as Karl Barth and Paul Tillich.[20]

Most theological specialists for evangelism and mission have dropped this distinction, not least for pragmatic reasons, since in the face of the existence of churches in almost every country in the world and the religious pluralism in many previously Christian countries the use of this distinction is in practice limited.

(3) The tension or breadth in the use of the term cited at the beginning follows from its history. Evangelism can today denote *both* a series of events in a church with missionary lectures in which the invitation of the gospel and the call to repentance is clearly expressed *and* the underlying thrust of all preaching and Christian activity which seeks to bring the gospel closer to all unbelievers.

The Silence of Major Theological Works

Almost everyone is talking about evangelism, both ecumenists and evangelicals, charismatics and liberation theologians. However, when one turns from the works of missiologists and specialists in evangelism to the textbooks for dogmatics, one encounters a curious hesitancy, if not a meaningful silence. But two of the greatest dogmatic theologians do address this issue briefly. In Karl Barth's *Church Dogmatics,* Volume IV.3.2, §72.4 ("The Ministry of the Community") there is a section which names evangelization as one of the tasks of the local church. Barth understands evangelization as "the announcement of the message to those in the more immediate environs of the congregation":

> Evangelization is the particular task unquestionably laid upon the church in every period of ministering the Word of God to the countless people who theoretically ought long since to have heard and accepted and responded to it, but who in fact have not really done so at all, or only at a distance and therefore in way which is meaningless as regards their participation in the cause of the community. Evangelization serves to awaken this sleeping Church.[21]

What is important for Barth in this context is that the evangelizing church says what it has to say, i.e. the gospel, and does so "in a glad and spiritual and peaceful way," and "that concern for spurious results should not lose track of its purpose by turning the proclamation of freedom into the propagation of a law, or the promise of life . . . into threatening with the terrors of hell!" But in spite of such danger it is certain that "a Church which is not as such an evangelising Church is either not yet or no longer a Church or only a dead Church, itself standing in supreme need of renewal by evangelisation."[22]

We find very similar tones in the work of Paul Tillich, who in the third volume of his *Systematic Theology* names evangelism as the third of the "functions of expansion of the church" alongside mission and religious education. Evangelism "is directed toward the churches's estranged or indifferent members. It is missions toward the non-Christians within a Christian culture. Its two activities, which overlap but are distinguishable, are practical apologetics and evangelistic preaching." According to Tillich, "evangelism by preaching is more of a charismatic function than is apologetics." Tillich also points out the dangers of evangelism, but concludes the short section thus: "However, it would be wrong to reject evangelism, or even an individual evangelist, *in toto* because of these ambiguities. There must be evangelism, but it should not confuse excitement with ecstasy."[23]

Except for these two works no other common textbook in dogmatics or comparable work, as far as I can see, speaks of evangelism. Even the missionary task of the church as such is often only treated very briefly.[24]

One need not turn only to dogmatics textbooks to observe how much can be written about ecclesiological questions without giving the missionary task of the church much attention; a glance in books on ecclesiology itself discloses the same thing. While Hans Küng, Jürgen Moltmann, Wolfgang Huber and Walter Kreck[25] only mention the missionary task of the church briefly, Ulrich Kühn at least dedicates an entire section in *Die Kirche* to the subject "The Sending of the Church into the World."[26] The Spaniard Miguel María Garijo-Guembe offers even more in his book *Gemeinschaft der Heiligen. Grund, Wesen und Struktur der Kirche*;[27] on pages 258–76 he discusses "Evangelization and its Implications" and pleads for evangelization in the sense of preaching as the actual missionary task.

Rather typical of the situation in the handbooks in practical theology is the (then East German) *Handbuch der praktischen Theologie*, in which Friedrich Winter treats missionary preaching on pages 279–82. Evangelism, he says, "wants to convert the baptized and the unbaptized to a personal decision of faith."[28] A short, positive statement on missionary preaching is underscored by 14 points which are intended to preserve it from the errors of conventional evangelism. Very pragmatically oriented, however, are the essays by Reinhard Linder, "Evangelism in the 'Volkskirche'," and Theodor Lehmann, "Evangelism in the Atheistic Society," in the (then West German) *Handbuch der praktischen Theologie*.[29] For Lindner evangelism is preaching "on the outside of the local church" and "outside of the church"; Lehmann maintains "everything boils down to the offer of a decision."[30]

The section "Sermon/Preaching" by Rolf Zerfaß and Herbert Poensgen in a similar publication from the Roman Catholic side is placed entirely under the rubric "Evangelization,"[31] which then receives a correspondingly broad definition:

> In contrast to the free church understanding of evangelization, which (in the form of the so called tent mission) aims at the conversion of the individual and so should be considered a particular form of pastoral care to those estranged from the Christian faith, in the newer concept of "evangelization" inspired by Vatican II, fresh reflection on the

mission of the church in today's world at large is taking place: "Evangelizing is indeed the grace and the actual call of the church, her deepest identity" (Pope Paul VI, *Evangelii Nuntiandi* 14). "Evangelization" thus represents a brand new paradigm of pastoral activity in which the preaching practice of local churches can be located and weighted anew."[32]

Two further quotations can indicate what that might look like in theory and practice:

> Evangelistic preaching is the announcement of God's rule; its original location is the "hedges and fences" (not pulpit or lectern); its horizon is the world (not the church); its basic model is the conversation (not the sermon in worship).

> The gospel preaches God's unconditional Yes to humankind; that is why Jesus was sent; that is why he for his part sent out disciples. Every mission and all power of the church is bound as regards content to this will of God. The church itself must "turn back" to this divine will again and again, i.e., it must dare in the name of God to believe in humankind.[33]

Thus we see that not only in specialized literature, but also in the standard works of systematic and practical theology the term evangelization/evangelism and the topic are defined very differently, insofar as they are considered at all. But before we make our own proposal for clarifying and using the term evangelism, we should remember that the word evangelism stems from the New Testament word *euangelizesthai* and also has its roots in the good news (Latin and German: *evangelium*) itself. An investigation of the biblical use of the term can, of course, not on its own change the language use as it grew through history. But it can help us to become aware of the historical and material depth of the term.

The Heritage of Biblical Language Use

The term evangelism is connected with the Greek word *euangelizesthai* and its use in the New Testament.[34] But this use is for its part rooted in the Old Testament to a great degree; the Greek version of the Old Testament translates the Hebrew verb *bsr* (Pi'el) with *euangelizesthai*.

The basic meaning of the Hebrew word is—in spite of the much discussed exception in 1 Sam 4:17—the bearing of good tidings.[35] One can order the theological-religious use of the term in three groups:

(1) The proclamation in worship of God's saving help of Israel: in Ps 40:10 as a component of a song of thanks, in Ps 96:2 in the call to praise

21

as an element of the hymn and in Isa 60:6 in the description of the procession of the peoples to Zion, which proclaims Yahweh's glorious deeds.

(2) The image of the herald of victory is transfered to the proclamation of God's already fulfilled saving help. In Nah 2:1 the heralds of good tidings proclaim peace, i.e. the liberation of the people from the threat of foreign rule and the restoration of all of Israel. Isa 52:7 adopts this wording; now peace, well being and saving help are announced to the people. For—so is it argued—the king is your God. According to Isa 40:9 it is the "Zion, herald of good tidings" who announces God's epiphany and his salvific rule. Characteristic of both references in Second Isaiah is that the heralds—as corresponds to the original meaning of the verb—say what has already happened: God has acted. Yahweh's victory and the in-breaking of salvation are the contents of the message.[36]

(3) The reference in Isa 61:1, which is so important for the New Testament, stands alone. The prophet first describes his commission, which he has received under the authority of God's spirit, with the phrase: "The LORD has anointed me to bring good tidings to the poor." The absolute use of the term is striking. What are the contents of the "tidings"? Are they described by the phrases that follow, or is "the proclamation of a word of salvation, and thus of a joyful message of God, . . . a primary element in the work of the prophet along with healing, liberating, comforting, saving, etc. and is itself a saving event"?[37]

It is striking how strongly the verbal element in the whole commission of the prophet is emphasized. The prophet is called to preach. But at the same time the observation remains valid that "to proclaim salvation is almost tantamount to summoning it into existence or bringing it about."[38]

Two elements come to light in Third Isaiah's commission: on the one hand, there is the closeness of God's salvific help for human beings' distress, whose misery has an external and an internal dimension;[39] on the other hand, there is the reference back to God's action as the decisive foundation of all of the great transformation which the prophet announces.

In the New Testament one can distinguish various layers of the theological use of *euangelizesthai* as well. The oldest use is to be found in the saying of Jesus in Q (Matt 11:5 = Luke 7:22) in which apparently Isa 61:1 was adopted to characterize the work of Jesus. In Luke 4:18, Isa 61:1 is explicitly cited as a programmatic reference to Jesus' commission. It is then not surprising that Luke-Acts is one of the two main focuses in the use of the term. According to Luke 4:43 Jesus proclaimed the gospel of God's kingdom (*euangelisathai tēn basileian tou theou*; cf. Luke 8:1, 16:16, Acts 8:12).[40] The form used by Matthew, *kēryssōn to euangelion tēs basileias* (Matt 4:23, 9:35, 24:14), has almost the same meaning.[41]

In Acts one finds a preference for a christological object for the contents of the proclamation: Christ Jesus (5:42), Jesus (8:35), the Lord Jesus (11:20), Jesus and the resurrection (17:18), or "the Word" (8:4, 15:35) or the promise (13:32).[42] The term can stand parallel to *didaskein* and *kēryssein* in this usage.[43] According to Acts 14:15 the content of the proclamation is "to turn from the non-existent idols to the living God" which shows that *euangelizesthai* has become a technical term for the salvific message in missionary preaching. The translation "preaching the good news" will therefore not in every case transmit the correct nuance of the term; the meaning becomes more general: "preaching the message of salvation."[44]

The absolute use of the verb in Acts thus circumscribes missionary preaching in its entirety (14:7, 16:10), whereby, in the cases in which geographic details in the accusative case appear as addressees, it is almost the transitive meaning of "evangelize" in the sense of "missionize" that appears to be reached (cf. 8:25, 40, 14:21).

The second main focus of the term is doubtless to be found in the Pauline letters. Here, too, *euangelizesthai* is a technical term for missionary preaching (cf. Rom 15:20; 1 Cor 1:17, 9:16,18, 15:1f.; 2 Cor 10:16, 11:7; Gal 1:8, 16, 4:13; Eph 3:8). In a few cases the aorist indicative expressly indicates the early proclamation of the Gospel (e.g. 1 Cor 15:1ff.; 2 Cor 11:7; Gal 1:8; 4:18). The content of the preaching is—often added in a tautological manner—the Gospel (1 Cor 15:1ff.; 2 Cor 11:7; Gal 1:11; cf. 1 Cor 9:18 also) or—to be deduced indirectly—word from the cross. Paul formulates this in a christological form only once, as to preach God's Son (Gal 1:16). One can recognize no difference in meaning from related expresions such as *katangelein*, *kēryssein*, *lalein to euangelion* (1 Cor 9:14; Gal 2:2; Col 1:23; 1 Thess 2:2, 9).

Romans 1:15, a reference that remains somewhat suspect on account of the contradiction of Rom 15:20 and the missionary horizon of its justification in 1:14, shows that *euangelizesthai* is not exclusively limited to missionary preaching—or did Paul want to pursue mission in Rome, too?[45] But the (admittedly hypothetical) wording in Gal 1:8f. shows that preaching the gospel in an existing church does not have to be an anachronism. Therefore Paul does not at all have to write in 1 Cor 15:1, as many translators opine, "I remind you of the gospel"; rather one can very well say what the Greek text means, "I proclaim/make known the gospel to you." This could be verified by a corresponding analysis of the continuing significance of the gospel for the church.[46] But this observation should not, however, divert from the recognition that the primary use of *euangelizesthai* also in Paul is the missionary context.[47]

To this degree *euangelizesthai* is always preaching which aims for acceptance, although this connotation of the term is not conclusively given in its use alone. But the context in 1 Cor 15:1ff. and Gal 4:13 and the larger thematic connection of 1 Cor 9:14-23 and 1 Thess 1:2–2:13 make this obvious. The fundamental preaching of the gospel is for Paul always an apostolic commission, but the church participates in this commission in many ways.[48]

In summary:

(1) The term *euangelizesthai* (to proclaim good tidings) has received its theological form from the Old Testament. It is particularly important to observe here that it not only is generally used when the good things God has done for some people should be passed on, rather that in Second and Third Isaiah it is closely connected with the announcement of God's eschatological salvific activity by means of which he turns the fortune of his people for the better and in particular helps the suffering, the desperate, the prisoners, and those with disabilities to new life.

(2) This thrust is picked up when Q and especially Luke summarize the preaching of Jesus and his disciples about the salvific coming of the rule of God with the term *euangelizesthai*. In this context it thus often appears together with the mention of the mighty acts in which the helping and saving reality of the rule of God become concrete and visible.

(3) In the post-Easter situation the term is then completely oriented toward the preaching of that which God has done through Jesus Christ and has its *Sitz im Leben* primarily (if not exclusively) in missionary preaching. Where the word is used absolutely it has received the meaning of preaching the Christ event as the message of salvation.

(4) The term *euangelizesthai* itself does not expressly include in its meaning the question of a response by anyone. The wider context of its use shows, however, that in the announcement of that which God has done for the salvation of humankind a question is always directed to the listeners, namely of how do they intend to react to this message. Since a person is so confronted with the seriousness of his or her situation, the translation "to preach good news" is not appropriate for all emotional connotations of the term. The basic definition of the Christian use of the term is "to preach the message of salvation."

The Theological Task

What is evangelism? It is not by chance that John Stott begins his Lausanne lecture "The Essence of Biblical Evangelism" with the citation of a deep conversation about the use of words between two persons in *Alice in Wonderland*.[49] For, as it so often is, the question here also appears not to be "What is evangelism?" rather "What do we want to understand by 'evangelism'?"

John Stott is admittedly of the opinion that an exact analysis of the biblical term *euangelizesthai* and its relevant field can grasp "the nature of biblical evangelism." In this manner one could avoid bringing "both ecumenical and evangelical thinking to the same independent and objective test" and "twisting words to suit our own pleasure."[50] Stott points out for example that the biblical term does not already include the intended result or much less the success of the evangelistic activity, as is commonly held in English language use, and shows that evangelizing in the biblical sense is not restricted to one particular method.[51]

But Stott does not consider two problems:

(1) The biblical language use is not uniform. Particularly in the current disagreement regarding whether evangelism is the generic term for all forms of the Christian community's gospel-directed encounter with the men and women of our time or whether it ought to mean missionary preaching in a narrower sense, the findings of an investigaton of the biblical usage offer only limitedly assistance. For the proponents of the first variant appeal, not without good reason, to Luke 4:18 and Luke 7:22 = Matt 11:6 where Jesus's complete activity in word and deed is summarized in the description "to proclaim the gospel to the poor," and the advocates of the second variant point to the use of the term in the missionary language of the New Testament with equally good reason.

(2) Biblical terms also have their own history which cannot be revised by simply determining what the correct biblical language use is. They enrich themselves by drawing on other biblical motives (in the case of evangelism for example, the close connection with the call to conversion which is hinted at in the New Testament but not terminologically fixed), and they penetrate into areas and issues which in biblical times did not exist (e.g. the problem of evangelizing anew nominal Christians). So the formative power of the history of the term "evangelism" finds its expression in general dictionaries and lexicons as well as in the compendiums of systematic theology. Proceeding from the biblical perspective, we could attempt to correct the language use which arises from this development when we consider it necessary. But it makes no sense to deny this development. This history is given, even if we attempt to dispute that it has used the term "evangelism" correctly.

The issue is therefore much less to say what the "correct" meaning of the term evangelism is as it is to say how we want to use the term. The basis for this decision ought to be the biblical roots of the word. But modern language use in its assorted variants is not to be neglected in so doing.

Against the background of this consideration I would like to opt for the following use of the terms "evangelism" and "mission":

In company with many others I use "mission" as the generic term for the whole mission of the church, i.e. for its existence, its words and deeds through which it, in faithful obedience to the commission of its Lord, devotes itself to the world.[52] This mission is fulfilled in the witness of the church (*martyria*), the service of the church (*diakonia*) and in the communion which the church lives (*koinonia*).[53] Not everything that the church does is mission. It lives directed toward God as well and has tasks in its own midst. But everything that it does and lives has a missionary dimension. As the expression of its missional essence, the witness, service, and communion of the church offer a multitude of possibilities.

Witness is fulfilled in the proclamation of the word (*kerygma*)—in public sermons as well as private conversations—and in the silent but eloquent faithfulness of those who live, suffer—and where it is necessary— die for their Lord. The diaconal work of the church takes place in care for the poor and the needy, in care and healing of the sick, in accompanying those who mourn, and in counseling those who are helpless, as well as in public engagement for justice, peace, and the conservation of the earth.

Koinonia lives in both the worshiping communion before God in prayer and eucharist and the organized cooperation of the multifarious gifts for mutual benefit as limbs of the body of Christ.

According to New Testament language use, evangelism is a part of preaching, part of the *kerygma*: It is the fundamental testimony of God's salvific act in Jesus Christ. It takes place in public sermons and private conversations. It is directed toward persons who are not yet acquainted with the gospel or who have not yet understood its fundamental meaning for their lives. It is in a special way oriented towards the men and women to which it is addressed, that is, it has as its goal that men and women very personally recognize and accept that which God has done as salvation and as a new foundation of their lives and live from it.[54]

Here I would like briefly to give reasons why I consider such a narrowly construed use of the term evangelism more appropriate and more useful for understanding than the broad definition in the sense of a generic term for the comprehensive mission of the church which is now rather common. This limitation stands in the service of terminological clarity and does not intend to devalue all of that which is additionally a part of the commission of the church.

(1) The term has its origins in a biblical verb of speech. It lives from its contents, from the message which it proclaims. This message and its orientation has a fundamental and elementary character. This means that its task involves more than the verbal mediation of its commission; rather it seeks communication with all dimensions of human life and human need. Nonetheless, evangelism as word event is the "heart" of mission[55] in so far as it names what saves and liberates humankind and that from which the Christian community and its members live.

26

(2) Proceeding from the essence of the gospel, evangelism is oriented toward hearers and receivers and thus has no respect for any boundaries. The message of salvation is for the poor and is to be preached to all peoples, and these are biblical models for its universality and its far-reaching implications. It is the announcement of God's act, which is for all and aims at change.

(3) In its history the basic preaching of the gospel has again and again been a critical and wooing question for all who live in the proximity of the church. They are asked to what degree the gospel truly represents the foundation of their lives. The heritage of the eighteenth and nineteenth centuries, which summarize missional and revival preaching, should not be simply discarded, rather be tested in its own right.

From this perspective I see three important tasks for theological reflection:

(1) What is the biblically justified message of evangelism and how does it speak to the situation of those addressed? What do we have to say when we evangelize—in the double sense of that expression: What *can* we say and what *must* we say?

(2) What implication does the acceptance of the message by the hearer have for its orientation and its effect? "Preaching for response" or, as it is sometimes more sharply formulated, "preaching for verdict" is one of the basic hallmarks of classic evangelism. How compatible is this characteristic with the essence of the gospel?

(3) What is the essential motivation for preaching the gospel? Does it stem from the church's instinct of self-preservation, the need of those addressed (and who determines what this is?), or the commission of Jesus, or are these inadmissible alternatives?[56]

A last word: I write my thoughts from the perspective of a central European. I want to learn from the experiences of Christians in Brazil, South Africa, India, or Korea. But I do not live there, and I do not have to preach the gospel there. I ask the readers to accept this limitation as a self-limitation and not as the absolutizing of my own standpoint. I hope that my presentation shows that the form of the proclamation may and must be different in different situations—but draws nonetheless in a discernible manner on the same source and remains the *one* gospel.

Chapter 2

The Gospel of Evangelistic Preaching

What is the gospel of evangelistic preaching? What do the messengers who preach the saving message say, and what need do they address?

To find an answer to this question, we must go back and ask what is the central message of the New Testament proclamations of the gospel. We shall further observe what situation they were spoken into and what significance this situation has for the formulation of the message. We shall consider what hermeneutical consequences for the orientation of the gospel today can follow from these observations, so that the gospel remains good news and the message of salvation and does not turn into a law of faith.[1] In the first step we shall analyze three basic forms of the New Testament message: the "gospel of the kingdom" of the Jesus tradition as the Synoptic Gospels hand it down; the "word of the cross" of the Pauline gospel; and the witness of the "incarnation of the Word of God" which determines the message of the Gospel of John and other early Christian traditions.

The Gospel of the Kingdom

It is characteristic of the Evangelist Matthew that he summarizes Jesus' message in the formula: Jesus "preached the gospel of the kingdom" (Matt 4:23, 9:35). Mark describes the relationship between Jesus' preaching the gospel and his preaching the kingdom of God in somewhat more detail in Mark 1:14-15: "Jesus came into Galilee, preaching the gospel of God, and saying, 'The time is fulfilled, and the kingdom of God is at hand; repent and believe in the gospel'" (cf. Matt 4:17). The formula in Luke 4:43, 8:1 (cf. 16:16) that Jesus preached the good news of the kingdom of God corresponds to this in content.[2]

Here we do not need to engage the exegetical question regarding to what degree such summarizing formulas reproduce Jesus' language use in an historically exact manner.[3] It is in any event clear that the proclamation of the imminent reign of God stood at the center of Jesus' preaching and ministry and that in Jesus' mouth this was the message of salvation, that is good news (cf. Mark 1:15, Matt 4:17, Luke 10:9).

Jesus' Message

Jesus' message is summarized in the Synoptic Gospels with the sentence: "The kingdom of God is at hand."[4] This sentence is different from a piece of information about the chronology in the course of apocalyptic events. It is the announcement of the redemptive nearness of God which is breaking in through Jesus' works. Jesus' saying, "But if it is by the finger of God that I cast out demons, then the kingdom of God has come upon you" (Luke 11:20 = Matt 12:28), is rightly viewed by many exegetes as a key to his self understanding. For it shows that Jesus is not only the herald who announces the approaching, or already initiated, commencement of the kingdom of God; Jesus considers himself to be the "representative" of the kingdom of God in whose works its liberating and redeeming reality has already broken in.[5]

A whole series of parables emphasize this connection between the unassuming commencement of the kingdom of God in Jesus' works and its overwhelming consummation.[6]

One can see from a whole series of central characteristics of Jesus' preaching and ministry that, in contrast to John the Baptist, who primarily preached the judgmental aspect of the approaching kingdom of God, Jesus interpreted the coming of the kingdom of God as a salvation event.

The Good News for the Poor

As we have seen, Isa 61:1 is used twice in the synoptic tradition as a summarizing characteristic for Jesus' ministry. In Luke 4:18 the passage is explicitly introduced as a quotation which Jesus in programmatic sayings pronounced to be fulfilled. In Q (Matt 11:5 = Luke 7:22b) the inquiry of John the Baptist is answered with the reference to Jesus' works, and preaching good news to the poor is named as the last element in this list. Two observations are important in this context: The reports of Jesus' works are not freely formulated as corresponding to the events; rather they obviously echo Old Testament descriptions of the time of salvation.[7] Partly corrected by the time of the text's transmission, the final position of "preaching the good news" in the listing shows that we are not dealing with one element among others here; this is the interpretative summary of Jesus' eschatological activity "which obviously is intended to describe the context for understanding his actions."[8]

But the relation of Isa 61:1 to Jesus' ministry was in no event just a retrospective interpretation of his miracles. At the same time it points toward a dimension of his preaching which is most clearly handed down in the Beatitudes.[9] In particular the first Beatitude associates comfort for the poor with the proclamation of the kingdom of God. The promise, "yours is the kingdom of God," is the certain promise of eschatological salvation.[10]

But who are the poor to whom Jesus turns?

The parellelism with the hungry and the mourning in the second and third Beatitude points toward social misery. Luke has underlined this with the connection with the cries of woe against those who are rich, full, and who laugh. But Isa 61:1 also stands behind the first Beatitude and with that the Old Testament promise of God's help for the poor.[11] Because the very Hebrew word àani/àanaw (= poor, miserable, bowed) which occurs in Isa 61:1 is also found in a series of psalms which are regarded as representatives of a late Old Testament tradition stressing the piety of the "poor," a long exegetical discussion arose around the question of whether the poor are socially disadvantaged or especially devout.

More recent investigations have shown that this is a false alternative. There is no doubt that, from the covenant code onward, the poor appear as "victims of social oppression" in many legal texts and prophetic sayings. But when one sees them together with "the brokenhearted" (Isa 61:1) and those who seek Yahweh (Ps 22:27, 69:33), they are also those who may hope for help from Yahweh.

One cannot relieve this tension by comparing "a poverty which was originally judged totally profanely with post-exilic spiritualized piety of the poor." For the Old Testament as a whole "the poor are not simply the poor, rather they are 'God's poor' who can expect liberation and joy to come from him" (Ps 34:19, Isa 29:19, 61:1).[12]

This is also the case with Jesus' attitude to the poor. The evangelists bring this out in different ways. Luke has the first Beatitude in the second person and so makes clear that Jesus' saying to the poor is not a neutral comment on the consequences of scarcity in economic terms; rather it shows him turning to persons who are in need and are hoping for help.[13] Matthew formulates the Beatitudes analogous to wisdom beatitudes in the third person, but sharpens the general observation with the addition *tō pneumati*. He describes the poor as persons "whose external situation is such that they have to expect everything from God, and whose internal attitude is such that they really do expect everything from God alone."[14] Poor in spirit means poor before God—but not just in a spiritual sense, rather such that economic misery, bodily hunger, and spiritual suffering become the place where God's comfort is experienced. Jesus does not idealize poverty, hunger, and tears. God will overcome them. He also does not develop a social program to rectify these problems, although some of his mighty acts alleviated the need in individual cases. Jesus announces God's eschatological help. And then again he does not just comfort them with the hereafter. For the promise of salvation is already valid now, as comes to expression in the words of the first Beatitude. God's concern and care are especially directed toward the deprived whose lives appear to be worthless.

31

The Healing of the Sick

As the programatic saying of Jesus in Luke 11:20 showed, Jesus considered the exorcism of demons to be of particular importance for his ministry as the representative of the kingdom of God. For the liberation of the demon-possessed from the demons who had enslaved them made tangible and manifest that the power of Satan is broken and God has realized his kingdom.[15] The Markan tradition primarily outlines Jesus' liberating omnipotence in impressive stories and sees in them representative demonstrations of his "teaching with authority."[16]

Healings of the sick are in principle distinguished from exorcisms; but there are *de facto* transitions between exorcistic and therapeutic actions in the tradition.[17] One can see from the fact that both phenomena are often mentioned in parallel in the summaries that for the early Christian tradition both forms of Jesus' ministry form a whole in the end. Jesus' action brings human beings, plagued by the power of evil and death, liberation and healing.

If one asks for the meaning of Jesus' miracles in the context of his message of the kingdom of God, one will have to give a simple response at first. They mean nothing other than that which happened in them: The kingdom of God which is breaking in through Jesus' ministry liberates from the destructive powers of evil. The handicapped can walk, see, or hear again; lepers are healed and re-integrated into the community; and even at the gates of death God's power proves itself to be stronger. Persons who were disabled are made whole; life that was threatened is sheltered; hearts that were possessed are set free. That is how God's salvific reign works, and it is the task of Jesus' actions to make this real.[18]

Therefore, the miracles are never called "signs" (*sēmeia*) in the synoptic tradition, rather "mighty acts" (*dynameis*). The synoptic tradition only names those signs miracles "which are intended to give witness to the claim of a savior or prophet sent from God and to awaken faith."[19] Jesus decisively rejected the demand to show a "sign from heaven" (Mark 8:11f., Matt 16:1, Luke 11:16; cf. Matt 12:38). He sees in this demand an expression of the disbelief which will receive no other sign than the "sign of Jonah," the call to repentance.[20]

The positive contrast to this attitude is the faith of those who seek healing from Jesus or their family and friends. "Faith" is in this context nothing more than the expectation, which is born out of bitter need and overcomes all resistance, that Jesus can help them.[21] The experience of help and healing it can then lend to individuals seeing and understanding more deeply, so that they encounter in Jesus the God of salvation and his holy nature. "Depart from me, for I am a sinful man, O Lord." stammers Peter

32

according to Luke 5:8 in the face of the miraculous catch of fish. Luke 17:11-19 tells in a likewise exemplary story how only one of the ten healed lepers returns after being healed, gives praise to God and thanks Jesus. The saying, "Your faith has made you well," applies only to him, so that the healing of the others almost appears to be a case of "unsucessfully treating the symptoms."[22] Other signals in the synoptic tradition indicate as well that one should not see Jesus' mighty acts in isolation, but that one can only understand them correctly when they are experienced as a part of the whole—as a part of the message of the salvific presence of God which Jesus lived.[23]

The Reception of Sinners

Luke 15:2 cites the Pharisees accusation against Jesus as being that "This man receives sinners and eats with them." That Jesus' table fellowship with a circle of notorious sinners was characteristic for Jesus ministry, but at the same time an affront is shown by the following saying from Q (Matt 11:18f. = Luke 7:33ff.), which doubtless goes back to the historical Jesus: "For John the Baptist has come eating no bread and drinking no wine, and you say, 'He has a demon.' The Son of Man has come eating and drinking, and you say, 'Behold, a glutton and a drunkard, a friend of tax collectors and sinners!'"[24] From the Markan tradition one can add Mark 2:16 where the "scribes of the Pharisees" are quoted in amazement with the indignant question, "Why does he eat with tax collectors and sinners?" And Jesus answers, "I came not to call the righteous, but sinners."[25]

Apparently, the term "sinner" has sociological meaning—at least in the quotations cited.[26] Well-known, notorious sinners are meant—people who are reckoned as "sinners" on the basis of the behavior or because they belong to a certain class. It is not possible to say conclusively who made up this group of individuals in a Galilean town or village. In any event, the Gentiles were reckoned among that group, as well as women who had the reputation of leading an immoral way of life,[27] and doubtless the group from which the Pharisee in Luke 18:11 distances himself: extortioners, the unjust, adulterers and tax collectors. The reason for this classification of the tax collectors is probably their frequent contact with Gentiles, but above all their reputation as extortionists.[28] One cannot conclusively say, in view of the New Testament reports regarding the "sinners," to what degree other groups are to be reckoned as the "sinners," e.g., persons with "dishonorable" occupations or indeed all who did not keep the Pharisaic rules.[29]

The term "sinner" doubtless had a social component. As in every society, in Judaism the members of the lowest classes were also in the most danger, under the pressure of their oppressive circumstances, to adopt deviant behavior and then, after having been so characterized, to fail in attempts to re-integrate themselves in the community.

But, as the inclusion of the tax collectors in this group shows, the economic issue is not the primary perspective. For even if the tax collectors of the New Testament were "Hellenist tax-farmers," they nonetheless belonged to the well-situated middle or upper class as regards their income.[30] Whoever wants to recognize as belonging to Jesus' company only the oppressed and exploited tax-collectors who worked for other, well-off tax collectors[31] has not understood how non-conformist Jesus' behavior really was: He turned to outcasts of all kinds and let them experience the nearness of God's salvific reign. His mission to all of God's people is to exclude no one (cf. Luke 19:10).

It was clearly offensive that the way Jesus promised these persons God's care and lived with them did not demonstrate with sufficient clarity his distance from their inappropriate lifestyle. As can be recognized in the later rabbinic tradition, even in Pharisaic circles there was an openness to the possibility that persons of this sort would return to God. They should, however, demonstrate the seriousness of their repentance with the corresponding behavior and make good their injustices. Jesus' opponents held against him that he did not demand this as the condition of their acceptance by God.[32]

To be sure, one finds in Jesus' words no indication of sweeping forgiveness of the "sinners" in the sense that they were only victims of religious structures of oppression and exclusion.[33] Jesus goes directly to these persons and makes them understand that God's call to enter into his kingdom is especially for them.

Unfortunately, we know precious little about what he said to them and what form his table-fellowship with them took. He called the tax collector Levi to join his disciples, and he invited himself to go to Zacchaeus' house.[34] Apart from these episodes we always just have the stories "after the fact"—as in the case of the woman who was a sinner (Luke 7:36-50), which appears to presume an earlier encounter of Jesus with this woman. Such is also the case in the parables in Luke 15 in which Jesus invites his critics to share in the joy that God's lost daughters and sons have been found again.

In the pericope of the adultress, which many later textual sources have inserted into the text of John at 7:53–8:11, we find a model narration of what Jesus' encounter with the "sinner" might have looked like. Jesus did not trivialize the woman's deed; rather he dismissed her with the admonition, "Go, and sin no more." But first he robs the indignant accusers of the competence to judge her with the allusion to their own sin. There is more going on here than just overlooking the sin with the excuse, "But we are all sinners," with a wink or a shrug of one's shoulders. But one detects this

34

more in the description of the character of the encounter between the persons involved than in the actual words spoken.[35]

In only a few places does Jesus speak of his authority to forgive sins. One reference is Mark 2:5, Jesus' address to the paralytic, with the unusual formulation in the present passive, "Now, in this moment, your sins are forgiven,"[36] which provoked the appropriate opposition of the scribes. Another example is Luke 7:48 where Jesus' words (here in the perfect passive) appear to seal what has actually already happened and in the woman's silent testimony of her love has been made manifest (v. 47). Notwithstanding all the difficulties which this pericope in its complexity presents for scholars who work historically,[37] it nonetheless makes impressively visible how humanly Jesus lived God's turn to sinners without renouncing its theological qualification and which opposition this provoked.

Now it has been doubted that the promise of the forgiveness of sins played a role in Jesus' ministry—and not only for historical-critical reasons, but also on the basis of fundamental considerations. "Jesus did not forgive sinners, rather he called sinners with whom he therefore ate and drank openly and with pleasure."[38] The thought of the mediation of the forgiveness of sins through some kind of priestly absolution by a mediator—as is critically objected—stands in contradiction to the absolutely unconditional acceptance of the sinner by God as Jesus lived it. But the acceptance of the sinner without express forgiveness appears to be the more radical and deeper action only in an abstract theological view. Actually, it is in danger of becoming superficial. Sin must be named; otherwise memories of it will be suppressed. The word of forgiveness becomes then a sign that God sees the need of the person who has sinned, takes this need seriously, and overcomes it.[39]

Of course it is true that, in Jesus' ministry, sin appears to be just *one* dimension of human need among others, and that at the same time he never goes searching for sin like an inquisitor.

The Invitation to the Devout

Jesus' mission to the sinners is described in several passages of the synoptic tradition in a remarkably exclusive manner. According to Mark 2:17 Jesus defends his dealings with tax collectors with the words: "Those who are well have no need of a physician, but those who are sick; I came not to call the righteous, but sinners." The conclusion of the parable of the lost sheep is similar: "There will be more joy in heaven over one sinner who repents than over ninety-nine righteous persons who have no need of repentance."[40]

There have been frequent attempts to understand these saying as irony.

35

Of course, no one is really just; everyone is a sinner and is addressed by Jesus' call to repentance. But this is understood only by those whose visible behavior and circumstances exclude all self-deception before God. The devout, on the other hand, remain prisoners of their own self-righteousness.[41] This interpretation, which has a lot going for it when one considers the entire Bible, does not, however, do justice to the passages mentioned. First of all, Jesus' turn to the sinners does not mean that the righteous have been disqualified. The picture of the physician and the sick proves this. It corresponds to the logic of Jesus' ministry that he first turns to those who are alienated from God with his message of the arrival of God's salvific rule. They must be called to enter, because they are outside. This does not imply any criticism of the others.

The conflict does not arise directly out of the question, "Are the 'righteous' sinners?" It arises indirectly out of their reaction to Jesus' behavior in regard to the sinners. Their question was, "Could one who was sent by God get involved so closely with persons who do not observe God's laws?" Concern for the continuing validity of divine laws, the open question regarding Jesus' legitimation and also possibly disappointment over failing attention on the part of the Galilean man of God led to his rejection just because of his contacts with the social and religious outcasts.[42]

Joachim Jeremias has correctly established that the historical location of a large group of Jesus' parables is here. They are "addressed, not to the poor, but to opponents" and justify the gospel of "God's mercy to the poor" to his critics.[43]

One can divide these parables into two groups. Those in the first group appeal for understanding of the message of God's goodness and invite one to share in this joy: the parables of the lost sheep and the lost drachma (Luke 15:3-10), the parable of the two debtors (Luke 7:41-43), and the parable of the laborers in the vineyard (Matt 20:1-15).

Jesus spelled out his situation and concerns most clearly and plainly, down to the very details of the parable itself, in the parable of the prodigal son or—as one should say more correctly—the parable of the two sons and the love of the father (Luke 15:11-32). Here the critics have been taken into the parable in the figure of the elder son and get a chance to speak in a manner that shows them understanding. In the events revolving around the younger son Jesus sketches how God in his deeds hurries toward those who are lost and receives them. In the figure of the elder son he invites his critics to share in the joy and truly to turn to God.[44]

This parable is of inestimable value for the evangelistic message, and not just because of the first part. For the twofold addressee of the evangelistic sermon—the person who has alienated himself from God and the person who, at least superficially, has remained close to God—is portrayed in the parable as the twofold addressee of God's words. Fundamentally, God encounters both in the same way: The father comes to meet both sons. But there is a difference nonetheless: The son who returns home from the misery of a foreign land confesses in the sanctuary of his father's arms his sins and is received with robe, ring and a banquet. The son who has remained home does not hear from his father that he has also done a lot wrong and is basically no better than his brother. Rather the father makes clear to him what the community with his father in his father's house means, and invites him to come in and join the celebration.

In terms of the dispute itself, Jesus does not make the righteous person into a sinner by pointing out to him his weaknesses and mistakes with painstaking detective work. This sanctimonious kind of behavior is alien to him. Instead he confronts the righteous person with his or her own claim of living in community with God.

Does this lead to the presumptuous attempt to determine for God the rules for his actions, or to openness for God's overwhelming and inclusive goodness? The test for that is how one reacts to the message of God's mercy to the sinner. The question of whether the elder brother also remains with his father in his heart is decided by whether he can share in the joy over his lost brother's return home!

While the parable of the two sons has an open ending with the sincere invitation of the father to his elder son to join the festivities, the second group of parables shows as a warning the consequences of a wrong decision. The story of the Pharisee and the tax collector (Luke 18:9-14), which contrasts the attitude of one who only expects help from God alone with that of a person who measures his value in comparison with others, belongs to this group.[45] It is the unmasking of a piety which lives from the negation of the other. Whoever cultivates this piety will always need the negative image of the sinner for his or her own justification. But by so doing he or she misses God.

The parable of the great supper (Luke 14:16-24) also belongs to this group. It emphasizes with great urgency that the invitation to God's kingdom is now being issued in Jesus' ministry. Whoever does not recognize this—and be it with the most respectable excuses—should not be surprised when he or she remains locked out and outsiders take his or her place.

The parable of the two sons (Matt 21:28-32) must also be seen in this context: "The 'Yes' of the righteous" comes to light described "in their 'No' to Jesus as 'No' to God" and "the 'No' of the sinners . . . in their 'Yes' to Jesus as 'Yes' to God."[46]

Indirectly all these parables underline how in Jesus' ministry God's mercy touches those who need it the most. *Directly* they address their winning and warning words to the devout of his time and invite them to

37

demonstrate their will to live in community with God by their "Yes" to Jesus' message and actions.[47]

The widespread rejection of this invitation leads then to the principal question of how righteous the righteous really are. In this manner Jesus' fate itself becomes a part of God's history of revelation by means of which God uncovers how things stand with a particular individual.

The Laying Down of His Life

Jesus' earthly ministry ended in his death on the cross.What does this mean in view of his message of the proximity of the kingdom of God? Is at least its anthropological dimension proved by Jesus' faithfulness to his mission? Or does Jesus' death itself have anything to do with God's salvific activity?

Whether Jesus gave an answer to this question himself and what it was is, as is well known, historically extremely controversial. Theologically one must in any event distinguish between the question of the meaning of Jesus' death and that which historians with their limited means can piece together out of the texts of the Gospels as a possible self-interpretation of the meaning of Jesus' death.

With a good number of exegetes, I am convinced that Jesus saw his approaching death as the consequence of God's positive decision for sinners embodied in his person and that he therefore interpreted it as the vicarious laying down of his life.[48] For our context it is of particular importance that in the very old summaries of the salvific meaning of Jesus' death in Mark 10:45 and the eucharistic tradition in Mark 14:24 derived from Isa 53:12 Jesus' death is described as occuring *hyper pollōn*, "for the many."[49] All the way through Jesus' rejection and death, his message and deeds, God's life-giving mercy is intended to have an effect on all humans beings.

For post-resurrection preaching of the "gospel of the kingdom" this raises the question to what degree it can directly pick up on Jesus' message after Jesus' death. This much is certain: For the disciples Jesus' death was not the last word and the last date in Jesus' history, a history of God's way with him for the salvation of humankind. The appearances of the resurrected one grounded their faith and the message: God has raised Jesus from the dead! That means God has confirmed Jesus' work, "justified" his person and ratified his mission.

But what does that mean concretely? Can they further pursue Jesus' authority to exorcize demons in the power of the inbreaking kingdom of God as if nothing had happened? What will become of the good news to the poor when he who lived it was put to death by "the powers of the world"? Or does Jesus' death and resurrection give that which he said and did a new quality and tap a deeper dimension in the realm of guilt and death for the message of the kingdom, a new dimension which the future community's preaching will never be able to give up?

To find an answer to these questions, we want first to ask a few historical-exegetical questions: Which mission did Jesus give his disciples, and how did they receive it after Easter and further it?

The Mission of the Disciples

We shall begin once again with an aspect in the ministry of the earthly Jesus, namely the sending out of the disciples, and then take a look at the conception of the post-resurrection commission of the community of the disciples according to the witness of the Synoptic Gospels and Acts.

Sending Out the Disciples

A solid part of the synoptic Jesus tradition is the report of the commissioning of the disciples during Jesus' earthly activity. Two traditions are distinguishable: the reports of the Markan tradition (Mark 3:13-19 = Luke 6:12-16; Mark 6:7-13 = Luke 9:1-6) and the tradition of Q (Luke 10:1-12, 17-20). Matthew combines both strands to make his missionary discourse (Matt 9:35–10:42).

As certain as one can be that this tradition goes back to the historical Jesus in its core, it is difficult to place it in his earthly ministry.[50] Is this a one time action of Jesus with symbolic meaning? This is the impression made by the tradition, particularly in Mark and Luke. Or does it found a permanent mission of the disciples in which their ministry accompanied its effectiveness? Or is it a programatic pre-resurrection anticipation of the post-resurrection mission, and if so what is the relationship between the commissioning and the disciples to the early Christian command to make disciples?

The answers to these questions are to a large degree determined by the method of interpretation used. If one analyzes the sayings about commissioning the disciples with the assistance of form criticism and sociology, they betray the predominant influence of a branch of early Christian mission work, which was denoted as "wandering charismatics" since the appearance of Theißen's investigations of the Jesus movement.[51]

If one considers the missionary discourses in terms of salvation history, they appear as the carrying out of Jesus' mission to Israel, an interpretation which Matthew particularly supports. The post-resurrection commissions then refer to a new stage of the mission among Jews and Gentiles.

In contrast, especially in charismatic circles, the commissioning of the disciples by Jesus is read as the programmatic foundation of the universal mission of the church, and this interpretation is carried over into the

39

post-resurrection command to make disciples as well. That is due to the particular form of the pre-resurrection commission. For the tradition reports unanimously of a "double commission" of the disciples by Jesus.[52]

In the choosing of the Twelve one can already read: "And he appointed twelve, to be with him, and to be sent out to preach and have authority to cast out demons" (Mark 3:14-15).[53] In the commissioning in Mark 6:7 the authority to cast out demons is granted, and then in 6:12-13 it is noted that "they went out and preached that men should repent. And they cast out many demons, and anointed with oil many that were sick and healed them." Luke 9:1ff. is formulated parallel to Mark, "And he called the twelve together and gave them power and authority over all demons and to cure diseases, and he sent them out to preach the kingdom of God and to heal," and 9:6 sketches how they carried this out, with the words: "And they departed and went through the villages, preaching the gospel and healing everywhere." In Q (Luke 10:9) the commission reads, "heal the sick in it [the town] and say to them, 'The kingdom of God has come near to you.'" And Matthew 10:7f. summarizes the entire tradition in a wide-reaching commission: "And preach as you go, saying, 'The kingdom of God is at hand.' Heal the sick, raise the dead, cleanse lepers, cast out demons."

The extension, "raise the dead, cleanse lepers," which stands in conspicuous contrast to the other tradition, is obviously formulated as an echo of the "works of Christ" in Matt 11:5 and underlines what determines the entire tradition of the commissioning of the disciples: The disciples carry on Jesus' ministry. The sentence, "He who hears you hears me, and he who rejects you rejects me" (Luke 10:16, cf. Matt 10:40), is a fundamental concept in the early Christian theology of mission which shows up in all layers of the tradition.[54]

The relationship between the mission to preach and the mission to heal is nowhere explicated. The Matthean version suggests that the healing and salvific actions unfold and make concrete the meaning of the announcement of the nearness of the kingdom of heaven. The mighty acts herald the miraculous transformation which God will initiate.[55]

But how is this mission to be continued after the radical turning point of the cross and the resurrection? Was it simply confirmed by the resurrected one, or was it received in a new form and further developed? The bearers and formers of the synoptic tradition offer different answers at this point which nonetheless reveal a common denominator.

Discipleship of the Cross—Mark

We do not know whether Mark, like the other Gospels, also originally contained a new saying of the resurrected one about the commissioning of the disciples after 16:8.[56] For what we now read in our Bibles as Mark 16:9-20 is, according to the evidence of the manuscripts, a later addition which was intended to bring the conclusion of Mark in line with those of the other Gospels. So this text, which many today regard as the mission command par excellence, in a certain sense, has an apocryphal character.

But even critical exegetes today no longer dispute that the pericope contains old early Christian tradition which probably gives us a look at very common and popular views.[57] Of all versions of the post-resurrection mission command, Mark 16:15-18 most likely adopts elements of the pre-resurrection commissioning of the disciples. But even in this text one can clearly observe a further development in comparison with the original elements. The contents of the commission to make disciples is solely the preaching of the gospel—as is emphasized—to all of creation. Whoever believes and is baptized will be saved; whoever rejects the message will be condemned. What is then named in v. 17*b* in partial dependence on the granting of authority to the disciples are the "signs" which "ensue as consequences"[58] to those who come to believe, i.e., which accompany them as authenticating and supportive signs.

One finds a similar promise to the disciples who have been sent out in Luke 10:17-19, though admittedly connected with Jesus' relativizing observation, "Nevertheless do not rejoice in this, that the spirits are subject to you; but rejoice that your names are written in heaven." Doubtless, we find in these traditions traces of a "charismatic" oriented mission in early Christianity which may well have formed the background for the work of Paul's opponents in 2 Corinthians.[59] Characteristic of the critical examination of this tradition in the texts of the New Testament is the concentration on the preaching of the gospel as the admission to the eschatological communion with God.

The genuine Markan answer appears once again to point in another direction. With Mark 8:27ff., Peter's confession, the conflict concerning the meaning of true discipleship begins in the Gospel. Mark 8:34–38 characterizes discipleship as discipleship of the cross and readiness to die as a martyr, an admonition which against the background of the rebuking of Peter and his rejection of Jesus' announcement of his coming passion is shown with especially impressive force. The story of the healing of a possessed boy (9:14-29) shows as one of its themes the powerlessness of the disciples, and it leads to Jesus' announcement that only prayer grants authority. Following that come the second prediction of his passion and the argument among the disciples about who was the greatest, with Jesus' answer, "If anyone would be first, he must be last of all and servant of all" (9:35), and the discussion about an unknown exorcist whom Jesus allows to cast out demons in his name. A section on discipleship in suffering and service as characteristics of discipleship (10:35-45) follows the third prediction of his passion as well.

So the perspective of the coming mission stands totally under the sign of confessing Jesus even under persecution. The eschatological address in 13:9-13 underlines this. It is not the successive overcoming of Satan by the disciples' authority that forms the horizon for preaching the gospel to all nations, but rather the impending general persecution (13:10). So it only follows that in Mark the first confession of Jesus as the Son of God from the mouth of a human being is uttered by the commander of the Roman execution squad in the face of Jesus death.[60]

Teaching What Jesus Has Commanded—Matthew

Whoever speaks of Jesus' mission command thinks of Matt 28:18-20.[61] Here the resurrected one's commission to his disciples is formulated in concise and impressive form. It is framed by Jesus' self-identification as the exalted Lord—"All authority in heaven and on earth has been given to me"—and his promise to his disciples—"And lo, I am with you always, to the close of the age."

The "authority of revelation" of the earthly Jesus (Matt 11:27) is now expanded to the comprehensive authority of the exalted *Kyrios* who accompanies his disciples on the journey. This grounds the universality of the commission which they now receive. But there is no talk here of transferring this authority to the disciples. Their mission is simply to make disciples of all nations. If God made him who taught with authority into the Lord of all things, then being his disciple is the way to the kingdom of heaven.

But how does one make men and women disciples of Jesus? In the Greek text two participles explicate the commission from Jesus.

(1) "Baptizing them in the name of the Father and of the Son and of the Holy Spirit." This participle doubtless describes the integration of humankind into God's comprehensive work of salvation.

(2) "Teaching them to observe all that I have commanded you." The good news of the kingdom which Jesus preached is his salvific command which guides humankind to God's justice.[62]

The whole area of exorcisms and healings is here excluded at first, and everything is concentrated on crediting salvation to baptism and acquiring salvation by discipleship in the footsteps of the master!

A glance at Matt 7:21-23 shows that this is not an accident; rather it is a characteristic feature of the Matthean reception of Jesus' message: "Not everyone who says to me, 'Lord, Lord,' shall enter the kingdom of heaven, but he who does the will of my Father who is in heaven. On that day many will say to me, 'Lord, Lord, did we not prophesy in your name, and cast out demons in your name, and do many mighty works in your name?' And then will I declare to them, 'I never knew you; depart from me, you evildoers.'"

The proof of discipleship does not lie in phenomena such as prophesying, casting out demons or doing mighty works—but in doing the will of God! In this context the call to do God's will is not to be understood as law. Whoever reaches for God's kingdom and his justice, whoever accepts the comfort and takes on the challenge of the Beatitudes, and whoever takes on the gentle yoke and light burden of Jesus' teachings enters into salvific communion with God and finds peace for his or her plagued and burdensome life (cf. Matt 11:28-30).

We cannot say for certain whether Matthew wanted to limit all that he has described in 10:8 as authorization of the Twelve to Jesus' earthly ministry. For the mission to the nations these signs must decline in importance in comparison with the message of kingdom in the form of Jesus' teaching.[63]

It is not the authority of the disciples which grounds and supports the mission command, but the authority of the resurrected one and his presence with his own people, and it is not by chance that in Matt 28:18-20 both are not identified. But as those commissioned by the resurrected one, the disciples carry the figure and the teachings of the earthly Jesus to the nations and open the door for all to live in discipleship to him. "To lead someone into the kingdom of God" is thus for the Matthean community "to direct someone to his or her place in the discipleship of Jesus."

Witnesses of the Resurrected One—Luke

In Luke's two-volume work we find two short commissioning sayings by the resurrected one.[64] In Luke 24:46f. not only are the death and resurrection of the Messiah emphasized as the fulfillment of the words of Scripture, but so too is the call to repentance to all nations with the goal of the forgiveness of sins. The disciples are "eyewitnesses of the previous fulfillments" and will therefore "also bear witness to the nations concerning this."(v. 48)[65] For this task God will arm them with the Holy Spirit, the "power from on high" (v. 49). This promise is taken up in the very much better known saying of the resurrected one in Acts 1:8: "But you shall receive power when the Holy Spirit has come upon you; and you shall be my witnesses in Jerusalem and in all Judea and Samaria and to the end of the earth."

The following characteristic features are important for the early Christian mission in Lukan perspective:

(1) Preaching is witness to that which God has done in Jesus Christ. That encompasses his earthly ministry as well as his death and his resurrection.

43

(2) The goal as regards the contents of the preaching is repentance and the return of humankind to God, out of which the forgiveness of sin grows.

(3) The power of preaching is God's Holy Spirit.

(4) The addressees of the preaching are "all nations," its horizon "the end of the earth," whereby admittedly—in accordance with Luke's salvation history—an order beginning in Jerusalem proceeding to Judea and Samaria is maintained.

It is instructive that Luke reports in Acts how this program is maintained.

(1) Already with the selection of Matthias to succeed Judas as apostle it is important that he was a witness of Jesus' earthly ministry and resurrection, and a remark along these lines comes in Peter's sermons. But Paul is also called to be a "witness" (26:16) and so is legitimated as the most important bearer of the good news to the Gentiles.[66]

(2) The sermons of the missionaries are conversion sermons. Granted that each has its specific emphases, this is the case for the preaching to the Jews as well as to the Gentiles.

(3) The Holy Spirit is the motivating force behind all missionary activity in Acts. That begins with the programmatic start in the miracle of the many languages at Pentecost and continues in the crossing of important thresholds in the missionary activity which are sketched in chapters 8 and 10, in the commissioning and sending out of Barnabas and Paul for the coming Gentile mission (13:2) and in setting the course for the work in Macedonia and Greece (16:6f).

(4) The narration of Acts follows the geographic program of the commission—at least as far as Rome.

The subject of the kingdom of God is not forgotten in Acts. Philip's sermon about "the kingdom of God and the name of Jesus Christ" (8:12) finds faith in Samaria, and even Paul "preached the kingdom of God and taught about the Lord Jesus Christ" (28:31; cf. 28:23, 19:8, 20:25). God's future kingdom remains the content of the preaching. But it is, "as the content of the preaching, immediately supplemented by the reference to Jesus or interpreted through him."[67] The name Jesus discloses the essence of the kingdom of God. The mission of the church, however, in no way continues the epiphany of the kingdom of God in Jesus' ministry in spite of its successes. "Through many tribulations we must enter the kingdom of God," says Paul according to Acts 14:22. Thus mission in Luke also stands "under the sign of persecution and suffering."[68] This is so true although Luke very much likes to tell of the numerous and astounding miracles which the missionaries perform in his story of the mission. But they are not the content of the preaching, rather accompanying signs which point to Jesus.[69] This is exemplified in 3:9-12 where the connection between healing and preaching salvation in the name of Jesus is impressively drawn out. The summary reports in 5:12-16, 6:7f. and 19:11f. are formed analogous to the corresponding reports in the Gospel (cf. Luke 6:18f.). Such miracles work faith (5:14, 9:36-42, 13:9-12), but they also provoke misunderstandings (8:13-24, 14:8-18) in which becomes clear that the miracles as such cannot be the message itself, but can just underline its salvific character.

Where Luke portrays the encounter of the message with individuals he has a preference for such persons who are searching for God: the Ethopian eunuch who was reading the prophet Isaiah on the way back from a pilgrimage to Jerusalem, Cornelius, the god-fearing Gentile centurion and Lydia, the seller of purple goods who found her way to the place of prayer of Jews. They are all men and women who are open for the encounter with the gospel. But also in the case of these persons it is God who does the decisive act (cf. 16:14).

In this manner even people who fall into an existential crisis completely unprepared can receive the gospel, like the prison guard in Philippi or—in a totally exceptional manner—the persecutor of Christians, Saul of Tarsus.

Preaching Like Jesus

The disciples' commission, which according to the witness of the synoptic tradition they receive from the resurrected one, is different from what the same Gospels portray as Jesus' ministry and nonetheless stands in close connection with it.

The christological concentration is unambiguous. The relationship of their commission and authority with "the name of Jesus" proves to be a relationship with God's activity in his person, that is, with God's deed *extra nos*. There is thus no double commission after Easter to preach and to heal; rather there is just the commission to preach the healing, teaching, suffering, and resurrected Christ.

This does not mean that miraculous healings and exorcisms did not play a role in the early Christian mission. They remain signs of liberation and had significant meaning particularly for the social effectiveness of early Christianity.[70] But the exorcist does not act in his own authority, rather "in the name of Jesus," referring to God's activity in him.[71]

The turn to the poor is also less a part of the fundamental message than it is part of the actual life of the church. The renunciation of possessions and holding everything in common as the life style of the young church are particularly emphasized in the Lukan work. In the Letter of James, which is to be considered within the wider realm of influence of the synoptic tradition, we encounter a church of poor persons which lives out of the promise of their election by God as "heirs of the kingdom" (Jas 2:5).

It is thus clear that the reports of the Gospels about Jesus' ministry

45

should not only be told as memories of a past time of blessing, but should also be read and heard as ways of making present the "good news of the kingdom." But it is equally apparent that there is no intention to adopt Jesus' messianic praxis directly and then to continue it, rather to imagine it indirectly through the mediation of Jesus' person and to see this image grounded in God's activity in him alone.

The Gospel: God's Response to Suffering

What is the gospel of the evangelists? We shall attempt to give a preliminary answer to this question. The Synoptic Gospels summarize Jesus' message as the "gospel of the kingdom." The in-breaking of God's reign means deliverance and salvation for his people, especially for those persons among his people who are alienated from God.

Jesus' call, "The kingdom of God has come near," is more than merely a piece of information. In his ministry, especially in the liberation of the possessed, the healing of the sick, and the care for the poor and the outcast, God's eschatological reign begins now to show its redemptive and healing effect.

The human need into which this message is spoken and into which it works is the suffering which grows out of the distance of men and women from God. Those addressed by the message are persons who suffer from the alienation of their lives. This is most obvious with those who are possessed by demons. The division of their person, the seizure of the deepest center of life's action by the power of evil to the point of self-destruction, makes clear with an extremely painful symptom in what condition humankind as such is. It is alienated from itself because its life, instead of being led by God's salvific rule, is subservient to the power of evil. Into the midst of this need Jesus speaks his liberating and redeeming word. The possessed are freed of their demons, and the sick are healed—indeed even such whose sickness not only means physical weakness, but because of the prevailing purity regulations also has social exclusion as a consequence. The poor who have been written off by the society as worthless, the hungry whose painful stomach and physical weakness hinders every flight of fancy, the mourning who cannot overcome the pain of separation and loss—Jesus promises them all God's presence and lives it for them. In his mouth it is not a vague putting-off tactic that God will supply their want; it is a promise that is dependable and a reality that can stand up to the test.

Despised women and men disqualified by their professions hear and experience through him that the contempt of society does not yet mean God's judgment upon their lives and find the strength for a new beginning.

It is thus—stated somewhat simplistically—the *victims* to whom Jesus turns.[72] This can be seen especially impressively in the center of his activity,

46

the liberation of the demon possessed. In contrast to pastoral-exorcistic practice as frequently exercised today these persons are not asked for the causes of their possession, not questioned about occult activities or accusations by parents, grandparents, relatives, or acquaintances and then once again declared to be guilty. Jesus' authority liberates without asking.

A person's sin is also a dimension of his or her misery. It is less the deep conflict between ethical claim and moral failure which comes into view in Jesus' encounter with sinners than the ambiguous area of human existence in which, in the struggle for survival and the banality of a wretched everyday life, only a moral *vita minima* can be lived.

But where this everyday life comes in touch with God's presence in Jesus' ministry the cry breaks loose, "Depart from me, for I am a sinful man, O Lord!" (Luke 5:8). Jesus' response to that is the promise of the presence in the epiphanal form, "Do not be afraid," and the acceptance of the sinner in the form of the call to discipleship.

Current observers of the situation in the favelas of South America or the townships of South Africa often report about the exemplary solidarity and humanity of the poor. These experiences should maintain their own value, although they could be juxtaposed with others that reveal the brutality with which persons struggling for survival treat one another. As far as exegetical issues are concerned, however, we must observe that in the Jesus-tradition there is not the slightest indication that it is because of their poverty that the poor are models or even "not sinners" and "subjects of the kingdom of God."[73] What is decisive is rather that in their want, they need God's presence. Therefore Jesus comes to them.

So his message of salvation also does not consist of accusations of others although the rich and the scribes are occasionally sharply criticized. It is God's presence alone which heals and frees.[74] The answer which God gives to human need in Jesus' ministry can scarcely be more fittingly summarized than in Matt 11:28-30. Jesus' call, "Come to me all who labor and are heavy laden, and I will give you rest," characterizes not only his preaching but his behaviour as well. His table fellowship with tax collectors and sinners and his service of liberation and healing were lived out invitations to the "exhausted" who struggled under the burden of sickness, poverty, suffering, and guilt.

The post-resurrection church took up Jesus' proclamation and yet did not simply continue it.[75] In so doing the church made clear that the rule of God does not come from simply persisting with Jesus' ministry. The "building up the kingdom of God," as it was phrased in the nineteenth century, terminologically has no basis in the New Testament. It is not the goal of the mission and evangelism of the church to build the kingdom of God.[76]

The permanent content of the gospel is, however, indeed that the kingdom of God has come near, and preaching is done in the expectation that God will erect his kingdom. This horizon is outlined when Rev 21:3f. sketches the goal of God's action with humankind. The words which the seer hears sound like the description of the fulfillment of that which God has begun in Jesus: "He will wipe away every tear from their eyes, and death shall be no more, neither shall there be mourning nor crying nor pain anymore" (v. 4).

On its journey from Jesus' messianic praxis to eschatological fulfillment the community of disciples is allowed to and must take up Jesus' call and carry on with it. The invitation to those who labor and are heavy laden, to those who are exhausted and overtaxed is also the foundation of its mission. It lives this mission in its service to the sick, the helpless, the captive and the needy, and in its fellowship, in the middle of which stands the table fellowship with the crucified and exalted Lord and which is so formed in its sacramental and human dimension by Christ's openness and sacrifice, and in its witness in which it tells about Jesus' invitation and passes it on.

Evangelism befitting the gospel is evangelism in service of this invitation. It relieves those of whom too much is demanded. It liberates the captive. It heals the sick and worn down and gives new courage to those who have failed. But it does that not on its own authority, but rather in the name of Jesus. "Naming the name" is the most important function of evangelism in the context of the integral mission of the church.[77]

A Hermeneutic of Discipleship

Jesus did not develop a hermeneutic. He assumed his hearers knew what he meant when he spoke of the kingdom of God. And nonetheless he did not just take over their preunderstanding. He taught about the kingdom of God in parables and showed it in his mighty acts.

The basis of the hermeneutic of the parables is the invitation of the hearer to agree with the message they bear. The "who among you" parables are particularly attractive examples of the identifying style of preaching with which Jesus draws his hearers with everyday stories and insights into the ministry of the kingdom of God. What Jesus says is intimately bound up with his works. Without directly depicting himself in one of the characters in his parables, his person and commission are the secret center of many parables.

We observe the same thing in Jesus' mighty acts. Their goal is to bring men and women into the salvific presence of the reign of God. And in just this way they provoke the question regarding his person: "Who is this man?"

Jesus turns around John the Baptist's question, "Are you he who is to come?" by answering with a reference to his ministry and concludes the list with the sentence, "And blessed is he who takes no offense at me" (Luke 7:19, 23)!

The "messianic secret" turns out to be the hermeneutical key to Jesus' message. That is the objectively correct contribution of the "parable theory" in Mark 4:10ff. As much as Jesus' parables are nothing other than an open invitation to declare one's agreement with his ministry, the secret of the kingdom of God is nonetheless disclosed only to those whose eyes have been opened to the significance of his person.[78]

How is this connection further pursued by the community of disciples? Must their preaching of the kingdom of God be replaced or supplemented by the christological message? How are they to make this bond understandable in its original sense?

Here we must once again recall the fundamental meaning of discipleship to be able to understand this. As we have seen, Jesus did not indiscriminately call all persons who encountered him to become his disciples. His call was to certain individuals as examples. In a Jewish context, following a master meant nothing more than becoming his student.[79]

Jesus' selection was not elitist. We never learn anything about any prerequisites for this profession, not even anything about the internal conversion of those called. There are no preconditions, just the call to the decision to orient oneself completely to Jesus. But this call does not first of all include an ethical imperative, rather above all the invitation to open oneself to a model of learning. This model of learning is based on simply "being with Jesus" (Mark 3:14), accompanying him, experiencing his authority, receiving his teaching, and sharing his way to the cross.[80] Particularly the last aspect, which in the face of the historical failure of the disciples sounds a bit strange, has special meaning. For the bond between recognizing Christ and following him in suffering, which is so impressively emphasized in Mark 8:27–10:52, holds true for the situation after the resurrection as well.

Understanding discloses itself in consent, but consent grows out of the openness for that which God performs in the person of Jesus. It makes sense that Matthew arranged Jesus' praise for the revelation of the message to the "babes" with the invitation to those who labor and are heavy laden (Matt 11:27-30). Understanding Jesus' message is understanding in consummation of the acceptance of that with which God gifts us through him. Evangelism in the spirit of Jesus is thus always an invitation to discipleship as the way of life with Jesus and so as the way of experience and understanding.

Evangelism in the spirit of Jesus is, however, at the same time consum-

49

mation of this discipleship by Jesus' disciples who by walking in his footsteps bring the message of the healing closeness of the kingdom of God to those persons who need it the most. For them, too, the hermeneutic needed to make the gospel understandable to others consists above all in "being with Jesus." It is not by chance that the life of the pre-resurrection group of disciples is not only the paradigm of being a Christian, but the seed of the apostolate, the missionary commission of the church. To make Jesus' message understandable means to live it, to show persons whose life appears to be worthless how much God loves them, to impress on persons who are injured, sick or handicapped how close to them God's help is—to live in such a manner that they are so made "whole." It is all the same whether God grants signs of miraculous healing or lets a person grow in suffering. Living Jesus' message means to make present God's liberating power to those held captive by addiction, possessed by compulsive ideas, burdened by occult experiences, or oppressed by their guilt—be it that one does this in prayer, with authoritative words of comfort and encouragement, or by patiently accompanying the sufferer.

Jesus' speaking in parables put the essence of the kingdom of God into words using the events of everyday life. Lived discipleship enables others to experience and understand the nearness and power of the kingdom of God in daily life. Such discipleship is not the kingdom of God, but lives it as a parable.[81]

The Word of the Cross

The message about the crucified and resurrected Christ forms the center of Pauline preaching. Where Paul formulates this message he does this in two ways. The gospel is the announcement of God's activity in Jesus' death and resurrection and at the same time the revelation of God's justice. Both aspects are inseparable, but nonetheless they must be distinguished.

The Proclamation of Jesus' Death and Resurrection

Paul had occasion in 1 Cor 15 once again to remind the church in Corinth which gospel he preached to them during his first period of ministry in the city and so became the foundation and content of their faith.[82] In his introductory remarks Paul characterizes this gospel as the message of deliverance which enjoys lasting validity. In so doing he appeals to a set formula which he had impressed upon the Corinthians and points out that what he passed on to the Corinthians he himself had adopted as tradition.

The last two references agree completely with the form critical observation that Paul cites a pre-formed piece of early Christian tradition in

vv. 3-5.[83] He probably adopted it from the church in Antioch which possibly had come to Antioch from Jerusalem. It is a catechetical summary of the Christian faith and possibly began with the words, "We believe that Christ died for our sins."[84]

In the summary Jesus' story is described in a double parallelism, and it is strongly emphasized that this is the story of the "Christ," i.e., the Messiah.[85] His death and his burial, his resurrection and his appearance before the Easter witnesses are named, and in so doing each first element in the list always receives the explanatory addition "in accordance with the scriptures." The death and resurrection of the Christ correspond to the will of God according to the witness of his word. The reference back to the Scriptures identifies Christ's fate as God's activity in the history of Jesus. That this event is anchored in human history is underlined by each second element of the double formula: The facticity of Jesus' death is secured by the reference to his burial; the reality of his being raised from the dead is verified by those to whom the risen Christ appeared.[86]

In the first element in the formula it is made clear that the gospel does not come to an end in the information about past events: "Died for our sins" describes the redemptive meaning of the facts named and so indicates to what extent this gospel is a message of deliverance and which significance the historical events have for the life of the hearer. In our context we may leave unexamined the fact that Paul uses this summary of early Christian preaching in what follows as the basis for a discussion of the reality of the resurrection of the dead. For us it is important that he is convinced that this formula outlines the missionary message as generally preached in early Christianity and is the basis and content of faith for all churches (v. 11).

In another passage as well, Paul characterizes his preaching of the gospel with the use of christological formulas. In the salutation of his Letter to the Romans, Paul apparently wants to introduce himself to the unknown church immediately as an apostle, and, significantly, he does this by giving a terse summary of his gospel. After having also established here that this message is anchored in the promise of the Scriptures (1:2), Paul characterizes his gospel as God's gospel of "his Son . . . Jesus Christ our Lord" and inserts as a more precise definition of Jesus' sonship a double formula, probably adopted as well, which describes Jesus as he "who was descended from David according to the flesh and designated Son of God in power according to the Spirit of holiness by his resurrection from the dead."[87]

Without soteriological explication christological "facts" are passed on here, which, of course, are not interesting as historical information about Jesus' descent and his individual *post mortem* fate, rather as "facts" of salvation history regarding his being anchored in Israel's history of promise and of his designation as eschatological Savior.[88]

The soteriological dimension of the message of Christ's being raised from the dead determines the description of the genesis of the Thessalonian church in 1 Thess 1:9f. as well. Here, too, Paul likely cites basic elements of the "gospel of God" which, according to 1 Thess 2:2, he preached in Thessalonica. Nonetheless, the use of a formula, which together with Acts 14:15-17 (17:22-31) and Heb 6:2 is at the same time a witness for a "preliminary monotheistic missionary sermon" to the Gentiles, cannot be proved with certainty.[89] The core of that preaching which founds churches and awakens faith is that "witness of God with a very definite content, namely the history of Christ."[90]

Elements of this method are also to be found in Acts 17:30ff.: The necessity and possibility of delivering repentance is founded on the designation of Jesus as the eschatological judge (cf. Acts 10:42, Rom 1:4). Also in Paul's missionary speeches before the Jews in Jerusalem the resurrection of Jesus (2:24; 3:15, 26; 5:30) and his designation as Lord and Christ or as leader and Savior found and make possible repentance and the forgiveness of sins. The retrospective look at the ministry and the death of Jesus (with the stereotypical formula: whom you have crucified/killed—2:23, 36; 3:15; 5:30) emphasizes like a banner the conflict between (and entanglement of) God's will to save the addressees and their guilt.[91] The same schema is also to be found in Peter's preaching before the god fearers in the house of Cornelius in Caesarea and in Paul's sermon in the synogogue in Antioch (cf. 10:40-43, 13:33, 37ff.), only that in an oddly distant and historicizing manner the death of Jesus is blamed on the Jews of Jerusalem alone.

In summary: The center of the early Christian Easter message, the testimony, "God raised him [Jesus] from the dead" (Rom 4:24f., 10:9),[92] is also the core of the early Christian mission message. It does not tell this news as an isolated historical fact, but rather in its eschatological significance. God has intervened in the kingdom of death and torn open the horizon of its fulfillment. Therefore Jesus' resurrection means "resurrection from the dead." At the same time God's action in raising Jesus from the dead discloses the significance of his fate. For Paul and the tradition to which he refers the significance is to be found in the meaning of his death for our salvation; through his death he has atoned for the sins of humankind and taken on humankind's mortal fate in its place.

For Luke and his tradition it is the ministry of the "Prince of Life" in signs and miracles and the unmasking effect of his murder by the citizens of Jerusalem which should make a direct impression on his hearers in the core of their being. Briefly put, missionary gospel in this context therefore means telling about that which God has done in Christ. That, however, is not the only dimension of the gospel which Paul brought out as a foundation of missionary activity.

The Revelation of God's Righteousness

Whereas Paul had cited his original gospel in 1 Cor 15 in the course of a debate with the church, he speaks of the other fundamental qualification of his gospel in a context which has somewhat more to do with our subject. In the introduction of Romans, Paul shows why he wants to preach the gospel in Rome—a delicate problem since according to 15:20 he actually just wants to minister where the name of Jesus is not yet known. But his preaching in Rome should be seen especially in the context of his whole missionary commission:

> I am under obligation both to the Greeks and to the barbarians, both to the wise and to the foolish: so I am eager to preach the gospel to you also who are in Rome. For I am not ashamed of the gospel: it is the power of God for salvation to every one who has faith, to the Jew first and also to the Greek. For in it the righteousness of God is revealed through faith for faith; as it is written, "He who through faith is righteous shall live" (Rom 1:14-17).

Paul gives two reasons for his willingness, indeed his inner drive, to preach the gospel to as many people as possible. His commission to preach directs him to all persons,[93] and also the gospel which is entrusted to him does not just announce God's activity in Christ (1:3f.); as a message it is itself God's creative power for salvation which delivers everyone who in trust opens him- or herself to it—Jews to whom this message was first directed as well as Greeks, i.e., the non-Jewish part of ancient society.

But what does Paul mean when he describes the gospel as *dynamis eis sōtērian*? In principle, *sōtēria* is for Paul deliverance from the final judgment whose sentence has already been passed for everyone (cf. 5:9; 1 Thess 1:10; Acts 17:31). Used absolutely, however, *sōtēria* also outlines in positive form the redeemed life in the coming communion with God, as is certainly the case in Rom 13:11: "For salvation is nearer to us now than when we first believed" (cf. also 1 Thess 5:8-9). This communion with God has already begun now in the acceptance of the gospel (cf. 2 Cor 6:2).[94]

The gospel is characterized in Rom 1:16 and in 1 Cor 15:2 as a message of deliverance. Its salvific effect is grounded here, however, not with the announcement of the soteriologically interpreted Christ event (1 Cor 15:3; cf. 1 Thess 5:9), rather with the description of that which takes place in the preaching of the gospel: in the Gospel God's righteousness is revealed.[95]

In traditio-historical perspective this statement is to be understood against the background of Ps 98:2, Isa 56:1 and the Qumran texts 1QH 4:16 and CD 20:20. The apocalyptic revelation of God's righteousness is the appearance of his faithfulness to his people in front of the entire world and the carrying through of his salvific help in spite of all opposition and all enemies. This revelation is now fulfilled in the gospel, and it is valid not only for Israel or the holy remnant in it, but for everyone who believes, or—as v. 17 formulates it—"through faith for faith," i.e., it is received on the basis of faith and has faith as its goal.[96]

Of course, the revelation of God's righteousness must be understood in christological terms as regards its contents. For Christ has been made our righteousness (1 Cor 1:30, also cf. 2 Cor 5:21). Paul shows that in detail in Rom 3:21-26 where, after the long excursus in Rom 1:18–3:20, he comes back to the revelation of God's righteousness again: God's righteousness *is* revealed.[97] God has demonstrated his faithfulness unto salvation "through the redemption which is in Christ Jesus" by granting expiation for sinners through Jesus' death. What God did in that act once and for all is now fulfilled in preaching about Jesus to those who are open to it in faith. The proclamation of the gospel pulls human beings into God's action and removes from their lives the claim of guilt that is past, but not yet overcome, and it leads them into a life in communion with God which is oriented toward the fulfillment to come.

The gospel of Rom 1:16f. is materially nothing else but "the word of the cross," which is named in the parallel in 1 Cor 1:17ff. as the content of Paul's evangelistic message and bearer of God's power and wisdom. It is also astonishing how the salvation event and preaching are linked in this passage. Because the world, in its wisdom, denies knowledge of God (1:21, cf. Rom 1:21), God decided to deliver those who believe through the "folly of what we preach." The gospel is also here the message of deliverance, but this message is "good news" in the "foolish sermon" which promises us that God was present in Jesus who was hung on a cross. Not the reference to the mighty acts which could verify the preaching—although the apostle later will speak of signs and miracles which accompany his preaching (Rom 15:19, 2 Cor 12:12)—and not the exposition of speculative or esoteric wisdom grants communion with God—although he will later speak of divine wisdom which one recognizes in Christ's cross (1 Cor 2:6-16)—the proclamation of Jesus Christ alone, and of him as crucified, leads to salvation.

In this passage, to be sure, the divisive effect of the gospel comes up, too. On the word of the cross part the ways of those who are about to be lost and of those who are being saved.[98] Nonetheless, even in this distressing conclusion Paul's horizon always remains universal: In 1 Cor 1:21 the believers as the object of God's salvific action stand in chiastic opposition to the world as the subject of knowledge which does not know God. Conversely, the Jews asking for signs and the Greeks seeking wisdom, for whom the crucified Christ is a stumbling block and folly, stand in opposition to those who are called, both Jews and Greeks, on the positive side, for whom Christ becomes God's power and wisdom.[99]

In 2 Cor 5:18-21 Paul shows most impressively that the cross and the "word of the cross," salvation event and proclamation, belong together. Verses 18 and 19 are parallels. First, the personal statement of the apostle: The renewal of life sketched in v. 17 has its origin in God alone who has reconciled himself with us through Christ and has entrusted us with the ministry of reconciliation—doubtless an allusion to Paul's radical change of heart in which he simultaneously experienced the overcoming of his unknown enmity against God and his call to be an apostle as "servant of the new covenant."[100]

Paul then continues, giving reason and possibly citing a pre-formed expression: "In Christ God was reconciling the world to himself, not counting their trespasses against them, and entrusting to us the message of reconciliation" (v. 19).[101] God's work of reconciliation which comes to fulfillment in the Christ event and the forgiveness of sins becomes concrete in the commission to be messengers of peace who call those who were previously enemies into God's peace.

Paul comments on these statements in chiastic succession. Verse 20 follows on v. 19b and describes the role of the apostle as that of an ambassador and authorized representative of God. Reconciliation which is truly reconciliation is not dictated, but rather offered to the enemy. Not that there would be anything more to negotiate or that indeed certain conditions would still have to be worked out, reconciliation is such that God's peace for humankind only becomes a reality in a person's life when he or she grasps God's hand which is extended in reconciliation. This reconciling hand of God encounters humankind in apostolic preaching. In this connection Paul dares even to speak of "beseeching on behalf of Christ" in the attempt to underline the urgency and sincerity of God's peace offer.[102]

It is noteworthy that what is obviously the contents of Paul's fundamental missionary message is said to a church which "as saints called in Christ Jesus" must be regarded as long since reconciled with God (cf. Rom 5:9). But in rejecting the apostle and turning to enthusiastic special doctrines, the Corinthians are clearly in danger of leaving the realm of reconciliation. So in 6:2 words are directed to them which we can assume to have been marks of early Christian missionary preaching and are used here to re-evangelize a church of the first generation.[103]

But we must still come back to 5:21, a verse which picks up v. 19a and in which Paul wants to explain what the ontological basis for God's act and word of reconciliation is. The paradigm "reconciliation" for the renewal of the relationship between God and humankind is taken from the profane realm: It is a peace agreement between two estranged parties which is put

55

into force unilaterally by the stronger.[104] Verse 21 tells how this peace agreement became possible and how the power of sin, which had stood as enmity between God and humankind, was broken and removed.

God has made him who did not know sin in his own experience the bearer of sin, to be "sin absolutely,"[105] so that "we," i.e., the apostle and the church, can become "ambassadors of God's righteousness." That means that Jesus stands between humankind and God. The deadly circle of suppressing guilt and blaming it all on someone or something else is broken. In Jesus' death on the cross human sin is designated and disclosed simultaneously in its enmity against God and against humankind and relieved of its death-bringing power. All who get involved with their own story in this identification process of sin and the sinless Jesus now become, for their part, "ambassadors of God's righteousness which is revealed in the gospel." To live from God's faithfulness unto salvation means at the same time to be formed and determined by it and to bear witness to it as the sphere of life in peace and in communion with God.

The Gospel: God's Response to Guilt

Our observations regarding the contents and essence of missionary preaching have shown a double aspect of the gospel. Both characteristics, however, do not stand unrelated next to one another; rather, they are closely connected with each other:

(1) The gospel as the message of God's activity in Jesus Christ reports about God's reconciling work in Jesus' cross and resurrection.

(2) The gospel as the inauguration of salvation makes God's faithfulness unto salvation present for everyone who hears and accepts the message.

Soteriologically both aspects are equally important. Anchoring God's work of salvation historically in the contingency of a human life and death sinks God's redeeming love deep into the reality of human existence. The message does not proclaim a Christ idea or a Christ principle, but God's concrete act in Jesus of Nazareth's life and death—without our assistance. The exclusiveness of God's work paradoxically grounds the universality of its validity. Because it took place *extra nos*, without us (when we were still sinners! Rom 5:8), God's act of salvation is for everyone.

But in addition to that comes the other aspect. In that preaching God's act of salvation reveals and makes present his faithfulness unto salvation, the historical events of cross and resurrection are not just isolated facts from the past; rather they become the present active reality of God's concern for us. Jesus' atoning death is not a deal concluded in the past in which debts were paid off; it is, as death preached, the present expression and effective reality of Christ's proexistence. In the perfect tense of God's revelation are bound together the aorist of salvation history and the present tense of the proclamation.

This is expressed soteriologically in the reformation formula: Justification takes place for Christ's sake by faith. It is a presupposition of the gospel's remaining the gospel that this circle is not sprung. We must point to what God has done for us once and for all in such a manner that this is good news and not a law of faith; and we must preach faith in such a manner that faith does not constitute the art of living, but holding on to God's work.[106] Here lies the challenge of evangelism in accordance with the gospel and evangelistic preaching of the gospel. Justification by faith for Christ's sake is not only the content of the message; it also describes its essence.[107]

Where this should take place depends on the addressee of the gospel. To what human need does this gospel want to respond? From what should this person be delivered? The addressee of the gospel is the person who is guilty before God and therefore sentenced to judgment. It is the person who is ruled by sin because he or she sins, for whom sin has thus become a second self and so separates him- or herself from God and communion with God (cf. Rom 7:13-23).

This takes place concretely in breaking God's commandments (Rom 2, 7:7ff.). That results fundamentally in enmity against God; for where human beings make their transitory created nature into the standard of behavior they become God's enemy (Rom 8:7). This basic attitude leads one into a double form of the conflict in which the law plays a decisive role in each:[108]

(1) The "antinomian" conflict: One follows the desire of the flesh and breaks God's commandment. One recognizes from the violations of the commandments in what condition humankind really is (Rom 3:20, 5:20, 7:7ff.; Gal 3:19).

(2) The "nomian" conflict: One attempts to fulfill the law as impeccably as possible and is seduced by that to trust in one's own religious achievement, "to boast in the flesh." One does not really seek God's righteousness, but one's own (Phil 3:9; Rom 10:1-3).

Paul did not set the two lines of thought systematically in relation to one another anywhere, so in some places it is an open question as to which conflict he means. It is important, however, that the message about justification is not just for those who ask after a just God. In the encounter with the crucified Christ even the *homo religiosus* who is self-certain and confident of his God experiences the fragility of the foundation of his life and his acceptance by God through grace. To what extent it is necessary to place a Christian proclamation of the law next to the sermon of the gospel is an open question which we shall pick up once again below. Paul indicates in Rom 2:15, however, that all these statements are not limited to persons who know the Jewish law. Every human being recognizes that he or she is

57

addressed. One senses the meaning which lies in the challenge of one's life to accomplish something and then by means of this accomplishment to be somebody. One experiences oneself, however, also as one of whom too much has been expected and who has failed, or as one who has protected oneself by absolutizing one's own accomplishments and (often) suppressing thoughts of the remaining deficits. The figure of the *homo religiosus* is thus also to be found in completely secular models, in his obvious failure as well as in his failure hidden under apparent success. It is therefore important to bring out the different dimensions of the action of justification and to put this into words in preaching.[109]

Justification means forgiveness and acquittal of concrete guilt. Guilt is a permanent existential factor of human existence. Guilt also exists in a society where almost everything appears to be allowed and thus superficially few guilty feelings are felt. Where the life of others is injured or destroyed guilt arises. It often remains unconscious, but has disastrous effects by projecting guilt on to "scapegoats"; it is compensated for in aggression or is held tight in unconscious self-punishment by neurotic illness. By promising men and women that God has overcome and cleared them of their guilt, the message of the cross opens the way for them to recognize and acknowledge their guilt and enables them, through the identification with Jesus's death, to overcome and assimilate their own guilt.[110]

Justification at one and the same time means accepting my own life, being valued by God, and being received into communion with him. The word of the cross opens up room for living with God which is not constituted by human accomplishments but by God's concern for us. His call is directed to the weak, the despised, and the foolish (in contemporary English, those who have the impression of always being "suckers"), those who have given up and those who have failed—thus all those whose guilt consists of not having made (or not having been able to make) of their lives what God put in it. The message of the cross and resurrection of Jesus tells them that God's weakness, which reaches them in their weakness, is stronger than all human power and that being valued in his love is worth more than whatever status social respect, wealth, or accomplishment could bestow.

Thus at the same time justification by grace means that it is possible to renounce securing one's own life. The word of the cross is therefore the urgent invitation to leave all the bunkers, armor, or protests of self-righteousness and self-representation before God and humankind. "The guilt of not being able to become guilty"[111] can also destroy a human life. The inability to accept one's own limits, to concede mistakes or accept help from others, the neurotic necessity to protect oneself with strict rules or standards suffocates every authentic life in relation to others and to God. For whomever lives such a life the message of the cross is a scandal. But where the affront is overcome and the message finds faith, it frees one for a life lived out of grace, a life which permits one to be merciful to oneself and to others and is thus filled with joy, love, and thanks.

A Hermeneutic of Authority in Suffering

At first glance, the "word of the cross" appears to be fundamentally closed to every human attempt to understand it and to every hermeneutic. Because it pleased God to redeem the world through the "foolishness of the sermon," preaching the crucified Christ appears as a scandal to the Jews and as nonsense to the Greeks. It becomes God's power and God's wisdom only for those who are called (1 Cor 1:21-24)!

Similarly, 2 Cor 2:15f. speaks succintly of apostolic preaching's being "a fragrance from death to death" to some and "a fragrance from life to life" to others. God alone, however, grants the competency to preach the gospel as the word that brings life (2:16b, 3:5f.).

But there is still another side of this event. In 1 Thess 2:13 Paul writes to the church in Thessalonica: "And also we thank God constantly for this, that when you received the word of God which you had heard from us, you accepted it not as the word of men but as what it really is, the word of God, which is at work in you believers."

Just before this he had looked back and described how that came to be: Paul had dared, although he had been mistreated in Philippi, to preach the gospel of God in Thessalonica. He did not make the financial demands of an apostle when he came; "But we were gentle among you, like a nurse taking care of her chidren. So, being affectionately desirous of you, we were ready to share with you not only the gospel of God but also our own selves, because you had become very dear to us" (2:7-8). That Paul's gospel "came to you not only in word, but also in power and in the Holy Spirit and with full conviction" (1:5) is thus also bound up with his readiness to suffer and offer his own life. For the Christians in Thessalonica followed his example (and that of the Lord) and have "received the word in much affliction, with joy inspired by the Holy Spirit" (1:6). And thus they became an example to others and living ambassadors of the message of faith.

When Paul writes to the Corinthians in the same manner that he "did not come proclaiming to you the testimony of God in lofty words of wisdom," rather was determined "to know nothing among you except Christ crucified" (1 Cor 2:1-5), then this means that there as well he was prepared to stand up for the strangeness of this message in this world with his whole life. In just this way the message and the messenger become transparent for God's power; in this way the "proof of the Spirit and of the power" is offered.

Whoever demands more "power" for authoritative preaching has not recognized how God's power works.[112]

Paul had to explicate this hermeneutic of authority in suffering in the conflict with hostile apostles whose ministry in Corinth had given rise to the impression that God's glory and transformative power was not sufficiently revealed in Paul's preaching. In this context the apostle passionately maintained that in his preaching the light of the creative word of God, which lit up in the form of Christ, shines on (cf. 2 Cor 3:18, 4:4b, 6). But the content of his preaching is not his own experience, but Jesus Christ as the Lord alone. The messenger is nonetheless a part of the message—but only as a servant (2 Cor 4:5). His ministry and his well-being are the "earthen vessels" in which God lays the treasure of his gospel in order clearly "to show that the transcendent power belongs to God and not to us" (4:7).

In the form of the preacher who is tempted and nonetheless protected, the power of the message, and its strangeness as well, finds its earthly expression. Which salvation the gospel grants—namely, life out of death (4:8-12, cf. also 1:8-10)—becomes comprehensible in this form.[113]

It is thus no accident that immediately following the leading statements of the apostle's evangelistic preaching in 2 Cor 5:20 and 6:2 there stands a description of his devoted service (6:3-10). That is not only apologetics; it is an existential hermeneutic of the message of the cross!

This is expressed in even more pointed form in the "speech of a fool" in 2 Cor 11:16–12:10 where Paul cites a saying of the Lord to him: "My grace is sufficient for you, for my power is made perfect in weakness" (12:9). The authority of the apostle originates in his powerlessness and the ill-treatment and afflictions, persecutions and fears which he bears for Christ's sake because Christ himself works and speaks through them.[114]

When Paul then writes in 1 Cor 9:22b, "I have become all things to all men, that I might by all means save some," this indicates less that the content of his message was flexible than it describes the messenger's proexistence which corresponds to the proexistence of the one who had commissioned him.

The Word Became Flesh

If we ask what the gospel of missionary preaching in the New Testament was, we must also consider another circle of tradition which is centered around the key term "the sending of the son." In the New Testament it is in traditio-historical terms not connected with the term "gospel," and in its more complete development it is not at home in missionary preaching. But in reference to the subject matter it makes a fundamental statement of the Christian message which is to be told all people.

It is above all the missionary aspect of the message of the Gospel of

John which one must consider here, but the form of this tradition in Paul and the Letter to the Hebrews must also be included.[115]

Salvation by Revelation

There is some controversy as to what degree the Gospel of John can be considered at all as a witness of the missionary message. Whereas earlier exegetes characterized the Gospel as virtually a "missionary writing," it has recently been maintained by more than a few that the book is more likely a "sectarian writing"—in any event, at least the written expression of the esoteric message of a church wrapped up in itself and referring only to itself.[116] Oddly, the textual tradition of the decisive word in 20:31 is hopelessly divided, so that it is not clear at first glance whether this concluding reference to the aim of the Gospel reads "[This is] written that you may believe [aorist subjunctive] that Jesus is the Christ, the Son of God" or ""[This is] written that you may live [or "remain," present subjunctive] in faith that. . . ."[117]

But one must distinguish between the question of whether the Gospel of John was composed as a missionary writing for outsiders and the question of to what degree, irrespective of its being addressed to such a group, it is a witness for the missionary dimension of the early Christian message anyway.

If the missiological slogan of the *missio Dei* as the foundation of all mission work applies anywhere in the New Testament, then it is to the Johannine writings.[118] The sending of the Son by the Father is the salvation event itself. In John 5:24 Jesus says, "Truly, truly, I say to you, he who hears my word and believes him who sent me, has eternal life; he does not come into judgment, but has passed from life to death." And in 17:3 at the beginning of the high-priestly prayer it is said even more trenchantly, "And this is eternal life, that they know thee the only true God, and Jesus Christ whom thou hast sent." Consequently, the existence and unity of the community of disciples, for whom the departing Christ prays, also serves the goal, "that the world may believe/know that you have sent me" (17:21, 23). And the Johannine post-resurrection commission saying accordingly reads, "As the Father has sent me, even so I send you" (20:21). The revelation of the Father in sending the Son is salvation and redemption for the world.

In the prologue of the Gospel the Evangelist stakes out the context of this statement.[119] By taking up the term *logos* which is so laden with meaning, he leads the reader into the area of tension between God, world, creation, revelation and redemption. In the *logos* the eternal God steps out of himself as the creating and revealing God. The *logos* cradles in himself life out of God, and as the light which gives life and illuminates humankind's

61

existence he shines into the darkness of men and women who stand far from God. The world, to be sure, does not recognize what the light lives from and does not accept its origin. But where the miracle occurs that persons receive God's living word, believe in "his" name, they are authorized to be his children, to belong to him alone.

In anticipation, right to begin with the Evangelist weaves into this first overview of the way of the divine word towards its goal the commission of the first witness of the *logos*, John the Baptist, who has come to bear witness "that all might believe through him."[120]

The incarnation of the Word is the message of the second part of the prologue, combined with the witness of the church to have encountered God's glory in God's only begotten Son and to have experienced divine salvation as eternal grace and "steadfastly lasting truth" in him.[121] In the Word become flesh—and that means, as the reference to John the Baptist makes clear, Jesus of Nazareth—the reality and presence of God is disclosed to humankind, namely his faithfulness and his mercy in the midst of a world which remains in darkness. The only begotten Son as the "interpreter" of the unseen God—that is the message which the book that follows this prologue is to unfold.

The missionary character of this message is shown above all in the first part of the Gospel. The first long section, 1:19–2:11, portrays in exemplary fashion how the witness of John the Baptist and the ministry of Jesus lead to the goal: Jesus reveals his glory, and his disciples come to belief in him (2:11). Woven into this report is also the story of how the witness goes on from one person to the next, how one disciple finds another, tells him about Jesus, refers him to Jesus, and how the encounter with Jesus then leads to a clear confession. Unlike the reports of the Synoptic Gospels, in the Johannine story of the calling of the disciples the initiative does not come from Jesus alone; in this manner it obviously ought to become a model of how to lead someone to Jesus.[122]

The next longer section, 2:23–3:36, will in contrast deepen the insights already gained. Proceeding from the conclusion obtained in 2:23 and in conversation with Nicodemus, it describes what the true faith is which opens eternal life. And in 3:22-36 the Evangelist once again reaches back to the witness of John the Baptist and following upon that grounds the possibility of faith in the witness of the Son alone.[123]

Jesus' encounter with the Samaritan woman, 4:1-42, has always been regarded as a textbook case of mission.[124] In a very striking way it connects the human situation and symbolic speech, the uncovering of personal guilt and a discussion of controversial religious questions with Jesus' self-revelation, and, typically, this encounter of Jesus with a single woman leads to others' coming to faith through her witness because they are led to their own encounter with him. But woven into this series of events is also Jesus' puzzling conversation with his disciples about sowing and harvesting, a conversation which undoubtably has a missionary dimension (vv. 34-38).[125]

The journey of a person to faith is then once again portrayed in detail in the healing of a man born blind, admittedly strongly against the background of the rejection of Jesus by the official representatives of the people. The inquiry of the Greeks who wanted to see Jesus (12:20ff.) gives occasion to express the view that Jesus' death will bear much fruit, i.e., that he will open the gate for all nations of the earth.

In the second part of the Gospel, whose main topic is Jesus' care and the consummation of his love for "his own" (13:1), the missionary dimension of the existence of the community of disciples in the world appears in brief but important passages. Verse 13:20 picks up the principle of the early Christian missionary theology; in 17:20-23 Jesus prays for those who come to faith through the witness of the disciples[126] and sees in the unity of the proclaimer and those come to faith the sign by which the world recognizes that he has been sent by the Father.

In 20:21-23 we find the Johannine version of the post-resurrection commissioning and authorizing of the disciples. Significantly what follows this is the scene with doubting Thomas, the disciple who "was not there," which apparently picks up the situation of the later hearers of the Easter message and therefore closes with the makarism, "Blessed are those who have not seen and yet believe" (20:29b). This saying also doubtless lends a missionary accent to the concluding verse of chapter 20.

The Gospel of John would thus like to pass on the gospel, a message of salvation which opens for humankind the way to communion with God, to "eternal life." But what is the content of this message? What does the one sent by the Father proclaim? What has he who has come from heaven seen and heard and to what does he bear further witness (3:32, 8:38)? What are the tidings brought by the one who dwells in the bosom of the Father (1:18)? Nowhere does Jesus report of these heavenly things; his message appears typically devoid of content. But it only appears that way. The message is the messenger.[127]

"He who has seen me has seen the Father," is the answer which Philip receives when he asks, "Lord, show us the Father, and we shall be satisfied" (14:8f.). It is preluded in many ways in the Gospel (cf. 1:18, 5:37, 6:40, 46, 14:7). For that reason the pure "I am" without any predicate can sometimes also become the content of the statement of faith (8:24, 28). "God reveals himself in Jesus, speaks and acts in him so exclusively that his salvation is visible and accesible only in Jesus. Because Jesus is perfectly God's voice, his Logos, the Old Testament revelation formulas can and must be on his lips since in them God reveals himself as the Saviour."[128]

But this statement does not remain abstract. The Gospel proclaims more than "the fact (German: *das Daß*) of the Revelation."[129] God's presence in Jesus becomes visible in the great miracles of the Gospel of John through which God's creative and redemptive glory shines. But these miracles are for their part "signs" which point further to the presence of divine grace and truth in the person of Jesus himself. Only where the help in superficial need becomes transparent for the entire wealth of divine life which is disclosed in Jesus does this help achieve its goal. It is no accident that a series of the "I am" sayings corresponds one-to-one with appropriate symbolic actions. The most unequivocal connection is that between 6:35, "I am the bread of life," and the miraculous feeding and its threatening misinterpretation; "I am the resurrection and the life" (11:25) is the key to the meaning of the raising of the dead; "I am the light of the world" (8:12) anticipates the interpretation of the healing of the man born blind, and in the first part of Jesus' conversation with the Samaritan womans hides basically an "embryonic" "I am" saying which for unknown reasons has not been formulated and could have been "I am the water of life." As here in regard to drawing water from the well, so all of Jesus' miracles are also

> parables of a greater reality, of a life which owes its existence to the communion with God, lives in it and is maintained in it. This reality of divine life came into the world through Jesus and will fill everyone who opens him- or herself for it. Everyday needs become transparent for life's true hunger and thirst, for internal paralysis and blindness, for spiritual death which all torture and threaten humankind and for which Jesus is the bread of life and living water, healing and eternal life because he gives humankind contact with the living God.[130]

Because a person who has faith in Jesus Christ steps out of the darkness into the light and out of the realm of death into the reality of a life in God, he or she already "has" eternal life. In the person of Jesus eternity breaks into time. The revelation of the Father through the Son is light and life, it is the truth which makes one free from sin (8:35). It is the reality of divine love which is represented and disclosed in the love of the Father to the Son and encounters the human world as perfect love in its consummation in Jesus' laying down his life (3:16, 36; 10:17; 13:1; 14:21, 23; 15:9-13; 17:23-26).

The horizon of this salvific action is universal: John the Baptist bears witness to Jesus, "Behold, the Lamb of God, who takes away the sins of the world!" (1:29). Verse 3:16 says programmatically, "For God so loved the world that he gave his only Son, that whoever believes in him should not perish but have eternal life." And the following verse underlines this: God sent his Son into the world "that the world might be saved through him"

(3:17, 12:47). The Samaritans confess, "This is indeed the Savior of the world" (4:42; cf. 1 John 4:14). The bread of God is that which comes from heaven and gives life to the world (6:33, cf. 51). Jesus is the light of the world (8:12, 9:5).[131]

Although many of these sentences may come from pre-Johannine tradition, in any event they offer a clear orientation for God's redemptive action, which is not simply wiped away by all that which still must be said about the world's reaction. Precisely the strict exclusiveness of a statement like 14:6*b*, "No one comes to the Father but by me," serves the universality of the sentence preceeding it in which Jesus responds to the question about the way to God, "I am the way, and the truth, and the life." That is "a classical summary of the Johannine doctrine of salvation which is based entirely on Jesus Christ. In Jesus Christ, the evangelist is saying, the invisible and incomprehensible God has, in his will to save humans, made himself so tangible and so comprehensible that they are able to reach the goal of their existence along this way, by accepting in faith the truth that has been revealed to them in Jesus Christ and by sharing in his life."[132]

The Redemptive Solidarity of the Son of God

One of the roots in the history of the tradition of the Johannine testimony of Christ is what Werner Kramer calls the *Dahingabe- und Sendungsformel* ("formula of giving up and sending").[133]

The basic form of the "sending" formula could have been, according to John 3:17, "God sent his Son into the world so that the world is saved by him." This formula is picked up in 1 John 4:9, "In this the love of God was made manifest among us, that God sent his only Son into the world, so that we might live through him" (cf. 1 John 4:10, 14). This formula of sending is also to be found in Paul. Perhaps in Gal 4:4f. he thus expanded an original formula which went, "God sent his Son so that we might receive Sonship." In Rom 8:3 as well we find the formula in altered form, a fact which possibly indicates that it was not a fixed formula but a model for formulations.

The similarly constructed *Dahingabeformel*[134] (formula of "giving up the Son") is to be found in John 3:16: "For God so loved the world that he gave his only Son, that whoever believes in him should not perish but have eternal life."

We find the next corresponding passage in Paul in Rom 8:32 where the "God for us" is explained by the sentence, "He who did not spare his own Son but gave him up for us all, will he not also give us all things with him?"

Galatians 2:20 (and Eph 5:2) also speak in a similar manner of the Son of God's "giving of himself": " . . . and the life I now live in the flesh I live by faith in the Son of God, who loved me and gave himself for me."

It is characteristic of the entire tradition that it is firmly associated with the title "Son of God."[135] Where God is the subject in the formula of "giving himself up," the unity of the Father and the Son is emphasized by a *monogēnes* or *idios*. God sacrifices himself in the Son.

Thus a second characteristic of the soteriological schema is important: It is almost always connected with a statement about the love of God or the Son (cf. John 3:16 and especially 1 John 4:9f.; Rom 8:37, 39; Gal 2:20; and Eph 5:2). In this manner the subject is linked with statements like Rom 5:8, "But God shows his love for us in that while we were yet sinners Christ died for us." Giving the Son up to the world and to death is the most profound demonstration of the love of the Father.

The salvific effect of sending and giving up the Son can be explained in various terms. 1 John 4:10 explicitly picks up the formula of sending and observes that God's love consists of having sent the Son as atonement for our sins; according to Rom 8:3 by sending the Son in the form of sinful flesh God "condemned sin in the flesh"; in Gal 4:4f. the Son is sent into human existence and placed under the Law to redeem those who are enslaved under the law so that they might receive adoption as children. Here the thought of comprehensively representing human existence is linked with the motif of redeeming, or buying free, a slave, as is similarly said in Gal 3:13 (here also with the motif of redeeming a slave) and 2 Cor 5:21.[136]

In contrast a more specific description of the salvific effect of such "giving up" is missing in the "giving up" formula. It is a matter of debate whether in John 3:16 more the "giving up" into the hostile world or unto death is meant. In Rom 8:32 the *hyper hēmōn* or the *ouk epheisato*, which play on the sacrifice of Isaac, ensure that the reader recollects of Jesus' sacrificial death.[137] Here, too, as with the other *hyper* statements in the tradition of the self-sacrifice of the Son of God (Gal 2:2; Eph 5:2,25; cf. Gal 1:4, Rom 4:25), particulary the thought of Jesus' expiatory death may well stand in the background. But the rhetorical structure and emotional connotation of the context in Rom 8:31-39 show that in the laying down of the life of the Son of God, God's will for salvation and work of salvation are meant to be described in the most comprehensive sense. It grounds one of the fundamental statements of the Pauline gospel: "God is for us" (v. 31). In the Son, God gives himself over into human suffering, even unto death, the most extreme and deepest problem of human existence. Thus Jesus' sacrifice guarantees God's Yes to us, even when all outward appearances appear to speak against it—or be it one's own sin (vv. 33f.), be it the most deadly or most joyful earthly experiences (vv. 38f.).

We find similar thoughts in other circles of tradition as well. In 2 Cor 8:9 Paul describes "the grace of our Lord Jesus Christ" with a terse sentence that in its chiastic construction reminds one of Gal 4:4f., "though he was rich, yet for your sake he became poor, so that by his poverty you might become rich." There can be no doubt that here the adoption of limited, transitory human existence by the one who comes from the abundance of divine existence is described as that which opens the way for humankind to enter into the riches of communion with God. 2 Cor 8:9 has rightly been decribed as a short summary of the christological hymn of Phil 2:6-11.[138] And yet Phil 2:6-11 does not explicitly make a soteriological statement; it just describes Christ's obedient way from existence as one equal to God into the lowliness of a human life all the way to the depth of death and God's response to this obedience in his being raised to *Kyrios* over all of creation.[139] But obviously he who is equal to God proves himself as Lord of the world in his humble and obedient adoption of the limits of a created existence with all its constraints and weaknesses; moreover, at the same time the healing fulfillment of human existence takes place in this. Paul has underlined this with the confirming and explanatory addition "even death on a cross." The adoption of human fate also includes the adoption of the curse which lies on the human race and is borne by Jesus in his death on the cross.

Romans 5:12-21 also belongs here. The obedience which Adam and with him all of humankind denied God Christ has lived out.[140] And yet— analogous to Phil 2:8—obedience is not geared toward following individual commandments; rather, it is "obedience in life" (*Lebensgehorsam*). Adam revolted against the limits of his created nature with which God's commandments confronted him and wanted to be like God. That is the original sin of humankind. In his place steps he who is equal to God, Christ, who sets himself under the limitation of created being and lets God be God. Through him God's gracious action heads up a new humanity which, justified by Christ, is received into communion with God (vv. 18ff.) and, taken out of the kingdom of death, participates in the abundance of the life-giving kingdom of God (v. 17).

All of these traditions are not cited in Paul or the Johannine writings in the context of missionary preaching; rather, they are used in teaching the church or in the doctrinal development of the Christian message. But they are obviously one fundamental aspect of the message of salvation which also achieves significance for missionary preaching.

In this context still another substantial correspondence must be mentioned, the "Son"-christology of the Letter to the Hebrews.[141] Sharply pursuing its christological line of argument, Heb 2:14-18 speaks of the salvific adoption of the human fate of death by the Son of God. Verse 14 emphasizes "the fact that Jesus did not shun the deadly fallenness of human existence. What cripples, humiliates and absurdly destroys did not remain a stranger to him."[142]

But it is just in "the paradoxical identity" of that which is the "glory of

God and bears the very stamp of his nature" (1:3) with the earthly nature of humankind "all the way down to physical frailty" that the power of death is broken.[143] The solidarity of the Son of God with his brothers and sisters in suffering and temptation is the foundation of his salvific action, of which the atonement for sin, which he fulfills as the true high priest (2:17f.), is also a part.

Thus the decisive key word for the christology and soteriology of the Letter to the Hebrews is mentioned. We cannot pursue the entire development of this theme here (cf. chapters 7–10). For our context the statements in 4:15–5:10 are important where the earthly way of the Son of God is defined as the fulfillment of his high priestly ministry. In his fate, the qualitative difference between divine origin and sinful human existence, out of which the power of complete atonement grows, and suffering in solidarity with human weakness, temptation and death are bound in a unity which only really reaches a person in distress and then opens the way to God's mercy and grace through which one finds help and salvation. This becomes especially impressive by its portrayal of the Son of God not as one who goes his way in total superiority and with inner distance, rather as one who "learned obedience through what he suffered" (5:8).[144] Obedience in life (*Lebensgehorsam*) capable of withstanding the fear of death—which the creature faces in the threat of its destruction as the consequence of its opposition to its Creator and Savior—grows out of the Son's proving himself in his earthly fate. His fulfillment of this obedience in offering his life becomes the foundation of the redeeming and salvific communion with God which is open to all who let themselves be formed by his ministry and example.[145]

Although the author of the Letter to the Hebrews regards the doctrine of Christ's high priesthood as a topic for the mature, the body of topics related to the obedience in life (*Lebensgehorsam*) of the Son of God which places him in redeeming solidarity with humankind is nonetheless a part of the fundamental statements of the early Christian message of salvation. It is also impressive how the connection is made back to the synoptic tradition. This is the case not only in view of the mention of the Gethsemane tradition and the allusion to the temptation story.[146] The motif of discipleship in the cross also appears in a very impressive variation in Heb 13:12-14.

When the Gospel of Luke emphasizes Jesus' divine Sonship in the infancy narrative with great vividness, but then primarily portrays the humanness of his way as savior of sinners and the poor and understands his passion according to the analogy of the suffering righteous one, then this may be a material parallel to the hymnic statements of Phil 2 and Heb 4f. about the Son of God's obedience and solidarity with humankind in the form of a story.

The Gospel: God's Response to Anxiety and Dread

The message of the incarnation of the Son is the message of salvation because it proclaims to humankind God's presence in the person and life of Jesus. It is the presence of life, light, grace, truth, salvation, of divine reality which says "Yes" to humankind in the midst of threats, darkness, sin, lies, and death. God's sending, giving and sacrificing his Son obviously means that God himself has in his love gotten involved in the needs of humankind. Particularly in an evangelistic context, it is important to observe that the statements of the New Testament regarding Jesus' divine Sonship primarily want to make clear that in his life and ministry the loving and redeeming God encounters us. Jesus' death is the proof of God's steadfast faithfulness and love (cf. Rom 5:8, 8:32). His word and ministry reveal God's glory, i.e., his salvific presence which creates and gives life (John 1:14). His life opens the way to God who through him is no longer the invisible and unapproachable God, but the proximate, compassionate, and merciful and helpful God (Heb 4:16, 10:19-22).

All these statements, however, are bound very closely to the historical figure of Jesus of Nazareth. They therefore assert and give witness to the presence of God in the reality of earthly life with its dangers from within and without, its transitory and limited nature, its heights and depths. In summary one can say that the message of God's redeeeming action in sending and sacrificing his Son is a response to humankind's anxiety and fear.

It is a bit daring to risk such a formulation in an investigation in biblical theology. For the term anxiety (*Angst*) is not to be found in the Bible in the subjective meaning of its modern use.[147] The term anxiety is nonetheless intended to serve as a summary of the human need into which the message of God's incarnation speaks. It is the subjective expression of humankind's "lostness," whereby "lost" is for the moment meant in a literal sense: humankind finds itself in a hostile world cut off from life in God. Humankind, which is in Heidegger's phrase "cast into existence"(*ins Da geworfen*), reacts with anxiety. This anxiety has many faces. As anxiety about survival, it can react very openly or very hiddenly to the insecurity of existence and can lead one to disassociate one's living space and food from that of others and even to attack them. As anxiety about losing what one has achieved and accomplished in life (in antiquity, fear of jealousy by the gods), it can sour one's joy about one's good fortune and lead to frantic attempts to safeguard everything in the secular area or also to religious activity at very diverse levels. It is anxiety, as Heidegger described it, anxiety about everything that restricts, and thus anxiety about "being-in-the-world" itself;[148] and it is anxiety, as Kierkegaard analyzes it, as the "dizziness of freedom" in which

69

"freedom gazes down into its own possibility, grasping at finiteness to sustain itself."[149]

Anxiety is related to guilt and sin. Kierkegaard has vividly shown how sin originates in anxiety and follows it. For that reason texts which speak of the soteriological significance of the incarnation of God in sending his Son certainly also do speak of sin. But anxiety and guilt are not identical, and thus these texts describe further dimensions of the lostness of humankind in an existence alienated from God, which we summarize with the term "anxiety." Its outward expression can be rebellion or resignation, manic overcompensation or depressive capitulation, compulsive safeguarding or hysterical complaining; its root is the separation of the creature from its creator. This separation makes the creation next to him or her into a "no man's land" and the world into his or her enemy—as much as he or she may lose him- or herself in the world, for lack of the true partner.[150]

God acts to address this need directly. In Jesus' being sent and his sacrifice, Jesus not only bears the sin of humankind, he also adopts the creaturely fate of humankind with its joyous and deeply endangered mixture of freedom and commitment. The obedience of the Son is not the attitude of one who servilely and timidly carries out orders. The obedience of the Son is demonstrated in his taking on the creaturely limits of a human being and fulfilling them in the lasting commitment to the Father with life from God. His freedom to sacrifice his life, through which he carried God's love into the darkness of death and also deprived of its finality, the abandonment by God in death results from this. Pursuing this path creates a place of trust in which those who stand by Jesus can themselves live in confident obedience.

"If God is for us, who is against us?" Paul asks the Christians in Rome (Rom 8:31) in the face of this activity of God. This is a rhetorical question and anticipates a certain and thankful "No one!" as an answer. In as far as evangelization is also always the new founding of a Christian faith that has become superficial, this invitation to trust in God's love, borne by the certainty of the Christ event, in the face of danger from internal and external threats, from apparently unlimited possibilities and limiting orders, is an element of the basic stock of evangelistic preaching. This question, however, cannot only be asked of Christians. Its power of conviction can reach all "before whose eyes Jesus Christ was publicly portrayed as crucified" (Gal 3:1) and who are promised that this is the way of God's love into their fears and their distress.

Jesus' promise according to John 16:33, "Take courage; I have conquered the world," was directed at his disciples. But the truth which it bears applies to all and is addressed to every man and woman who feels like he or she is being ground to pieces between the millstones of the forces and conditions of this world.

That is the good news of the incarnation of God: "For because he himself has suffered and been tempted, he is able to help those who are tempted" (Heb 2:18).

Paradigms for that which takes place in God's action for the salvation of humankind in this circle of tradition are the motifs of childship and freedom. The radical change from being a slave to law and sin to the freedom of sons (i.e., legally responsible, grown children) stands in the middle of important statements of our circle of tradition (cf. Gal 4:1-7, John 8:30-36). This new relationship to God is thus not a formal, legally recoverable legal status; rather, it is formed by the spirit of childship, of complete trust in the Father (Rom 8:14, 17; Gal 4:4-7). This "freedom of the glory of the children of God" is now hidden under suffering and transitoriness as the conditions of earthly existence. But where God's spirit performs its liberating task "the breaking in and realization of the new world"[151] is already fulfilled now, and there the pledge of future completion is received.

By entering into the limits of creaturely existence in Jesus, God also takes care of humankind's destructive hubris, its "God-complex,"[152] which at root means that because God became a human being, we do not have to be God. If humankind accepts its role in creation as God's created counterpart in this manner, hope for all of creation and its salvation can blossom.

Without mentioning the word "childship" the same event is described in the conversation between Nicodemus and Jesus in John 3:1-21, which is very important particularly for evangelistic preaching and theology. Being "born anew" as being "born from above" is here simultaneously demanded as the condition of entering the kingdom of God and as a miracle promised in baptism and the Spirit. Through the ministry of the Spirit, the reality of a new existence before God grows out of faith in God's generous love in sending the Son.[153]

Considered psychologically, rebirth is thus first of all a "regression," a step back into complete dependence on God. But it is therapeutic regression: It involves learning the lost fundamental trust, healing inspection of errors committed, and dealing with guilt in the sign of the cross and under its protection, thus growing into a mature "childship," which is lived in freedom and responsibility in the knowledge of that trust and the authority of God.

Rebirth, becoming a child of God, being a new creation (2 Cor 5:17) thus does not mean that one flees from an unloved and mistaken identity into a new existence which has nothing to do with the old one. Our history, e.g. our genetic nature or early childhood formation, is not simply obliterated. The new identity is won by the new relationship to God into which the old existence is taken up. One sets aside everything which constituted the old existence as "old": the framework of relationships in sin and law which separated it from God. That is the "old nature" which through the encounter with Christ can be set aside and in whose stead the "new nature" ought to be put on, Jesus Christ himself, who has created a framework of relationships for our lives, the childlike communion with God (Col 3:9). In so doing not only is a new relationship to God established, but also a new relationship to, and a new style of behavior between, human beings. (Col 3:11-15, Gal 3:27f.).

Paul describes the intimate relationship between a fundamental reforming of a personality before God and the daily living out of this fact in the reality of a human life in very pregnant form in Gal 2:20: "It is no longer I who live, but Christ who lives in me; and the life I now live in the flesh I live by faith in the Son of God, who loved me and gave himself for me." God grants humankind in Christ a new existence. He grants it not as a "habitus," a new basic genetic endowment or behavior programming; he grants it by giving himself in the life and death of Jesus as the loving God, the liberating and encountering partner of enslaved and lost human beings. That is the message of salvation of the gospel.

A Hermeneutic of the Spirit and of Love

"Come and see" says Philip to Nathanael in response to his skeptical question, "Can anything good come out of Nazareth?" (John 1:46). The Samaritan woman speaks similarly to her fellow Samaritans: "Come, see a man who told me all I ever did. Can this be the Christ?" (John 4:29). What the participants say here is the agenda of the gospel itself. "The incarnation of God establishes that speaking about the incarnate one can no longer abstract his teaching from his person . . . , rather that it can have nothing else in mind than bringing about an *encounter* with the incarnate one."[154]

Weder had correctly proposed "to regard the incarnational thought of the Gospel of John as hermeneutical instruction for its interpretation."[155]

I have already pointed out the points of contact, indeed the partial overlapping of the miracle stories and the "I am" sayings. In them becomes visible who Jesus is and what his coming into the world means: an encounter with the ground and source of life! Stories and metaphors invite one to "think with one's eyes," "to consider the earthly reality from the perspective of its transcendental ground."[156]

The same is true, *mutatis mutandis*, for the hermeneutic profile of the tradition in Paul. The "hymnic" element which is also everywhere bound up with it originates in the wonder about that which God has done. By describing Jesus' path and portraying God's activity, the hearers and readers find placed before their eyes how deeply and comprehensively God's love

72

has taken on human distress. The rhetorical questions in Rom 8:31ff. underline the persuasive character of this tradition.

To be sure, the figure of Nicodemus in the framework of the Gospel of John shows in exemplary fashion the difficulty of truly grasping the significance of this event. Although the decisive sentences about the work of the Spirit (3:5-8) are formulated soteriologically and not hermeneutically, they have nonetheless again and again led to the thesis that only one who has been led by the Spirit and born again in it truly understands the message. But in such a case we would be stuck in a hermeneutical circle, and the question how one can enter this circle would be of fundamental importance particularly for evangelistic preaching.

One can indeed observe that the statements about the sending and the sacrifice of the Son are often bound up with the motif of the reception of the Spirit. But this takes place in a clear relation. In John 3 a new reference to God's inexplicable working of the Spirit does not follow Nicodemus' question, "How can this be?" (v. 9), rather a reference to the coming of the Son and faith in him. The Christ event is the foundation of the new birth.

Similarly, Gal 4:4-6 first describes the sending of the Son as the beginning of the father-child relationship and then describes the sending of the Spirit into the hearts of the children as the existential fulfillment of the new relationship to the Father. This is even more distinctively recognizable in Rom 8 where, in light of the context and the contents, in v. 3 one would already expect the sending of the Spirit to be named as making possible the new obedience. But even there sending the Son "in the likeness of sinful flesh" as the foundation of a "life in the Spirit" is once again trenchantly placed at the beginning. The dwelling of the Spirit in the "mortal bodies" of those who belong to Christ is the consequence of God's incarnational action (vv. 9-11). It is the ground of hope in a future life, energy for new activity and internal witness to the new relationship to God.[157]

The clear determination of what the Spirit does is also grounded in the close relationship to the Christ event. Romans 5:5 says perfectly clearly, "God's love has been poured into our hearts through the Holy Spirit," and as proof for this statement, points to the fact that God has proved his love for us in Christ's dying for us when we were still sinners (v. 8). What happened in Jesus' death for all men and women once and for all becomes reality here and now through the workings of the Spirit in the center of their being as individuals.

What does this mean for a hermeneutic of missionary preaching?

At first glance a clear order appears to be given: preaching the message of God's redemptive activity in Christ, faith which places one in communion with Christ, reception of the Spirit which grants certainty that one indeed belongs to God.[158] But a closer analysis soon shows that such a stringent account does not do justice to the many dimensions of the event. In 2 Cor 3 Paul characterizes his missionary commission as *diakonia pneumatos*, as ministry which gives the Spirit—and thus life.[159] And the puzzling sentences in 3:16ff. then say very clearly: Whoever turns to preaching about Christ that has been formed by the Spirit, his or her eyes will be opened and his or her perspective made open to the presence of the glory of God in Jesus Christ.[160]

John 16:8-11 also speaks of the disclosing and convicting work of the Spirit, whereby it remains undecided as to what degree this has a condemning or redeeming effect on the world.[161] In any event, however, the Spirit as champion of the messengers makes sure that it is unmistakably clear what the message is about.[162]

It is also precisely at this point then that the great distance between the world and those who belong to Christ becomes clear. The farewell discourses impress this upon the hearers and readers with special emphasis. At first glance it may appear paradoxical that this distance is so strongly emphasized particularly in the wake of the incarnational tradition. However, the reason for this is easily apparent: Where God's love descends so deeply into human existence the difference between "flesh" and "spirit," between God's way and the "schema of this world," i.e. the system in which humankind has become entangled through its sin, comes to light in all its harshness.

But, then again, the power and the profile of the Christian witness results from just this difference.[163] The love of the disciples among themselves and their unity lets the world recognize that the Father has sent Jesus into the world as the bearer of his love (John 13:34, 17:23).

74

Chapter 3

One Gospel, Many Situations

The Identity and Relevance of the Preaching

At first glance the missionary message is, as we have shown, diverse and varied. That is not really surprising. The New Testament is not a missionary writing in which the fundamental gospel is presented with a consistent orientation towards a certain circle of listeners or in the most generalized form possible.[1] It is a collection of writings for certain churches which cite this basic missional gospel in very different situations and utilize it for theological or teaching purposes; thereby, they obviously also reach back to fundamental forms of this gospel which were different from the very beginning. Nonetheless a unity is recognizable. This unity will be shown in the following section, but we shall also ask whether it is possible to recognize reasons for the differentiation and what hermeneutical conclusions for our preaching can be drawn from them.

The One Gospel

In "Pistis und Soteria," a study that is extremely important for our topic, Egon Brandenburger has observed that "from the the beginning the motif of 'sending,' 'commission,' linked with a message to proclaim, was characteristic" for early Christianity. This is the case "in spite of different forms of content of the basic message. In the circle of tradition of the Palestinian mission this was, 'The kingdom of God has drawn near'; in the circle of tradition of Jerusalem-Hellenists-Antioch this was, 'God has raised Jesus from the dead,'" a formula whose development we especially encounter in Paul.[2]

To these one can also add the Johannine tradition, whose local origin is unknown to us. Its fundamental message is "Jesus is the Christ, the Son of God" (John 20:31). The motif of sending (17:8, 20:21) is not directly linked with the commission to bring the message; the connection arises indirectly through the confession of those who encounter Jesus (1:34, 49; 4:25f., 42; 6:69).

Besides this motif of sending and the message one can note further common structural features: the question of repentance or faith as the response to the message, and the "horizon of the apocalyptic judgment of doom" which in the Johannine tradition has been radically drawn into the actual present moment of decision.[3] The structural agreement is an indication of the internal unity of the message: God's unconditional turn to lost humankind as preached and lived by Jesus.

The gospel of the kingdom has its soteriological high point in the Beatitudes of the poor, the word of the cross in the justification of the godless, and the message of the incarnation of God in the promise of God's steadfast love. God's existence *for us* in Jesus Christ, which is proclaimed, is the basis of the "Immanuel" of the Matthean account of his birth. The internal unity of this message is also shown by diverse connections of assorted motifs, especially in Paul with his interweaving of the message of the cross and sayings about Christ's being sent and sacrificed; but one can find similar connections in the emphasis on the election of the poor and meek in the synoptic tradition and Paul or in the contact between statements about the preservation of the human nature of the Son of God in the Jesus tradition and the tradition of the earliest Christian confessions.

This gospel has a prehistory. Creation stories and primal history, patriachal narrative and exodus tradition, deuteronomistic history and exilic prophecy, are all, each in their own way, portrayals of God's turning to humankind and his people in a manner which overcomes everything. Basic statements of the belief in creation and examples of God's leading persons in the Old Testament will thus always be a part of evangelistic preaching. That is not intended to level out the difference between Old Covenant and New Covenant: Israel's task was preservation, the task of the church is mission.[4] But both bear witness to God's intervention for his creation by their existence and their confession.

This message also has a posthistory. In the development of the trinitarian and especially the christological dogma, the reality of the redeeming presence of God in human existence is doctrinally fixed. Particularly in Athanasius one can feel the seriousness of the soteriological consequences involved in the disagreements about Jesus' person: "God himself brings in Christ salvation to humankind"[5]—that is what had to be held on to. Athanasius's slogan—"He [God's *logos*] became human, so we could become divine"[6]—reveals besides the strength of such an incarnational soteriology its weakness as well: As much as the total salvation which encompasses every dimension of human existence is emphasized, the consummation of salvation at the same time threatens to be transferred to the purely transcendent. But that would narrow the biblical witness in which the encounter of the redeeming reality of God with the entire breadth of human need is addressed.

In Jesus' life and death God encounters the suffering of men and women, bears and forgives their sin, and delivers them from the anxiety of alienated creatures. This suffering is made up of all the different dimensions of human lostness, which penetrate and condition one another; in this lostness God goes to his creation in Jesus' sending, ministry, and death.

This salvific activity of God also has a temporal extension. What is breaking in in Jesus' proclamation of the nearness of the kingdom of God, what in the resurrection of the crucified one proves to be valid and effective will be consummated in God's apocalyptic action. That is also a basic common element of the missionary message of the New Testament.

The basis and power of this message lies in the certainty that "God is for us," which is guaranteed by Jesus' message and his offering of his life for us. The reality of God's proexistence reaches human need in its entire complexity and breaks through the power of sin which draws its power from the isolation and egocentricity of humankind.

The mission of the church of Jesus Christ, whose witness, communion, and ministry is filled and formed by God's existence *for us*, is grounded in this. This message is, however, also above all the basis and content of the evangelism in which the church inwardly and outwardly names and bears witness to that from which it lives and which delivers humankind: God's merciful care in Jesus Christ.

The Origins of the Differentiation

From our own presentation is obvious that we encounter the gospel in the New Testament in various forms in spite of this clearly recognizable inner unity. What is the origin of this differentiation? Does it suffice to give a *traditio-critical* answer?[7] It can describe how Jesus' message and the tradition based on it developed on the fertile ground of apocalyptic expectations of salvation, but also how they, and their contents, were formed by Jesus' unique claim to authority. It can explain how—starting from Jerusalem under the influence of Jesus' death and resurrection—his fate was interpreted as a salvation event, whereby the interpretive categories were first adopted from the tradition of the Suffering Servant to which the further motifs from the circle of Old Testament and early Jewish statements about atonement soon came. Paul adopted this interpretation, but radicalized it through the influence of his own experience of being called. The formation of the message in the Gospel of John has its roots in early Jewish wisdom theology for which there are already the beginnings in the Jesus tradition in the Synoptic Gospels and which are expanded to a theocentric theology of commission in the Gospel. In a very specific recasting of the given traditions the Gospel of John unites the narrative Jesus tradition and the kerygmatic preaching of Christ in early Christianity. Whether the Gospel is to be located in the debate with an incipient orthodox Judaism or with the beginnings of Gnosticism is a matter of great controversy in New Testament research.[8]

This explanation of the differentiation of the message remains strongly bound to the descriptive and tends to show more the origin of some interpreting motifs than the actual reasons for the new formulation. An interpretation in terms of *salvation history* could help us further, although one must certainly consider that the differentiations of the message made there will not necessarily coincide with the results of traditio-critical research on the strands of tradition.[9]

Using the criteria of salvation history, one would have to distinguish between the sayings of the pre-resurrection and post-resurrection mission to Israel and the message for the Gentile mission and the Gentile churches. As far as I can see, the peculiarity of the Johannine portrayal is not taken into account in analyses in terms of salvation history since it is mostly harmonized with the testimony of the Synoptic Gospels.[10]

An important element of the salvation-historical approach is that, according to its own claim, it rests upon a conception of revelation history: God reveals himself and his salvation in the course of a story, and he does this with an "orientation to the addressee"—a view which in an extreme case can lead to a denial of the significance of the Jesus tradition for the Gentile church of today.[11]

On a quite different theological plane, "addressee oriented" is the *sociological* interpretation which explains the variation of the message in accordance with the economic conditions into which it is preached. Thus Jesus' preaching and the oldest Jesus tradition are formed by the poverty and oppression of the population of rural Galilee.[12] The Jerusalem theology of atonement and the Pauline doctrine of justification are rooted in the living conditions of the lower middle-class in urban areas; however, the radicality of the word of the cross could also be a coded protest against the oppressive violence of the military power of Rome.[13]

The Johannine message could then under certain circumstances be depicted as a response to the isolation of the individual in the mass society of large Hellenistic cities and an escape from the severity of their social conditions.[14] But there have also been other very different attempts to "locate" the Johannine message, for example as the testimony of churches under pressure from a Jewish majority in the area ruled by Herod Agrippa II.[15]

This short overview shows some of the difficulty involved in giving information about the relationship of the form of early Christian missionary preaching to its original addressees. What is it that determines the development: the unfolding and differentiation of the message on the basis of an inherent logic and dynamic which rests upon the interplay of salvation event and models for its interpretation already available in the history of tradition, *or* the necessity of a response to very specific challenges by new addressees?

The answer to this question is of considerable importance for hermeneutics. Jürgen Moltmann has described the current crisis of faith of Western Christianity as a crisis of relevance and identity and has thus, at the same time, named the fundamental prerequisites of the authority of evangelistic preaching: identification with the original message of salvation of the gospel and relevance for the hearer in his or her situation in life.[16]

Does the New Testament help us with the task of maintaining the identity of the gospel and simultaneously bringing out its relevance for a particular circle of listeners in new situations? At at least one point one could expect to obtain exemplary information on how preaching adapted itself to listeners with totally different premises, namely the transition from being a mission to the Jews to being a mission to the Gentiles. What can we discern from the texts?

A Different Gospel?

In Gal 2:7 Paul reports that the recognized leaders of the church in Jerusalem saw (and accepted) "that I had been entrusted with the gospel to the uncircumcised, just as Peter had been entrusted with gospel to the circumcised." Are two different forms of the gospel envisaged here?

In so far as the exegetes do not from the very beginning consider "gospel" to be a noun of action with the meaning of "to preach the gospel," they agree to a large extent that Paul did not mean two different forms of the missionary message in regards to content. Stuhlmacher writes, "Both forms of the gospel are, in the Pauline perspective, united by the proclamation of the free grace of God realized in Christ. What can only distinguish, but cannot ever divide both forms is the high regard for and position of the Torah on the way of salvation that is now revealing itself."[17]

But even the differentiating characteristic must be relativized because—as Stuhlmacher correctly observes—one can in no case ascribe to the Torah salvific significance. However, it is then not a constitutive element of the message of salvation itself; rather it can in any event be named, as in Rom 3:21, as a witness of the gospel.

This alone corresponds to Paul's other testimony as well. In Gal 2:15ff. he makes clear in a free-wheeling repetition of his words to Peter in Antioch that even the Jews—although "not Gentile sinners"—can only be justified by faith in Jesus Christ. And the brusk rejection of another gospel in Gal 1:6-9 under no circumstances permits the conclusion that Jewish Christians could have another gospel while Gentile Christians could not.

Paul also postulates complete agreement between himself and the apostles in Jerusalem in the basic missionary proclamation in 1 Cor 15:1-11: "Whether then it was I or they, so we preach, so you believed" (v. 11). And in Rom 1:16 he notices that the gospel is the power of God which delivers all who believe in it, the Jews first and the Greeks likewise. Thus for Paul there is doubtless only the one gospel of God's redeeming and justifying action in Jesus Christ, which is basically preached in the same way to the Jews and the Gentiles. Of course, where he comes to speak of the condition of non-Christians he can differentiate between Jews and Gentiles. When in Rom 1:18–3:20 he describes the deterioration of humankind in judgment, he describes the Gentiles in a manner different from the Jews.[18] But here, too, Paul likes to bring out elements both have in common: the Gentiles have written on their hearts what the law requires (2:15), and in Gal 4:3 and 4:8-10 slavery under the law is set parallel to the rule of the cosmic elements as they were represented by the old gods. Religious motifs of the non-Christian past of the Gentile Christians is as good as ignored, and particularly the two letters which were most clearly written to predominantly Gentile churches (Galatians and Romans) contain the most detailed references to the message of the Old Testament. This, of course, mirrors the special situation of these two letters, but also points to the fact that many of these Gentile Christians probably did not come directly out of pagan traditions, but were won from the circle of "God fearers" who had already left their pagan past behind them.[19] Nonetheless, it remains puzzling that at no point in the Pauline letters do we find a serious discussion of any particular phenomenon of Hellenistic religiosity, rather just now and then a placative rejection and disqualification typical of the current Jewish polemics.

What is the relationship of all this to Paul's well-known statements in 1 Cor 9:19-23 in which he describes in a very impressive manner how thoroughly he becomes like the Jews, the Gentiles, or the weak to win them for the gospel? One must, as is well known, read this carefully stylized passage very closely.[20]

(1) The issue is—as v. 19 makes clear—not the question of the adaptation of the gospel, but the renunciation of the apostle's own freedom for the sake of an effective mission. That corresponds to the context which, in connection with the problem of eating meat that had been offered to idols, wants to encourage and call the Corinthians to have consideration for one another.

(2) The first concrete example, "To the Jews I became as a Jew," is not continued, as the proverb suggests, with a parallel, "To the Greeks I became as a Greek"; rather it is expanded for greater precision: "to those under the law I became as one under the law—though not being myself under the law—that I might win those under the law. To those outside the law I became

80

as one outside the law—not being without law toward God but under the law of Christ—that I might win those outside the law" (vv. 20*b*, 21).

Thus Paul does not embrace a simple strategy of conforming to what he encounters. The inner identity of the apostle and his message is not marred by the different forms of this message in encounters with different persons. His living as a Jew among the Jews does not nullify his freedom from the law. His refusal to impose the Mosiac law upon the Gentiles does not change anything about his inner bond to Jesus and his commandment and Paul's desire to lead his listeners into the kingdom of Christ.

(3) In the section under consideration, the gospel appears not as a variable, but as a constant (cf. vv. 14, 16, 18, 23). The odd wording in v. 23, "I do it all for the sake of the gospel, that I may share in its blessings," shows clearly that "gospel" in this context is more than the fixed text of the message. It is the epitome of God's movement toward humankind. The "apostle's turning to the hearer just picks up the turning of the gospel to humankind."[21]

These observations lead to the correct understanding of the section:

> When Paul makes himself a slave of humankind, this means that he preaches the gospel to them unabridged, but with total personal commitment in such a manner that they can understand it in their respective situation and by means of that come to faith . . . He adapts himself, not the message, to his listeners and is so a true witness of the gospel.[22]

Günter Bornkamm has attempted to concretize the manner in which Paul lives this way on the basis of 1 Cor 7:17-24:

> In the light of the Christ message he does not accept the different material *standpoints* of Jews and Gentiles; however, he understands each different position as the historical location where the 'call' of each individual by the gospel takes place.[23]

The message of the gospel, that God's love knows no preconditions and seeks everyone at the place where he or she is lost, determines the apostle's practice in his own life. He goes the way of the gospel and comes to the Jew, bound to a life under the law. And he shares the yoke of the commandments and prohibitions with him or her and bears witness in word and deed that he is freed from the scrupulousness of defining his status before God by the fulfillment of the law.

He goes to the Gentile, whose life is running away through his or her fingers, because the restraining border of God's commandment is missing. And he does not shun contact with him or her and his or her sphere of life and bears witness in just the manner that a life in commitment to Jesus is free and fulfilled.

When one imagines that Paul wanted to continue to pursue this missionary praxis in the religiously mixed cities of Asia Minor, then it is clear that conflicts were preordained. For outsiders who could not recognize the center out of which he lived, his behaviour must have often appeared equivocal and inconsistent.[24] So it was certainly the source of some persecution and distress. But just that is for Paul a necessary consequence of a consistent translation of the gospel into life.

The "Conversion" of the Evangelist

According to Paul's own testimony this missionary hermeneutic has its origin in the encounter with Christ through which he was called to be an apostle. With the calling of a zealot for the law and persecutor of the church to be the apostle to the Gentiles (cf. Gal 1:13-16) the die for his later activity was already cast.[25] In the encounter with the resurrected one as the crucified Messiah his pride in the law was shattered; in it begins his life in grace alone; here are the roots of his conviction that God's love, which chose death on the cross as its sign, knows no preconditions, seeks every human being where he or she is lost.

The complete re-evaluation of his self-understanding, as Phil 3:7-11 describes it, is the existential side of his recognition that God's merciful care in Jesus Christ is not only for the Jews, but also for the Gentile. But because the truth of the sentence that God is not only the God of the Jews, but also the God of the Gentiles (Rom 3:29) does not have its origin in general thoughts about monotheism, but is disclosed through God's justifying action in Jesus Christ, all reflection about to what degree this God could have already revealed himself in the pre-Christian religiosity of his Gentile listeners is missing in Paul. Such thoughts would only obscure the direct and unconditional nature of God's revelation in Christ.[26]

Walter Hollenweger has spoken of the "conversion" of the evangelist in many of his publications on evangelism and understood by that not only the initial call to do missionary preaching, but also the turn away from the understanding of the gospel formed by one's own religious culture and the turn towards an understanding of the gospel that first discloses itself in the encounter with the "evangelized."[27] The paradigm for this is Acts 10, Peter's encounter with Cornelius. His exegesis of this story is impressive; also impressive, to be sure, is how what stands in this story is continually mixed with what Hollenweger would like to say on this subject.

Doubtless, Peter learns something in this story, namely "that God shows no partiality, but in every nation any one who fears him and does what is right is acceptable to him" (v. 34f.). But he does not learn this "in dialogue with persons of another faith,"[28] rather through a series of visions which

82

God granted him and Cornelius, whereby one must consider that Cornelius was "an upright and God-fearing man, who is well spoken of by the whole Jewish nation" (v. 22). And thus Peter also preaches in Cornelius' house as he had always preached.

It is also correct that at the end of this sermon those present are anointed by the Holy Spirit before an express call to repentance has been issued, and this is enough for Peter to baptize them. "Discovering what the Holy Spirit is already doing,"[29] however, does not refer to the pre-Christian life of Cornelius and his household, but to that which happens under the preaching of the apostle. This is certainly unusual enough and is doubtless intended to make one thing clear at a decisive point in the history of mission: It is God who shows the Gentiles the way. But, in any event, this opens up no completely new categories of receiving salvation. The Jerusalem party acknowledges much more than just the material substance of the event when they say, "Then to the Gentiles also God has granted repentance unto life" (11:18).

But detailed exegetic criticism here is not intended to cover up a correct concern of Hollenweger. The example of Peter shows that evangelists who are open for God's guidance must allow themselves to be corrected in their ideas about the proper adressees of their preaching and the proper form of response to this preaching. That such corrections can be triggered not only by special visions, but also open eyes and ears for what God's Spirit does in the life of another person, certainly does not contradict Luke's intention. Openness for the surprising work of God is one of the charismata of a true evangelist.

Where this also means a correction for the message, it leads neither Peter nor Paul to adapt new religious insights, rather always to concentrate on what is essential, the message of God's free grace. In this manner the preacher learns not to preach him- or herself, not to make his or her own ideas about the most fitting manner to receive the gospel absolute, but to preach Jesus Christ alone as Lord. And exactly that grants the listeners the space to have their own thoughts and be themselves before God. Human and religious biography, social circumstances, and cultural influence are taken seriously without making them a topic for themselves in preaching.[30]

The Significance of Extra-biblical Knowledge of God

Now it is known that there are only a few examples in the New Testament where in missionary preaching or even in dogmatic explanations the possibility of extra-biblical knowledge of God is pointed out and taken up. The least ambiguous example of this is in Paul's speech in the Areopagus, Acts 17:22-31. According to Luke's report, Paul picks up an old altar inscription, "To an unknown god," and then, following Stoic patterns of argument, develops the doctrine of the *one* God as the Creator and Sustainer of the world and concludes this line of thought with a quotation from the hymn to Zeus by the Stoic philosopher Aratus. The call to repentance begins with motifs from Old Testament polemic against idolatry and aims towards the allusion to God's having installed the resurrected one as judge over the entire world.

The prominent location and the fact that this is the only sermon Paul preached to Gentiles which Luke reports leads to the supposition that he attributes programmatic meaning to this speech. Thus Paul preached in the stronghold of education in Greece, and thus should one preach before educated Greeks.[31] Irritating in this regard are only the relatively modest results of this sermon. Or is it perhaps an example of how one should *not* preach?[32]

Yet against this hypothesis it can be said that Luke does not offer a counter-example—using, say, a sermon in Corinth. He knew that in Athens a church was not founded immediately and he stuck faithfully to this historical fact. But he did not want to let the opportunity pass to offer an example of a sermon before Gentiles there. Therefore throughout the history of interpretation this sermon has been understood as a model for taking up indigenous concepts in missionary preaching.[33] After the first critical questions by Calvin, it was not until recently that doubts arose regarding the theological propriety of the argumentation—often, to be sure, mixed up in a methodologically disastrous way with the question of its agreement with the preaching of the "historical" Paul.

Before we allow ourselves a judgment about this, we must first examine whether and then to what degree the sermon on the Areopagus "takes up" knowledge of God found in Greek philosophy.

(1) The first observation is that as regards content no statements of Stoic philosophy are directly taken over. Rather, they are offered in the form in which they have been transmitted by Hellenistic Jewish theology. Thus the first re-forming of these concepts by biblically based thinking had already taken place.[34]

(2) More important is a second observation: Neither in terms of formalities is Paul's line of argument directly based on the heathen knowledge of God. "What therefore you worship as *unknown*, this I *proclaim* to you" (17:23).[35] What Paul thus afterwards proclaims as "natural" knowledge of God, i.e., knowledge one can derive from creation and its order, is unknown to his listeners—despite a quotation from one of their poets! Paul also does not appeal to the better knowledge of God of the philosophers in contrast to the worship of images by the people. The criticism of worshiping images of gods is directed at all listeners.

What Paul admittedly does in this speech is to bring out the correct question, which stands behind the wrong, religious answer: The question about the living god. And he does this, to be sure, with the assistance of Stoic concepts as the Hellenistic Jewish theology transmits them.

(3) Then the call to change one's ways is decisive—in the truest sense of the word. Its clarity is not softened by recourse to natural knowledge of God, but sharpened. The possibilty of recognizing God is given—but what have human beings made of it? The optative in v. 27 emphasizes the hypothetical character of what is described there as the goal of knowledge of God in his creation.[36]

The meager success of the sermon on the Areopagus is thus no "accident." Rather it is the consequence of a self-authorized religiosity and the call to turn back to the one, true God coming into conflict with one another.

The break between knowledge of God as actually possible on the basis of creation and the actual, inappropriate worship of God by humankind is emphasized much more sharply in Rom 1:19-23. It is a matter of controversy whether or not Paul is taking up motifs out of his missionary preaching here. We shall still have to deal with this when we talk about the meaning of the announcement of judgment for evangelistic preaching.[37] In any event Paul's remarks function not only as a positive example of taking up knowledge of God already at hand, but also as an indictment which underlines that humankind cannot be excused: Men and women could have recognized God; but they put the creature in his place and thus in the final event made themselves gods.[38] Humankind has fallen victim to the temptation "to make the infinite finite" and thus manifested that what concerns human beings "the most in their relationship to the divine is above all their own self."[39]

In the prologue to the Gospel of John, the text, which in terms of its content has done the most for attempts to link the Christian message with the thought of antiquity, although it does not present itself formally as such, we find the same basic structure as well. The light of the *logos*, which as life from God illuminates all that has been created, is not received by humankind. "He was in the world, and the world was made through him, yet the world knew him not. He came to his own home, and his own people received him not" (John 1:10f.). It is also made clear here that first the incarnation of the *logos*, the revelation of God in Jesus Christ grants humankind the redemptive illumination of their existence.[40]

But as much as all these texts show what is inappropriate about humankind's self-generated religiosity, a decisive hint is nonetheless implicit in them: As wrong as the human answer to the question about God may be, the question as such is correct and fitting, and the answer of the gospel takes up this question. It does this in opposition to the answers already offered, but it does this in the conviction that those addressed know what is being talked about. They have failed to achieve knowledge of the true God, but the preacher may proceed from the assumption that his or her listeners possess the necessary categories of thought to be able to understand what he or she wants to tell them.

Points of Contact and Conflict: An Excursus

Two questions have been heatedly discussed in the last sixty years on the basis of this observation: Which position must (or may) one grant this "pre-understanding" theologically and in missionary preaching? Can such a "pre-understanding" also be presumed in persons who have nothing to do with religion as commonly understood?

It was **Emil Brunner** who with his articles "The Other Task of Theology" and "The Question of a 'Point of Contact' as a Problem for Theology" gave the cue and "fighting word" for the debate.[41] For the sake of a missionary theology and pastoral work he demanded a Christian natural theology as "the other task of theology." In opposition to a "false apologetic wary of making contact" with a knowledge of God already present, which he identified with the attempt to prove God's existence,[42] Brunner sees the "most elementary form of 'making contact' . . . in the human *capacity to be addressed*, which is given in created human nature." "The *humanitas* as personal being, the ability to speak, the ability to think, freedom, *Du-Bezogenheit*, a relationship to the transcendent, responsibility is the formal, indeprivable image of God which points towards the determination of living in communion with God, in love. . . . The experience of failing the standard of the moral law, the knowledge of guilt, the dubious human knowledge of God and of oneself is just in its dubious nature the point where the word of God, which calls one to change one's way of thinking, pulls one upright and makes everything all right, can take up human knowledge of God and existence." The process of taking up elements of human knowledge is thus dialectic: "Both points are true: The gospel can only be preached and believed in a certain continuity of human knowledge of the world around himself. And: The gospel can only be proclaimed by completely breaking through this continuity."[43]

This concept provoked vigorous dissent from **Karl Barth**. As early as the *Church Dogmatics* I/1 he opposed a theology which instead of being interested "in the divine message itself as it has gone out and been received" is interested "in the exhibition of a point of contact for the divine message."[44] His essay "No! Response to Emil Brunner!" turned into a vehement protest against every form of the effort to make a supposed human "ability to reveal something" into a subject for theology and preaching. Every positive

86

evaluation of such a point of contact must unavoidably put the doctrine of justification by faith in question.

For his part, Barth must face the question of whether he really takes the hearers of the gospel seriously when he offers the advice to treat the unbeliever "as if their rejection of 'Christianity' was not to be taken seriously. It is only then that they can understand you, since they really see you where you maintain that you are standing as an evangelical theologian; on the ground of the doctrine of justification by faith alone."[45]

At the same time **Karl Heim** published the first volume of his great work, *Der evangelische Glaube und das Denken der Gegenwart. Grundzüge einer christlichen Lebensanschauung* [*The Evangelical Faith and Contemporary Thought: The Rudiments of a Christian View of Life*], with the title, *God Transcendent: Foundation for a Christian Metaphysic*.[46] In the context of the portrayal of a "Christian view of life" the "Christian philosophy" "only has a negative task. It must 'disarm' all soothing illusions that a person has. It must mercilessly uncover the impossibility of everything that a person has undertaken to find a secure place in which he is safe from the question about eternity, which every passing moment demands of him once again. This negative cleaning up operation is, however, only a means to an end. It is only there to make room for the positive moment that we cannot bring about, that only takes place when God lets it happen, namely for the testimony of Christ in the New Testament, which today just as at all times in history must be expressed without any justification or excuse in the simple factual language of the Apostles."[47] But this negative cleaning up operation nonetheless is eminently important: "If every human attempt to liberate oneself from the arbitrariness of one's life is unmasked as a circular argument, if the individual is once again put back in his original despair to stand before the question, 'What, then, ought we to do?' then the ear is open once more for the words which Jesus said to those whom he called to follow him."[48] Chapter headings like "God or Despair" indicate some of the suggestive power of Heim's argument. It is interesting that just at this point Adolf Schlatter begins his criticism; he feared that evangelistic preaching would now make it its goal to drive people to despair.[49]

But a second line of thought can be traced through all of Heim's work: "Where the Christian faith has been forced by the claim of science either into the past or into inwardness, it has the task of setting forth its inherent possibility for thought—in no case the necessity of thought—and to demonstrate the possible foundation of a world view which does not have to stand in opposition to the scientific picture of the world."[50] Heim does not derive from this any direct human knowledge of God. The "God of that which has come into being," who would be recognizable in nature, "remains the *deus absconditus*":

As much as he as Creator of the world is also present everywhere in the sphere which has become, a human being encounters him as the primeval-Thou only in the world of becoming, in Jesus Christ. Jesus Christ is God's Thou, and as such he approaches humankind. To become an "I" with this Thou, entails conversion.[51]

It is astonishing to observe that **Rudolf Bultmann**, who has addressed this topic in a series of publications since 1933, is basically not opposed to Karl Heim's efforts. In his 1933 essay, "The Problem of 'Natural Theology,'" Bultmann first comes to the conclusion that "Even the natural man can speak of God because in his existence he knows about God. . . . In knowing theoretically about existence, he knows its historical nature and to this extent he also knows about God."[52] Humankind enquires about God and nonetheless falls victim to the danger of making "the idea of God serve his own self-established freedom. [But] While un-believing existence cannot of itself change to existence in faith, it still, since it is historical existence, has the possibility of understanding the Word of proclamation which imparts a new quality to the moment. The *question* is not the *answer*, even though the un-believing existence always yields to the temptation to interpret it as the answer. Only faith can say that the question is the answer; and when it says this, it is doing 'natural theology.'"[53]

However, the actual point of contact for Bultmann is to be found somewhere else, namely in the observation that the existential analysis of existence shows structures of existence which "are also valid for existence in faith."[54] It is true that, for philosophy, that which theology characterizes as unbelief is "the original freedom in which existence is constituted."[55] But because philosophy knows of the freedom of existence, it also knows of faith. Thus, "unbelief, as the choice of freedom which grounds human existence, is from the very beginning oriented toward faith."[56] In his essay, "The Question of Natural Revelation" (1941), Bultmann developed this idea further: "*Knowledge about God* [which is inferred in the idea of God in general] *is in the first instance a knowledge which man has about himself and his finitude, and God is reckoned to be the power which breaks through this finitude of man and thereby raises him up to his real nature.*" The Christian faith must, first of all, confirm this knowledge:

This too, according to Christian belief, is meant by the term 'God'—the power which liberates a human from his finitude; and the act by which God does this in the Christian belief system is called the revelation of God. But it asserts that only on the basis of this revelation does a human have a knowledge of God which is not just about *humans*, thus involving a *concept* of God, but is about God *himself*.

88

On the basis of its knowledge *the Christian belief therefore criticizes not the non-Christian inquiry about God—it can only penetrate into it and illuminate it—but first and foremost the answer which the non-Christian question constructs.*[57]

In "Points of Contact and Conflict" of 1946 Bultmann deepens this approach and attempts to clarify the paradoxical nature of the necessity and simultaneous impossibility of connecting God's activity in humankind dialectically. He writes, "the revelation of God is God's conflict with a human in his religion. . . . Yet it is, paradoxically enough, in the very conflict that the point of contact is created, or rather revealed. . . . human's conflict with God is the point of contact for God's conflict with him. A human's sin is the point of contact for God's contradicting Word of grace."

Because sin has seized humankind completely, there is not a single point of contact in humankind: "The human in his existence, taken as a whole, [is] the connecting point." From this follows the second statement. Because human existence always appears in concrete historical form, preaching must take notice of its respective self-understanding. For "the conflict must actually be understood *as a conflict.*" But that means that "the form in which at any given time humans' understanding of existence has been expressed, the expression which his conflict with God and the question of real being has found for themselves is the point of contact—and therefore in a special way, his religion, his conception of God, his ethics and his philosophy is the point of contact."[58]

There is no question that this position has a biblical foundation. The problem is that in pursuing this Bultmann has not avoided the danger of making the point of contact the central issue of understanding and reducing the contents of the message of salvation to the bare "fact" of Jesus' having come and died on the cross.

The concept of "correlation" takes the place of that of a "point of contact" in the *Systematic Theology* of **Paul Tillich**:

The answers implied in the event of revelation are meaningful only in so far as they are in correlation with questions concerning the whole of our existence, with existential questions. Only those who have experienced the shock of transitoriness, the anxiety in which they are aware of their finitude, the threat of nonbeing, can understand what the notion of God means. Only those who have experienced the tragic ambiguities of our historical existence and have totally questioned the meaning of existence can understand what the symbol of the Kingdom of God means. Revelation answers questions which have been asked and always will be asked because they are "we ourselves." Man is the question he asks about himself, before a question has been formulated. . . . Being human means asking the questions of one's own being and

89

living under the impact of the answers given to the question. And, conversely, being human means receiving answers to the question of one's own being and asking questions under the impact of the answers.[59]

Tillich wants to substitute this method for the "supranaturalistic" method in which there is no mediation to the human situation. "But man cannot receive answers to questions he has never asked." However, he also rejects the "naturalistic" or "humanistic" method of liberal theology because "It derives its answer out of human existence, unaware that human existence itself *is* the question." And he wants to correct the "dualistic" method which wants to combine natural and biblical revelation. The method of correlation solves its dilemma "by resolving natural theology into the analysis of existence and by resolving supranatural theology into the answers given to the question implied in existence."[60]

Admittedly, in this method "there is a mutual dependence between question and answer. In respect to content the Christian answers are dependent on the revelatory events in which they appear; in respect to form they are dependent on the structure of the questions which they answer. God is the answer to the question implied in human finitude. This answer cannot be derived from the analysis of existence." But it determines the form of the answer so that a new understanding "of the traditional symbols of Christianity is achieved which preserves the power of these symbols and which opens them to the question elaborated by our present analysis of human existence."[61]

But that is the unanswered question to Tillich's form of the "point of contact." On the one hand, his formulation of the Christian message achieves "an astounding relevance" again and again. On the other hand, the question of the identity in respect of content of his definition with biblical statements arises just as often, i.e., "doesn't the question actually program the answer?"[62]

In so far as it leaves the paths of the traditional, Thomistic dominated natural theology, the "question of being as the characteristic of human structures of existence" in recent Roman Catholic theology, is an important starting point for the ability of humankind to be addressed by revelation.[63] **Karl Rahner** writes, "Man is the radical question about God which, as created by God, can also have an answer, an answer which in its historical manifestation and radical tangibility is the God-Man, and which is answered in all of us by God himself."[64] Rahner ventures this statement, which, at the point cited, is derived from thoughts on God's incarnation in Christ, in the claim of a "transcendental experience" that is constitutive for humankind. It is an experience of transcendence "in which the structure of the subject and therefore also the ultimate structure of every conceivable object of knowledge are present together and in identity."[65] With this transcendence "the knowledge of God is always present unthematically and without name."[66] Simply said, this means that all human existence is created as individual existence oriented toward God and is also, consciously or unconsciously, experienced in this manner. "The attempt is made in every religion . . . to mediate the original, unreflective and non-objective revelation historically, to make it reflexive and to interpret it in propositions. In all religions there are individual moments of such a successful mediation made possible by God's Grace, usually when the supernatural, transcendental relationship of a human to God through God's self-communication becomes self-reflexive. Through these moments God creates for man the possibility of salvation also in the dimension of his objectivity, his concrete historicity"[67] But such "objectifying self-interpretations of gratuitous revelation"[68] succeed only partially. "It always exists within a still unfinished history, it is intermixed with error, sinful delusions and their objectifications, and these once again co-determine the religious situation of other people."[69]

The unparallelled high point of all revelation is the incarnation of the *logos*. "In Jesus, God's communication to humanity in grace and at the same time its categorical self-interpretation in the corporeal, tangible and social dimension have reached their climax, have become revelation in an absolute sense. But this means that for us the Christ event becomes the only really tangible caesura in the universal history of salvation and revelation"[70]— nothing more, but also nothing less! As impressive as this inclusion of the world of religion in the event of revelation may be in its systematic consequences, the tension with the corresponding biblical statement is extremely high.

Wolfhart Pannenberg, who dedicates two detailed chapters in his *Systematic Theology* to the question of natural knowledge of God and the truth of the religions, stays closer to the biblical statements here:

> How can we call that primordial awareness even a nonthematic knowledge of God? How can Paul say that all of us know God? This becomes understandable when we consider that it is part of life to give new meaning to what we have experienced in the light of later experiences. . . . from the time of Moses, the exodus, and the conquest, Israel knew that God had appeared to the patriarchs as their God even though they had not known him as Yahweh. Similarly, he is present to all of us from the very first and is known by us, although not as God.[71]

One can see many indications that the religious relationship is "constitutive for the humanity of humankind," although this is disastrously suppressed in modern, secular culture:

> The universal presence of religious themes corresponds to the feature of human behavior that is described as openness to the world, eccen-

tricity, or self-transcendence. In individual lives this finds historical concretion in the relevance of so-called primal trust to the process of building personality, to the constitution of identity.

In this regard one might well speak of a religious "disposition" which is inseparable from humanity. But the truth of religious statements about the reality and operations of God or the gods does not necessarily follow from such religious disposition. Even when, in distinction from purely anthropological definitions of religion, a reference to divine reality is constitutive for religion, we cannot infer the existence of God from our human religious disposition.[72]

Following a very detailed discussion of the question of the truth of the religions, Pannenberg comes to the conclusion that "the religious relationship always stands under the threat of the ambiguity that the self might be the main concern in the relation to deity. The starting point for this is the finitude of the sphere or the form in which the deity manifests itself and which can be brought into other comprehensive associations and localized there. In the process what gets lost sight of is actually the infinity or absoluteness of the deity. It is exchanged for the finite form of its manifestation."[73] Not until the event of God's revelation in Christ is "the making of the finite of the Infinite which characterizes the religious relation of humanity to God . . . transcended. . . . But as the experiences of history show, this does not protect the members of the church against the perversion of religion into magic."[74]

It is notable for the significance of the topic that **Eberhard Jüngel**— who comes out of Barth's position, but stands in constant conversation with Rahner and Pannenberg—has also taken up the question of natural theology in several publications.[75] In these articles he consistently keeps a firm hold on the rejection of a preparatory natural theology by dialectical theology. This demands not only the "logic of faith," "which denies that the *ground of faith* and *certainty of the content of faith* can be grasped apart from faith," but also "the stringency of thought." But one must indeed "consider and bear responsibility for the problem which natural theology represents," namely "that of the universal claim of the word 'God,' especially in a theology of revelation."[76] With this statement the task of all evangelistic preaching is also outlined which asks every woman and man about her or his relationship to God and faces the problem whether this question can and may be made plausible to the listeners.

"That a human being is a human being and not a cat" obviously gives rise to more theological thoughts than Karl Barth wanted to allow.[77] Responsibility and guilt, anxiety and worry, knowledge of the immense possibilities and at the same time the narrow limits of human existence as well, especially the knowledge of one's own death, all of these are structural characteristics of human life which hint that human beings are oriented toward an other. It is no accident that these manifestations of human existence are almost always given religious meaning, and it would not be difficult to show that even in a post-Christian society there are forms of secularized religiosity in which this orientation of human existence takes form.

All of these are indications for the ability of humankind to be addressed by the message of the gospel, but they are only indications and nothing more. It is not difficult to interpret them in a different way. Thus has, for example, **Horst-Eberhard Richter** in his book *All Mighty: A Study of the God Complex in Western Man* described in a fascinating manner the disastrous course of humankind in the modern period which set itself in God's place and now threatens to perish from its fantasies of omnipotence which function as substitutes for religion. For a Christian this sounds like a brilliant confirmation of what is said in the story of the fall about the deadly consequences of the temptation of wanting to be like God. But Richter draws totally different consequences from his analysis. Not saying "Yes" to God, rather saying "Yes" to death, is "the prerequisite for the destruction of the myth of man's omnipotence and for the achievement of a human mean between impotence and omnipotence."[78]

This conclusion will hinder no one who wants to enter into serious conversation about faith with men and women of our time from taking up such findings and incorporating them into his or her thought. The points of contact with the analysis of human need as found in the message of the Bible are too evident.

But what a Christian should consider forbidden is the construction of a preceding system which proves regardless of the biblical revelation that humankind is dependent on God. Our review of the proposals in systematic theology on this question has not just shown the fundamental problems of such an undertaking. Everywhere that the issue of point of contact has become a topic in and of itself, the message threatens to be swamped by categories that are inappropriate to it. An increase in relevance of the message may not be purchased at the cost of its identity.

To this degree, Barth's warning not to ask humans about their ability to be addressed, rather to tell them the message is justified, then as now.[79] That, however, must at the same time be tied to the readiness to take the addressees of the message totally seriously in their situation. In trust that there is no human life without reference to God, the preacher addressees his or her contemporaries, takes up the variety of their self-interpretations and places the interpretation of the gospel next to them in comparison, confirmation, question or opposition—in the hope that this interpretation will become evident to his or her listeners.

We find this form of dialogue in exemplary fashion—if perhaps sometimes a bit crudely—in the preaching of the New Testament to Jews and Gentiles. The preacher and his or her partner in conversation give time and attention to the presuppositions of the other. People "under the law" are taken seriously in their striving to do God's will. At the same time they will be asked about their falling short of the will of God that shows up either in violating concrete commandments or—more subtly—in the pursuit of their own righteousness, the self-constitution of their place before God by their own achievements. The followers of non-Jewish religions are asked about the discrepancy between the actual intention of all religiosity, the worship in thanks of the transcendent God, and the practical exercise of their cult to manipulate the divinity.

The reference to the catastrophic consequences of egocentricity for the common life accompanies the interpretation of the conventional worship of God as idolatry of the self. In any event, men and women are addressed as religious beings (*homines religiosi*) who fall short of what they seek as the other, namely the living and true God. This does not become evident, however, in an independent proof, rather in connection with the reference to the revelation of this God in Jesus Christ.

It is thus not possible to derive a typology for contemporary preaching from the basic models of the New Testament, although what was said to the Jews back then would, with the necessary alterations, also have to be said to Christians today, and what characterized the early Christian sermon to Gentiles ought in many points also to be said to followers of the new heathen religions. But we shall find the problem of people who want to justify their life by their own achievements—before whatever judge—among atheists as well and shall also have to diagnose the modern variants of idol worship among Christians.

But the fact that men and women feel and perhaps even understand what it means when they are asked about their responsibility, their guilt, how they deal with fulfilling and failing in the tasks and plans of life and thus are also always asked about the other in their lives, about God, is an expectation which the evangelist bases on his or her faith in the unity of Creator and Redeemer, an expectation he or she sees corroborated on some clues observed in human behavior, but confirmed primarily in the miracle of faith.[80]

The Attempt of an Evangelistic Hermeneutic

Heinrich Leipold summarizes his article "Anknüpfung I" ("Point of Contact, I") in the *Theologische Realenzyklopädie* in the following words:

> The discussion about a point of contact has made evident what cannot be the issue in this question: not a Pelagianizing anthropology; not the recognition of true natural knowledge of God which could supplement

or compete with the knowledge of God in Christ; not the attempt to manipulate faith with a technique of making contact; not playing down the scandal of the word of the cross. Every attempt to make contact with human preconditions of understanding has its limit in the fact that faith as an event between God and humankind is beyond human grasp. . . . That "becom[ing] all things to all men" of which Paul speaks in his classic formulation of the problem of the point of contact in 1 Cor 9:19ff. takes place "for the sake of the gospel"—not in renunciation of the gospel, in a consideration which wants to redeem humankind by *bringing the gospel home* to men and women in every way possible. Making contact in this sense means getting involved with the interpretive situation of the person to whom one wants to talk, demonstrating solidarity with him or her even in the process of bearing witness to the gospel. The issue here is the *human* process of offering the word and bringing the word offered home to the hearers, the human responsibility for bearing witness to it fittingly and for hearing it fittingly.[81]

This result corresponds to our observations about the hermeneutical approaches of the New Testament preaching tradition. Where discipleship, apostolic suffering and brotherly and sisterly love become the key terms "the human process of offering the word and bringing the word offered home to the hearers" stands at the center from the very beginning. Thus is also clear that for an evangelistic hermeneutic the issue is more than just finding the most comprehensible evangelistic manner of speech. The issue is a fundamental dimension of missionary existence: making comprehensible for the men and women we encounter what God has done and does for us and for them.

The "Presence" of the Evangelist as the Presence of the Gospel

The basic question of an evangelistic hermeneutic is how do I translate the redeeming message into the language and thought of my fellow human beings in such a way that this message also reaches them. We cannot and are not permitted to "make" persons come to belief under the influence of our preaching. But it appears to be our task to make them understand what we mean when we preach Jesus Christ to them.[82]

However, at the outset of these reflections a conflicting question must be asked. In principle God in Jesus Christ has already reached all of humankind with his salvific action. Because "while we were yet sinners Christ died for us" (Rom 5:8), it follows that "we are convinced that one has died for all; therefore all have died" (2 Cor 5:14). I encounter the human being for whom Christ died not just in the sister or the brother in the

Christian community. I meet him in every person with whom I come together; in Jesus' death the love of God has already reached everyone.

If the Letter to the Hebrews demands that we go "outside the camp" and bear the burden and the humiliation of a life in the profanity of our world, then that is a way to him who suffered "outside the gate" (Heb 13:11-13). Through Jesus' life and death God in his love is already there, in the midst of the godlessness of humankind and all the internal and external misery to which this godlessness gives rise. In this sense all evangelism is follow-up work, literally following the way of God to humankind.

It is important for the evangelizing church to know that Jesus has already reached our fellow human beings. It relieves us from the tension of thinking we have to begin at point zero or look for a point of contact under all circumstances. The decisive point of contact of evangelistic preaching is that which God has already done for humankind.

But it is just as important to realize that many persons do not yet know this and that the biblical way to make them conscious of this is to bear witness of it to them in word and deed. The basic relation of God's salvific action in Christ and preaching the message of salvation is the lifeblood of evangelism. By coming to humankind in Jesus' footsteps, telling them the message of salvation and living with them, the messengers of the gospel open the way for them to the reality which God has long since created to their salvation.

It is no accident that variants of a "theology of the messenger" show up in all important layers of New Testament tradition. "He who hears you hears me," we read in Luke 10:16; "As the Father has sent me, even so I send you," in John 20:21; "So we are ambassadors for Christ, God making his appeal through us," in 2 Cor 5:20. His disciples "represent" Christ; in his name they have the authority to tell and make present to others what he lived through on their behalf. This authority to "represent" him, however, remains closely tied to the commission, yet less to a particular authoritative wording of the message, than to the authentic reproduction of its essence. The commission to represent Christ means the same thing as the instruction to find one's place amidst the need and distress of this world and live the gospel there. The existential seizure of the messenger by the message of God's existence for others in Jesus Christ is a basic element of the New Testament tradition of discipleship (cf. Mark 8:34, 2 Cor 4:7-15, Heb 13:13).[83]

That leads to a first principle of a biblically based hermeneutic of evangelism. The key for the presence of the message in humankind is the transparency of the person, life, and word of the evangelist for the message itself. We can only make the reception of the poor in God's kingdom comprehensible if we ourselves are ready to receive help; we can only preach the justification of the godless if we live from grace ourselves; what the glorious freedom of the children of God means can only be mediated by those who are borne along by child-like trust in God. The issue is not about being a sort of moral example; it can also be especially important to deal with one's own weaknesses and shortcomings openly where God's forgiveness and compassion is preached. It is also not a matter of making one's own experience the Archimedean point of our preaching from which we squash every question about the reality of that which has been preached. "For what we preach is not ourselves" (2 Cor 4:5)!

But what the messenger experiences and suffers can become the medium of understanding so that they are a part of the proclamation, "as your servants for Jesus' sake." The preacher makes clear, "I myself eat the bread that I offer the hungry." Here the issue is not just the psychological power of the personal conviction of the individual who wants to convince others. The sharing of the gospel binds together personal experience and the proclamation of salvation and thus is constitutive for every form of missionary existence.

For the sake of the transparency of that which the gospel promises and grants us *extra nos*, the dimension of the word—preaching and hearing—also remains fundamental. As much as silent action can and must also be an expression of the presence of the gospel in the world for the mission of the church as a whole, where the foundation and the source of such activity become important, Jesus Christ must be mentioned.[84]

But a second principle of an evangelistic hermeneutic also arises from the approach outlined here. If the message of the gospel is at its core nothing other than promise and fulfillment of God's existence for us in Jesus Christ, then the questions of identity and relevance of the message can no longer be regarded as diametrically opposed demands; rather, they converge in the demand that the proclamation be authentic. Identity with the original gospel of the New Testament and relevance for contemporary men and women often constitute two contradictory goals so that as a matter of course nearing one causes us to distance ourselves from the other. But where the gospel is taken seriously as the revelation of God's redemptive turn to humankind, a new perspective comes to the fore. The deeper I sink into the character of this message and the more sincerely I represent it, the more relevant it becomes for persons in need. The theological insight in this matter, of course, does not automatically produce a change in the way our fellow human beings hear the gospel. The insight must be lived, and its truth is not demonstrated by immediate successes but is disclosed in its fulfillment. But the connection between a head-long involvement with the gospel and radical openness to the need of one's fellow human beings can be seen in any number of biographies of Christian individuals and groups. A deepened identity with the gospel can in that context certainly entail the renunciation

97

of suggested human safeguards of one's identity that are often put forward. Jesus' debate with the Pharisees and Paul's struggle for a gospel without Law are biblical models for this which will repeat themselves again and again. And out of this deepened identity grows an existential consummation of the correlation of message and situation. It does not consist of superficial analyses of need; rather, an internal relationship between the gospel and human need grows out of our sharing the life and suffering of the men and women of our time. In the ministry of the messenger the incarnation of the word (which took place in Jesus Christ once and for all) happens anew again and again. The "presence" of the evangelist or of the evangelistic church in the world mediates the presence of the message of salvation.[85]

The message which is formulated out of this presence makes reference to the situation, but is not conditioned by it. We have gotten to know New Testament paradigms for their differentiated orientation of the gospel to a range of addressees and have observed at the same time how they refer to a clearly recognizable center in spite of the differences. These paradigms will also again and again offer models for preaching the gospel today which enable us adequately and specifically to address the needs of our time. We must and may talk differently about guilt and forgiveness with someone dying of AIDS than we would with a successful business man who can proudly look back at the accomplishments of his life, even if it is true for both that God wants to take mercifully their lives in his hand. And both must not degenerate to "types" for us whom we then offer prepared formulas; they must remain unique human beings to us who first disclose the purpose and shortcomings of their lives in our hearing of what they have to say.[86] The message for a mother who fights for her own survival and that of her children in the favelas of Brazil will differ in form and content from that for a woman of the European middle class who actually has "everything" and for just that reason asks what the meaning of her life is. And yet active support in the struggle for survival of the one and the fight with world-weariness of the other can be sustained by the same source, namely by the promise, "God says 'Yes' to your life however much external oppression and internal depression may scream 'No' at you."

The question of meaning is, incidentally, a good example for the possibilities and problems of making "contact" with the questions of our time.[87] The question of meaning is not a biblical question, and there are still today many people on this earth whose external circumstances do not allow them the leisure to ask the question. Nonetheless, it has become the question of life or death for many men and women of the satied society of the northern hemisphere and doubtless encapsulates a hidden yearning for God. Whoever takes this seriously will try to give a biblical answer to the question. But, on the other hand, whoever also takes the biblical message seriously, cannot simply, in the form of a particularly user-friendly offer of meaning, give an appropriate answer, such that the hearer can now also salve his conscience with this answer and proceed to enjoy his or her abundance. If the question of meaning is confronted with the full radicality of God's love, it will also bring the egoistic elements of the question to light and force our lives into the salvific restlessness of the challenge of the love of God. Only in this manner can one really give the question of meaning an answer.

The Presence of the Spirit

What we have described in the previous section as the "presence" of the evangelist in the various situations of human life could also be called the necessity of presence of mind which recognizes at the right time where someone is really lacking something and what the right word and the proper act at the right place are. In a fitting play on words Eberhard Jüngel has brought presence of mind (German: *Geistesgegenwart*) and the Spirit's presence together.[88] A double reference is to be found in this word play in our context. For the decisive dimension of every biblically based hermeneutic is pointed out to us, namely that all true understanding of the word of God is worked by God's Spirit. At the same time, however, it is maintained that this does not simply place the irrational next to the sphere of the rational in an effort to make the message comprehensible. As Jüngel, following Karl Barth, observes in another place, isn't the Holy Spirit truly "the most intimate friend of common sense"?[89] Whoever observes the truly gifted evangelists—be it among the great speakers or be it among the hidden witnesses in everyday life—will find confirmation of this sentence. Knowledge of human nature and a sixth sense for what a particular person or group needs are nourished and formed by the love of God which the Holy Spirit has poured out into their hearts. Interpretation of the Bible justified with critical thinking and intuitive grasping of what is to be said in a certain moment from God's perspective are not opposites; rather, they are complementary kinds of openness for God's speaking that we have to hear and pass on.

The presence of the Spirit in the hermeneutical process is described in different ways in the New Testament. In Acts, in which the promise of and anointing with the Spirit represents the foundation of all missionary ministry, the overwhelming power of the work of the Spirit can step to the forefront (particularly in Acts 10:44-48). But its quiet power of persuasion can also be described in the comment that God opened Lydia's heart (16:14).

In Paul the "demonstration of the Spirit and of power" is intimately connected with preaching Christ crucified (1 Cor 2:1-5). As much as Paul emphasizes that he preaches in power and not just in words (cf. 1 Thess 1:5,

1 Cor 4:19ff.), he by no means intends the performing of miracles which then additionally verify or even supercede the word of the cross. The miracle is just that the word of the maltreated apostle about the hanged savior of the world is believed by anyone and accepted as God's word, and in this Paul sees a demonstration of the power of the Holy Spirit.[90]

In the synoptic apocalyptic discourse in Mark 13:11 one finds Jesus' promise, "And when they bring you to trial and deliver you up, do not be anxious beforehand what you are to say; but say whatever is given you in that hour, for it is not you who speak, but the Holy Spirit." Primarily this is a promise about the Christian responsibility in court. But the context clearly shows that the support of the Spirit in missionary preaching is also meant. This understanding of the motif is taken up in the Johannine farewell discourses where the S``pirit is described as Jesus' and the disciples' "Counselor" (*parakletos*) who will arm the disciples as Jesus' witnesses and convict the world as regards its true situation (John 15:26ff., 16:7-14).[91]

The work of the Spirit in preaching, therefore, does not release the preachers from their responsibility for the witness that is their task and that they formulate in their own words. But it does relieve them from the pressure of thinking that they ought to or could convince their listeners of the truth of their message. They can leave the actual work of persuasion up to God's Spirit freeing their preaching from a tense and forced demand for performance and in so doing leading to a true *parrhesis*, confident authority trusting in the effectiveness of the Spirit.[92]

The preacher's openness to the hermeneutical ministry is manifest humanly in two ways: in prayer, and in the communion of the church.

In the act of prayer the unity of both the identity and the relevance of the message is consummated in a special way by the one praying turning him- or herself completely to the God who revealed himself in Jesus Christ and taking up into this relationship all persons and all needs which he or she encounters in intercessory prayer as their advocate. We must intensify forms of prayer in which we in adoration and praise open ourselves completely to God and then think through and discuss everything before God that moves us. In an intercessory prayer, which is more than the presentation of possible premeditated solutions, rather a prayer which wrestles with God and God's word for the salvation and well-being of persons known and unknown, lies the source of inspiration for beneficial acts and intelligible words.

The process of "distinguishing between spirits," however, is consummated in the communion of sisters and brothers of the church. Evangelists are often loners, individualists, with all the positive and negative sides of practicing artists. For just that reason they need the corrective of the church, not only on the human level, but also on the spiritual level, by living their gift (*charisma*) as a member of the body of Christ. The New Testament does

100

not know the slogan, "Every Christian a missionary!"[93] In the face of the dominating role of apostolic preaching, the image of a missionary or evangelizing church recedes into the background at first; the tasks which are bound to the service of an "evangelist" are also not easy to discern.[94] But in analogy to the statements on prophetic speech which correspond to the service of the evangelist in some regard, one can distinguish a double function which the communion of gifts (*charismata*) in the body of Christ has for the hermeneutical ministry of the Spirit:

(1) In the final analysis it is not the words of an individual which lead one to understand God's call; the life of the church, her worship service, and her orientation towards her Lord are the more comprehensive aids to understanding. Thus Paul presents the church in Corinth as an ideal situation in which an unbeliever or outsider is so examined and convinced by all members that he or she confesses, "God is really among you" (1 Cor 14:23-25).[95]

(2) Thus the church has a critical function for the inspiration of an individual. Whether or not evangelistic preaching is in accord with the faith and thus with the gospel is not decided alone by tangible success, but as the shared responsibility of the Christian church. It is just this wrestling with the truth of the gospel which, under the direction of the Spirit, becomes an eminently hermeneutical process.

The Reflection of Theology

Considered in soteriological terms, as we have said, all mission and evangelism is follow-up work that comes after what God has already done in Jesus Christ. This is particularly the case for the theological work that accompanies it. The starting point of Pauline theology is Paul's encounter with Christ and the charge to preach to the Gentiles which is connected with it and not vice versa. One can even get the impression that the actual terminological formulation of the theological principles of the Gentile mission without the Law was first provoked by the debate with the opponents in Galatia. To be sure, the conviction about the universal validity of the gospel was thus given a form that, for its part, has led missionaries to cross new boundaries again and again.

As we have seen, explicit dialogue with Hellenistic religious thought has been taken up nowhere in the New Testament. The early Christian apologists, who were not content to defend Christianity against accusations of its opponents but went on to enter into a positive conversation with Greek philosophy, were the first to take on this task. This was an obviously necessary, but dangerous path; for one "can scarcely overlook that they pursued the dependence on classical philosophy too far, up to the point where the dynamic of the Christian message was diluted and its central statements were obscured. This danger, which is apparent in retrospect, at that time remained unrecognized."[96]

Nonetheless, this danger should not discredit the task of Christian theology to give everyone an account of the "presuppositions, limits, meaning and basis of the sentences of the Christian confession."[97]

For an evangelistic theology it would doubtless be helpful if the accounts of systematic theology and especially dogmatics would not regard it as their task just to contribute to understanding inside the church, but would also give an account of the faith to those beyond the church. The theologians will avoid the errors of earlier apologists if they reflect upon what God has done in Christ in intensive conversation with contemporary science and culture instead of trying to develop a prolegomena which is independent of the revelation in Christ, in the sense of "another task of theology." That does not exclude the possibility of their accounts then turning into vanguards for preaching by opening new hermeneutical horizons for the preaching ministry. That may even be the case if these accounts pursue paths which in retrospect have been shown to be too dangerous for the general public!

The Announcement of Judgment

In all that we have said about the biblically based content of evangelistic preaching thus far, we have scarcely mentioned judgment. Does the Christian church just have salvation to preach? Is it not said that the usual kind of evangelism speaks too much about judgment? And is not the component of many evangelistic addresses which generates anxiety and fear on account of which some Christians consider themselves victims of evangelism found in this talk of judgment? In any event, this appears to be the background for the following statement of a study consultation of the Conference of European Churches on "The Mission of the Churches in a Secularized Europe": "Without limiting the seriousness of judgment or the mysteriousness of God, our main task is preaching the gospel of the merciful, loving and liberating God."[98]

This corresponds to the New Testament evidence we have thus far highlighted in this chapter. But what remains unanswered is whether, next to the main task, there is still another task of preaching which by its testimony holds onto "the seriousness of judgment." We have already briefly noted that the eschatological "horizon of the threat of judgment"[99] is constitutive of early Christian missionary preaching. We now want to investigate in detail what this means for the preaching of the gospel.

The Disclosure of Standing Under Judgment

The interpretation of Rom 1:18 is of fundamental significance in deciding whether the announcement of God's threatening judgment is a part of the message of the gospel. Paul has given reasons in 1:17 why the gospel is the power for salvation, and then continues, "For the wrath of God is revealed from heaven against all ungodliness and wickedness of men who by their wickedness suppress the truth."

When and where this revelation of the wrath of God will be realized is a matter of controversy in the interpretation. There are three alternatives:

(1) The revelation of the wrath of God is consummated like the revelation of the righteousness of God (v. 17) in the proclamation of the gospel. And here there are two further possibilities:

(a) The proclamation of the gospel must preceed the proclamation of Law and judgment, so people can become aware of their guilt.[100]

(b) The proclamation of salvation through the judgment consummated in Christ always includes the disclosure that humankind stands under judgment as well.[101]

This solution does justice to the parallelism of verses 17 and 18; the strongly emphasized opposition between the revelation "in the gospel" (v. 17) and the revelation "from heaven" (v. 18) makes this solution questionable, however.

(2) The revelation of the wrath of God will take place in the Last Judgment, i.e., *apokalyptetai* is a present tense with future meaning.[102] What speaks for this solution is that in Paul *orgē theou* always refers to the Last Judgment. This solution would also leave aside the difficult problem of how one is to conceive the present revelation of judgment if it does not take place in the proclamation. Against this alternative, however, is the fact that *apokalyptetai* can scarcely have different temporal meanings in verses 17 and 18. The relation between the (future) revelation of the wrath of God and God's having already given up humankind to its lust (vv. 24, 26, 28) is not clear in this solution. That leads to the third alternative.

(3) The revelation of the wrath of God is evidenced in the present-day events all over the world, a reality that weighs on humankind whose symptoms one can infer from the results of God's having turned humankind over to the consequences of its egoism and godlessness.[103] This solution leaves open the question of how humankind can recognize its situation and that which is revealed from heaven. The context of vv. 16-18 suggests that for Paul the revelation of God's wrath in judgment is not the content of the gospel, though it is nonetheless first disclosed in light of the gospel.[104]

Otherwise, in its decisive point there is no difference for us between alternative 2 and 3 (and to a certain degree 1b as well): The announcement of judgment is not directly a task of preaching the gospel. As an explanation for the necessity of salvation, however, humankind's standing under judgment is mentioned. This is not just the case with Rom 1:16ff. Egon Brandenburger formulates as the results of his investigation of the relevant passages that "The prophetic *kerygma* [which is to be proclaimed in missionary preaching] is not (primarily) a threatening with judgment with the chance of conversion and faith, but (primarily) a message of salvation (*euangelion*) with the constitutive horizon of threatening judgment."[105]

In the New Testament texts this horizon is most often presupposed as given. The fact that humankind stands under God's judgment is considered evident. The question of whether we have examples of Paul's missionary preaching before us in Rom 1:18–3:20 in which he argumentatively supported this evidence, is a matter of controversy.[106] One will scarcely be able to deny a connection with it. The material problem is there in any event: Can it be the task of preaching the gospel, and does it have to be the task of preaching the gospel to tear down the façade that provides men and women with false security and thus to open their eyes for the horizon of judgment which threatens their lives? In the first step towards an answer to this question we shall pursue some basic elements of the biblical message of judgment.

The Biblical Message of Judgment

The Preaching of the Prophets

The concept of judgment in the Old Testament is very complex. Since we are interested in questions regarding the "preached" judgment, for the most part we shall restrict our analysis to the prophetic message of judgment. Nonetheless, at the beginning of our analysis we must point out two terminological aspects: When the Old Testament speaks of God's judgment, it can mean salvation or doom for the one addressed. God's judging includes not only his punishing judgment, but also a salvific redirecting of his people and all of creation.[107]

Conversely, there are tradition complexes which we count as statements of judgment in which nonetheless there is no forensic terminology to be found. There are other categories in which God's reaction to the improper behavior of his people can be expressed, e.g., the emotional language of God's "wrath" or the reference to the consequence of the causal relationship between one's behavior and what follows from it which God lets take its course.[108]

Among the unexpected results of more recent exegesis is the observation that not the call to repentence, but the recognition of the people's unavoidably standing under judgment lies at the origin of the tradition of the literary prophets.[109] As "original texts" of literary prophecy, Amos 7:1-8, 8:1ff., 9:1-4, Hos 1:2-9, and Isa 5:1-7, 6:8-12 speak very clearly here. This has a pre-history. The sayings of Nathan to David (2 Sam 12:7-12) and of Elias to Ahab (1 Kgs 17:1, 21:17-24) are early examples of such concrete announcements of judgment. And even in the book of Jonah, which tends to be dated somewhat later, the prophet has no other commission than to say, "Yet forty days, and Nineveh shall be overthrown!" (3:4). Where there is talk of repentence in the oldest tradition, this takes place in the reproachful observation, "yet you did not return to me" (Amos 4:6, 9; Isa 30:15ff.; Hos 11:1-7). To the extent that reasons for the imposed judgment are named, they are primarily social injustices, lacking trust in God, superficial observance of the cult and idol worship. How the judgment will be consummated remains vague. Natural disasters, devastating losses, and deportation are mentioned. But although these are all events "in history," what is actually going on in them remains clear: the merciless confrontation of the people with its Lord.

Jeremiah and Ezekiel pick up this message anew. Their commission is also at first just to announce judgment. True, Jeremiah especially wrestles again and again with a change in the behavior of the people (cf. Jer 4:1-4, 7:3); but even he must draw the conclusion that "they have refused to repent" (5:3). Thus he himself is forbidden to intercede for the people; the judgment, whose consummation in the political situation can be named very concretely, is unavoidable.

Next to the three motifs which are adopted from earlier prophecy, three accents are particularly important: the deceptive security in the unjustly claimed assurance of Yahweh's protective presence among his people must be destroyed; the relationship between God and his people is portrayed very pointedly in the categories of love and faithfulness on the part of God and faithlessness and contempt on the part of the people, and consequently the motif of the wrath of God as justification for the judgment grows in significance.[110] Thus particularly for the prophets it is "least of all a dynamic or juristic automatism as model [that is] decisive than the personal reality of the hurt, offended, disregarded and thus 'justly' angry Lord of his people and the world."[111]

In the face of the suffering that Jeremiah and Ezekiel are burdened with by the severity of this message, the question which in view of the earlier literary prophets could not be suppressed arises all the more drastically: Why should they preach judgment? What was the intention of their message if one could no longer reckon with a change in the fate of the people? Is the "announcement of an approaching turn in history," which—as Amos 8:2 predicts—brings the end of the people Israel, really their "actual message"?

105

Hans W. Wolff, whose research has provoked this question, has attempted to answer it and formulated as his conclusion, "that the comprehensive actual content of the prophetic message is to be seen neither in the call to repentence nor in the announcment of the radical change in history as such, but in the cry, 'Prepare to meet your God'; or still more accurately in the announcement, 'Whatever you do—your God will not pass you by; there is no way to evade him.'"[112] The announcement of judgment is thus intended not only to inform God's people of a pending, unpreventable event, but also to "open the dialogical encounter of the God of Israel with his people."[113] This also explains the hidden but repeatedly manifested hope of the prophets that in the encounter with God, even in certain circumstances in passing through judgment, the possibilities of a new salvific communion between God and his people might open up. Here one might include Amos's "perhaps," but primarily the return to his people of the God who is overcome by the love surging up in him, as Hos 11:8ff. depicts.[114]

This does not mean a premature pardon, but the renunciation of complete destruction. In judgment lies the beginning of a new communion; God will heal the faithlessness of the people and thus make its return possible (cf. Hos 14:5-9).

In this manner the hope the people might be made new grows from the inside (Jer 31:31-34; Ezek 11:14-21, 36:16-32). This is then also the first sign for the hope of God's creative grace for the people, as that is particularly impressively portrayed in Ezek 37:1-14: Life from the dead is grace passing through judgment, in New Testament terms justification of the godless.[115]

The announcement of judgment is thus a call to encounter with God, but simultaneously a call to confrontation with oneself and the true condition of the people. It is the encounter with the holy God, who does not let himself be manipulated by a cult, who loves justice and hates injustice and oppression, who fights for his people with the exclusiveness of true love, but for just this reason does not give it up to the destruction it deserves, rather in passing through judgment creates it for himself anew. Nonetheless, the term "salvific judgment" would be too slick for all the pain, suffering, and destruction that happens in this process of conflict.

However, at one point an entirely new outline for the concept of judgment grows out of the experience of the events of the year 587 BCE. In opposition to the accusations that the collective responsibilty of the people for generations is unjust,[116] Ezek 18 and 33:10-20 emphasize the individual judgment of every person and thus link it to the pressing and personal invitation to return to God. No one must bear punishment for another; everyone can find his or her own way to God and thus to life. A further concept is thus suggested, but not expressed, namely that it is not the total balance of one's life that is finally decisive—not in the sense of the sum total of good or bad works, but in regard to the question in what direction the life of a particular person stood in the final event.

The line which begins here practically invisible then appears clearly for the first time in Dan 12:2: The Last Judgment at the resurrection of the dead at the end of time brings to light what sort of life every person has actually led.[117]

John the Baptist, Jesus, and the Synoptic Tradition

John the Baptist picks up essential elements of the prophetic message of judgment. The announcement of the inevitable and unavoidable judgment and the polemic against the deceptive security of a wrong-headed understanding of election are fundamental for his ministry.[118] They determine his ministry to such a great degree that the question has been posed whether his preaching had aspects of salvation at all. To be sure, if that had not been the case, preaching and performing the "baptism of repentence" would have been meaningless.[119] But as much as the tradition allows a somewhat more accurate look in the first place, the "baptism of repentence" certainly does not mean that those so baptized evaded judgment.[120] Being dipped under water possibly symbolizes being dipped into the "floods of judgment," and the confession of sins linked to it is "judgment doxology." In this case the baptism would be an eschatological act of applying a seal to deliver the baptized when they must pass through judgment.[121]

Jesus, although he received the Johannine baptism, did not share this understanding. His preaching and his ministry are formed by the conviction of the salvific nearness of the kingdom of God. Its promise sounds so unconditional in his mouth that the question surfaces again and again as to whether the concept of judgment could have had a place in his preaching at all.[122]

There are two points in the oldest tradition of Jesus' sayings in which a statement of judgment gets established whose meaning is then unfolded in the further tradition of the synoptic tradition.

(1) There are the sayings which express Jesus' pain that so many close themselves to his ministry and do not enter into the renewed communion with God which he makes available to them.[123] Matt 11:20-24 = Luke 10:13-15 and Matt 23:37-39 = Luke 13:34f. are witnesses of Jesus' fighting on behalf of his hearers. The parable of the great banquet (Luke 14:16-24) underlines the danger of exclusion particularly for those who were actually invited. Judgment is here nothing other than effective self-exclusion from salvation. Since the decisive element is Jesus' ministry, the problem is also christologically formulated—possibly even by Jesus himself. The saying about confessing and denying the Son of Man (Luke 12:8f. and parallels)[124] and the parable of the vineyard (Mark 12:1-12) are proof of this. Against

the background of the motifs of Deuteronomic preaching of judgment, the parable in particular sketches Jesus' being sent as God's last and decisive call and Jesus' path as the embodiment of the God who asks and seeks, but it also simultaneously marks the deadly consequences of rejection.[125]

Jesus, who lived the inviting, sheltering, and healing nearness of God is thus—as the Lukan introduction formulates in anticipation (2:34)—"set for the fall and rising of many in Israel, and for a sign that is spoken against."

His murder is the reason for and sign of the judgment of the Jewish people. While Matthew appears to see in that a (preliminary) conclusion of God's history with Israel and considers the judgment to be consummated in the destruction of Jerusalem,[126] Luke sees in this the reason for the decisive call to repentence to the people of Israel (cf. Acts 3:12-26).

(2) The second starting place for the topic of judgment in Jesus' teaching is to be found in the question about the responsibility which arises as a consequence of the encounter with the God of mercy. The parables of the talents (Matt 25:14-30 = Luke 19:12-27) and of the unmerciful servant (Matt 18:23-34) can be cited as examples. Especially the Matthean tradition emphasizes these elements. The insertion of the motif of the wedding garment in the parable of the marriage feast (22:11-13) and the pointed warnings in 7:15-27 at the conclusion of the Sermon on the Mount show this. A series of parables that only appear in Matthew emphasize assorted aspects of the concept of judgment as well: The parables of the tares among the wheat and of the fishing net and their interpretations (13:36-43, 47-50) warn about judging too quickly with a reference to the final judgment; 25:31-46 names the standard in the judgment of the nations and so identifies in a unique way the orientation on those in need and Jesus; 20:1-15, on the other hand, maintains that before God the issue is not the accumulation of good deeds, but that he grants his care to everyone who hears his call.[127]

Especially the last two examples, which cannot be ascribed to any system, demonstrate the function of the concept of judgment in the Jesus tradition. It is not intended to lead one to make new calculations about or become afraid of whether and how one could pass God's judgment; rather it ought to direct one's entire concentration toward the encounter with God revealed in Jesus and the task for one's life that it discloses to one. However, to be able to give this perspective the necessary deeper dimension, the auxiliary line of the concept of judgment appears indispensible.

Paul and Early Christian Mission

In Pauline preaching the concept of judgment is to be found under three aspects.[128]

(1) The knowledge that all of humankind stands under judgment is the dark background of the preaching of salvation. Here Paul doubtlessly has

recourse to constitutive motifs of early Christian missionary preaching. The salvation which he preaches is deliverance "from the wrath to come" (1 Thess 1:9f.). This conviction is—as we have seen—also the background for Rom 1:16–3:20 (cf. further Rom 5:9 and 1 Thess 5:9).[129] In Paul's writings "wrath" no longer has any emotional connotation and is practically a synonym for judgment. The term describes God's No to all injustice and sin of humankind which will be spoken in the final judgment (1 Thess 1:10, Rom 2:5-10), but already weighs upon humankind as fate (Rom 1:18, 1 Thess 2:16).

As our analysis of Rom 1:16-18 has shown, the revelation of righteousness and of the wrath of God does not take place in the same way. "Not wrath *and* righteousness are preached, but righteousness as deliverance in the face of wrath which is already at work."[130]

It was, however, not evident to all hearers of the early Christian missionary sermon that they were living under the fate of judgment of destruction. We do not know for certain what and how much the preachers did to prove this to them. The argumentation of Rom 1:19-31, 2:1-16; Acts 17:29-31; 1 Thess 1:9ff. and the set "formulas of warning" in 1 Cor 6:9-11, Gal 5:19-21 (cf. Col 3:6 and Eph 2:5, 5:5) betray traces, however, of such a practice.[131]

However, one may not forget that in the context of his letters Paul never speaks of humankind's standing under judgment from any perspective other than that of the gospel, from the perspective of deliverance that has already begun. It is necessary to speak of this because as cruel reality it threatens human life; but it never takes place as if there were no gospel.

(2) And thus we encounter the second aspect of the concept of judgment in Paul. In the event and preaching of the cross the motif of judgment is doubly present. The cross is the sign of the judgment upon sinners which Christ suffered. He "became a curse for us" by taking upon himself the fate of one cursed by the Law (Gal 3:13, cf. 2 Cor 5:21). God sent "his own Son in the likeness of sinful flesh and [as a sin offering] for sin, [and] he condemned sin in the flesh [of his Son]" (Rom 8:3).

In the word of the cross, the proclamation of Christ who died for our sins, humankind is thus confronted with the judgment upon their lives, but as the judgment carried by Christ. The proclamation of the cross reveals both: How humankind really stands before God—and that "God has not destined us for wrath, but to obtain salvation through our Lord Jesus Christ" (1 Thess 5:9).[132]

In faith in the crucified one a person professes his or her faith in this judgment, and in baptism he or she is taken up into what it works (Rom 6:3-11). The function of baptism as a doxology of judgment as in the activity of John the Baptist is thus taken up once again in a form which gains its depth from the christological dimension.

But it is precisely here that the conflict begins. Because this message is an insult to human self-esteem, it is rejected.[133] Thus the message not only becomes an occassion of deliverance, but also of perishing (1 Cor 1:18; 2 Cor 2:15f., 4:3f.). Paul never fleshes this out to a threatening full-fledged picture of judgment,[134] but it remains a painful limit of his preaching: Whoever rejects life granted by Christ chooses death. "Such a separation is already an event of judgment."[135]

(3) The third aspect of the concept of judgment has nothing to do with missionary preaching, rather is expressly directed toward Christians. It has attained such special attention because the judgment according to works addressed here (2 Cor 5:10, cf. Rom 14:10) appears to contradict the Pauline doctrine of justification. But in such a case the "limited function" of these texts is not recognized.[136] However, above all what is not recognized is that neither "justification by faith" nor "judgment according to works" are principles which can be calculated on the anthropological level. They are dimensions of the encounter with God whose merciful will determines human life in justification and sanctification. And vice versa: Those who do not "remain in God's goodness" but make their own faith into a work on the basis of which they despise others must reckon with losing this goodness themselves and falling under judgment. God's judgment of others never becomes one's own justification. Justification lies in God's free grace alone.[137]

This knowledge widens the apostle's perspective: At least for Israel the unlimited breadth of divine mercy (Rom 11:25-31) shows up on the other side of the horizon of judgment which had been obliquely referred to in Rom 9–10. And in the formula, "God has consigned all men to disobedience, that he may have mercy upon all" (11:32), the alternative of "judgment or salvation" appears to be overcome for all.

The Johannine Writings

In the writings which according to tradition are from John one finds the two most contradictory views of judgment in the New Testament. According to the view of the Gospel of John the decision for salvation or damnation is made in the encounter with Christ and his word. A special future act of judgment on the part of God is unnecessary. Whoever believes comes to the light (3:21), has passed from death to life (5:24) and *has* eternal life (3:16 and similar passages). Whoever does not believe is already judged (3:18) and the wrath of God rests upon him or her (3:36). Even if some passages nonetheless speak of the Last Judgment (12:48, cf. 5:28ff.), this

110

does not change the fundamental view: Now, in the encounter with the Word, the ways to judgment or to life part.[138]

What the Gospel of John clearly denies, the Revelation according to John offers in excess. Two different levels of the act of judgment are described:

(1) We find the first level in the letters in which prophetic sayings of judgment and comfort to seven early Christian churches are assembled. Having been identified as a saying of the risen Lord by the "messenger formula," the admonition to remember the reception of the gospel and to repent, which is underlined by a "conditional threat of judgment,"[139] follows a verdict on the condition of the church (accusation). It is not insignificant that the letters are placed at the beginning of a book at whose conclusion the portrayal of the judgment will stand. The judgment will begin with the house of God.[140] "This prophecy is concerned with the fate of its respective hearers in light of the fact that the apocalyptic judge will soon come and judge everyone according to his or her works. Its admonition and its comfort always serve to prepare the church for the judgment soon to come. The special emphasis of all statements of this prophecy lies in its being authorized as the speech of the one who will hold court in the end."[141]

The fact that in the saying of judgment and the saying of comfort the encounter with Christ is fundamental safeguards this preaching against casuistry. Behind the causal connection between act and consequence of the conditional threat of judgment stands the personal authority of the living Lord of the church who woos it and calls it back to himself. To observe this is also important for evangelistic preaching, which has liked to refer to the prophetic message of the letters and also always understood itself as a call of alarm to a sleeping, luke-warm or self-contented church.

(2) However, in Revelation we see a second level of judgment in the description of the judgment of the world. This is effected in two series of images. The first (19:11-21) describes the "judging" of the coming judge of the world as overcoming all powers that are enemies of God, draws its images from the world of war and battles and is materially oriented on the erection of the kingdom of God.[142] The other is oriented on the motifs of the final judgment as they are given in Dan 7:9f. and is materially directed toward the responsibilty of the individual for his or her life and his or her actions (20:11-15). The last mentioned text, to be sure, has one difficulty. Among the books which will be opened at the day of the judgment a clear distinction is made between the "book of life" (20:12a, 15) and the books whose contents form the basis for the judgment according to works (20:12b, 13). Books of judgment are known in the apocalyptic tradition and are kept in heaven to list human misdeeds.[143] The "book of life" or the "book of the living" is in contrast an Old Testament metaphor which proceeds from the

assumption "that God has a register of the living and that from time to time he strikes out from this register those who are to die" (Exod 32:32ff.; Ps 69:29, 139:15).[144] But the concept has been so expanded that those who belong to God are listed in God's book.[145] Not the works are the basis of the entries in this book, but God's merciful election (cf. Rev 13:8, 17:8), which to be sure, is not to be understood as predestination in a narrow sense. Even the Christian is threatened by the danger of being stricken from the book (3:5).

Both perspectives, judgment according to works and judgment according to the book of life, stand in a tension which is hard to resolve. Do we have the *concursus practicus*[146] that the "believers show by their own lives that they are in the Book of Life,"[147] or must the tension remain in order to describe the dialectic of the lasting responsibility of humankind and the final decision in God's merciful election?[148] According to 20:15 the final court of judgment is, in any event, the book of life.

Which kerygmatic function do these reports of the judgment of the world have? They are, first of all, information for the church which should fortify against temptation in the face of the uneasy question of whether God will really keep the upper hand. Simultaneously implied in that is the admonition to faithfulness and sticking it out. We do not know whether Christians also used this knowledge in discussions with outsiders to sketch for them the awful end that threatens them.[149]

Summary

The concept of judgment is a constituitive element of biblical theology. It follows not only as a consequence of the causal relationship between one's behavior and what follows from it (= *Tun-Folge-Zusammenhang*) or as a "postulate of practical reason." It is an expression of God's sovereignty and humankind's responsibility before him as his creation. From this fundamental conviction follows the tension in that which is named as the standard of judgment, namely the relationship to God on the one hand and the deeds of a person on the other—in New Testament terms, on the basis of faith or according to works. A final systematic reconciliation of these two perspectives is not sought in the biblical tradition since it is not an issue of naming criteria that humans could use, but involves an encounter with the living God.

The announcement of judgment in preaching can exercise differing functions. It can disclose that the hearers stand under judgment, warn of the threatening judgment, appear under the sign of the judgment which has been overcome, and point out the danger of scorning God's love and remaining in the area in which the death sentence is still in force. Within the New Testament, it thus stands in the shadow of the proclamation of salvation in the literal sense that it shows the dark consequences of rejecting light and life out of God and reminding the hearers what the true circumstances of men and women without God are.

The Necessity of the Concept of Judgment: An Excursus in Systematic Theology

"The concept of judgment is one of those topics about which contemporary systematic theology is intentionally and unintentionally silent." This pithy saying stands at the beginning of an article by **Konrad Stock** on "God the Judge: The Concept of Judgment as the Horizon of the Doctrine of Justification."[150] In it Stock sketches the origin of this omission in Albrecht Ritschl's theology. But he also notes that voices of protest against this omission already arose in so-called dialectic theology. Thus the concept of judgment is also (if sometimes only briefly) in most of the "classical" systems in systematic theology.

In his textbook on eschatology, *Die Letzten Dinge*,[151] **Paul Althaus** puts the significance of decision in the center:

The moment in which God's rage and forgiveness in Christ tries to win one for complete truthfulness, one's total abandonment to his forgiving grace, can only be understood as the moment of a *decision* that dominates simply everything: The Yes or No to Christ means life or death. Christian eschatology can thus not renounce the idea that human history will have *one of two conclusions*, depending on the experience of one's conscience with Christ. The Either-Or, which I see placed before me by Christ, the unconditional contrast between faith and un-faith, in which I should decide, cannot be a game. In the idea of two conclusions, of a definitive parting of the ways, Christian theology secures for itself something that can never be given up: the meaning of our life as a decision about our relationship to holy God, the eternal seriousness of this decision. . . . The decisional character of life thus means the possibility of two conclusions of history, in salvation or damnation, the winning or losing of life" (pp. 187f.).

A doctrine of the *apokatastasis*, "when it makes the claim to be an exhaustive description of the end," would thus be a claim to "know-it-all." The seriousness of the decision, the possibility of eternal damnation must remain visible, and in pastoral care and invitational preaching "those whom the decision thus approaches" must be reminded of that.

But one may not make a "theory about others" out of that, and insofar as persons "are beyond the reach of our love and efforts to win them for God or are unapproachable in their dullness and rejection, we commend them— as we do all of humankind including ourselves—to God's guidance which insures that everything turns out all right." The view toward the end is thus "determined by two things: that we know that all persons are continually faced with the decision, and that in and above every decision we believe in God's omnipotent grace."[152]

Karl Barth also dedicates several longer passages of his *Church Dogmatics* to the question of judgment. In II/2, §35.3.4, he deals with the determination of the elect and the rejected and §39 treats "The Command as the Judgment of God." In IV/1, §61.2.3, he discusses "The Judgment of God" and "The Pardon of Man." The tone of his remarks can be concisely summarized: God has judged humankind in the death of Jesus Christ. He is the only damned one; in him all men and women are elected. In the proclamation of the word of the cross all persons learn that the judgment of Jesus Christ is judgment of their "former self" with complete works.

But precisely in hearing this, they learn about their acquittal for Christ's sake. Barth dismissed the charge that this must necessarily lead to the doctrine of *apokatastasis* and refused to commit himself either fundamentally to limit the number of the saved or to expand it to include all human beings. This would be a case of failure to "respect the freedom of divine grace."[153]

Emil Brunner, who was among the first to formulate this question for Karl Barth,[154] for his part comes very close to Paul Althaus's solution and sees in the concept of the judgment of the world and that of universal salvation two perspectives which stand irreconcilably next to one another but are both irrenounceable: "In the two terms Final Judgment and Universal Salvation God's communication of himself as the Holy One and God's glorification of himself as the Loving One achieve their most complete form of expression."[155]

Shortly after the war **Helmut Thielicke** wrote an essay entitled "Judgment and Affliction" which examined the "question of the 'concrete' sermon of judgment," and he included it practically unchanged in Volume II/1 of his *Theological Ethics*.[156] The conclusion of this investigation is that the church's message of judgment

> . . . must preach *krisis* and *soteria* simultaneously, that it is the message of reconciliation and the promise of affliction in one—simply because the Son of God, who is present in every word of a sermon of judgment, has not come to judge the world, but to save it. Judgment can also be a means to save, simply because it is the Father of Jesus Christ who carries it out and because this Father "loved the world." The judgment only ceases to be a "means" and turns into a *final* judgment when the savior is thrown out of the court. Then this "very stone which the builders rejected" will become a stumbling block and a cause of outrage.[157]

In this sense Thielicke regards holding onto two results of the judgment as theologically unavoidable: First, "it gives the present moment of decision the eschatological weight of the unconditional," and second, "any attempt to dissolve this dualism of eternal life and its opposite intellectually . . . ends with a problem that is no less severe."[158]

In his *Systematic Theology* **Paul Tillich** interprets "the symbol of ultimate judgment" in a completely different manner. "[H]ere and now, in the permanent transition of the temporal to the eternal, the negative is defeated in its claim to be positive. . . ."[159] This leads to a totally changed meaning of judgment for the individual in comparison with the usual interpretation:

> From the point of view of the divine self-manifestation the doctrine of twofold eternal destiny contradicts the idea of God's permanent creation of the finite as something "very good" (Genesis, chapter 1). . . . The doctrine of the unity of everything in divine love and the Kingdom of God deprives the symbol of hell of its character as "eternal damnation." This doctrine does not take away the seriousness of the condemning side of the divine judgment, the despair in which the exposure of the negative is experienced. But it does take away the absurdities of a literal understanding of hell and heaven and also refuses to permit the confusion of eternal destiny with an everlasting state of pain or pleasure."[160]

Because of the complexity and ambiguity of all human being, for Tillich there can be no either-or in regard to the life of a particular individual. The fate of the individual is taken up into the fate of humankind and all being in all of its manifestations. "He who is estranged from his own essential being and experiences the despair of total self-rejection must be told that his essence participates in the essences of all those who have reached a high degree of fulfillment and that through this participation his being is eternally affirmed."[161]

Gerhard Ebeling begins with the "postulate of practical reason" in the short section "Judgment" in his *Dogmatik des christlichen Glaubens*. "How strongly does world history awaken an honest, well-founded desire for judgment, for re-installing rights that have been trampled in the dirt, for distributive justice."[162] Then, however, he tersely develops the meaning of the New Testament statement

> that the judgment of the world has been handed over to Jesus Christ. That means, to begin with, that the one who will execute judgment has, through his path to the cross, first himself undergone the judgment which will sweep over the world. That means, further, that the gospel

of Jesus Christ is a serious matter. The gospel is not some subordinate issue that we could be indifferent about; the gospel is the ultimate issue, that which is the measure of all things.

From this follows, in opposition to Tillich, that "it is a question of a total or comprehensive verdict, of an Either-Or, of being accepted or being rejected, but it is not a question of weighing sins and excuses, of a lighter or more severe punishment, of a mixed verdict: partially guilty, partially innocent. Here it comes to a clear and definitive distinction without any shadow of doubt." When one speaks of judgment according to works, then the issue is "what has been reality in one's life, what one has done. But Jesus Christ as the Judge understands the connection which links deeds and faith. . . . Judgment according to works leads all justification by works *ad absurdum*" and points toward "justification by faith alone."[163]

Konrad Stock, with whose essay we began these reflections, himself begins with Rom 1:20ff. "In the history of his turning to humankind, God is faced with the twofold experience of being dishonored by humankind and sharing in the experience of the dishonor which men and women inflict upon one another in the actions of others which they then must bear." Under the "wrath" of God he understands "God's indignation and wound caused by this twofold . . . experience of human history." God's "judgment," however, consists in "God's not hiding his indignation and hurt, but for the sake of his own self-regard letting them become a human experience that is not hidden and that nothing can hide." "Judgment is the metaphor for the definitive situation in which God confronts a person with his or her life history and once and for all commits him or her to the consequences and thus identifies him or her with this life history." But "God forestalls [this fatal situation for humankind] in the death of Jesus Christ. In just this manner he decisively and conclusively resists the power of evil; in just this manner he asserts himself in his intention to turn toward the world of humankind." Christ's cross "is the form of divine resistance and opposition to the power of evil which creatively distinguishes human life history from its own disaster and declares it not guilty for its own disaster." In this "new determination the concept of judgment is a . . . permanent theme of the gospel." "Faith hopes for the eschatological presence of God in the world of humankind which is determined by the name of Jesus Christ. Faith hopes for this because just where the power of human evil must become visible the greater power of divine goodness will be disclosed at the same time."[164]

This brief review shows that we cannot renounce the the concept of judgment, but it also shows its problems. Which ideas and consequences follow from this for biblically based missionary preaching?

(1) The question of judgment is a universal question shared by all of humankind. Not every asks it; many are sceptical about whether or not there will be any kind of "poetic justice," but in their very scepticism they underline the inherent question about judgment. The concept of judgment is thus not the rod of an abusive divine pedagogy which one would do better to leave standing in the corner. It is simultaneously the expression of a longing for justice and overcoming evil and of knowledge of true responsibility. But as a postulate of a human sense of justice alone, God's judgment is neither real nor just. In the encounter with the word of the living God his judging proves to be a necessary dimension of the relationship between Creator and creature.

(2) Christian talk about judgment is speech which follows the crucifixion of Christ. Even in the Revelation according to John the judge of the world whom God enthrones is none other than "the Lamb who was slain."[165] Speaking of humankind as lost without mentioning its being delivered by Christ is thus inappropriate. But it is the cross which maintains the knowledge of humankind's being lost. On the cross the guilt of all of humankind is disclosed, of the men and women who due to envy, hate, laziness or cowardice let him who lived God's love among them end his life on the gallows. On the cross the condemnatory power of the law which places the sin of humankind under the curse of separation from God shows itself. Human transgressions and God's wound are revealed in the death of Jesus because God himself takes both upon himself in suffering.

(3) Talk about humankind's being lost is an invitation to life through Christ. It does not threaten with future punishment which God could exercise; rather, it discloses the true situation of a person who does not seek refuge in the sphere of grace opened by Christ but remains bound by the fate of his guilt, separated from life in God. It refers to the earthly symptoms of the transgressions in a human life, the hell on earth which human beings make for themselves since God renounced his power. And it refers to the final encounter with God which can be characterized by the joy of consummated communion with God or the pain of spurned love and a wasted life. Biblically oriented talk about judgment, however, will also announce that God's judgment does not just mean taking stock of an individual's life in which—neutrally and so to speak automatically—will be shown what has come out of an individual life. It is much more the case that it is a part of the process of establishing the rule of God over a fallen creation through which all evil and ungodliness will be overcome. In that lies hope for all, a hope which does not make the seriousness of the question about individual responsibility and behavior superfluous.

For evangelistic preaching a twofold problem remains here: How can it make contemporary hearers conscious of this responsibilty, and how does it mention the exclusiveness of salvation in Christ?

Preaching the Law?

There is a long tradition of evangelistic preaching which proceeds on the assumption that individuals first must be led to a recognition of their guilt and sin by preaching the law before they can truly understand the meaning of the gospel. One of its most convinced representatives was John Wesley. In his sermon "The Law Established Through Faith, I" he disputes that with the proclamation of the gospel, i.e. "speaking of nothing but the sufferings and merits of Christ," all the goals of the law are fulfilled. For this has the purpose of "convincing men of sin, the awakening of those who are still asleep on the brink of hell. Here and there, there may have been an exempt case. One in a thousand may have been awakened by the gospel. But this is no general rule. The ordinary method of God is to convict sinners by the law, and that only." In an allusion to Matt 9:12 he says, "It is absurd therefore to offer a physician to them that are whole, or that at least imagine themselves so to be. You are first to convince them that they are sick; otherwise they will not thank you for your labor. It is equally absurd to offer Christ to them whose heart is whole, having never yet before been broken."[166]

In a letter to an unknown layman he describes the correct method of preaching.[167] When one begins to preach in a place, one should first give a general explanation of God's love for sinners and his readiness to deliver them, but then the law should preached in the most forceful and demanding form possible and the gospel should be shown more or less only from a distance. Only when more and more are convinced of their sins, should one also offer—in careful doses—the comfort of the gospel.[168]

The conversion sermon of Pietism corresponds to this. Preaching the gospel should first awaken the hearers so that the law can truly shatter them and lead them into despair over their guilt; it is just at this point that it comes to true "acquisition and realization of grace."[169] It is obvious that with this method there was the danger of using preaching about law and gospel as a psychological instrument for conversion.[170]

Fundamentally, this conception can appeal to Luther's understanding of the second use of the law (*usus secundus*), the theological (*usus theologicus*) or educational use (*usus paedagogicus* or *elenchticus*). The law has no other task than to convict humankind of its guilt and to speak its verdict. "To those who are bound and in despair under the law as the word of wrath, distress, pain, the hour of judgment, [comes the gospel and preaches] to them Christ, who bears the sins of the world and fulfills the law, as their righteousness, sanctification and salvation."[171] The decisive difference is that for Luther this event is not oriented on one once and for all experience; rather, it describes a permanent dialectic to which the *simul iustus et peccator* anthropologically corresponds.

How does Paul speak about the problem considered here? It is well known that the opposition of law and gospel does not exactly correspond to Paul's language use terminologically in which law and Christ (or faith) confront one another.[172] But materially this antithesis is, as Otfried Hofius has shown in a vivid investigation of 2 Cor 3, the core of Pauline theology.[173] The *palaia diathēkē*, God's old "covenant," is the law of Sinai, which as letter, as "that written and ordained," binds the sinner to his sin and speaks his or her death sentence. The *kainē diathēkē*, however, God's new "covenant," comes into being through the spirit which gives life, the spirit "which dedicates that salvation—including the forgiveness of sins and new creation—which was decided in the salvation event of Jesus Christ's death on the cross and resurrection and is disclosed in the word of salvation of the gospel in a manner that awakens faith."[174]

The task of the apostle is the "ministry," "which proclaims the gospel that was fulfilled by God's spirit and in the power of the spirit is creating our hearts anew and thus makes that word known in which God himself 'reveals'—in a manner that awakens faith—that in Christ's death and resurrection our acquittal was issued that we might live." This stands in opposition to the "ministry of Moses" as *diakonia tou thanatou* and *diakonia tēs katakriseōs*, as a ministry "which brings up God's killing law in an effective manner and validly executes its death sentence."[175]

The fundamental question is then accordingly, "Must evangelistic preaching discharge the ministry of the apostle as well as the ministry of Moses?" The answer to this question must clearly be "No." In the actual meaning of the word, the law is not "preached"; it is already there. It demands, condemns, and kills by its very existence. True, where one knows the law and its commandments one can come to recognize one's sin, but the law can just as well be misused to construct one's own righteousness. For Paul no direct path led from a sermon on the law to recognition of Jesus Christ. "Only . . . in the light of the gospel is the Torah from Sinai recognized as that which it in truth is—the killing *letter* which a person *outside of Christ* always has before him- or herself, but *in Christ* has definitively behind him- or herself."[176]

Thus it is not preaching the law that works the consummation of this knowledge, which for Paul is clearly a basically once-and-for-all, decisive breakthrough, but the interpretation and illumination of one's life under the law in the proclamation of the gospel. The distinction between "preaching" the law and disclosing its effects may appear to be a subtlety which will scarcely have any meaning in practice. And yet this distinction is the key to distinguishing between preaching which makes men and women ill and preaching which can show them how ill they are even though they may feel totally healthy, preaching which thinks it must first shatter its hearers and preaching which reveals the inner brokenness of persons without God and heals.

But how does a contemporary individual experience the workings of God's law? Paul has already pointed out that what the Torah means for Jews is "written in the heart" of non-Jews. How does a secularized individual of our time experience this demand of God on his or her life?

In an interpretation that is particularly enlightening for evangelistic preaching, Gerhard Ebeling has shown how the reality of life as such turns into an experience of the law for humankind.[177] In a variety of tasks, borderline experiences and encounters a person experiences that much is demanded of him-or herself, often too much; such a challenge promises to give his or her life meaning and content. However, it leads a person to self-justification through "self-deception and self-appeasing"[178] or to resignation and despair in the face of failure and discontent. There are more persons who have fallen victim to the arresting and deadly verdict of the law in this manner than we would think proceeding on the basis of a perspective limited to moral issues.

Ebeling, however, has also pointed out that this interpretation is only biblically legitimate when we succeed in referring the diffuse demands and challenges of the reality of life to the fundamental demand of the law as the revelation of God's will, as it is summarized in the great commandment of love.[179] The reality of life as experience of the law can speak very unclearly, if not deceptively.[180] It is simply not so obvious that and how we recognize God's will in it. But it is the background of all experience, the background against which persons understand that God approaches them as a demanding God: They feel that a task could be hidden in the gift of life and that a call to be modest and give account of one's actions lies in the demarcation of life. But they must be told that in this God encounters them as their Creator who assigns them responsibilty for their lives. This is, however, not a task that should first be performed without the gospel. It is the encounter with Jesus Christ which also discloses this dimension of their relationship to God in its profoundest sense to humankind. His obedience in life reveals how life as a creature was meant as life before God and in communion with others. His cross uncovers what humankind has made of it. Because the crucified one bears the curse of the law, the consequence of misguided human existence, the work of the law and its origin in human life becomes visible in the proclamation of the gospel. Where the cross is preached thus also always makes audible how a person stands before God in regard to his or her wisdom, power, reputation, or piety. Preaching grace which only "superficially heals the damage" is out of the question. That "the word of God is living and active, sharper than any two-edged sword . . . and discerning the thoughts and intentions of the heart" (Heb 4:12) applies particularly to the word of the cross. Adaptating a thesis of Hans-Martin Barth, one could thus say: "The sermon about Jesus Christ in which that in my being, action, and unaction I am rushing towards my death, (a fact that in its radicality first becomes perceptible in that sermon), and that I require a deliverance which I cannot procure (or even just appropriate) on my own" points toward the law. However, "the sermon about Jesus Christ in which I am told that I have been brought to the way to life and that my origin in the way of death is incapable of impairing, much less preventing this" proves to be the gospel.[181]

The reference to the law and the proclamation of the gospel may receive different emphases in different circumstances.[182] But "the ministry of the new covenant" is always essentially a "ministy of reconciliation."

Extra Christum nulla salus

"All are lost without Christ." Such sentences, or similar ones, are among the basic claims of traditional evangelistic preaching. As regards its contents, it is covered by weighty statements in the New Testament like John 14:6 or Acts 4:12. Nonetheless, there are two diametrically opposed interpretations of this truth. One is exclusive: Only a person who comes to personal faith in Christ is delivered.[183] This interpretation suggests itself against the background of the call to decision in the Gospel of John (3:18; 12:47f.). The other is inclusive: Because "there is no salvation apart from Christ. . . . and God has really, truly, and seriously intended this salvation for all men . . . every human being is really and truly exposed to the influence of divine, supernatural grace which offers an interior union with God and by means of which God communicates himself whether the individual takes up an attitude of acceptance or of refusal towards this grace."[184] On the basis of this thesis Karl Rahner has spoken of anonymous Christianity.[185] Karl Barth's doctrine of election is also an example of such an inclusive interpretation of the *extra Christum nulla salus*. It can appeal to passages like Rom 5:18f. and 2 Cor 5:14 in which the reality of God's act of salvation in Jesus for all humans is announced.

Of course, objections have been raised repeatedly against the statement as such which in both versions is considered presumptious or imperialistic in different ways.[186] The reason for that is obvious: On the one hand, it appears inconceivable that all persons who have never heard of Christ, or who have only been superficially reached by the message and thus have made no decision of faith, should be lost before God. On the other hand, in the encounter with persons of other religions and world views a wealth of mature humanity and knowledge of God often opens up to which Christians also cannot deny their respect. So John 14:6 and Acts 4:12 are not understood as generally valid conclusions, but as expressions of subjective certainty, and the verdict regarding a person's life is set under the sign of Lessing's parable of the ring.[187] Is there a way to deal with these statements of the Bible which remains faithful to its message without simply negating the critical questions?

To begin with, it must be made clear that the issue is not the claim of Christianity's absolute truth; for just this reason the extension "*extra ecclesiam nulla salus*"—which has no biblical witness—must always be regarded very critically. Where Christ is and works is not something that we decide.

At the same time one must recognize that the claim of exclusivity for salvation through Jesus Christ constitutes "an unheard of provocation" for those close to the Christian community then and now.[188] That in a society as religiously tolerant as the Roman empire it could come to persecutions of Christians is causally connected with this provocation. But the provocation appears necessary for the sake of the matter at hand. "As soon as talk about God moves into the context of an exclusive claim for Jesus, God takes on the concrete features of the one who as the creator of the world has started to look for and love those whom he has created in an unfathomable and irrevocable manner. This provocation of the concrete God is an attack on all indefinite talk about God and on all fuzzy syncretism. For it is the invitation to praise the God who has broken into this world and to hope for the consequences for the future which follow from that." For just this reason a profound tolerance lies in the exclusive claim for Jesus which we are not to turn into our own human claim of power. "Where human beings move into the spotlight of Jesus Christ's claim, they are recognized as loved by God, and thus as fellows whom we are neither to hate nor to idolize, but to love. But in that the provocation is given that in the midst of all absolutizing of programs one asks with all passion about the fellow and primarily about the weak, hungry, and guilty neighbor."[189]

The certainty of that which is absolutely valid for me bears the challenging demand that it is also valid for all others. In this manner the exclusivity of Jesus Christ is lived inclusively.[190] Therefore, as important as a person's response to the message is, we have to be very restrained in our judgment about the quality of the response and shall with humility leave it up to God, just as we may commend to his righteousness all those who have never heard the message.[191]

The Prophetic Commission of Evangelism

Because evangelistic preaching in pointed form proclaims the liberating, healing, and renewing power of the gospel for all, it has always in similarly pointed manner asked the church and its members whether they really live out of the power of this gospel and let it form their speech and action. It is not the law itself which here must speak anew to the Christian community, but it is the measure of the gospel which must be asserted and which in a new manner represents God's will as intended in the law.

The seven letters in Revelation are the permanent paradigms of such Christian prophecy which asks what is really to be found behind established religiosity, missionary, or diaconal hustle and bustle and permanent church growth—not to mention the wasting away of churches caused by quarrelsomeness, lethargy, or lack of faith.

It is precisely in this context that the accusation is made in evangelical circles that in sermons sin is no longer called sin. One must be careful in entertaining this accusation. It refers almost exclusively to the area of sexual transgressions in which the examination of human sin was traditionally sought. In principle this is biblical and necessary since the powers of sexuality work destructively instead of creatively in human community where they are not lived in a manner ordained by God. But it is suspect when at the same time naming greed, exploitation, and desire for power as sin is denounced as political misuse of the sermon, especially when it does not address individual transgressions, but collective misconduct. If sin is called by its name, then it hurts—and not just the other persons.

Of course, such preaching is in danger of becoming legalistic and thus making human behavior a condition of salvation. Where it passes on Jesus' judging, critical word, it always takes place as a call back to the gospel, to Jesus Christ. Thus it is also a sort of "crosscheck" for an orientation of the gospel that itself is correctly directed at a certain target group. Is it oriented just toward the needs of the hearers: Has it comforted the poor in their need and salved the consciences of the rich, or has it taken both up into the transforming dynamic of the gospel of the kingdom of God?

But what is fundamentally valid for this aspect of evangelistic preaching is valid also: The reference to human transgressions is an indicator of life's basic need which lies deeper; the goal of all preaching is to deliver the hearers from this. As the prophets of the old covenant drew the people into the encounter with the holy and zealous God, the prophetic word in the new covenant calls us to the encounter with the merciful and redeeming God whose love, like his holiness and his zeal, has been revealed in the cross of Christ.

Open Questions and Necessary Implications

In chapters two and three of this book we have inquired into the New Testament foundations of evangelistic preaching. This investigation has showed a very clear concentration on the redeeming message of the gospel

123

of Jesus Christ. In contrast to this, reservations might arise from evangelistic praxis: Is this not a theoretical reduction which as such cannot be maintained in the daily practice of missionary conversations? Do we not also have to name presuppositions which are necessary for understanding the gospel? Should we not also consider the implications and consequences of the message for the life of those who are called to Christ and then include them in the preaching?

This is to be briefly examined here. We shall begin with the question of basic axioms or "general conditions" in which law and gospel can be recognized as talk about God. "The invitation to act comes only after an adequate base of knowledge has been given," writes Francis Schaeffer,[192] and James Engel has proposed a scale of attitudes which influence the evangelism process and in which every stage builds upon the other. At the lowest end of the scale is "Belief in a higher Being." Must this level first be achieved before the next ("Partial knowledge of the gospel") can be attempted?[193]

The Proclamation of the One God

The problem considered here is not limited to American pragmatists. In 1963 a theological conference as distinguished as the Fourth General Meeting of the Lutheran World Federation officially came to this conclusion:

> Contemporary men and women no longer ask "How do I get a merciful God?" They ask a more radical, more basic question; they simply ask after God—"Where are you, God?" Humankind no longer only suffers from God's wrath, rather from the impression of God's absence; it suffers not only from its sin, but also from the senselessness of its being. It no longer asks whether God is merciful, but whether God really is.[194]

Must not evangelistic preaching especially take up this challenge and first of all preach that God exists before it speaks of one's responsibility before him and then finally of forgiveness and justification?

In addition there is evidence that early Christian mission work among Gentiles took such steps into account in its preaching. Heb 11:6 declares that "whoever would draw near to God must believe that he exists and that he rewards those who seek him." Consequently in 6:1 "repentance from dead works" and "faith toward God" appear as the first two steps among basic foundations of "the elementary doctrines." In turn, Paul's central statement in the sermon in Lystra corresponds to this, "We . . . bring you good news, that you should turn from these vain things to a living God who made the heaven and the earth and the sea and all that is in them" (Acts 14:15), as does his description of the beginnings of the church in Thessalonica, "how you turned to God from idols, to serve a living and true God" (1 Thess 1:9). Was there a monotheistic mission sermon?[195]

There can be no doubt that the tradition recognizable here has points of contact with monotheistic Jewish missionary sermons. However, it is questionable whether early Christian missionaries used these motifs without preaching about Christ; 1 Thess 1:9 proves the opposite. "It is not a preliminary monotheistic sermon, but rather a witness of God filled with a quite definite content, namely the story of Christ, that awakens faith. The church's faith in God is the faith grounded by the gospel."[196]

This is also fundamentally true for the traditional faith and confessional formulas which Paul cites and which describe God's activity through Christ. "It is not some traditional concept of God, not God as Creator or benevolent Father, stands at the center of these old statements of faith, but *the* God who acted eschatologically in Jesus Christ. What is confessed about God becomes known in looking at Jesus Christ."[197] Thus one can say in general about the connection between christology and theology in Paul that "God is not verified in metaphysical, existential or universal historical terms, but is defined in christological terms."[198]

These observations mirror paradoxical facts: On the one hand, against the background of the Jewish tradition in the Old Testament the New Testament speaks self-evidently of God's words and action; on the other hand, *who* God is is revealed through God's disclosure in Jesus Christ, in his life, his death, and his being raised from the dead.

That leads us back to the question with which we began. Setting aside the problem of whether the question of a merciful God is the only and the truly proper presupposition of the message of justification, one must in any event doubt that the question of God's existence "in and of itself" is more radical than the question of his relationship to us.[199] This indeed becomes clear in the sentences cited at the beginning of this section: "Contemporary men and women" do not ask whether something like "God" exists. They want to know whether God enters into a relationship with their lives, comes into existence in their presence. But this is the way in which the Bible speaks of God's being.[200] It is being for us in creation and salvation. God is love, love which reveals itself in Jesus and his death on the cross in all of its profundity.[201]

The linguistic investigations of the possibility of Christian talk about God underline this as well. They can be justified as meaningful only out of the ontological relationship of the basic Christian experience, i.e, "in the experience of Jesus as God's form of direct address."[202]

These exegetical and systematic insights bring significant relief for the praxis of evangelistic preaching. In conversation with our contemporaries, we shall indeed not overlook the impressive persistence of the concept of

God in the religious thought and experience of humankind and shall just as alertly take up into our dialogue their denials of God in their intellectual and emotional argumentation. But it is not our task first to make theists out of our dialogue partners before they can become Christians.[203] We may and must rely upon the power of the witness of our experience of God in God's speaking and acting in the fate of Jesus and the history of his people. Our faith that "God exists" is always simultaneously the confidence that as "God for us" he also steps into existence for our contemporaries. The proof of God's existence is offered in nothing other than preaching the gospel.

The Reliability of Holy Scripture

All of what we know about God's action in Jesus Christ we know from the Bible. The credibility of our preaching is thus dependent upon the reliability of what it says. We are eager to establish this reliability from the very beginning with a corresponding doctrine of Scripture so that we might have solid ground under our feet. It is no accident that the second paragraph of the Lausanne Covenant treats the authority of the Bible. Similarly, in numerous evangelical publications on evangelism one can find the comment that only absolute fidelity to Scripture can be the foundation for success in spreading the gospel. And doubtless, the insistence upon the absolute inerrancy of Holy Scripture in modern fundamentalism is grounded in missional concerns: Only in this way can the preachers and the hearers be guarded against uncertainty from the very beginning.[204] There are theories of practical evangelism concepts whose premise is that the conversation partners should first be convinced of the reliability of Scripture by formal arguments (for example, fulfilled prophecy) before preaching with content, which should be based on this proof, can begin.

Here, too, we must first inquire about the statements of the New Testament itself, and in so doing we reach two conclusions. On the one hand, there is no "article on Holy Scripture" in the early Christian confessions of faith and witnesses of missionary sermons.[205] On the other hand, these witnesses and confessions quite understandably refer to Scripture, especially when they are addressed to Jews.[206]

In practice early Christian mission among Gentiles benefited from often beginning with the so-called "God-fearers"—persons who already were conversant with the writings of the Jews.[207] But nowhere can one observe a fundamental transition such that the early Christian missionaries felt the need first of all to lay a foundation with a doctrine of Scripture. The early Christian witnesses take their trust in the authority of Holy Scripture along with them into their new surroundings and count on this authority's demonstrating itself as evident on the basis of the persuasive power of the message.[208]

This also applies for contemporary missionary preaching. One cannot pass on the gospel to others when one is not guided by a basic trust in the reliability and authenticity of the biblical message which tells us about this gospel. Evangelistic preaching pushes the concern of Holy Scripture by preaching the biblical gospel, telling about God's history with his people and bringing to life for the hearers the persons with whom God speaks and interacts in the Bible. It refers to the biblical reports about Jesus and puts central sayings of the apostles or the psalms in the center of its preaching. It does not shy away from referring to the authority of Scripture as God's direct call to humankind, but it does not demand antecedent faith in this authority which could turn into a precondition of faith in Christ.

In use of Scripture which is appropriate to the gospel, the Bible may be as human as it is and may be taken seriously in its history and historically bound nature, in its apparent and actual contradictions. And through this it will unfurl its power as God's word spoken to humankind in speaking of its own most fundamental subject—God's redeeming act in Jesus Christ.

As successful as formally securing the authority of Scripture may be—because there are many people for whose psyche such a form of security is very congenial—theologically it nonetheless stands in danger of making faith in Jesus Christ dependent upon the truth claim of a particular doctrine of Scripture.[209] Conversely, it is not intended to deny that historical-critical research has *de facto* contributed a great deal to uncertainty regarding missionary preaching by its unavoidable relativizing of historical events. However, a more rigid view of Scripture does not help here, just reflection upon the good news itself.

The Question of World View

Human beings who are addressed by the gospel do not live in isolation. More or less consciously they carry with them a picture of the world in which they live. They have a relationship to nature and to culture. What does the message of God's act in Jesus Christ mean for this relationship? Does it have nothing to do with it, or does it just have one connection which is conveyed through an understanding of existence, or does something like a new "world view" follow from it?

In practice this question is taken up by more than a few evangelists who not only preach judgment or salvation, but particularly in regard to the origin of the world and its end sometimes pass on rather detailed information in order to give a biblically grounded world view. They thus take on the task of an apologetics which, on the one hand, does not pretend to be able by the use of rational arguments to lead one back to revelation, but on the other hand, does want to show that when one begins with the revelation of God a consistent and logically comprehensible view of nature, history, and society is possible and necessary which can be worked out in critical discussion with the natural and human sciences as well as the humanities, all of which operate without the hypothesis of God.

The theological legitimacy of such an undertaking has been emphasized from quite different quarters. Against the background of a fundamentalistic understanding of the Bible, Francis Schaeffer and Amos Wilder-Smith have, with different emphases, outlined the program of a Christian "world view" in which the fight against the doctrine of evolution plays a decisive role. For Schaeffer that is not just a consequence of faith, but virtually a precondition, since according to biblical teaching "knowledge is needed prior to salvation."[210]

Proceeding from totally different presuppositions, Karl Heim had attempted in his multi-volume work *The Evangelical Faith and Contemporary Thought* [*Der evangelische Glaube und das Denken der Gegenwart*] to develop "An Outline of a Christian View of Life [*Grundzüge einer christlichen Lebensanschauung*]." To be sure, in so doing he did not regard the biblical statements to be material rivals of the results of the modern natural sciences; rather he sees them as useful complements, whereby he strongly depended upon the incipient dissolution of a mechanistic-materialistic world view in the natural sciences.[211]

Heim did not really start a movement with his approach although many appeal to him. In his book *Foolishness to the Greeks,* Lesslie Newbigin comes very close to Heim's concerns.[212] Here Newbigin sketches how it is the task of missionary preaching not only to penetrate into the private sphere of faith, opinion, and values but also into the "world view of modern western culture" including all of what scientists and politicians tend to call "facts."[213]

And finally—much to the surprise of the world of theology, but faithful to the motto of his *Church Dogmatics*, Anselm's sentence *fides quaerens intellectum*—even Karl Barth has expounded in Volume IV/3 how, in light of God's revelation in Jesus Christ, the creaturely world, cosmos, and nature, "also indicate their own *lights* and *truths* and therefore their own *speech* and *words*."[214] Christian Link picked up these ideas and under the title *The World as Parable* presented studies on the problem of natural theology which plead for a theology of nature that has its origin in the statements about incarnation in John 1:14 and "accepts responsibility for faith in the sphere of experience." The theological claim which he thus formulates is especially significant for missionary preaching. "The truth of revelation is indivisible; it disregards the borders drawn between philosophy and theology. It cannot be limited to an isolated sphere of *faith* and yet be suspended for the sphere of *knowledge of the world*."[215]

In the context of this book it is not possible to discuss these approaches individually. Here it is only intended to note two dangers and one suggestion. The fundamentalist approach is obviously in danger of making into an object of faith a system, which one passes off as the biblical world view, but *de facto* is actually an idiosyncratic alloy of a biblical framework and modern observations about nature. Doubtless, a text like the priestly account of creation intends to pass on knowledge about nature. And—as Gerhard von Rad has emphasized—one cannot simply separate cosmological and theological statements from one another.[216]

But it would falsify the very statement of this account if one would replace of the confession of God as Creator of the entire cosmos with the demand to regard as true all details mentioned here, even in the context of entirely new knowledge about nature. To understand this confession correctly, one would doubtless have to confess it anew with all the means of contemporary natural sciences.[217] But that is difficult because these are characterized by methodological atheism.[218]

The danger of using God as a "missing link" to close the gaps in the causal chain of explanations of the natural sciences is lurking for whomever might take on this task. But, in the first place, this does not correspond to the comprehensive claim of biblical statements on creation, and, of course, such attempts also prove to be in need of frequent revision when science once again can deal with such issues without recourse to the "hypothesis of God."[219]

Thus arises the suggestion that an evangelistic theology addresses to systematic theology. It needs help to show the significance of revelation in conversation with the world view of the natural and human sciences. The charge that contemporary theology operates with the "concept of divided truth"[220] is a weighty one and must be refuted.

The Church as a New Space for Life

One of the most important results of the discussion about evangelism and mission in the last fifty years was the discovery of the local church as the vehicle and instrument of mission. The emphasis upon "mission as a structural principle"[221] of the church as a whole turned into the foundation of the conception of missional church growth which, on the one hand, enables a church to work beyond its walls and, on the other hand, so forms it that it can develop into a new area of social life for persons who are touched by the gospel and are seeking a home and orientation.

The church's turning into the "social form of the gospel" corresponds to early Christian practice. In baptism persons are taken into the Body of Christ and thus bound not only to Christ, but also to the members of a church. The merciful acceptance by God without any regard of one's origin, status, or sex is practically lived in the Christian community. Its significance for the performance of mission and especially of evangelism in the sense of embodying the gospel can thus scarcely be exaggerated.

Nonetheless, an important qualification must be made. The church is not the content of the proclamation or of the confession of faith.[222] In itself it has no soteriological standing. This observation is not a cheap excuse for the ecclesiological deficit of some evangelistic activities. But the existence of the church and of local congregations is not an element of the gospel that ought to be named as a supplement to the proclamation of Christ. Proceeding from the basis of the New Testament, just the opposite is the case: In its existence and in the form of its life and ministry the church of Jesus Christ is testimony of the effectiveness of the gospel.[223] The task is to realize this in practice.

Reappraising the Past

The promise that God forgives those "now" who accept it in faith is a biblically grounded, fundamental element of evangelistic preaching. In the past it has often been linked with the demand for a full confession of one's sins. As a consequence of the recognition that Jesus unconditionally accepted sinners and renounced any kind of inquisitorial pressure for a comprehensive revelation of transgressions, a general promise of forgiveness is usually deemed sufficient today. Thus one may well trade one extreme for another. The vertical dimension of the divine promise must have an effect in the horizontal dimension of a human life story, and to do that it needs help reappraising a past loaded down with guilt and formed by suffering.

The offer to make a comprehensive confession covering all of one's life, in which transgressions and not already healed wounds are revealed, ought to continue to be a part of evangelistic work. The biblical grounds for it lie not only in a series of isolated statements of important Old and New Testament texts such as Ps 32:1-5, Prov 28:13, Acts 19:18, 1 John 1:9, and Jas 5:16, but also in the fundamental conviction of the biblical message that the forgiveness of sins is not just a declaratory act, but includes overcoming and coping with one's accumulated guilt.[224] When one does this, the culpable failures of other persons and inexplicable blows of fate a person has experienced in his or her life are included in the encounter with Jesus Christ so that what in charismatic circles is called—with good reason—"inner healing"[225] can be consummated. Telling about the life journeys of men and women of the Bible can offer beneficial models for identification. Clearly, that is primarily the task of (possibly long-term) pastoral care. In evangelistic preaching the door to this journey could be opened. It will be even easier to open the door to this journey into one's own past if this has its place not only in short-term special events, but also occurs in the Sunday sermon and personal conversation.

Coping with the Present

Where a person is placed in communion with God the issue at hand is not just overcoming the past. One must also cope with the present. Must evangelistic preaching have standards for recognizing a person's present responsibility and helping him or her to fulfil it?

In Matt 28:20 "keeping Jesus' commandments" is expressly named as the contents of missionary teaching. In contrast the missionary kerygma in Paul appears to be determined purely by the promise of salvation in Christ. But since it is reasonably certain that, especially in missionary sermons for Gentiles, the way of life of the hearers was sharply criticized,[226] one cannot assume that ethical questions remained reserved for the imperative of congregational instruction alone, while missionary preaching limited itself to the soteriological indicative. Although our sources, which are documents of instruction for churches, do not admit of proof in detail, one can proceed on the assumption that in the development of the missionary kerygma in Paul the "ethical imperative" was also a part of it. God's salvific act in Christ and the gift of his love in the Holy Spirit ground a new way of life.[227]

For persons whose lives are running through their hands like water because they have no internal structure, no external limits, and no clear goals for their activity, it can be good news to hear that in his love God wants to use and form their lives, and that he gives them help to find their bearings and guidelines for coping with their lives. It is no accident that "superior ethics" was one of the essential missional factors of the early church.[228]

For the entire early Christian tradition, at the core of such "navigational assistance" stood the commandment to love one's neighbor; it summarized the ethical demand of the law, and in its being grounded in Christ's love it was no longer a law one could never fulfill, but a directive that gives life (Eph 5:2, 1 John 4:7). In so doing the early Christian missionaries proceeded on the assumption "that this love implies a clearly defined content and criterion of behavior and does not form an abstract formal principle."[229] Showing the perspectives of a life which can be lived in responsibility before God and one's fellow humans is thus one of the essential tasks of evangelistic preaching.[230] To be sure, it must be careful not to let the need of some contemporary hearers for clear, authoritative directions (for which others must bear the responsibility) seduce it into preaching legalism.

Making Sure of the Future

In my youth, an evening dedicated to discussing apocalyptic questions was one of the standard topics of a week of evangelistic meetings. Today the picture is more diverse. While in certain groups these topics continue to be pursued with great confidence and good crowds, they are almost completely avoided by some preachers. This applies not just to speculations about the chronology of apocalyptic events; even basic statements of the biblical hope for the future appear to have become victims of widespread insecurity in view of eschatology.

The message of salvation of the New Testament is eschatologically imprinted through and through. Salvation is deliverance at the final judgment, the consummate communion with God, and the establishment of the kingdom of God over all of creation. Of course, the same is true of the other side. The salvation to come is grounded in God's act of salvation in Christ and is present for humankind in the salvation event and preaching. For just this reason the certain hope in the fulfillment of one's life and of all of creation in God's apocalyptic act is one of the basic statements of Christian preaching and one of the foundations of Christian existence (Rom 5:5, 8:18-25; 1 Cor 15:19; 1 Thess 4:13; 1 Pet 1:3).

The hermeneutical difficulties of rending the biblical statements about the future with their heavily apocalyptic language in comprehensible terms for contemporary preaching are immense. But the temptation is also immense to say more in response to the pressing questions of our contemporaries—"what comes after death?"—than the biblical witness offers. We shall find a path between embarassed silence and unauthorized speech when we bear witness to the basic statements of biblical hope: Nothing can separate us from the love of God—not even death (Rom 8:38f.). That is the certainty that forms our individual lives and maintains itself even in death.[231] God will be all in all when this world reaches its goal (1 Cor 15:28). That is our hope for history and nature. And because we know the essential characteristics of God's rule, namely justice, peace, and joy (Rom 14:17), we encourage those who live without hope and any goal to approach and work toward this end—exactly because we know that God alone works the fulfillment.[232]

The Message of Salvation—A Summary

What do we have to say in evangelistic preaching? Nothing more than the message of the gospel of Jesus Christ: God "has visited and redeemed his people" (Luke 1:68). In Jesus of Nazareth, God took upon himself the limitations of a creaturely life in the fullness of his love, bore human suffering, fear, and guilt, and liberated men and women from the affliction of their alienation from God. In Jesus' ministry and resurrection, God's salvific rule breaks into a world of evil and death. In Jesus' death, God's love flows into human hate and guilt and thus frees all men and women of the death-bringing spell which burdens their lives.

132

Good news for the poor, freedom for the captives and those who are oppressed, healing for the sick, forgiveness for sinners, hope for the desparate, justification of the godless, and resurrection of the dead—these are the "key words" of the message of deliverance, and are thus in the final analysis all the exposition of one fundamental saying: "God is for us human beings in Jesus Christ!" Because this is the meaning and content of the gospel, "all preaching of the gospel . . . [is] missionary preaching."[233] For this message applies to all persons and thus must reach all to whom it applies. It proclaims the peace which God has made. It discloses that humankind lives in enmity with God (and with itself), and calls all to reconciliation with God. The goal of the gospel is that a person, just as he or she is, allow him- or herself to be taken up into God's peace. And the task of evangelistic preaching is to deliver God's invitation to every woman and to every man personally and in as understandable and attractive way as possible. For it is an invitation to live, and is thus vital. That is what we have to say, and that is what we try to live—for ourselves and for the others.

Chapter 4

Divine Action and Human Response: The Biblical Evidence

God's unconditional love for each human being in his or her need is both the theme and content of the salvific message of the New Testament. This gospel is thus both the content and basis for all evangelistic proclamation.

But is God's affirmation really unconditional? Without a doubt, it is true that God's activity on behalf of human beings is not made dependent upon any preconditions. God reconciled us while we were still enemies. But is there perhaps such a thing as a "post-condition"—a condition after the fact, which must be met in order for God's work in the human person to take effect?

The gospel is the power of God for salvation for all who believe (Rom 1:16). And what is the gospel for those who do not believe—"a fragrance of death to death" (2 Cor 2:16)? As the secondary conclusion to the Gospel of Mark says with perfect clarity: "the one who does not believe will be condemned" (16:16). Is the human answer therefore decisive?

For a theology of evangelization this question is of fundamental importance, for it is after all the historical proclivity of evangelistic proclamation that it seeks to lead human persons to a verbalized response, to a personally confessed faith, in order to bring them to participation in the salvific action of God.

How biblical is this insistence on the human response? This is the question which we will pursue in this chapter. It is appropriate, then, to use the concepts of repentance/conversion and faith as leitmotifs for the matter at hand.

A number of questions will follow from this. How can a theology of grace be maintained if the human decision is allowed a high rank? In chapter five we will reflect on this question. How responsible is the call to decision in the light of all the biographical, psychological, and sociological factors which are involved in such decisions? This is the material which will concern us in chapter six. The principal question, however, is this: How does God's saving activity in the good news achieve its purposes in human persons?

135

Human Love for God in the Old Testament

The basic formulations of God's promise of salvation in the Old Testament are simultaneously unconditional and coercive. God speaks to Abraham: "Go from your country and your kindred and your father's house to a land that I will show you. I will make of you a great nation and I will bless you and make your name great, so that you will be a blessing" (Gen 12:1-2). And Moses is told, "I am the God of your fathers, the God of Abraham, the God of Isaac, and the God of Jacob . . . I have observed the misery of my people in Egypt and have heard their cries on account of their taskmasters" (Exod 3:6-8).

God's salvific activity creates a relationship to God out of which unavoidable consequences grow. This finds its classic formulation in the first commandment: "I am the LORD your God, who brought you out of the land of Egypt, out of the house of slavery; you shall have no other gods before me" (Exod 20:2ff.).

Life according to the commandments of God is one consequence for humans from God's salvific action which, for the first time, constitutes his fellowship with the people. It is not the precondition for God's presence that we keep his commandments; rather God's action is the preliminary gift which makes keeping the commandments in some sense possible.[1]

Faith

In a very few yet obvious places in the Old Testament the behavior which appropriately grows out of fellowship with God is described as faith. Among them, Gen 15:6 carries purely declarative character: "And he believed the LORD and the LORD reckoned it to him as righteousness."[2]

In Hab 2:4 a conditional meaning augments the declarative. The sentence "The just shall live by faith (faithfulness)" Zimmerli assigns to the "conditional declarations of life."[3] The reference to faith and trust as the sole possible attitude toward God has an immediately relevant context in Isaiah. "If you do not stand firm in faith, you shall not stand at all" (Isa 7:9) is the message in connection with the threat in the Syro-Ephraimitic war.[4] A parallel passage in Isa 30:15 makes the fact clear, however, that faith is not thus a matter of (substitute) performance by the human agent, but rather the attitude of being open to God's help, where the divine message is one of "returning and rest," of being "in quietness" and "trust" as the source of salvation and strength, linked, nevertheless, with the observation, "But you refused. . . ."[5]

The fact that the missionary aspect of the concept of faith can also be found in the Old Testament has only recently been given proper attention by the exegetes.[6] In Jonah 3 the reaction of the people of Nineveh to the unrestrained proclamation of judgment of the prophet Jonah is described as follows, "And the people of Nineveh believed God; they proclaimed a fast, and everyone, great and small, put on sackcloth." (3:5)

Faith here means first of all no more than taking seriously the prophetic message.[7] But precisely this taking seriously leads them into a genuine penitence and to a clear repentance which turns away the divine threat of judgment.[8] However, this repentance is obviously not intended as "conversion." The people of Nineveh do not become Jews. Their repentance is more a model, perhaps even a provocative challenge to Israel.[9] In contrast we read in Jdt 14:10 (NJB), "Achior, recognizing all that the God of Israel had done, believed ardently in him and, accepting circumcision, was permanently incorporated in the House of Israel."[10]

Thus the Old Testament use of the concept of faith provides the decisive elements for its New Testament meaning, even if "the matter of faith" still finds expression in a wide variety of forms in the Old Testament.[11]

Conversion

But how does God react toward his people when they have broken fellowship with him or do not live accordingly? We have already addressed this question from one side in our section on the proclamation of judgment. Here we must address the other side of the question: What behavior is expected from the human side in order that the fellowship with God can once more become a healing living-space of the people?

This is the theme of the early prophetic writings, and they are not satisfied with simply enjoining the keeping of the commandments. Certainly demands such as the following find their central place in their message: "But let justice roll down like waters, and righteousness like an everflowing stream" (Amos 5:24). But the realization of this is no longer possible given the inner constitution of the people. Much more profound change is necessary; a radical conversion is required. The question of "conversion" thus becomes a central theme of their proclamation.

But the question remains: to what degree and with what purpose? In this regard there is no agreement among the exegetes. Consensus does exist that "conversion" in the preaching of the prophets in its religious use remains a very concrete concept. It is a matter of the change of direction of all of life, a matter of turning away from false behavior and false gods and the turning to God, indeed turning back "to the beginning which Yahweh made with his people as a whole."[12]

This is reinforced by the fact that there are not only religious grievances but above all social abuses which motivate the call to conversion.

137

For the early prophets above all what function the theme of conversion had in their preaching remains controversial. The "classical" interpretation of the prophets assumes that the prophets call the people to conversion in order that they may avoid the judgment. The theme finds its place in a word of "admonition." This view was especially forcefully represented by Martin Buber, who wrote, "The true prophet does not proclaim any unavoidable misfortune; he addresses the potential of the moment for decision and does so in such a way that his message of disaster impinges upon this decisive potential."[13]

Against this view H. W. Wolff has addressed his fundamental essay, "Das Thema 'Umkehr' in der alttestamentlichen Prophetie." He has observed that in the earliest tradition of the prophetic writings the theme "conversion" does not find its context in the words of admonition or threat. Rather, it appears in the context of "scoldings" which announce judgment because Israel has not repented and, on the other hand, in words of salvation which present God as the originator of the conversion of the people.[14] The call to conversion is not an admonition motivated by threat of judgment, but "solely an invitation to [partake in] the salvation prepared by Yahweh."[15]

The open question of this interpretation relates above all to the messages of Isaiah and Amos. Did they have no other task than to announce to the people the unavoidable judgment? To what degree did they assume that the admonishing call for conversion had already been spoken and find it necessary to affirm its failure? Or is there yet a glimmer of hope, as L. Markert assumes of Amos, in not wanting to exclude the notion "that Amos here and there hedges the timid hope that his hearers might yet change their behavior" (cf. 5:4, 24).[16]

In any case the tension remains, the dialectic nature of which is clearest in Hosea. He must say about Israel, "They have refused to return to me" (11:5 cf. 11:7). But he is also permitted to call out in God's name, "How can I give you up, Ephraim? How can I hand you over, O Israel? . . . My heart recoils within me; my compassion grows warm and tender. I will not execute my fierce anger; I will not destroy Ephraim; for I am God and no mortal, the Holy One in your midst, and I will not come in wrath" (11:8ff.).[17] The diversion of the fate of the people lies in the inextinguishability of the love of God which—even if following the judgment—draws the people to itself anew. (cf. 3:1-5).

The prophetic word was the voice of outsiders and remained that even after the fall of the northern kingdom in Judah. The fate of Jeremiah is a touching example of this. Not until the catastrophe of 587 BCE did a profound change come. The judgment which the prophets had announced had now hit Judah and the whole people; their message had been demonstrated to be true. Precisely in their exile, where the loss of all assumed guarantees of salvation—most especially the loss of the land and the temple—had to be suffered in all its consequences, God spoke through the words of the prophets to the people that he had not given up on the people, not even in judgment, and that he would receive the people back into fellowship.

This promise of salvation is unconditional. Ezekiel speaks of it most impressively in 37:1-14 in the visions of the revivified people rising out of the graves. But also in 11:14-21 and 36:16-32 we find the promise of the homecoming, connected with the pronouncement that God will renew the inner nature of his people so that it would be able to follow his commandments.

Alongside this Ezekiel also makes a conditional promise of life in chapter 18 and in 33:10-28. "But if the wicked turn away from all their sins that they have committed and keep all my statutes and do what is lawful and right, they shall surely live; they shall not die" (18:21). He connects his promise with the admonition "get yourselves a new heart and a new spirit! Why will you die, O house of Israel?" (18:31).

Despite a different accentuation of the prophet's word in chapters 18 and 33 both passages are equally under the sign of the promise of life.[18] In the call to conversion even the "grumblers" are "shown the freedom of God which desires life even for those who quarrel with God,"[19] and the prophetic disputation pursues those who are in rebellion against God, ending in the appeal, "Why will you die, O house of Israel? For I have no pleasure in the death of anyone, says the Lord GOD" (18:31b, 32a).

In a certain sense Ezekiel 18 and 33 are the Old Testament magna carta of evangelistic proclamation: the urgent address to the individual, the warning of a false security of salvation among the pious, the point about the responsibility of each generation and the promise of the possibility of conversion to life for everyone, the review of the relationship to God on the basis of correct and incorrect societal behavior, and finally the urgent query, "Why do you want to die when God gives you life?"—all of these are part of the fundamental expressions of evangelistic proclamation.

Such a call becomes one-sided and narrow whenever it forgets that even as early as Ezekiel the "conditional promise of life is anchored in an unavoidably obvious way in an encompassing promise of life with an unconditional beginning and end of the history of the people of God."[20] Walther Zimmerli has emphatically appealed that we eliminate

neither of these two promises of life from the Book of Ezekiel for the sake of the other . . . however much they may stand in a palpable and logically irreconcilable tension one with the other. This tension must truly be a part of the innermost being of the prophet: the life of the

139

house of Israel—and thus also that of every member of the people of God—is from its very beginnings only possible through their God's free and incomprehensible proclamation of life. At the same time their life is only comprehensible in conversion and renewed obedience before God's justice.[21]

We can observe the same phenomenon in Second Isaiah, although the unconditional promise of salvation seems to stand totally in the foreground at first glance.[22] Even in Second Isaiah, however, the joyous message is not simply proclaimed to the people via heralds; rather also through words of disputation it struggles to reach the people in the despair of their exile.[23] With this prophet also this leads to the invitation "I have swept away your transgressions like a cloud, and your sins like mist; return to me, for I have redeemed you" (Isa 44:22).[24] The conclusion of Second Isaiah is also most impressive. The unconditional promise to the people in chapter 54 flows into the call of chapter 55: "Ho, everyone who thirsts, come to the waters; and you that have no money, come, buy and eat! Come, buy wine and milk without money and without price" (55:1). "Seek the LORD while he may be found, call upon him while he is near" (55:6). No conditions are formulated, but accepting salvation is a part of its realization.

The Choice of the People

In two passages outside of the prophetic writings in the Old Testament the people are especially urgently called to decision for or against Yahweh. In Deuteronomy 30 after a renewal of the covenant obligation, proclamation of blessing and curse and the covenant renewal in the land of Moab, Moses puts before the people the choice between life and death:

> See, I have set before you today life and prosperity, death and adversity. If you obey the commandments of the LORD your God that I am commanding you today, by loving the LORD your God . . . then you shall live . . . But if your heart turns away and you do not hear . . . I declare to you today that you shall perish; you shall not live long in the land (Deut 30:15-18).[25]

Something similar happens in Joshua 24, at the renewal of the covenant at Shechem. Joshua says to the people:

> Now therefore revere the LORD and serve him in sincerity and in faithfulness; put away the gods that your ancestors served beyond the River and in Egypt, and serve the LORD. Now if you are unwilling to serve the LORD, choose this day whom you will serve . . . but as for me and my household we will serve the LORD (Josh 24:14-15).[26]

Here we must observe two things. First, nowhere in the Old Testament is it said as urgently as in Deuteronomy that the election of the people by Yahweh is anchored in nothing but the "Love with which he loves his people."[27] The choice of the people is their response to God's free choice of them.

Second, we must see that the stories are not the historical report of the first moment when the people makes its free choice. A people which has repeatedly run away from its God is once more given the possibility of making a decision. The history of failure is rolled back once more into the history of the beginnings of the saving action of God. Of course, the dark clouds of judgment which pile up from wrong choices are no longer to be overlooked and are burdensome. Yet the basis of a decision remains the fact that God wants life. Accordingly we find the promise of conversion in Deut 4:29ff.; 30:1-10, which stands in close connection to the conversion sermon of the Deuteronomic history.[28]

Conversion in Early Judaism

The conversion sermon of the Old Testament was carried over from early Judaism. The Pharisaically molded rabbinate developed out of it an attitude of penitence which can be compared in many points with Luther's penitential theology. Penance (*teschuwa*) means to turn back to God daily.[29] But the prerequisite of God's action before the reaction of the human agent is not forgotten. This is evidenced in the fifth benediction of the "Eighteen Benedictions": "Cause us to return, O Lord, unto Thee, and let us return anew [in repentance]."[30]

Alongside it there stood the apocalyptic theology of repentance of the Qumran community which turned away from the rest of Israel as "repenters in the wilderness" and understood turning to God as turning back to the law of Moses in which one was bound to the fellowship of the community in law and in property.[31]

John the Baptizer also belongs to this eschatological conversion movement. To a great extent his message corresponds to that of the writings of the early prophets. He also assumes that the judgment is unavoidable. Israel is lost and "has wasted its prerogative to salvation. Conversion requires therefore not only confession of individual sins, but also admitting this lostness and thereby a radical departure from all which is past, including that from which Israel previously drew its salvation and assurance of salvation ."[32] "By this logic conversion includes radical acknowledgment of God, whose wrath toward Israel is just."[33]

Solely in the "radical forfeiture of every assurance of salvation . . . does John see one last chance for salvation."[34] His baptism is a baptism of conversion in as much as it symbolizes salvation by means of judgment and thereafter.

Jesus showed the seriousness with which he took the Baptizer's message of encounter with God by his own baptism. And yet he did not perpetuate this message unchanged.

Accepting the Reign of God—The Message of Jesus

In accordance with the task we have set ourselves we cannot deal only with Jesus' call to conversion in this section. We will much more attempt to comprehend all motifs which describe the meaning of the human answer to Jesus' word and work.

The Theme of "Conversion" in Jesus' Teaching

The significance of the call to conversion for the preaching of Jesus is viewed as a matter of extreme controversy. Whereas Schniewind declares, "Jesus' whole preaching is a call to penitence, a call to conversion,"[35] W. Trilling asserts, "The word *metanoia* is not typical of his message."[36] The majority of the exegetes today would likely tend to Trilling's position. On the one hand, the reason for this can be found in the fact that the proof texts for the concept are relatively few (as we will see soon enough). On the other hand, however, it seems to have been one of the more irritating features of Jesus' ministry that he did not call sinners to some difficult path of repentance, but simply accepted them by eating and drinking with them. For this reason a number of exegetes consider it to be verging on a perversion of the message of Jesus when Luke recants the saying of Jesus which we find in Mark 2:17 as "I have come to call not the righteous, but sinners" and transmits it in the form "I have come to call not the righteous but sinners *to repentance*" (Luke 5:32).[37]

With a view to forming our own judgment in this controversy we first need to look at the passages in the Synoptic Gospels in which the concept *metanoia* (*metanoein*) occurs.[38]

Mark 1:14f. and Matt 4:17 offer a short summary of the message of Jesus. In the process Mark seems to be seeking accommodation to the missionary proclamation of the early church,[39] while Matthew seeks to make Jesus' call parallel to the proclamation of the Baptizer.[40] Both passages will have to be set aside for the moment.

The problematic nature of Luke 5:32 has already been mentioned; the *eis metanoian* seems to be an addendum from Luke's pen. This observation also throws suspicion on both 15:7 and 15:10. Since the two parables in Luke 15:4-6 and 8f. describe how an animal or an object is found, rather than how a human being is brought to conversion, many exegetes assume

142

that the interpretation relating to conversion in vv. 7 and 10 is secondary.[41] Whether this is an accurate judgment or not must still be examined.

In contrast there are no formal problems about the origin of Luke 13:1-5 in the proclamation of Jesus. In their content the passage is very close to the preaching of the Baptizer.[42] Not just a few who have lost their lives in spectacular catastrophic events are guilty; the whole of Israel stands under judgment which can only be escaped through decisive conversion.

The evidence from the Logion source points in the same direction: Matt 11:20-24 = Luke 10:12-15, the "woe-saying" upon the cities of Galilee, and Matt 12:41 = Luke 11:32, the reference to the repentance of Nineveh as a contrast for the behavior of the contemporaries of Jesus.[43] Both of these Logia have the same scope: mourning and announcement of judgment in the face of the refusal to accept the message of Jesus by people to whom he had brought it in word and deed. The words reflect the missionary awareness of Jesus:

> His kerygma is finally the eschatological word of God. To let yourself become involved with Jesus' teaching and his deeds of power would be the conversion which is now required. In content Jesus' idea of conversion is therefore to be seen in close connection with the reign of God, whose salvation Jesus announces, promises, and brings about.[44]

As we seek an overview of the evidence concerning *metanoia* (*metanoein*) in Jesus' teaching, we find the paradoxical result—even if not a totally surprising result against the background of the prophetic tradition—that Jesus speaks most clearly of the conversion that is denied and its consequences. But what does the positive aspect look like? When Jesus "called sinners"—to what was he calling them? For he certainly expected from them some sort of answer, otherwise his woe-saying against the cities of Galilee would be meaningless.

A first answer to the question is found in the trilogy of parables in Luke 15. Even if the trilogy has been put into its present form and edited by Luke, it still very poignantly shows a fundamental situation of Jesus' preaching.[45] The common point of the three parables is the joy of God when the lost one is found and the accompanying invitation to everyone to rejoice about it.[46] Appropriately, Luke 15:1ff. characterizes the situation into which these parables are spoken. Jesus is having dinner with notorious sinners, who "have not yet shown any sign of that which we normally call conversion. Jesus, however, interprets his table fellowship with them as a finding again of the lost, by which can only be meant the restoration of that fellowship with God which was ruptured by sin. This is an incredible claim. For Jesus thus asserts that God has broken through, here and now, on his own accord

143

to the sinner, without waiting until the sinner has created the necessary predisposition which was thought necessary at that time."[47]

While the material of the parables of the two sons gives Jesus opportunity to describe this state of "being found again" as the return of the prodigal son into the house of his father, the parables of the lost sheep and the lost coin sketch the picture of a passive "being found." Exactly this is the point of the pre-history of the joy of God in all parables. What is decisive is not what the human agent does, but what happens to him or her. Yet Jesus does not tell this as a general truth, but against the background of experience in which he encounters persons who let this happen. And because the human being is neither a sheep nor a coin, this would seem to imply a human compliance, as it is portrayed in the parable of the prodigal son in a marvelous intertwining of image and content. But the interpretations in Luke 15:7, 10 say nothing other than this: The fact that people allow themselves to be found, is itself conversion in Jesus' sense![48]

In Luke 19:1-10 the evangelist tells us a story as an example of how this process of being found can take place and to what totally natural consequences it leads us. The closing logion (v. 10)—"For the Son of Man came to seek out and to save the lost"—ties this story with Luke 5:32 and Luke 15 and thereby underlines what Luke means when he understands Jesus' call to sinners as the call to conversion. It is the challenge to let oneself get involved with Jesus, who "invites himself in" to a person in his search for the lost. But that is exactly the content Jesus intends for conversion: "life out of the gift of salvation, 'to live from forgiveness.'"[49]

The Gift of the Reign of God

Having established this, we find ourselves near to other sayings of Jesus with which he describes the appropriate reaction of human beings to the immanence of the reign of God, as well as the salvific action of God which will encounter us there.

Mark 10:15 quotes Jesus' saying: "Truly I tell you, whoever does not receive the kingdom of God as a little child will never enter it." Most exegetes consider this to be a genuine saying of Jesus.[50] The simile "like a child" is obviously to be related to the predicate of the sentence: "to receive, as a child receives a gift," i.e., to allow oneself to be given something, to stretch out one's hands toward the gift full of expectation, to be able to rejoice over it without reservations. Only someone who turns toward the reign of God with such an openness and undivided relationship and receives it into his or her life will participate in the reign's fulfillment.

From its content this saying aims at a "conversion appropriate to the gift of the grace of God" and "is to be put in close proximity to the ideas of

144

seeking (Matt 6:33; Luke 12:31) and happy discovery of (Matt 13:44-46) the reign of God."[51] The double parable of the treasure in the field and the pearl show once again, though from another side, how Jesus handles the matter under discussion.

The parables' vitality is due to the argumentative contrast between two contradictory human experiences. The one is mirrored in the story told. The inestimable value of the pearl or the treasure, a value beyond all that which the finder now owns, as a matter of course and almost inevitably leads to the action described in the parables, through which the finders put at stake their whole wealth and resources in order to come into possession of their find. But the willing reader will also sense the other experience for which reason all of this has to be told: There are enough people alive who are lacking in courage and remain indecisive, who would never go in for this risk (which is really no risk at all). It is in this that we find the significance of both parables: encouragement to do what ought to come as a matter of course![52] For the reign of God this means: The overwhelming and inestimable value of the reign of God leads all those who encounter it in Jesus' words and deeds to get involved in it with their whole lives. "From the deeds of the reign of heaven flow the deeds of human persons, just as the call of Jesus almost matter-of-factly brought with it the leaving behind of boat and house and tax-collection table" (Matt 4:18-22; 9:9).[53]

The fact that Jesus tells of such not-so-obvious matters of course in his parables is part of his forward-pressing invitation to existential agreement with his message, which is characterized by his telling of parables.

The Example of the Call to Discipleship

For Jesus the call to discipleship is not identical with the call to salvation. It doesn't affect everyone; many, in fact, are even expressly excluded from that path. But what happens to disciples who leave everything to follow Jesus is, to a certain degree, a living example told about what it means to allow oneself to be determined by the proximity of the reign of God. Thus in an especially emphatic manner Luke 5:1-11 tells about the acceptance of one sinner who has been overpowered by the mercy of God as this shines forth in Jesus' deed of power and, at the same time, of that sinner's calling to be a disciple of Jesus.[54]

This is not only true for the "successful" stories of the calling of the individually named disciples. It is true especially also for the calls about whose results we are unsure or which are negative. The hard words which Jesus finds for two potential disciples in Luke 9:59-62 not only speak of special conditions for discipleship, but also of a decisiveness and consistency of life under the reign of God.[55]

The paradigmatic elements in the story of the rich person who asks Jesus what he must do in order to inherit eternal life are especially clear. For this person, who can say with good conscience that he has kept all the commandments from his youth on, Jesus names the one thing which he is lacking: to let loose of his riches and to live in the freedom thus won as a disciple of Jesus. The problem of wealth and its power to lay claim to people is dealt with in the tradition of Jesus' teaching with a radicality which, according to Mark 10:26 brings his disciples to the disgusted interjection, "Then who can be saved?" The answer to the question typically once more leads us away from that which is demanded of human beings in response to what God does: "For mortals it is impossible, but not for God; for God all things are possible."(v. 27).[56]

Summary and Prospect

Jesus proclaimed and lived out the imminence of the reign of God in remarkable freedom and openness as the presence of the mercy and goodness of God. Without preconditions he promises the poor, the hungry, and those who mourn God's realm and God's aid; he sits down at the same table with sinners and tax-collectors in order to celebrate with them God's acceptance of them, he forgives sinners, drives out demons, and makes the sick well. But even Jesus expects that this will have its effect in the lives of those who are thus addressed. He notes gratefully that people are gaining confidence in God through him,[57] encourages them to draw the (obvious) conclusions from their encounter with God's reign, and makes it plain in the example of his disciples how incisive the changes might be which prove necessary as a result of discipleship. His call to repentance is the great invitation for all who need the nearness of God most urgently and thus calls into question all who listen to him with indifference or a wrinkling of the nose. Jesus awaits an answer and speaks of the painful consequences for all who reject his call and his work.

A further important aspect must be added. The tradition of the proclamation of Jesus cannot be viewed in isolation. The fact that Jesus' claim was rejected and he was handed over for crucifixion is a fact which cannot be avoided in the question of the content and meaning of his ministry. For the question of decision arises anew in the light of his death. Has Jesus' claim been proven invalid through his death? Or is it confirmed in the sense of his extreme fidelity to his own concerns? Or if—as the proclamation of the primitive church insists—this dying was the God-willed end of his way, has human resistance finally and forever been circumvented by divine love and has the question of human decision for Jesus been decided by God himself, or does this question pose itself now in the most radical and fundamental way possible?

God Grants Repentance—The Acts of the Apostles

Since Luke continues motifs of the synoptic tradition in the Acts of the Apostles, an analysis of his presentation will follow here, although from a literary or tradition-historical view we should treat Paul first.

The Goal of the Message

In no other New Testament writing do we get as clear an answer to the thematic we are covering as in the Acts of the Apostles. The mission addresses of the apostles have been constructed according to a clear schematic, which as a rule closes with an unambiguous instruction to the hearers of what they have to do. Thereupon follows a report on the reactions of the listeners.[58] In varying combinations the call to repentance,[59] conversion,[60] baptism,[61] and faith[62] in the name of Jesus Christ are named as the goal of the proclamation. Further, the goal of this activity is forgiveness of sins, which is unanimously described as *the* soterological happening for the human hearer.[63] In the portrayal of the positive reactions what is most commonly mentioned is that people come to faith and receive baptism, often enough, however, only the one or the other of the two processes,[64] but also that they have turned to God, received the Word, or given heed to what was said.[65]

A differentiation between these individual concepts is not easy;[66] apparently each concept can describe the whole process of devotion to God. The only thing that is clear is that on the side of the challenge it is the call to repentance and conversion which dominates, while on the side of response it is more often the coming to faith or baptism which are mentioned. Understandably, the "conversion to the Living God" or to "the LORD" is mentioned only in reference to the heathen.[67] Nevertheless there is no differentiation between the concepts of repentance and conversion; thus in the Acts of the Apostles a double event is described under the concept "conversion": the "turning around" in Judaism which is a "return" to the God of Israel who acted in Jesus, and the conversion of the heathen to Christianity as a "turning to" the one true God, who reveals himself in creation itself and in Jesus of Nazareth.[68] Acts does not allow much visibility to the tension which is thus contained. On a changed level, however, it recurs in contemporary evangelization, in as much as it also calls Christians to a "turning back" and "return" to the properly understood faith of their childhood or their forebears while calling non-Christians to turn away from their gods or ideologies and to turn toward the Father of Jesus Christ and calling both of these "conversion." This is the heritage of the prophetic message and of the proclamation of John the Baptizer, in which people's claim to collective salvation is rejected and they are challenged to a unique personal encounter with God, which is the same for all persons, no matter how its form may vary with the story of their lives.

God's Deed and Human Deeds

The point of departure for the missionary message of the Acts of the Apostles is the resurrection of Jesus.[69] For the Jews this documents the injustice of the judgment against Jesus (3:15), for the heathen it reveals the living God and the one whom he has sent as judge of the world (17:31). In both cases the resurrection finds its place on the horizon of eschatological judgment and responsibility before God. But the resurrection of Jesus bears witness to God's intent for salvation: The fact that the one guiltlessly condemned did not remain in death opens new living space for those, as well, who have made themselves guilty. Through the exaltation of Jesus to the position of Prince (of Life) and Savior, God grants Israel return and forgiveness of sins (3:15; 5:31)

Parallel to this we find the commentary of the leadership of the congregation at Jerusalem to the granting of the Holy Spirit to the heathen in Caesarea: "Then God has given even to the Gentiles the repentance that leads to life" (11:18). Strictly speaking, of course, the intention in both cases is the possibility of repentance. But precisely the second example shows that this possibility is filled with divine dynamism, which presses on to its realization.[70] The theological evaluation of these passages is a matter of controversy. Conzelmann writes on the theme of "calling" to 3:16, 26:29 and 16:14: "Faith, and repentance are understood as God's work,"[71] while Taeger holds the opposing view: "We should not contradict the fact that repentance happens with the powers, the will, the decision of the human agent, for it is precisely the powers, the will, and the decision of the human agent which Luke addresses." "The decisive step—in every regard—must (and can) be done by the human agent himself."[72]

Obviously both positions are one-sided. The human response grows out of the action of God alone; God's salvific action accomplishes its goal, however, whenever the human person lets it happen in him or her by turning to God. This involution of one with the other finds marvelous expression in 3:26: God "raised up his servant, he sent him first to you, to bless you by making each one of you turn from your wicked ways."[73]

The Exemplary Tales

Forms of God's working and the free response by humans are evident also in the examples of individual conversions.[74] The conversion of Paul of course takes a special place in this regard, for he is overcome by the appearance of the resurrected one in such a way that we can no longer talk of a decision, but only of an induction into Christian living (cf. Acts 9:17f.; 22:16).[75] The same can be said for the "conversion" of the God-fearer Cornelius, in whose case the human answer is replaced by the outpouring of the Holy Spirit—which is clearly identified as a special case in salvation history.[76]

Much less dramatic is the course of the conversion of the Ethiopian eunuch: After Philip has "proclaimed to him the good news about Jesus" (8:35) on the basis of Isa 53:7f., the listener to the sermon responds at the sight of the next brook or pond, "Look, here is water! What is to prevent me from being baptized?"[77]

Similarly, the story of Lydia in Philippi, of whom it is told that while she was listening to the preaching of Paul, "The Lord opened her heart to listen eagerly to [or: take seriously] what was said by Paul." There is no report of her conversion, but the story continues immediately. "When she and her household were baptized, she urged us, saying 'If you have judged me to be faithful to the Lord,[78] come and stay at my home'" (16:15).

The story of the prison warden in Philippi shows similar emphases. To his desperate question "What must I do to be saved?" he receives the brief answer, "Believe on the Lord Jesus, and you will be saved, you and your household" (16:31). Then the story continues "They spoke the word of the Lord to him and to all who were in his house. At the same hour of the night he took them and washed their wounds; then he and his entire family were baptized without delay. He brought them up into the house and set food before them; and he and his entire household rejoiced that he had become a believer in God" (16:32-34). The "deed" of the decision is not mentioned, only the result counts for anything: to be baptized and to rejoice in "having come to faith"![79]

A few notable motifs shape these stories. They emphasize the power of the proclamation of the word through which God works in people.[80] They underline that this can happen without precondition and immediately.[81] They report only indirectly of the decision of the central figures, as if they do not wish to permit the "action" of the human agent to have any weight of its own. And they also include—wherever possible—"the household" of the central figure in the decision made.[82]

Although Luke may emphasize the call to repentance, to conversion, and to faith through the sermons of the apostles and may also make clear from the phenomenon of unbelief that he is concerned with the free decision of the human agent, yet this human decision at no time becomes the center and the foundation of Christian life, but rather the result of what God has effected.

By Faith, and Therefore by Grace—Paul

For Paul the concepts of repentance or conversion hardly play a role. What there is to say theologically about the acceptance of salvation comes to expression at great length through his concept of faith. Yet there is also a series of non-terminological phrases which describe the reaction of persons to the message of the gospel. These phrases also will be considered in the following overview.

Saving Faith

Paul shares the language use common to a broad stream of tradition in the mission of the primitive church, in which the accepting the message of salvation and thereby becoming Christian are described by *pisteuein* in the aorist mood ("coming to faith").[83] Pauline evidence for this is found in Rom 13:11 (cf. 10:14); 1 Cor 3:5; 15:2, 11; and Gal 2:16.

The origins of this terminology was hotly argued.[84] According to the evidence of Jonah 3:5, Jdt 14:10, and Wis 12:2, it would seem to have been used in Hellenistic Judaism especially for the conversion of heathens to the God of Israel. Thus the concept was taken up by Hellenistic Jewish Christianity, perhaps here as well at first exclusively for the conversion of heathens to Christianity.[85] Later it was Paul who suspended this distinction and viewed precisely this "coming to faith" as the unifying bond between Jews and "Gentile sinners" (Gal 2:15ff.).[86]

From this origin the concept of faith is extremely closely bound to the kerygma to which faith gives answer. This is evidenced in 1 Cor 15:1-11 and above all in Rom 10:9, where also we find a citation from a creedal statement of the primitive church.[87] In the sentence, "if you confess with your lips that Jesus is Lord and believe in your heart that God raised him from the dead, you will be saved" we find standing side by side the original acclamation (homology) of the primitive church, *Kyrios Iesous*, "Jesus is Lord," and the central confessional statement of the early proclamation, "God raised Jesus from the dead." Through the juxtaposition of these two sentences they mutually interpret one another. The identity of this Jesus, to whom those who confess submit themselves in a legally binding way, is made plain by the reference to his resurrection by God. The confession of Jesus as present Lord shows that faith in his resurrection is more than assent to the truth of a historical fact.

But in what way are faith and its confession conditions of salvation, as seems to be expressed in this conditional sentence? Is a "hurrying effort of faith" necessary to be saved, as H. Schlier put it? What is the relationship between justification by faith and justification by grace?[88]

Justification by Faith

We can observe relatively easily how Paul develops the concept of faith found in the primitive church. He is able occasionally to use the present participle *hoi pisteuontes* analogous to a widely used usage in the primitive church with the meaning "believers" or "Christians."[89] But, in the antithesis to trusting in one's own accomplishments and to the demand for wisdom and demonstrable evidence (1 Cor 1:22), he makes from this ecclesiastical formula the precise definition of the existential behavior which is appropriate over against the salvific action of God (thus 1 Cor 1:21; Gal 3:22).[90] Precisely this concept of faith becomes the anthropological characteristic for the fact that the separation of Jews and Gentiles into the "collectives" of salvation on the one side and of damnation on the other has been broken down; God's justice, God's righteousness applies to everyone who believes (Rom 1:6; 10:4; plural: Rom 3:22; 4:11).[91]

What is to be understood under this designation as "faith" is described by two constitutive characteristics:

(1) Faith describes the attitude of a person which is appropriate to the justifying activity of God. Paul explicates this idea especially carefully in response to the Galatian false teachers who demanded of heathen Christians that they would need to be circumcised and received into God's covenant with Abraham. *Hoi ek pisteōs*, those who live by faith, are Abraham's children (Gal 3:7f.). This contrasts sharply with those who live by works of the law and who, by trusting in their own accomplishments, thus reap death.[92] The contrast between faith and works prevents faith in itself from becoming some sort of substitute accomplishment demanded of people. Paul makes this clear in Romans 4 with the example of Abraham. In contrast to the usual Jewish interpretation he concludes that God's reckoning Abraham's faith as righteousness is not recognition of some accomplishment of Abraham, but is rather the gracious acceptance of one who expects everything from God and nothing from himself.[93] For this reason the sentence applies: It depends on faith that it may rest on grace (Gal 4:16). Abraham's exemplary faith, as described in Gal 4:18-22, is not human heroism, but an expression of full trust upon God who makes the dead to live, creates out of nothing, and justifies the godless. The faith that God resurrected Jesus from the dead also has this same character (4:24f.). Whoever opens him- or herself to God's activity in Jesus Christ makes the fundamental existential determination to live totally from the promises of God.

(2) Thus we have arrived at the second characteristic. Justifying faith is always *pistis Iēsou Christou*, acceptance of what God has done through Jesus Christ. Even if we cannot maintain the turn of phrase as a *subjective genitive*—"the faith *of* Jesus Christ"— in our translation, the kernel of truth

151

of this view remains even in its translation as an *objective genitive*— "faith *in* Jesus Christ." The content of faith is not, strictly speaking, its object, but rather much more its source.[94]

Paul has most urgently made this plain in Rom 3:21-26, where justification by faith, by grace, and for the sake of the redemptive deed of Christ are woven together most inextricably. God's reconciling activity in the death of Jesus is the foundation of faith, which makes faith possible at all.[95] Thus Paul can occasionally use the formula "faith came" (Gal 3:23) where we might expect "Christ came."[96]

Accordingly, in Rom 10:17 faith comes from hearing the proclamation; proclamation itself proceeds from the *rhēma Christou*, from the word of Christ which proclaim his deeds and which he himself authorizes. "Faith owes nothing to the decision of the believer, but (only) to the word from without which urges itself upon the believer's ear and heart."[97] Thus it is that faith as "attitude" is nothing less than holding fast to what God has given.

Faith and Baptism

The baptismal theology of Paul is essentially a memorial of baptism.[98] This has to do with the character of his letters as letters to specific congregations, but it is not easily explained in its specificity only by this circumstance.

The statements in Rom 6:3, 1 Cor 12:13 (cf. 6:11), and Gal 3:27f. all emphasize what has validly happened to a Christian in baptism, namely, the initiation into the area of validity of the salvific action of God in the death and resurrection of Jesus. Remembering the baptismal event is thus the clearest possible expression for the reference to that which has happened to the Christian at God's initiative and which applies to his life. It is the clearest expression of a personally relevant indicative which remains connected with the concrete, unique process of baptism: You have been effectively received into the sphere of influence of the salvific activity of God.

If from this point of departure we ask what the relationship of baptism and faith is, we come to a remarkable conclusion: Although there can be no reasonable doubt that baptism is carried out on believers, there is not a single passage in which Paul brings faith and baptism into an explicit, temporally ordered, conditional relationship to one another, in which he might, for instance, say, since you have come to faith, you have received (or were able to receive) baptism.[99]

Paul does not require one specific act of faith as a prerequisite of baptism, nor does he make baptism a necessary completion of faith. Faith and baptism are two complementary sides of receiving salvation,[100] in which

152

baptism presents more strongly the objective ordering of the salvific act of Christ to an individual, while faith is described more in its significance as a subjective occurrence in which a person relies on God's promises and his work in Jesus Christ. Thus there is no "remembrance of faith" in the sense of a referring to the personal decision of the individual at his conversion.[101]

It is highly questionable to attempt any abstraction from the fact that the New Testament baptism was missionary baptism connected with a consciously executed change of life's direction and to assert that evangelistic proclamation today should in contrast take the form of a recollection of baptism, especially in "mainstream" churches. Exegetically, we must first test the premise whether the subjectivity of this change of life's direction really plays no role for Paul.

The New Understanding of Oneself

We need to reconsider Paul's experience of the call. The three reports we have in his letters are significantly different in their emphases. Two of them emphasize what happened to Paul in his encounter with the Resurrected Lord; in Gal 1:15f. his call as a missionary to the heathen is in the foreground; in 1 Cor 15:8-10 it is his call to be a witness to the resurrection. Contrasting with them we have Phil 3:4-9, the only report which we might properly describe as a report of Paul's "conversion."[102] For this passage deals with the radical change of direction in Paul's self understanding; the character of this change is lifted up with all clarity as a personal decision and as a conscious change of his inner attitude. If it were not for the agreement in Phil 3:6 and Gal 1:13f. (cf. 1 Cor 5:9), one could properly ask if the same event is intended. But Paul is apparently able to let the two stand side by side: what God has done for him—without there being any positive pre-conditions to pave the way on his part—and what God's action has triggered in his own will and thought. The inner connection is easily reconstructed: Paul persecuted the early (Hellenic) church because its proclamation of the Crucified One (and that means, according to Deut 21:23, one of the accursed) as Messiah was blasphemy.[104] God's revealing the crucified Jesus to him as God's own Son, i.e., as the one with plenipotentiary powers for the eschaton, triggered in him a fundamental rethinking of his assumptions. Through his cursed death Jesus bore the curse which the Law would have laid upon us all. Simultaneously the law was discredited as a path of salvation, justification on the basis of works was exposed as self-righteousness, and the righteousness of faith was acknowledged as a justification given by God.

But even if this new self-understanding may be described as Paul's decision—expressly emphasized by the accountant's talk of profit and loss—it is nevertheless not the case that Paul describes anew his own way. The source of his decision is Christ and his encounter with him, and its destination and goal to achieve fellowship with Christ: Justification in faith is justification in Christ.[105] And what does this mean for the act of faith? Is faith the "divine decision"[106] or human decision?

God's Sovereignty and Human Decision

The question raised cannot be answered simply. It is precisely when he clearly addresses the question that Paul gives no clear answer. In Romans 9 and 10, where the question is Israel's lack of faith, two answers stand side by side. Romans 9:6-29 places in the center the sovereign decision of God to call or to make defiant: "So it depends not on human will or exertion, but on God who shows mercy" (Rom 9:16). Alongside this, however, stands the accusation against Israel that Israel has fallen short of the goal of its path to God because it has not let its life be determined "on the basis of faith" but rather "on the basis of works," although the proclamation of faith has reached Israel (Rom 9:30–10:21). God's sovereignty and the human agent's responsibility for his own reaction are not, therefore, mutually exclusive.[107]

A similar tension confronts us in Rom 5:12-21. In carrying out the parallel "Adam and Christ" in verses 18f., sinful humanity molded by Adam finds its complete counterpart in a new humanity justified by Christ. The universality of grace corresponds to the universality of sin. On the other hand, in the passage describing the incomparability of sin and the gift of grace, all those who will exercise dominion with Christ are described as persons, "who *receive* the abundance of grace and free gift of righteousness." It would certainly introduce an emphasis not intended by Paul if we were to translate *lambanein* with "accept" instead of "receive."[108] But even so the digression remains important: Righteousness and life are gifts of God and in a certain sense faith is also a gift (Phil 1:29). But at the same time faith is the completion of the reception in which God's gift reaches its goal.

Gerhart Friedrich formulated the possible limitation of this view very carefully. "Persons cannot give themselves gifts. But a person can reject a gift. Persons cannot have faith on their own account, but they can avoid following the call of the gospel and be disobedient (Rom 10:16). Although human agents do not have the capacity to acquire faith, they have the power of negation of faith."[109]

A person can say "no" to God's "yes." But must someone say "yes" in order for God's "yes" to accomplish its purposes? Is it sufficient not to have rejected God's gift, or must it also be accepted—or would this question itself already pose an unacceptable condition?

The call to faith places no other condition than the request to a beggar to cease making his hands into fists, but to open them and to allow his empty hands to be filled. Fulfilling this condition is no reason for pride. To continue the image: A donor does not hide his loaf of bread behind his back and only show it when the intended recipient has passed the test of his obedience and his faith by opening his hands. The bread is offered, and it is the easy access to the bread itself which opens the hand or the mouth of the hungry. So it is that faith is God's work, and yet a human deed.

Paul shows this dialectic clearly. The gospel of the righteousness of God for all who believe is that which is proclaimed. What is described, however, is faith as the faith in one who justifies the godless (not, however, the one who justifies believers). Faith leaves no room for itself in the equation, but acknowledges owing all to God.

Paul characterized these two elements in Gal 4:9, as well, in looking back to the conversion of the Galatians through an intentional self-correction: "Now, however, that you have come to know God, or rather to be known by God." Their subjective acknowledging of God, the decision for the true God, finds its foundation in God's acknowledging them, i.e., in God's gracious election. Therefore the opposite also holds: The assertion that God is reconciling the world to himself does not say it all. Reconciliation includes its appeal to those affected: Let yourselves be reconciled with God.[110] We can summarize this dialectic in the single sentence: The proclamation of the gospel has as its purpose human faith, but faith does not talk about itself, but about all that God has done through Christ.[111]

It is worthy of note that the later or Deutero-Pauline writings hold fast to this dialectic. Ephesians 2:8f. expresses this in an especially fruitful way: "For by grace you have been saved through faith, and this is not your own doing; it is the gift of God—not the result of works, so that no one may boast." And in 1 Tim 2:4ff. the universality of God's intention for salvation und the question of the recognition of faith in humans is summarized in the classic formulation: "[God] desires everyone to be saved and to come to the knowledge of the truth. For there is one God; there is also one mediator between God and humankind, Christ Jesus, himself human, who gave himself a ransom for all."

All Who Have Faith in Him—John

As Klaus Haacker writes in the article "Glaube II" in the *TRE*, "Johannine theology reflects on the fact that in the encounter with Jesus a decision is required."[112] In contrast with the Synoptic Gospels John speaks very much more about faith and unbelief. To describe the positive decision there is a series of equivalents: "to see, to recognize, to come to Jesus or to accept him." What significance does this decision have for the salvation of the human person and how does it come about?

The Purpose of the Message

The purpose of the message is formulated in John's Gospel with all clarity. It begins with the witness of the Baptizer for the light of the *logos*, "so that all might believe through him" (John 1:7). And it ends in 20:31 with the remark that the report of the signs of Jesus was written "that you may come to believe that Jesus is the Messiah, the Son of God, and that through believing you may have life in his name." This ties the witness of John the Baptizer and John the Evangelist to the meaning of the sending of the son of God, whom God gave into this world, "so that everyone who believes in him may not perish but may have eternal life" (3:16). Corresponding to this is a saying at the end of Jesus' public ministry: "I have come as light to the world, so that everyone who believes in me should not remain in the darkness"(12:46). Faith in Jesus Christ is the way to fellowship with God, to light and to life, indeed faith is itself life. "Whoever believes in the Son has eternal life" (3:36; 5:24; 6:47; 11:25f.). For, as it is formulated in the high-priestly prayer, "this is eternal life, that they may know you, the only true God, and Jesus Christ whom you have sent" (17:3).

The Way to Faith

How do you come to faith? The answer of the gospel is: by witness and sign.[113] John 1:35–2:11 is a model tale of how the disciples are led to faith through the witness of John the Baptizer, mutual encouragement, and the experience of the miracle at Cana. This pattern recurs many times (2:23; 4:35; 8:30; 9:38; 11:45; 12:42; 20:29-31). But it also becomes evident that such faith can be superficial and easily shaken. It must be deepened in order to be a truly saving faith. That is the issue in the conversation with Nicodemus (3:1–21) and in the dialogue with the Jews who had become believers (8:31-59). The conversation with Nicodemus impresses upon us that eternal life begins at that point where a person allows his or her life to be filled with the free, indeterminable, and wonderful action of God and also acknowledges the Son of Man who was exalted upon the cross as the true revelation of the love of God. John 8 promises freedom to all who, in their encounter with Jesus as the Truth of God, "see through" their own lives and see their own insistence upon religious guarantees and their own search for personal honor as the self-powered animosity to God laid bare for what it is, i.e., as sin. This insight can be bestowed by the signs of Jesus, if they are recognized as signs of the sovereignty of God encountering them in Jesus. The saying is true for this reason, "Whoever believes in me believes

156

not in me but in him who sent me." (John 12:44; 17:3) Wherever Jesus' work and word become transparent for the glory of God, true faith grows.

For this reason faith after Easter is only indirectly dependent upon signs. They are part of the witness of those who confess, "We have seen his glory" (John 1:14). Despite 14:12-14, the Gospel of John does not perceive any immediate continuation of the signs of Jesus through his disciples. People come to faith through the word of the disciples (17:20) and the "greater works" are not still more spectacular miracles, but aim at the unbarring of the soteriological message of Jesus in the post-Easter proclamation.[114] So the hearer is told, "Blessed are those who have not seen and yet have come to believe" (20:29).

Faith and Unbelief as Crisis Events

The sentence, "Whoever believes has eternal life," has its down side: "Whoever does not believe is already judged." The Son of God has been sent into the world to save persons, not to judge them (3:17; 12:47). But in as much as people close themselves to him and his ministry, they become their own judgment. They do not allow themselves to be brought into the light of fellowship with God, but they remain in the darkness characteristic of distance from God, and they refuse to take the step from the reign of death into the arena of divine life and remain corrupted to death. So faith or unbelief constitutes the final decision about one's life, and on the last day—so far as John speaks of it—nothing will be established except what has already happened.[115]

And yet for the Gospel of John salvation and damnation, life and death are "not parallel alternatives."[116] The Gospel does not call us to choose between life and death, but proclaims salvation, namely the gospel of "the healing deed of God for the salvation of the whole cosmos, which proceeded through Jesus Christ." It is derived from "the pre-decision of God for the Salvation of the world." "Since, however, faith is a free deed and decision of the human agent, the possibility remains that human beings may reject God's offer of salvation, that they may take offense at the Word of God made flesh, trip and fall and in the process call down judgment upon themselves. In these decisions of rejection the human agent misses out on Jesus Christ and, in him, God and his own salvation, and thereby his own very self. The possibility of judgment remains until the definitive end of all ages."

Does faith thus become a condition for salvation? Is there something which human beings have to do by their own strength in order to turn toward God's salvific action?

The grammatical structure of the central expressions of the gospel concerning faith and unbelief, which for the most part are formulated with

157

conditional participles, seems to imply this. On the other hand, the total structure of a sentence like John 3:16 with its interpreting contradistinction between the love of God for the world as the source of God's salvific action and the goal of such action that all who believe in him have eternal life, rules out an interpretation of faith as an exclusionary condition. Is, perhaps, the concept of faith in John's Gospel less a condition of salvation and much more a description of its subjective realization?[117] This view, however, runs up against the phenomenon of unbelief. Why does the salvific will of God not find realization in those who do not believe?

The Advance Decision of God

The "riddle of faith" is given a dual explanation in John.[118] In the unbelief of people it becomes clear how people really are: "For all who do evil hate the light and do not come to the light, so that their deeds may not be exposed" (3:20). But whether in faith or unbelief it is not simply the ethical behavior which is revealed. Therefore, the positive statement declares, "But those who do what is true come to the light, so that it may be clearly seen that their deeds have been done in God" (3:21). Thus behind the different behaviors of human agents—and thus behind faith or unbelief—is God's working. "No one can come to me unless drawn by the Father who sent me" (6:44, 65).

The significance of this statement is clear: Human beings cannot create their own salvation, not even through their faith. All who come to Jesus come to see that they have not taken this path out of their own strength, but that the love for the Father has brought them there. It is not a synergistic cooperation of divine and human work at which we are looking, in the sense of an additive relationship of both, rather that "everything that the Father gives me will come to me" (6:37).

But who are those whom the Father has given to the Son (cf. 17:2, 6, 9, 12, 24)? Is it a carefully counted circle of the predestined,[119] and why don't the others belong to this circle? "You do not believe, because you do not belong to my sheep. My sheep hear my voice"—so the message of John 10:26f. Are there people who are "from God" (8:47) or who "belong to the truth" (18:37) and therefore "hear" God's word and Jesus' voice, i.e., accept them in faith, and others who are not "from God," but from the devil (8:43f.) and for whom Jesus' speech therefore remains inaccessible? Or do they qualify as children of the devil because they have refused by free decision the claim of God in Jesus?[120]

It is a difficult task, in the light of these texts, to follow Blank's argumentation when he asserts, "The theology of revelation in John's gospel makes the seriousness and broad consequences of human freedom apparent in its full extent. Exactly at this point this theology holds to the authentic line of Biblical religion at whose core lies the free dialogue of God with human beings."[121]

Freedom for John is not the prerequisite of the personal decision for or against God, but the consequence of the acknowledgment of divine reality in one's holding fast to the Word of Jesus (8:31f.). A person "is not free to decide about his salvation. The world has already decided about itself."[122] This is, however, not the consequence of a cosmic, inevitable fate, which pre-determines humanity, but the consequence of sin in which human beings entangle themselves (8:35). To whom, then, does the call to faith apply? Only to a circle of the elect, or to all?

Faith—God's Work, and Human Response

The fact that rejection and acceptance of the message do not stand as the juxtaposition of two pre-programmed ways of behavior is evidenced in two paradoxical assertions of the Gospel of John. In the hymn to the *logos* in 1:11f., we read, "He came to what was his own and his own people did not accept him. But to all who received him, who believed in his name, he gave power to become children of God." The rejection of the Revealer is total.[123] The fact that the miracle happens and people nevertheless open themselves to the working of the *logos* is not valued as an independent occurrence, but it leads into what the *logos* effectuates.[124] Precondition and consequence at the level of grammatical logic seem to be absolutely reversed at the level of facticity. This tension is mirrored again in the two explanatory glosses of the Evangelist (12*d*-13). In chiastic relationship to 12*a-b*, verse 12*d* characterizes the recipients of divine childhood as those "who believe in his name" and verse 13 those who "receive" him as ones "who were born, not of blood or the will of the flesh or of the will of man, but of God." Anticipating John 3:1-16 the miracle of new birth, of the creation of a new existence through God here is named as the cause of the acceptance of the revelation, but at the same time it is made clear that this is realized at the level of human subjectivity in faith in his name.

We find a parallel train of thought in 3:32f., where it is said of the witness of the Revealer, "yet no one accepts his testimony. Whoever has accepted his testimony has certified this, that God is true." Here also we find "the juxtaposition of that which is to be expected in human and earthly terms, and that which the reality and truth of God nevertheless effects, which gives the witness of the Revealer its power."[125] The human side of this process, the acceptance of the message, becomes transparent for that which is its basis: the truth of God, which reveals itself in the word of the Revealer.

Against the background of these observations it is probable that the

159

mention of faith in him whom he has sent as a "work of God" (6:29) denotes not only that work which God expects,[126] but above all the work which God effects.[127] Yet we must immediately add that this working of God never occurs except in the witness of Jesus. "Faith comes into being out of the proclaimed and witnessed Word."[128]

The paradox of these relationships finds its most pointed expression in John 5:25: "Very truly, I tell you, the hour is coming, and is now here, when the dead will hear the voice of the Son of God, and those who hear will live." The voice of the Son of God "targets" the "spiritually" dead and they can hear (!) and, insofar as they hear, they will live. The miracle of the word of God which wakes from the dead and the quest for an "active" hearer as human response are involuted in one another.[129]

It is therefore to be taken seriously when in the Gospel the call goes out time and again, "Let anyone who is thirsty come to me" (7:37) and when in the sermons of Jesus the antithetical conditional participial sentence repeatedly calls out for the basic decision for humankind.[130] The fundamental decision of God in sending the Son is clear: "For God so loved the world that he gave his only Son, so that everyone who believes in him may not perish but may have eternal life" (3:16; 12:46).

Thus the human "yes" rests alone on God's "yes." The fact that there is also a "no" to this "yes" becomes the evidence of the true state of human beings, as well as a constant appeal to humans, to perceive their responsibility in a fitting answer to God's working.[131]

The Call to Repentance Addressed to the Early Christian Community—Revelation

The message of the letters to the seven churches, which we have already dealt with briefly in our overview of the proclamation of judgment, must be mentioned once again in this context. While it is not really a matter of an initial missionary proclamation, yet it is in the strict sense of the word a "proclamation of awakening" (cf. 3:2) which shakes up a Christian community which has become self-satisfied and calls it back to its Lord. The call to *metanoia* is both the call to penance in the sense of humbling oneself and regret for particular wrong behavior, as well as a call to repentance in the sense of a return to the origins of their existence as a congregation. It is precisely this emphasis—the recalling of "the love you had at first" (Rev 2:4) and the remembering of all that the community has received and heard (3:3)—which takes up an important motif of Old Testament prophecy.[132] The emphasis upon the common responsibility of the community reminds us of prophecy, as well. The call to repentance applies to all, even if manifest misbehavior is evident only in some. Yet the sayings about those who

160

conquer also recall the call to the individual. In each case the call to penance of the letters to the seven churches is a call to a clear change of behavior of both the community and the individual, a change which is to have a clearly recognizable temporal beginning and lasting consequences.[133]

God's Action and Human Response—Summary

The biblical message of God's speaking and acting is aimed at eliciting a human response. Because it is the biblical view that human salvation depends on God's granting fellowship to humans, God's salvific action achieves its purposes whenever human beings permit themselves to be received into this fellowship. On the human side, fellowship with God has been destroyed. Nevertheless God created all prerequisites for Israel to live in fellowship with him; and some words of Jesus seem at first to reckon with the possibility of a life of the "just" in fellowship with God.[134] But what the prophets repeatedly had to take into account finally becomes obvious in Jesus' death. Even religious persons fall short of the will of God, because they are ultimately not concerned about God, but about themselves.

Because God in his love does not, however, will the death of the sinner, he grants to human beings in the sending, death, and resurrection of Jesus both reconciliation and fellowship without a single precondition. Jesus' proclamation of the proximity of God's reign and the apostolic preaching of the incarnation of the son and of the revelation of the justice of God is both promise of salvation and invitation to let it happen to those who hear. Thus Israel receives the call to return into the fellowship founded for it by God, and non-Jews receive the call to turn toward the fellowship with God which has been opened to all persons in Jesus Christ.

In this it is clear that obedience to the call of God cannot be reckoned as any sort of accomplishment, as a "work." Rather it is God who grants repentance, and his activity in Jesus Christ is the foundation and the enablement of faith.

Therefore we find in almost all layers of early Christian proclamation a paradoxical, but theologically fully meaningful situation. Human persons are addressed regarding their repentance, their faith, and their 'yes' to God's action; missionary preaching aims for a clear, unique change of life's direction; and Christian nurture and teaching assumes such an event. But in retrospect it is not the human conversion or decision for faith, but solely God's salvific activity which is the object of memory and reassurance. The Pauline self-corrective, "Now, however, that you have come to know God, or rather to be known by God" (Gal 4:9) encapsulates this relationship between subjective experience and divine action in a nutshell.

Yet in terms of the ordering of divine and human activity questions still remain open for systematic reflection. This is all the more true because in all levels of tradition the opposite side of this status quo is addressed: The possibility does exist of rejection, of denial, and of the human "no" to God's "yes." And this "no" is effective. The pronouncement of judgment makes it clear—as is given special emphasis in John's Gospel—that, although the judgment is not against humans because of their disobedience, yet the judgment takes seriously and "makes firm" the decision of human agents themselves to remain in "darkness," i.e., outside the life-creating and sustaining fellowship with God. The rejection of the message of the cross, which does yet announce God's reconciling action for all persons, remains as a burdensome and unsolved riddle hanging over the proclamation of the New Testament love of God which overcomes all resistance.

Two assertions are important in conclusion: In the act of conversion and of faith human beings are given a new self-understanding which permeates even the roots of their existence and transforms them. Their very being is then no longer centered in their own ego, their own situation or piety, but instead their lives are incorporated into the action of God with humankind and with the world. Thus the reaction of an individual is no longer a goal in itself and the main theme, but it rather belongs to God's activity, to his reconciling, saving, and liberating action which is for all persons.

To this first observation comes a second: Strangely enough, even in the late writings of the New Testament the problem of being Christian in the second or third generation is never mentioned. May we conclude from the remark of Paul in 1 Cor 7:14 and the frequent references to the baptism of whole "households" in the Acts of the Apostles that children of Christian parents were simply assumed to be Christians? The few extant witnesses to this topic from the first, second, and third centuries only allow the conclusion that members of succeeding generations were neither seen as automatically Christians nor viewed simply as non-Christians who had to be evangelized in the same way as the heathen.[135] In a church which did not yet stand under a Christian society's pressure to conform it must have necessarily come to a decision about the question of who would want to remain in the "house of the Father" and who would not.

162

Chapter 5

Salvation and Decision:
A Systematic Reflection

Inherent in the complexity of the biblical evidence itself the question of the significance of the answer to God's redemptive action for the salvation of human persons receives an extraordinarily controversial treatment today. It is obviously difficult to bear the tension which the biblical witness offers. Everything seems instead to urge the alternative form of the question: Is it finally God's decision for humankind which is decisive or the decision of a human being for God? When the final balance of a person's life is at issue a further question arises about the relationship between the singular conversion to God and standing fast in faith and in love. Let us first concentrate on the first question, coming back to the second in the course of the chapter.

Classical Theology of Evangelization

The view of the theology of evangelization as it is found predominately in "evangelical" circles is made clear in Articles 3 and 4 of the Lausanne Covenant[1]:

(3) *The Uniqueness and Universality of Christ*
Jesus Christ, being himself the only God-man, who gave himself as the only ransom for sinners, is the only mediator between God and people. There is no other name by which we must be saved. All men and women are perishing because of sin, but God loves everyone, not wishing that any should perish but that all should repent. Yet those who reject Christ repudiate the joy of salvation and condemn themselves to eternal separation from God. To proclaim Jesus as "the Savior of the world" is not to affirm that all people are either automatically or ultimately saved, still less to affirm that all religions offer salvation in Christ. Rather it is to proclaim God's love for a world of sinners and to invite everyone to respond to him as Savior and Lord in the wholehearted personal commitment of repentance and faith.

Additionally Article 4 complements the above regarding the essence of evangelism:

(4) *The Nature of Evangelism*

To evangelise is to spread the good news that Jesus Christ died for our sins and was raised from the dead according to the Scriptures, and that as the reigning Lord he now offers the forgiveness of sins and the liberating gift of the Spirit to all who repent and believe.

It would be possible to bring numerous citations to support this conviction. The evangelists of the nineteenth century emphasized human responsibility especially strongly. This was true of the preacher of the gospel. Charles Finney said that "The preacher is a moral agent in the work: he acts; he is not a mere passive instrument; he is voluntary in promoting the conversion of sinners." And this is true in an even greater sense for the hearer of the message; Finney stresses

> the agency of the sinner himself. The conversion of a sinner consists in his obeying the truth. It is therefore impossible it should take place without his agency, for it consists in his acting right. He is influenced to this response by the agency of God and the agency of men.[2]

To "tell him [the sinner] that conversion is the work of God and he ought to leave it to Him . . . is all wrong"; "The sinner is not to be told to pray to God to do his duty for him, but to go and do it himself."[3] It is therefore necessary to make the person aware at every possible opportunity of the seriousness and the urgency of the decision. The story of Dwight L. Moody, who failed to call his hearers to decision precisely on the eve of the great Chicago fire, is one of those admonitions which recur again and again in the literature of evangelism.[4] So it is that more recent authors also emphasize that "A person is free to answer God's call to salvation."[5]

Not without reason, this view claims its substantiation in the biblical message itself. Where the call to conversion and to faith is formulated, it is obviously assumed that it is humanly possible to respond to this call or to refuse it.[6] But this view also points us to substantial problems which show that its single-mindedness is not totally justified by the biblical message. God's activity in Jesus Christ becomes for this viewpoint an "offer," the "possibility of salvation," which becomes reality only through human decision.

If we say—to put it in its most pointed form—that Jesus is only present as "a potential savior, because he offers salvation to all, but is not the actual savior, because not all accept his offer,"[7] then we immediately see the difference from the biblical claims about the redemption which happened in Christ. The accusation of synergism hovers threateningly above this form of Protestant theology. And this leads to the question as to the foundation upon which the assurance of salvation rests: upon an experience, namely the experience of one's own decision, or upon the work of God in Jesus Christ?[8]

The Variant of Theological Existentialism

Anyone coming from pietistic-revivalistic circles in the 1950s and 1960s to study theology at the universities encountered, alongside various strange ideas, a familiar one, namely the word "decision" as the expression of the fundamental turn of life of a Christian. Taking Søren Kierkegaard as their point of departure, and in dialogue with existential philosophy, the representatives of dialectical theology had taken over this concept in diverse ways. Kierkegaard himself had made of "the 'decision' of individual inwardness, of immediacy . . . of individual self-awareness the very criterion of the truth of all 'essential' knowledge, i.e., all knowledge oriented to existence itself."[9]

Having chosen the category of "decision" for describing conversion and faith, it would be necessary to clarify what significance the revelation of God in Jesus Christ has as its goal and content. Karl Barth manages this most clearly of all, for whom the decision of God for each human being, which has been made once and for all time in Jesus Christ is both the basis and the content of the individual's decision of faith. With a higher degree of dialectic, and yet similarly, Emil Brunner yokes "the human answer of decision" with the "divine creative address" as the common, constitutive form of personal decision.[10]

Formative for the concept of decision are, in each case, the ontological assumptions: For Barth this is an "ontology of divine self-revelation," which assumes "God as the subject which decides for itself;" for Brunner it is an "ontology of the 'Thou-I' relationship or the 'call-answer' relationship," which assumes "the human being, as well, as basis for decision."

For Bultmann the concept of decision is itself a sustaining foundation of the ontology. For the truth-claim of the biblical message—whether Jesus' proclamation of the imminence of the divine reign or Paul's word of the cross—encounters all human beings, as Bultmann sees it, in the question of how they want to understand themselves in the presence of God—and thus in their own presence. Thus, on the one hand, the decisions of human agents are not their own because they owe the opportunity for decision to a call from outside themselves. Simultaneously, however, the very essence of the human agent before God is constituted in this decision: "Through his decision the human agent becomes a sinner or one of the just."[11] However, the event itself to which the decision of faith refers cannot be grasped in the framework of the ontology which Bultmann assumes; to speak about it in other terms than those of existential interpretation or direct, existential

165

encounter would be an objectifying speech which falsifies the actual meaning of the message. Ernst Fuchs carries the ontologically narrow path of existential theology yet further when he—taking the matter to extremes—writes: "Our faith is allowed to and ought to decide about the existence of God."[12]

In his own way Tillich also radicalizes the concept of decision in as much as he broadens the biblical teaching about justification of the sinner to include justification of the doubter, who in the genuineness and radicality of his very struggle for the truth is standing in the truth itself. Tillich goes yet another step when he finds in "the courage of being" that "absolute faith"—which stands beyond what has previously been understood as faith in or doubt about certain, specific articles of truth and which can face down the anxiety of doubt and meaninglessness. "The faith which makes the courage of despair possible is the experience of being grasped by the power of being, despite the overwhelming experience of non-being." This faith does not have any particular content; it is indefinable, "it is simply faith—individual, absolute." It is a faith "which has been deprived by doubt of any content which nevertheless is faith and the source of the most paradoxical manifestation of the courage to be."[13]

For me there remains a strange air of tragedy in these efforts. In their attempt to allow the doctrine of justification to be consistently valid in all realms of life and to understand clearly that the *sola fide* does not require a *sacrificium intellectus*, but is rather to be subordinated to the *sola gratia*, they rob faith of its concrete content and submit it to the danger of finally being nothing other than pure human decisiveness in favor of being. Of course, neither Bultmann nor Tillich want to do that, but the question whether faith does not indeed become a "work" precisely because it is robbed of its concrete object is a justified question to be addressed to all their propositions.[14]

Especially in Bultmann's work what is evident time and again—strikingly parallel to a certain pietistic-evangelistic view—is that the gospel is interpreted as a "possibility for salvation" which becomes reality by virtue of the "yes" of the human agent.[15] So it is that the question remains unanswered whether the priority of grace through Jesus Christ is sufficiently emphasized and preserved in all of this.

God Effects Everything

Those theologians who, under all circumstances, want to hold fast to the priority of the grace of God over every human decision in the salvation event, have, in the course of church history, essentially found two possibilities for doing this. The first of these is the doctrine of the *apokatastasis pantōn*, universal salvation, which was, however, in the case of its first representative, Origen, expanded into a synergistic purification doctrine and which is not often taught publicly, since its foundation in Scripture is rather limited.[16]

The second is the teaching of gracious, divine choice according to which it is solely a question of divine election whether a person comes to faith and to salvation. Almost all major theologians of grace in the history of theology, e.g., Augustine, Zwingli, Luther, and Calvin, were led to this doctrine, but were then also forced by the logical consequences of the doctrine to accept the rejection by God as the basis for unfaith, i.e., a double predestination to salvation and to damnation.[17]

That does not, of course, keep these theologians from talking about faith. Especially Luther, for whom the dynamism of the biblical message breaks through the systematization of the doctrine of predestination time and again, recognized the dialectic of the matter:

> *Sola fide*, therefore, excludes not only human works as a basis for salvation, but it also includes the person who has turned away from God in the work of God. From this point of departure we can understand that faith can be seen both as the work of God as well as the work of the human person.[18]

At this point Lutheran orthodoxy has, for the sake of clarity, "cleaned up" Luther's teaching. So it is that we find the following infamous sentences in the Formula of Concord: "But before man is illumined, converted, reborn, renewed and drawn by the Holy Spirit, he can do no spiritual things of himself and by his own powers. In his own conversion or regeneration he can do as little to begin, effect, or cooperate in anything as a stone, a block, or a lump of clay could."[19] Here *sola fide* is taken absolutely seriously. However, the Formula of Concord reveals a certain inconsistency when it finds that the damnation of the godless is "based in their active rejection of the Word."[20]

We find a synthesis of the doctrines of predestination and universal salvation in the doctrine of election of Karl Barth. In Christ all are elect and this eternal decision of God for all human persons, which is revealed in Jesus Christ, precedes every human act of decision:

> The revealed truth of the living God in His quickening Spirit finds its content and form in the fact that it is He first who is for man and then and for that reason man is for Him. God precedes, therefore, and sets man in the motion to follow him. He says "Yes" to him when man says "No," and thus silences the "No" of man and lays a "Yes" in his heart and on his lips.[21]

The same can be said of faith. Of course, faith is a "human act." But that needs to be defined more precisely: "Faith is the human activity which is present and future, which is there, in the presence of the living Jesus Christ and of what has taken place in Him, with a profound spontaneity and native freedom, but also with an inevitability in the face of his actuality."[22] It is with a special sharpness that Barth rejects talk of faith as a native possibility of human beings:

> With the divine No and Yes spoken in Jesus Christ the root of human unbelief, the man of sin, is pulled out. In its place there is put the root of faith, the new man of obedience. For this reason unbelief has become an objective, real, ontological impossibility and faith an objective, real, and ontological necessity for each and every person.[23]

So Barth has much to say about the significance of repentance and faith as the working of the Spirit in the life of individuals, and proclamation has, undoubtedly, the task of making people aware of that which has always been true for him in Christ; a special salvific significance alongside that which God has done in Christ can not, however, be attributed to human faith. The approach of Karl Barth has been taken up by many more recent authors with various justification and accentuation. For example, Hans Weder writes, in his *New Testament Hermeneutics*:

> Exegesis of the New Testament is not supposed to bring the individual into the position of decision, to the point where he, like Hercules, must stand at the parting of the ways. Rather, exegesis has to make him aware of the Word which has preceded him, i.e., of the Word which carries his very existence, which he cannot overtake with his decision. . . . The divine Word . . . points me to that which has already be granted for me, and my decision can, at the most, be the decision to push aside that which has been granted me. Whoever is grasped by the divine Word will have just as little to decide as Paul outside Damascus. There is a very important asymmetry here.[24]

Ingolf U. Dalferth makes an even more pronounced assertion:

> Whoever has faith can only be the recipient of the effect of this event which addresses him, without being able to influence it from his side, let alone inaugurate it. The person who is addressed by God in Jesus and who perceives this address by means of the Spirit is characterized in his total passivity (Rom 3:28, 4:5); he is for his part totally uninvolved in his faith . . . In the faith-event the person is so exclusively an affected beneficiary that he or she cannot per se participate in this event in any way, either actively or passively . . . This event is, after all, nothing which said person did or allowed to happen, per se, but in

the strict sense of the event that which first makes this person wholly existent at all.[25]

Thus we ought not be surprised that the study of the Protestant Church in Germany entitled "Shaping Christian Life" [*Christsein gestalten*] also says,

> If the sinner is promised justification through the Gospel, then this is an act of unconditional grace. The condition for this grace has been fulfilled in Jesus Christ . . . Every legalism which makes of faith a demand and would raise it to the condition of this justification contradicts the sole efficaciousness of divine grace in justification and would make of faith a work.[26]

The high reformatorial pathos of these sentences is, admittedly, called into question when, alongside the statement "On the basis of the sovereignty of the word of God, faith attains its shape in freedom," there also appears the modern, relativising statement "Faith is finally undefinable."

Of all of these expressions of highly respectable theological intention we must for clarification finally ask the simple question: To what degree can the majority of New Testament expressions regarding faith still find a meaningful exegesis in the light of these standards? It is correct that the "Coming of Faith" in Gal 3:23 is described as a reality of salvation history which precedes every human decision, or that Rom 10:17 says that faith comes from proclamation, that Phil 1:29 sees faith as a gift of God and that 1 Cor 12:3 identifies the confession of Jesus as Lord as the work of the Holy Spirit.[27] But precisely faith is never presented by Paul as clearly the work of the Spirit,[28] and the very significance of the word "having faith or believing" in itself ought to forbid our banning every human participation from the concept.[29]

Let us recall our exegetical assertion of faith as the "condition" of justification, while we simultaneously note that it is apparently extremely difficult to hold together in systematic terms, on the one hand, the fundamental priority of the grace of God and, on the other, the call to repentance and to faith, which is, however, equally biblical in its foundation,[30] without finally assigning the decisive role to human beings after all.

Free Grace or Free Will?

The example of George Whitefield and John Wesley, two great evangelists of the eighteenth century, shows that it is possible to hold very different positions in the doctrine of grace and still be involved in similar intensity in evangelistic proclamation. Their lives were bound together at many points. In their common time at Oxford the Wesley brothers were the spiritual leaders of the young Whitefield. But Whitefield was the first from their closer circle who experienced an evangelical conversion, winning assurance of salvation by faith alone. By precept and example he encouraged Wesley to pursue outdoor evangelistic preaching. In contrast to Wesley he had become convinced that only the doctrine of double predestination took proper account of the fact that persons are saved through God's grace alone. Although the two of them had agreed not to carry their dissension into public, Wesley published his sermon "Free Grace" in 1739, in which he vehemently attacked the doctrine of predestination.[31] Whitefield answered with an open letter.[32]

Wesley attacked the doctrine of predestination for two reasons: He considered it totally irreconcilable with he fact that Christ died for all persons and with the will of God as stated in 1 Tim 2:4 that all persons should be saved. Further he could not understand how it is possible to call people to repentance if you know that God has already determined that some come to salvation and the others to damnation. He considered to be "scriptural" only the proclamation of the free grace of God, i.e., grace which is valid for all.

Whitefield's answer to the second question is simple: The proclamation of the Word is the means which God has ordained for calling those whom he has chosen to himself. This is the assignment of evangelistic preaching. The answer to the first question can ultimately be summarized in one point: Only when God is allowed the freedom to determine whom he saves and whom he submits to their just (!) punishment, can it be said that the salvation of human beings comes solely from God and from his grace. Thus he accuses Wesley: "You plainly make salvation depend not on God's free grace, but on men's free will."[33] In that case Christ has died in vain and every proclamation and every invitation to faith in him is in vain.

It is true enough that this accusation does not find its appropriate target in Wesley—at best, only indirectly. For Wesley is no defender of free will. Even the possibility of participation in salvation in an act of will for faith is created by God. It is the work of God's prevenient grace, the light which shines in the darkness. The "free will" of human beings is not natural, but supernatural.[34] The question of why there are people who do not take advantage of this reality which God has set at their disposal remains open; it is, however, clear that persons of faith owe the possibility for believing not to themselves, but to God.

Since Wesley knew from his own experience that assurance of salvation and being a child of God are not the result of a decision of will, but are received as a free gift through the working of the Spirit, he differentiates in his evangelistic and pastoral activity between that which a person can do with God's help and that which remains solely the work of God.[35]

While Wesley clearly felt that progress from the "faith of a servant" to the "faith of a child of God" was necessary for salvation during his early period, at the end of his ministry he was no longer so sure whether human judgment was in a position to draw such distinctions about one's own or others' experiences.[36]

A further important corrective affected a theology fixated on a single and unique conversion experience:[37] Conversion and justification put a person on the way to sanctification. Sanctification is equally a work of grace which molds and perfects the life of a person.[38] In this sense, a purely backward-oriented piety looking only to one's own conversion is made untenable and a forward-looking perspective given which trusts, full of hope, in God's action in one's own life.

Judgment and Decision

Before we attempt to conclusively answer the question which formed the point of departure for this section, we need first to deal with the "negative" aspect of it: To what extent does the rejection of the message bring down judgment and damnation on a person? The theme of judgment, which we have already dealt with exegetically and systematically, reappears here under this special aspect. The alternatives which offer themselves in response to this question can be characterized by two quotations:

> Go into all the world and preach the gospel to all creation. Whoever believes and is baptized will be saved; but whoever does not believe will be damned (Mark 16:16).

> In the face of this the preacher has the opportunity . . . to teach the assembled congregation awe before God, who leaves them absolutely free, demanding nothing, giving them life, joy and mercy—an offer which they can accept or ignore. In this, ignoring the offer is not immediately to be understood as being under punishment, but rather as a genuine chance of the exercise of freedom which God indeed gives us.[39]

Both statements require some clarification. According to the witness of the Bible taken as a whole, the judgment which impinges upon someone who rejects the message is not an additional punishment or sanction which God imposes on lack of faith. The Gospel of John expresses this fact most clearly: "Whoever does not believe is already judged" (3:18). If people do not take the step from darkness into the light, from death into life, and thus remain in the darkness, then God's judgment remains in effect for them and is carried out in their separation from God (3:36). It is then not a question of "imposing punishment" because of ignoring God's offer, but rather a matter of pointing out the consequences which follow from refusal of fellowship with God.

171

Yet it would be too superficial to assume that Stollberg's question is thus dismissed. For he indeed points us to a difficult problem which needs to be solved in the systematic theological exegesis of the New Testament message of grace. Is the message of the salvific action of God in Jesus Christ a limited offer of amnesty which depends upon the acknowledgment of this action and which expires when it is rejected?[40] Or has God effectively propitiated the guilt of humanity on the cross of Jesus, so that it continues to remain evident in the cross what guilt and judgment mean, but the evil which Christ bore can never again fall back on human beings, as if nothing had happened?[41]

This question cannot be easily decided, since both alternatives are true to elements of the New Testament proclamation. Without doubt the salvific message of New Testament proclamation is more than an offer of amnesty. In Jesus' death the sinner has been legally judged and sentenced, the punishment has been meted out, and the presence of the love of God guaranteed even in the abandonment by God which is death. The message of Jesus' death and resurrection speaks of the reality of reconciliation which has occurred in Jesus.

On the other hand, the possible refusal of the human being to respond is neither banned from the world nor simply ignored. In view of what God has done for humankind it is clearly an "impossible possibility" (Karl Barth), but that does not make its frightening reality any less real. The fact that it is precisely the word of the cross which has been a *skandalon*, a snare which causes persons to trip because of their will to self-assertion against God, simply lays bare the true human condition and is seen in the New Testament witness in all its deathly earnestness. The fact that God takes humans seriously in their "no" to God's "yes" can therefore not be ignored in today's message, either. The warning against unhealthy consequences of the rejection of the message or of insisting on remaining undecided ought not to be confused with anxiety-creating threats of punishment (however hard it may be subjectively to draw a clear line of separation between the two, as we could easily demonstrate with examples from strategies of education or preventative medicine).

Yet the preacher will not be able to avoid a final decision on fundamental issues. A proclamation which speaks solely of the love of God, but in the process emphasizes the greatness of the offering and the sacrifice of Christ can seem to threaten or to be paternalistic. Anyone truly wanting to make the love of God known to people will not hesitate to face this accusation. Conversely, an offer which finally remains something which the person addressed may take or leave at liberty can have little significance and little effect. A proclamation which takes God's grace to be of vital importance and decisive for life will not be able to avoid the question of what rejection of the message may mean; rather, it has already implicitly answered this question in a certain sense. Yet it must continue to reflect upon the "asymmetry" of the salvific event and its opposite[42] in Jesus Christ, which is found in the circumstance that there exists no human being for whom it is not permitted to express the assurance that Jesus Christ died for him, that God offers him the hand of reconciliation and accepts him without condition. The possibility of remaining closed to this truth has not thus been glossed over, but is presented in its painful consequence, its veritable "impossibility."

Reprise: By Faith, Therefore By Grace

When we survey the systematic reflection in more recent Protestant theology on the biblical witness regarding conversion and faith, we can recognize a basic tendency. The priority of the salvific action of God before every human response and, thereby, the priority of divine grace over every human action is clearly underlined. Conversion and faith are always a "re-action" of humans to the saving action of God.

However, diverse judgments are made about the theological weight to be given the action of humans in this connection. Wherever fundamental theological reflection takes place, there is hardly room for a synergistic *partim-partim* (in part God acts, in part the human being). Even H. Burkhardt, who follows closely in the heritage of the pietistic-revivalistic school, formulates the thesis thus: "The decision which finds its expression in conversion is not a human accomplishment, but the gift of God."[43] For Burkhardt this assertion in no way frees humans from responsibility, "for (a person) is indeed called to conversion. He may well experience this initially as completely his own agency. He is active in his conversion to the highest degree." "The person definitely experiences his own conversion as a decision of his own will." But in this decision the person recognizes that the decision is nothing other than "a possibility given by an inner renewal, a hidden working of the Spirit of God."[44]

In the act of conversion, therefore, a change of perspective occurs comparable to the Pauline course correction in Gal 4:9: The ones who are called to conversion and faith recognize that God has long since anticipated their human decision and already decided in their favor, and this alone is the basis for their salvation.[45] This holds together the appropriate dialectic of the biblical witness noted previously.

Nevertheless there is a dominant trend in the more recent exegetical and systematic literature which instead emphasizes the full passivity of humans in the process of faith. Although they indeed avoid such coarse expressions as claiming that the human being behaves as a "lump or a stone," yet drawing on Rom 4:5, 17 in content justification by faith is often described (not totally falsely) as *creatio ex nihilo* and thus the human is seen as being "involved in this event neither actively nor passively (!)."[46] So it would appear that the slogan "by faith and thus by grace" has to be taken with radical seriousness, but the price paid is that the original meaning of words like "to have faith, to believe," or "to repent" as active, intransitive verbs can no longer be maintained.[47] The distance between this view and the biblical witness becomes the clearer when we recall that these verbs are frequently used in the imperative in the New Testament, that is, appealing without a doubt for an action or a behavior of human agents.

So we see that we cannot solve this question so easily; rather it is good to recall the word of such a reliable witness as Augustine, whom John Wesley actually quoted: *Qui ergo fecit te sine te, no te justificat sine te* ("The one who created you without your aid will not justify you without your participation").[48] Human beings have gotten involved in God's salvific action in our thinking, feeling, and willing. The tension in the biblical dialectic between the fundamental "pre-" of the grace of God, which itself makes conversion possible, and the responsibility of human beings, whose "yes" or "no" God will not simply overlook, can and must be asserted.

Paul Althaus has appropriately noted that this dialectic is reflected in the distinct metaphors of the terms "new birth" and "conversion":

> One and the same process is called "new birth" inasmuch as it is supposed to describe the work of God in us, and "conversion" in as much as it is reality only in the human act which is grounded in God's activity. We are not, therefore, dealing with two acts which can be arranged one after the other in an "order of salvation," but with one and the same event, a paradoxical unity of a single divine and human deed, but so that the human part is totally based in the divine, both born of it and encompassed by it. We are not referring to a cooperation between God and human persons, but to the activity of God in as far as it determines our will and activity and thus places us into a life where we are responsibile for ourselves.[49]

On this foundation we can make some important basic assertions about the theology and practice of evangelization.

The Call to Reconciliation

Evangelistic proclamation happens like all other missionary endeavors in the trust that God effects faith. That the proclamation "as announcement of God's decision" "calls to decision"[50] appropriately describes the paradoxical, but deeply significant task of evangelization. "Faith," as H. Weder correctly says, "is not a subjective human possibility, not a spiritual activity which I could force myself to do. Faith arises where that which saves appears."[51]

Precisely for this reason the proclamation calls to repentance and to faith, "elicits faith from people," and "provokes," as Jesus did, the response to the saving and helping action of God.[52]

Jesus' parables are both the measure and model for such proclamation, through which he leads his hearers to inner agreement with him with the simultaneously compelling and inviting power of the logic of everyday images and unusual circumstances and empowers them "to make a right decision."[53] It is in this plenipotentiary power that the apostolic word of reconciliation takes place, which bears the message that God has reconciled the world to himself and, at the same time, calls to his hearers with the "authority of the bidding Christ": "Let yourselves be reconciled to God" (2 Cor 5:20).[54]

A proclamation which calls us to the acceptance of salvation, to personal faith, and to concrete repentance with the urgency of the love of Christ, does not once more put the human agent to work, but is a tool to enable God's work on the human being to reach its goal. It is one part of the way which the God who seeks us takes toward us; it is the voice of the one who calls the lost in order to find them.[55]

Liberation to Repentance and Faith

Evangelistic proclamation is therefore nothing else than such a provocation to a response, an invitation to agreement and an urgent petition to reconciliation. Its aim is that its hearers accept God's saving activity as the reality which shapes and determines their lives. As the voice of the bidding Christ it assumes that we have the freedom of decision.

That people would dare to open their empty hands and allow them to be filled by God is not their own accomplishment; God's giving hand which even now is truly stretched out to them in the proclamation of the gospel, effects it. And yet it is an act to which they must be called and encouraged: letting go of the ideological straws they grasp at, letting go of the perishable possessions—whether material or philosophical—to which they so desperately cling, to relax the fist clenched in impotent rage, and to draw near to God's outreached hand.[56] In as much as the proclamation of Jesus Christ tells people that they are reconciled and justified in Christ, it shows them the basis and the foundation of faith and calls them simultaneously to take their stance full of trust on this foundation and to base their lives in Jesus Christ.[57]

In evangelization in accord with the gospel the call to faith is, thus, simultaneously the opening of faith and the liberation to conversion. This does not mean that such a proclamation need not speak of the danger in which a person stands without God, the danger of losing his life and

175

succumbing to death. But where urgently petitioning love sets the tone this will never become an anxiety-producing threat, but only and always a deeply concerned warning.

The Variety and Unity of Faith

How persons are reached by the message and how they articulate their affirmation of it is described in the New Testament in manifold ways. Here we find reports of persons who by virtue of unavoidable necessity have been overcome by God, as for example Paul or Cornelius and his people; then there are those who have recognized the defect of their lives by virtue of the confrontation with God's wondrous activity and who have then been shown the way into discipleship and faith, as, for example, Peter (cf. Luke 5:1-11) or the prison warden in Philippi; or there are those for whom hearing the word of Scripture and its exposition so opens their hearts that they become convinced of the truth of the gospel, e.g., the Ethiopian eunuch or Lydia of Philippi.

All these reports have two things in common, however: They tell how God and his word work on or in a person and how this effects the consciousness and the action of the person in question. Paul, overcome by the appearance of the resurrected Christ, makes clear decisions about his own self-understanding (cf. Phil 3:7-11) and Lydia, whose heart God has opened so that she can pay heed to what Paul says, demands that her faith be acknowledged. Wherever God's word reaches its objective, this cannot remain unnoticed—not for the person in question, nor for his or her fellows. Or, to quote John Wesley, "None is a true Christian 'till he experiences it."[58]

There are two points at which the New Testament nails down this experience: profession of faith and baptism. What we have traditionally called the confession of faith is in turn two elements, according to Rom 10:9: the publicly spoken acclamation "Jesus is Lord," with which a person places him-or herself in a legally binding way under the lordship of the *Kyrios*, and that conviction which reaches into the innermost part of a person which sees that in Jesus' resurrection God's creative power has overcome the reign of sin and of death.[59]

It is extremely important to Paul to show that this faith and this profession is nothing which is demanded out of a person's own capacity, nothing which must be sought for at great distance. "The word of faith which we preach" is near to human persons; it has been put in their mouth and into their heart, and is thus also much more than a subjective conviction of the persons of faith, namely the expression of the reality into which they have been placed.

176

It is thus no accident that we lack any formal definition of this act of confession of faith.[60] Nevertheless it is totally unambiguous: The goal of proclamation is the personal affirmation of a person through which he or she makes the message his or her own, lets his or her life be "founded" in God's salvific activity and entrusts him- or herself to the reign of the resurrected Lord.

Even today this affirmative response can take various forms. The profound and far-reaching change of life of a drug addict and the in-breaking of grace into the life of an official who is caught by his own self-righteousness; the quiet infusion of the message by a terminally ill patient and the experience of acceptance by God which a single mother has in the supportive and encouraging fellowship of Christians; the public affirmation which has been provoked by the call of the evangelist to decision and which ends the long search for the right path; or even the liberating recognition that one need not be converted (according to some particular pattern), but may simply live on the basis of God's affirmation of the sinner—all these are forms in which God's grace reaches people and in which a profession of faith can find expression.[61] It is not the form which is decisive: The dramatic conversion of some prominent sinner as reported on television or in the newspaper is in no way more worthy than the private, silent, acquiescent nod of someone near death. What is decisive is the content of the event: God touches the life of someone in such a way that a personal experience and confession result. In the "yes" of the beloved, God's love attains its goal.

The New Testament expression for the fact that it is less the human agent who is effecting the acceptance of the message than it is God who is acting upon that human recipient is baptism. Christians let themselves be baptized and are reminded what God has done for them in baptism. In missionary situations where the message of the gospel encounters people for the first time, where they come to faith and are baptized, the sequence and relationship of faith and baptism are clearest. Where children grow up in Christian families and congregations and live, with greater or lesser awareness, within the framework of faith during their childhood and youth, this sequence and becomes more difficult. For even in congregations where the normal practice of infant baptism, which reaches back at least as far as the fourth century, has been rejected, the question still remains: Can the church baptize children on the basis of a desire for baptism which grows out of childhood faith, or must the church wait for a particular sort of conversion experience?[62]

Here we are helped by our recognition that New Testament evidence indicates that faith and baptism always stand in a relationship to one another, but are never identified with one another.[63] Thus under certain circumstances infant baptism can be a legitimate expression of prevenient grace and the "pre-" of the indicative of God's salvific activity in human persons, and in this manner it can raise the question of faith for the one being baptized and elicit from him or her a personal "yes" to God's acceptance.[64]

The opposite may also be true—that baptism reminds the person who is baptized following a confession of faith that it is not his or her confession which saves, but that whereon he or she believes: Christ died for our sins.[65]

The answer "I have been baptized" to the gospel's question about a person's faith can, as with Luther, be synonymous with the decisive "yes" to the message of grace and the profession to want to live only from that which God would provide. But it can also mean—and this is the way the evangelization movement has repeatedly experienced it—a diverting of the claim of grace from the life of the baptizand by reference to the legalistically fulfilled ritual. The recollection of baptism by itself cannot fully encompass the content and the intention of the New Testament call to conversion and to faith.[66] The question of the personal attitude to that which has happened to the baptizand cannot be left out of the equation. Wherever this question is raised in a manner appropriate to the gospel message it will make clear that I, through the question, only accept what God in Christ has done for me and attributes to me (or has already granted me) in the act of baptism.

The Singularity and Necessity of Conversion

It is at this point that most systematicians diverge most obviously from the witness of the New Testament. Whereas in the New Testament, as a rule, conversion and coming to faith appear as clearly recognizable biographical moments which separate "then" and "now," contemporary theologians would rather warn us not to share this point of view, unless we are dealing with a clear context of mission to the "heathen." They emphasize much more strongly, with Luther's first thesis—which admittedly was formulated in a totally different context—that conversion means practicing daily repentance.[67]

Althaus asserts provocatively, "In contrast to the pietistic law of a singular and particular conversion we admit readily to being 'unconverted,' i.e., as those who need to be converted daily."[68] So we see the reservations clearly noted: There is concern that a particular experience of conversion will be demanded and that this experience will serve as the foundation for assurance of salvation.

G. Ebeling, who also points out this aspect of the matter, does, however, note that in the metaphor of "new birth" it is a singular process which is being addressed. "The significance of new birth is intended to be just as absolutely once and for all as is the event of birth itself."[69] Corresponding to this is the non-repeatability of Christian baptism. "The question of

178

whether subjectively a singular biographical turning, the singularity of conversion, corresponds to the objective event of baptism, is open to debate."[70] But Ebeling does not, therefore, avoid the issue by asserting that new birth has already taken place in baptism, but he speaks rather of a "fundamental change" in the life of persons in which the old creature without salvation becomes the redeemed new creature.

Theologically it is absolutely essential to hold fast to this point. The affirmation of the gospel is valid for the whole person; the appeal "let yourselves be reconciled with God" is aimed at the complete "yes" of persons and, in the light of the urgent proximity of the reign of God, the call to conversion aims at the immediate and unconditional human decision. The goal of the proclamation of the gospel is basically to arrive at consistent and decisive commitment to God. This is just as true for the "church's internal situation" as for the "missionary situation." It is, however, necessary to lend this fundamental theological statement greater precision in three respects:

(1) Even what has to be asserted as theologically fundamental may unfold variously in the reality of human life and may and must not be formed into any sort of biographical law. Turning to God and the acceptance and reception of the good news for one's own life can take place in one longer process of growth or in several chronologically non-contiguous experiences of radical change. The feared question of some Christians about which one may have been their "real" conversion is misplaced. It is part of the essence of the concept of conversion that it is not the method of the change, but the path into the right direction which is decisive. Therefore the question of the necessity of a conscious decision is to be subordinated to the question of the necessity of intentional fellowship with God in faith in Jesus Christ. Wherever this fellowship with God does not constitute the load-bearing foundation of life—whether in the person raised a Christian or in a non-Christian—turning to God is necessary to "turn aside" the "need" of life [German: *Not-wendig*].[71]

(2) From this first point follows a second: Conversion and coming to faith are the beginning of a journey. This is the journey of a life filled with love by God and led by this love, the direction of which is marked by the assignment with which Jesus has sent us to our fellow humans and the destination of which lies in perfected fellowship with God in eternity. To remember this beginning can occasionally be of significance when it is a matter of reflecting upon that which has determined our journey from its origins. But perpetually to return in thought and feeling to this point of departure or, indeed, to make it a permanent resting place, would be to turn the meaning of conversion into its opposite. Without birth there can be no life, but life which persists in the newborn stage would hardly be more than vegetating.

(3) Yet we must clearly point out the limits of this image. The life of a new creature in Christ is always threatened by the possibility of falling back into the previous existence. Although there is no such thing as the static dialectic of *simul iustus, simul peccator* in the New Testament,[72] there is still the awareness of the need to constantly admonish all those who have "put on Jesus Christ" to lay aside their old being and put on the new.[73] The fundamental insight into the singularity of turning to Christ dare not be, at this point, the Procrustean bed into which we force the often much more complicated biographical reality; but it can offer a line of orientation to which we look in time of crisis for life and faith. It is no accident that Paul, when he talks of the necessity of preserving and maintaining the Christian on their journey to their destination, always starts at the beginning of the journey; assuredly, he does not speak of the beginning which a person has made, but rather of the "good work which God has begun" in us, which he will also perfect (Phil 1:6; 1 Cor 1:8ff.).

The Broader Horizon

As regards what has been considered in chapters four and five, the individual stands sharply in the foreground. This could be criticized as an individualistically narrow view. In this regard we need to keep in mind two further points of view.

First, we must remember that the perceived narrowness is first and foremost a limitation for the purpose of definition. We have been looking at evangelistic proclamation as the form of missionary activity which most especially speaks to individuals and their personal lives. This does not exclude us from also considering other areas and dimensions of human life as the goal of our missionary assignment.

Second, despite all justifiable criticism of Western individualism, we need not be ashamed to assert that one dimension of God's activity toward human beings is the salvation and redemption of the individual, of the particular person, unique in history and fate,[74] to whom God promises his love and mercy. The gospel speaks to me in the depths of my existence, God accepts me just as I am with my guilt, my fears and anxieties, and my suffering, takes me into his protecting hand and fills my heart with his love. The fact that a person can avow this so very personally is one of the most precious treasures which the gospel has to offer, and it should not be maligned or despised.

Yet a one-dimensional Christian existence would be flat, without a firm stance, and impotent. Therefore, let us here mention the other three dimensions which open themselves to those who have been touched by the gospel and which encompass the broader horizon of life with God.

180

(1) For the person whose eyes and ears God has opened to the gospel, God also opens God's own being in the endless richness of his grace. All those who allow themselves to be introduced to the praise of the God of grace gain a perspective for the perfection of God's reign in which God becomes "all in all" (cf. 1 Cor 15:28; Rom 11:33-36). This protects us from making our own experience of salvation and our own redemption the center of all salvation history. Numerous hymns of Charles Wesley could teach us how to make the praise of the all-encompassing grace of God and gratitude for personal redemption the basis and motivation for evangelistic proclamation.

(2) All those who have been put into the effective sphere of the death and resurrection of Jesus Christ by the grace of God discover themselves thereby to be in the midst of the fellowship of the Body of Christ. The church of Jesus Christ is not a club of like-minded persons, but the fellowship of sisters and brothers that is constituted by Jesus' death. Characteristic of them is, therefore, not the uniformity of their experiences of faith and their gifts, but the cooperation of manifold charisms for the common good. All who live from grace can be gracious to one another and offer one another mutual acceptance, just as Christ has accepted them (Rom 15:7).[75]

(3) Whoever truly hears the message of God's salvific activity in Jesus Christ will not fail to hear that the extent of this message and of the salvific activity of God which they proclaim is as wide as the world. "God so loved the world" (John 3:16) or "God was reconciling the world to himself" (2 Cor 5:18)—in this or like manner important fundamental expressions of the New Testament proclamation formulate the goal of God's salvific action. It is into this horizon that the person of faith is drawn. Conversion and faith happen very personally, but they never remain private.[76] The prototypical case is the calling of Paul. Corresponding to the radicality of the grace which he personally experiences as a reorientation of all his values, there is the universality of the message entrusted to him. The more intensively someone experiences "God for me," the clearer "God for you" will appear to him or her.[77] The brothers and sisters for whom Christ died are not all to be found in the congregation, the church; there are those people in distress to whom Jesus takes us on his way to the poor and the rejected.

The "second conversion to the world" that is often mentioned among followers of Bonhoeffer can, at best, be a construct to help us see both sides of the issue. Strictly spoken, our turning to the world is already included in our conversion to God, because it is conversion to the God who saves the world through his love. Anyone who is redeemed from self-justification, self-pity, and self-doubt will gain unencumbered vision and unfettered hands for the people round about him or her.[78]

181

Chapter 6

Conversion and Life History: Biographical, Psychological, and Sociological Aspects

How does the call to conversion and reconciliation show itself in the lives of individuals? What effect does it have in a life story affected by many influences and what does it actually cause? In light of these critical questions we need to go beyond our biblical evidence in a sort of "cross-check" to inquire of the significance of conversion and preaching for conversion for the biography of individual persons. In so doing we shall take special note of psychological and sociological aspects.

Here again we are immediately confronted with the question of the definition of concepts. "Conversion" in the sense of phenomenology of religion has a much more comprehensive meaning than the biblical concept upon which it is based. It denotes not only the decision for a change of direction, but every experience of religious (or philosophical) nature which leads to a profound new orientation and renewed foundation of personal life.[1]

In the Christian realm this experience has always appeared in two different forms which A. D. Nock describes as follows:

> The turning back to a tradition generally held and characteristic of society as a whole, a tradition in which the convert was himself reared but which he has left in skepticism or indifference of violent self-assertion; and the turning away to an unfamiliar form of piety either from a familiar form or from indifference.[2]

Various suggestions have been made to differentiate these two forms with different concepts, e.g., R. Travisiano's suggestion that the first form be called "alternation" and only the second "conversion."[3] But, as Nock notes, there is such a fluid border between the two forms that such a differentiation could never establish itself.[4]

183

Paradigms of Church History

We are familiar with a number of conversion experiences from church history—experiences which have become paradigmatic because of their great consequences for the church. They have been publicized in very obvious places in autobiographical documents and have had long-lasting effect, both by virtue of this publication but also by virtue of the life's work of those named.[5] For our study let us outline briefly the conversion experiences of Augustine (354–430), August Hermann Francke (1663–1727), John Wesley (1703–91), and Paul Claudel (1868–1955).[6]

Augustine's decisive life change[7] took place when he was thirty-one years old and was the end of a crisis of meaning of longer duration which had already led to a theoretical affirmation of Christianity, but which had finally been frustrated by Augustine's inability to truly live a Christian life, i.e., to master his own compulsions. The final step took place as he read in Rom 13:13 of a divine, personally understood calling to a life in accord with the will of God (i.e., in chastity and abstinence), which bore within itself the power for its own realization. For Augustine this meant an existential concretization of the theoretically acknowledged truth of Christianity.

August Hermann Francke[8] was suddenly overcome by radical doubts in God's existence while preparing a sermon on John 20:31 at the age of twenty-four after eight years of theological studies which had been marked by a search for the true Christian life. After days of profound struggle he appealed to God in prayer, "whom I do not yet know nor trust," and "as in the turn of the hand, all my doubts were gone, I was assured in my heart of the grace of God in Jesus Christ, I could not only call God 'God' but 'my Father' as well."

John Wesley[9] had already turned to a life of intentional Christianity on the occasion of his ordination as a deacon in 1725. Experiences on the sea passage to Georgia and as a parish priest in the colony there—a ministry he experienced as a great personal failure in many ways—threw him into a deep crisis and left him doubting his previous Christian life, based on personal piety. After his return from Georgia, the Moravian Peter Böhler convinced him that according to the witness of Holy Scripture justification could come only from faith, and that such faith is given to a person in an instant. But it was only in hearing the reading of Luther's Preface to the Epistle to the Romans in a small religious assembly that he concluded: "I felt I did trust in Christ, Christ alone for salvation, and an assurance was given me that he had taken away *my* sins, even *mine*, and saved *me* from the law of sin and death."

If the "conversion" of all these so far named was the end of a long searching for God and for the assurance of salvation, the case of Claudel[10] was rather the opposite. As an eighteen-year-old agnostic, out of pure curiosity, he attended the Christmas mass in Notre Dame.

> In a moment my heart was taken, I *believed*. I believed with such a powerful inward affirmation—as if my whole life were being ripped upward—I believed with such a strong conviction, with such undescribable certainty that no place was left open for even the slightest doubt . . . It is true! God exists, he is there! There is someone, a being with personality like me. He loves me and he calls me.

There followed upon this experience a four-year struggle between the philosophical convictions of the young Claudel and the truth which he had encountered through this experience and which he found affirmed in the Bible.

As different as these experiences appear to be in detail, they have some important common characteristics:

(1) In no case is the "conversion" triggered directly by a sermon (aimed, for example, at decision).[11] But in the background—with the possible exception of Claudel—there lies a theoretical knowledge of the promise of the biblical message.

(2) In no case does the personal decision, one's own deciding, stand at the center of the experience. The fact that it is God who grants the assurance is so strongly in the foreground that some have expressed doubt that we should call this kind of faith experience "conversion" at all.[12]

(3) The experience of new life given by God effects a fully negative judgment upon the previous course of life.[13]

(4) Although the affected were fully aware of the exceptional quality of their experience and the gift-character of the faith based upon it, the call to personal faith becomes a central emphasis for all of them in their further proclamation. This is true, of course, especially for August Hermann Francke, who founded the "conversion theology" of Pietism,[14] and for John Wesley, who, for a longer time, viewed the experience of a faith assured of its salvation as essential to that salvation itself.[15] But it is also true for Augustine, as evidenced by the significant role which the theme of conversion plays in his work on catechisms,[16] as well as for Claudel, who was active in evangelistic work especially among artists.[17]

Conversion as a Phenomenon of Adolescence

How strongly the work of Francke, Wesley, Whitefield, and others has led to a unique significance being attributed to conversion in church history may be seen in the first studies of the psychology of religion. E. D. Starbuck published his book *The Psychology of Religion: An Empirical Study of the*

Growth of Religious Consciousness in 1899 (third edition, 1911); more than half of it was dedicated to the phenomenon of conversion. In his empirical studies he observed that, statistically seen, conversion had become a phenomenon of adolescence. The frequency curve showed a steep peak for male subjects at 16 years, and at 13 and 16 for the females. Social pressure is named to no small degree among the motivations for conversion. This is truly no surprise since the study took its subjects primarily from Baptist and Methodist students at the end of the nineteenth century in the U.S.A., i.e., shortly before the peak of the Second Great Awakening with its "revival meetings." The pressure of the masses was so great because in the Protestantism of revival "conversion . . . often has become a ritual of initiation with a set pattern of behavior on the part of the so-called convert and the members of the congregation."[18]

Starbuck did not, however, see this as a negative development, but noted that, for those who experience conversion, in comparison with other youth who do not, conversion was an acute phase of the search for meaning in adolescence which achieved in the shortest time what the others without conversion could achieve only through a longer phase of development.

The interviews which Hans Leitner carried out in a Methodist youth group in Leipzig in 1928 give intensive insights into such a youth "culture" of conversion.[19] The sociological analysis of Billy Graham events of the 1960s led to similar conclusions. Among those who went forward for decision, teenagers from middle-class, church families were over-represented, which led the researchers to the assertion that "normal conversion" was a "socially programmed event."[20]

We ought to be careful not to judge these phenomena totally negatively. Erik H. Erikson characterized the time of adolescence with the key words "identity vs. role confusion," which corresponds to Fowler's stage of "synthetic-conventional faith."[21] Both point out how important it is for this age-level to attain to a self-worth and a world view which is in definite consonance with an accepting and accepted group. So it is that in the United States the discipline of religious education as influenced by developmental psychology has demanded that the role of conversion for a mature Christian faith not be underestimated. Conversion so understood is "a significant aspect of a long process in the growth and maturation of faith by Christians with the Christian family" or, in other words, "a radical turning from 'faith given' (through nurture) to 'faith owned' (through conversion)."[22]

Regression and Progression

At the beginning of the twentieth century, the discipline of the psychology of religion was interested, although not solely, in the evangelical, statistically measurable, "normal conversion." More attractive was that which the Anglo-Saxons tend to call the "mystical conversion," for which Paul's conversion is the prototype. William James dedicated his research to this form of conversion above all, and attempted to clarify its genesis with all its extraordinary peripheral displays from the presence of unconscious psychic processes.[23] He did not understand this psychological explanation as a substitute for the theological one, but as a supplement to it.

The matter was different for Sigmund Freud, who was convinced of his ability to identify the underlying, unconscious processes much more precisely. In a short study he explained a conversion experience which someone had reported to him as a religious disguise of an underlying Oedipal conflict.[24] Erik Erikson's *Young Man Luther*[25] picked up the train of thought, viewing the crisis-filled religious development of the young Luther as a confrontation with Luther's image of his father and with authority, further enhancing the psychoanalytical approach with the social-psychological aspect; alongside the Oedipal conflict was the open conflict with authority with which Luther had to deal. Erikson expanded on Freud, seeing the religious confrontation with conflict not as a dislocation or dismissal of conflict, but as genuine coming to terms with conflict.

Psychoanalytically trained eyes have naturally not been blind to the fact that certain other famous "converts," e.g., Augustine and Wesley, exhibited a marked attachment to their mothers, whereas the role of their fathers was more residual.[26] J. Allison identified a similar constellation in a study of students at two Methodist theological seminaries in the United States.[27] In a comparison of one group of students who reported a strong conversion experience with a control group which did not, there was evidence to a significantly high degree of a weak father figure and a mother experienced as ambivalent—simultaneously attractive and smothering. In turning to God a helpful father-attachment occurs in whose protection the criticism of one's own father can be ended—thus stabilizing and limiting the relationship to one's mother as well, so that a fruitful dealing with issues at conscious and subconscious levels becomes possible. Here we find, empirically documented, the therapeutic character of a psychological "regression" triggered by a conversion or new birth.[28]

"Drift," "Brainwashing," or the Search for Meaning

All of these observations make it clear that persons in the process of conversion are dealing not only with themselves (and their God). In his book *Religion and the Roles* H. Sundén was the first to make this approach the basis for a comprehensive theory of conversion in the light of the psychology of religion.[29] He called attention to the fact that an orientation to a new

187

meaning always has a social side and that conversion often means a change of roles.

This theme comes to the forefront of American sociological research toward the end of the sixties and the beginning of the seventies in light of the rise of the Jesus movement and the so-called youth religions. A vigorous debate over the degree to which conversions in this arena may be viewed as the result of a kind of "brainwashing," i.e., a massive, psychological re-education, whether the cause may rather be a "drifting" due to personal problems or whether the decisive motivation was the convert's active search for new offers of meaning, found expression in a plethora of empirical research and theoretical studies.[30]

Additionally we have important individual observations regarding the "conversion careers" of many young people who found their way from middle-class homes into the protest movement and the drug scene before experiencing a religious conversion to groups of the Jesus movement or one of the new religions.[31] A further study found wide recognition which showed how much, in the case of the Jehovah's Witnesses, for example, conversion reports (and experiences!?) are molded by the expectations of the receiving group.[32]

In the last few years attempts have been made to develop integrative concepts from the very divergent observations, studies, and research approaches. So it was that Lofland and Skonovd put together a list of six "conversion motives,"[33] to which they assign various degrees of social pressure, temporal duration, and emotional excitement, various emotions, and diverse sequences of acceptance of faith convictions and participation in the life of the new religious group.

They distinguish between the following types of conversion: "intellectual" (the seeker after God), "mystical" (surprised by God, e.g., St. Paul or Claudel), "experimental" (those who "try out" a new religious socialization), "affectional" (who are attracted by the warmth of a fellowship), "revivalist" (the less frequent dramatic conversion under the influence of suggestive proclamation and the group experience), and "coercive" ("brainwashing" under extreme force).

B. Kilbourne and J. T. Richardson describe the various types even more disparately.[34] They assign eleven individual types (in part identical with those of Lofland and Skonovd) into four fundamental groups which are constituted by the coordinates active-passive or intrapersonal-interpersonal.

It is important to note that these types do not necessarily indicate different experiences of conversion, but perhaps only reflect different aspects of their research. The authors see in conversion a particular form of socialization which distinguishes itself from others by virtue of "the local emphasis on self-change (e.g., a change in world view) in a religious or quasi-religious setting and the kind of social audience reaction to that self-change."[35]

Of special interest for us in this connection is the question of how close the conversions of the revival meetings or the so-called "new religions," with their origins under massive emotional stress, come to the so-called forced conversions. Although the authors see the lack of external force as the decisive distinguishing characteristic,[36] in his much discussed book *Battle for the Mind*, W. Sargant had already compared the conversion methods of revivalist preachers like Jonathan Edwards or John Wesley with the brainwashing of a Communist prisoner-of-war camp.[37] In all the excitement surrounding the issue, it has often been overlooked that he also placed the treatment of war neuroses by means of hypnosis or insulin-shock in the same context, i.e., he assigned them a therapeutic role under strict indications of deprogramming through physical or psychological stress of an otherwise unmanageable past. This calls to mind the relatively high success rates of invasive methods of conversion practiced by fundamentalistic groups among drug addicts. Kilbourne and Richardson therefore make the suggestion "to conceptualize the so-called brainwashing procedure . . . as a form of ideology healing."[38] It is, however, to be feared that such "healing" will not lead to true liberation, but to new dependencies. The danger of becoming allergic or immune to the Christian message by such methods may, in any case, not be overlooked.

Development of Faith and Conversion

In his highly respected work *Stages of Faith* (1981) J. Fowler described six stages in which the development of the religious and philosophical attitude of a person occurs. Following the early childhood phase of an undifferentiated "faith" in the mother-child symbiosis there comes first the stage of "intuitive-projective" faith, followed by "mythical-literal" faith (in primary school age), then "synthetic-conventional" faith (in puberty and early adolescence), "individuative-reflective" faith (in the young adult years), "conjunctive" faith (often achieved at mid-life or old age), and "universalizing" faith (the ideal goal of "self founded in God" which is seldom achieved).

This is not the place to elaborate and discuss these stages. Yet it is important for our context that Fowler dedicates a major portion of his work to the phenomenon of conversion.[39] He points out that "conversion" can be either the change of the content of faith convictions within a given stage of development (most especially the third) or a step from one to another in connection with an existential crisis—or both at once. In so doing, Fowler arrives at a very sophisticated understanding of the phenomenon of "conversion" which can help, for example, to recognize and evaluate the possibilities and the limits of a conversion dating to youthful years and to nurture further development to a mature faith. The actual theological aspect does, however, take a subordinate role in Fowler.[40]

Identity Through New Beginning

In his novel *Stiller*, which circles around the problem of the flight of a man from himself and his longing to be someone else, Max Frisch has his protagonist write down the following lines:

> With the clear recognition that I am a totally insignificant and inessential human being, I nevertheless keep hoping that I am, precisely by virtue of this insight, no longer insignificant and worthless after all. Basically, in all honesty, I still hope in all things for transformation, for flight. I am simply not willing to be insignificant. I actually only hope that God (if I should encounter him) would make me into a different—a richer, profounder, more worthy and significant—personality. Therein lies, most likely, that which prevents God from appearing as a true existence to my presence, i.e., to become experience-able. For my *conditio sine qua non* is that he should repeal me, his creation.[41]

In these words we have both a psychological and a theological problem described: What does the conviction of being a new creation in Christ mean for our relationship to our "old man," i.e., to our past? Is the past obliterated (and perhaps thereby, from a psychological point of view suppressed) or is the secret of the new existence to be found in the unconditional acceptance of the old by God?

Gremmels has written an essay with the rather daring title "Self-reflexive Interpretation of Conflicting Identifications as in the Example of the Apostle Paul (Phil 3:7-9),"[42] in which, against the background of the sharp contrast between Paul's old and the new self-understandings in current Pauline exegesis, he strongly underlines the question, "whether, in the light of the soteriological change of status connected with faith, the putting off of the 'old person' by the 'new person' should be understood as an eliminative or a re-interpretative process."[43] He himself answers this question in saying "that the 'new person' is determined by the progressive acceptance of the 'old person' in re-interpretative acquisition, which means, under one aspect of identity theory, that the expression 'killed' may not be misunderstood as the 'throwing off' of older identifications."

Indeed G. Theissen has made it seem probable that the tension between the self-presentation of Paul in Phil 3:7–9 and the "I-report" in Rom 7:7-21 are explicable by the fact that in Romans 7 the processing of a subconscious legal conflict is evident.[44] D. Stollberg and D. Lührmann have demonstrated in a very penetrating exegetical and psychoanalytical interpretation of Gal 2:20 how ego loss and identity gain are interlaced in Paul's encounter with Christ.[45] I consider it extraordinarily important that the proclamation of the new existence in Christ know of this profound dimension of human life.

It would be worth considering what significance the promise and the necessity of a new beginning in Christ have for the psycho-structural character formation of persons as described by F. Riemann.[46] For the "hysterical" types the offer of new beginning is itself the great possibility; these people need it and must yet learn at the same time that life (with Christ) is more than a chain of new beginnings. The "depressive" types will agree from the depths of their heart that they must become someone different; they would like to convert—but they cannot. They need the insistent promise of acceptance of their lives by God which applies—without any psychic "high" on their part. The "compulsive" types have ordered their lives and erected their security systems; only in the destruction of their protective houses will the call and the offer of a fully new beginning reach them. The "schizoid" persons, on the other hand, need the non-pressuring warmth of the love of God which allows them time and space to believe that God's mercy applies especially to them in their highly scrupled self-limitation.

These characterizations ought not to mislead us to adjust the proclamation "according to prescription" for the various human types. On the other hand, it should lead us to take care not to "make too much" of evangelistic preaching. Anyone wishing to break down the fortress of compulsiveness, would first destroy the depressive inwardly; mediate, perhaps, a masochistic lust-experience to the hysterical; and scare off the schizoid. We ought not and cannot "make" the message be accepted. It is our task to proclaim the message of reconciliation clearly and always keep in mind how different the people are to whom we deliver it—in full confidence that it is valid for all. In our pastoral work our knowledge of psychological differentiation will, however, be extremely useful.

Consequences

And thus we have arrived at the question of the significance of this confusing myriad of points of view from the humanities and social sciences for theologians and preachers. I will attempt to summarize this in a few short theses:

(1) "Conversion" as a fundamental change of life is a phenomenon of human existence which is not limited to the Christian sphere. It corresponds to the human longing for fully new beginnings and for a changed existence

which is based on a new identity. In this regard it is not only the (alleged) human possibility for making decisions and beginning anew on one's own power which are in view, but precisely that new beginning which is granted from outside us, which transcends our own possibilities.

(2) Every fundamental change of life occurs—as does everything else human—in an interweaving of intra- and interpersonal causes, conditioning and consequences. Social sciences describe various dimensions of this happening, but offer no complete explanation for it. God's activity takes place in the immediate, immanent context of life, and simultaneously transcends it.[47]

(3) Extraordinary conversion experiences have been understood in the arena of Christian tradition as examples and paradigms of divine action.[48] The fact that they are retold and passed on is an encouraging witness to the possibility of new beginning which God grants fundamentally to every person.[49] Where these are made to be binding models of behavior, they seduce us to accept simulations or become repulsing, legalistic demands upon us.[50]

(4) A sudden and marked conversion is not the only form of the life-determining effectiveness of the grace of God. We must take into account that there are character types for whom such a possibility is rather more distant but who, nevertheless, will be able to reach a decisive turn of life in their own way on the basis of the gospel. But take care! The Spirit moves where it will and statistical divisions can be totally meaningless for the individual case (not only "hysterical" types can convert!).

(5) Therefore this important reminder is in order: The call to conversion and the invitation to reconciliation is based solely in the message of the gospel. We proclaim neither psychograms nor socialization models, but Jesus Christ as "God for us." It is good to know something about the psychic and social contexts. For it helps us to understand people better, offers us possibilities to support and nurture them, makes us aware of dangers of manipulative or counterproductive behavior and should therefore be an admonition, especially for the theologians, to find their way back to the core of their message and, with all that knowledge about humankind in mind, to search for God's saving word for men and women.

Chapter 7

Motivation and Method:
Why and How to Evangelize

Internal and External Motivation

Evangelization seems to be the need of the moment. In rare show of unity Pope John Paul II and the Lausanne Movement, the Anglican Lambeth Conference and the United Methodist Church exhort us to special evangelistic efforts in the last decade of the millennium.[1] What are the motives? Concern about diminishing influence of the churches, strengthened by a fascination with the imminent turn of the millennium? Concern for people who might be lost without the saving message? What kind of motivation is necessary that it may not stop at such appeals, but that missionary attitudes and evangelistic involvement may grow at the level of the local church and in the life of individual Christians?

If we cast a look into the New Testament we will see that the motivation there can be described in manifold ways. Even in the short passage of 1 Cor 9:16-23 Paul mentions a whole series of motives for his missionary activity. According to v. 16 the task of preaching the gospel is a divine imperative which has been laid upon his life; in vv. 19-22a he turns his attention to various groups of people as if he were one of them in order to "win" them, and in v.22b all this happens in order to "save" at least a few. In summation he says (in v. 23), "All this I do for the sake of the gospel in order to participate [together with others] in it."

Among the motives Paul mentions—it should not be difficult for us to recognize—is the fundamental motivation upon which the call to missionary activity is based both in the New Testament and in today's world. Let us present them briefly, question their significance for today, and above all seek to understand their rationale so that the biblical instructions (or ecclesial necessities!) which come to us from outside might also become the inward consequence of a life proceeding from the gospel.

Obedience to the Assignment

What Paul experienced as an unavoidable divine imperative over his life—the assignment to missionary proclamation—was, according to the conviction of the primitive Christian church, the mandate of the resurrected Lord to all his disciples. The mission command of Jesus in Matt 28:16-20—in the Anglo-Saxon tradition referred to very emphatically as "The Great Commission"—in many missiological publications remains to this day the most important element of motivating missionary paraenesis, although reservations are also heard against a biblicistic foundation of mission on an "order."[2]

In fact the mission assignment of Jesus to the "eleven" applied, according to conviction of the Evangelists as well, not only to the narrow circle, but "to the whole successive Jesus-congregation."[3] This congregation realized the assignment outwardly primarily through its wandering apostles.[4] The remarkable thing is, admittedly, that the whole early church was convinced that this commission was intended only for the circle of the first apostles, which had in turn missionized the whole *Oikumene*—the whole known world.[5]

This conviction may well be caused in part by the fact that the letters of the New Testament contain practically no missionary teaching. Nowhere do we find admonishment to the congregation and their members to actively carry forth the good news.[6] The congregation was missionary in its effect simply by virtue of its existence. In "all the world" they talk of their faith (Rom 1:8; 1 Thess 1:8); the congregation is to be "a letter of Christ . . . acknowledged and read by all people" (2 Cor 3:2f.).

Corresponding to this are the words of the synoptic tradition which promise disciples, "You are the salt of the earth . . . you are the light of the world (Matt 5:13).[7] Even here the talk is at first strongly indicative: "The city built on a hill cannot remain hidden." And yet a question arises in these words of Jesus: What happens if salt becomes ineffective and light is hidden under a basket? Can salt become saltless? This seems impossible. Can God's congregation become ineffective? Obviously there are impossible possibilities, the dangers of which Jesus' admonition reveals.

Thus it is that the imperatives of Jesus' words of commission continually remind his disciples of the fact that missionary activity is not a matter of their discretion. Neither do they describe some assignments among others. They establish that the commission is part of the very essence of the congregation.[8]

The Inner Compulsion

The most beautiful expression for the inner necessity for missionary proclamation is found in Peter's words in Acts 4:20: "We cannot keep from speaking about what we have seen and heard." One's own experience provides the unavoidable urge to communicate the message of God's

194

salvific action in Christ. Many who were healed by Jesus behaved accordingly: They made public—often despite an explicit prohibition to do so—what Jesus had done for them (Mark 1:45; 5:19f.; 7:36). It is the same with the content of Paul's justification of his missionary activity in Rom 1:14-17: He is under obligation to share with all people the message of salvation which has touched him personally in his encounter with Christ. So it is that for him the urgent command of the Lord Jesus Christ (the *ananke* of 1 Cor 9:16) and his inner urge to preach are one.[9]

D. T. Niles has summarized in an oft-quoted phrase: Evangelization means one beggar telling another where to find bread. It is precisely at this point the question arises why this happens so little. Often enough we can quite easily forego talking about what we have experienced with Christ. Only for newly converted persons does it seem to happen now and again that they are so excited by what they have experienced through the gospel and the Christian community that they cannot quit talking about it to all their friends and acquaintances, hauling them along to church, where such enthusiasm often turns out to be a source of embarrassment for the congregation. But it is exactly by this means that missionary breakthroughs occur even today.

But what about the rest of us? Have we experienced nothing? Has it been so long ago? Or do we think we have learned that one "does not live by [the] bread [of the gospel] alone" and therefore no longer consider the whole matter terribly important?

It will be the fundamental question asked of the evangelistic effectiveness of the church of Jesus Christ whether it succeeds in fanning this fire of the "inner necessity" to flame again and again—this fire which cannot remain silent about that which is our only comfort and consolation in life and death. And it is clear that it cannot be done with admonition, but that only through the encounter with the saving power of the gospel itself can this be a compelling consequence.

Saving the Lost

If we were to research the question of the most effective motives for missionary efforts in this century, we would probably discover two sets of themes. The one encompasses the consciousness that those persons who have not been reached by the gospel and have not accepted Jesus Christ as their Lord and Savior will be eternally lost. This idea was the decisive motivation for the ever new efforts to reach the "unreached peoples" which has molded the Evangelical mission work of this century in particular and continues to motivate many Christians in their evangelistic efforts and concerns for the salvation of their own family members and friends. That

195

is why many evangelists are convinced that strengthening this awareness is the most important aid to motivation for evangelization.[10]

The basic idea of this motivation is admittedly profoundly biblical. The commissioning of Jesus and his messengers has as its goal saving the lost (John 3:16; Rom 1:17; 1 Cor 9:22; 1 Tim 2:4). Theologically (and psychologically) more difficult is the negative formulation of this idea, which makes the salvation of the lost dependent upon our evangelistic efforts. That can awaken extraordinary powers in certain phases of missionary awakening: It depends on us and our efforts, whether people are saved or whether they are lost! But the idea can also have a demotivating function: Many Christians experience in their own families how fruitless their efforts are and how problematic it is to make distinctions between the "saved" and the "lost."

In the light of what is finally only a very small degree of effectiveness in Christian missionary activity and of its great defeats (e.g., in the Islamization of ever more Christian territories), thoughtful Christians must ask themselves whether the God who "wants all people to be saved" has left the fate of the fulfillment of his wish totally up to the success of our "missionizing."[11] Wherever people hold fast to this motivation, it often degenerates to a formalism of fulfilling an obligation: We have to see to it that all people can hear the gospel sufficiently clearly that they can make a decision. What decision they reach is their own responsibility.[12]

That is why we need to allow a positive formulation of this motivation thoroughly to take the place of the fear-producing negative version: We are coworkers of the saving grace of God, persons who have been commissioned and empowered to pass on to others the liberating message of God's reconciliation. Wherever those feelings of impotence, which often overcome us because of all the misery round about us, would try to lame us, pondering the fact that it is God who wills the salvation of the lost and who gives plenipotential power to our words of peace and deeds of love can protect us from lethargy and resignation. When the total lack of interest of our contemporaries for the gospel threatens to discourage us, we allow ourselves to be guided by the word and example of Jesus in finding the "sick" who have need of the doctor. To know that all need this help does not mislead us to a generalized complaint or to passing judgment but enables us sensitively to identify the symptom of the hidden human need which we encounter.

The Ecclesiological Interest

The second enduring motive for missionary activity is the ecclesiological concern for growth of one's own church or, more precisely, one's own congregation. The church growth movement has studied the factors which lead to rapid and continuing growth of congregations and has thereby given a mighty push to forms of missionary work which have as their goal such growth.[13]

The biblical rationale for this motivation is narrow. Nowhere in the New Testament is the numerical growth of a particular congregation the declared goal of missionary endeavor, and there is no promise made that God will reward particular behavior with such growth. Rather, growth is described clearly in the Acts of the Apostles as God's free gift (cf. 2:41, 47; 5:14; 6:7; 11:21, 24).[14]

In contrast the socio-psychological rationale for this motivation is excellent. It presents us, to a certain degree, with the application of the applied marketing principles in the field of mission.[15] Therein lie both its strength and its danger. From a spiritual point of view, the growth and the success of a congregation are ambiguous phenomena. They can be a consequence of sacrificial servant ministry and missionary activity, powerful proclamation of the gospel, and openness to the stranger and the needy. But they can also be the expression of a consistent application of methods of work completely oriented to felt needs and group egotism. The controversy about the significance of "homogeneous groups" is one symptom of the conflict between successful methods and the truth of the gospel.[16]

Yet we cannot and ought not to try to exclude the ecclesiological interest in evangelization. The fact that there are no Christians without Christian community means that winning a person for Christ is always also winning him or her for a congregation.[17] Conversely, for a person who has found a home, understanding, and help in a congregation it will be one natural concrete expression of the call to reconciliation to invite others into this congregation (but not, of course, the only possible concrete act!).

Sharing in the Gospel

In our search for the fundamental motivation for our missionary existence, which keeps the fire of "inner compulsion" aglow even when our first enthusiasm has long since passed, we return to that sentence of Paul's: "I do it all for the sake of the gospel, so that I may share in its blessings." (1 Cor 9:23). Paul does not only mean "that share which he wants to have, together with those whom he has converted, of the salvation of the gospel which he has proclaimed."[18] He is really concerned about his participation in the gospel as a whole, in its essence, its path, its message, and thus, of course, also in the salvation which it bestows. Both belong together indissolubly. It is, therefore, helpful that he talks of his missionary motivation in a context which focuses upon a totally different concern, namely that of showing consideration for other Christians who have scruples about eating meat offered to idols. Both of these elements, consideration for others and missionary openness, have their roots in one of the most central insights of the Christian faith: The truth that God is "God for me" can be effective and vital only where I discover the God who is "God for you" and "God for the others" and follow him.[19] Our personal absorption in the gospel of the love of God and our turning to people for whom this love is given as much as for me are the common center of a vital Christianity and assure, like the two chambers of our heart, proper "circulation" of divine grace in our lives. Like love, the gospel becomes richer and larger when we share it with others. We cannot store energy; we must use it and live in order to experience it; we must give it away in order to have it. Whoever becomes awe-struck because of the immanent presence of God in Jesus Christ will have to share that awe with others in order to continue in that presence. Such a person will have to share—for his or her own sake and for the sake of the others—and so also for God's sake. This is the rationale of our missionary existence!

The Praxis of Evangelism

The goal of this book is to establish a biblical foundation for a theology of evangelism. The missionary praxis of Jesus and of the primitive church has been investigated with a view to finding its significance for the theological baseline of its message. I am convinced that such does not offer a ready-made model for contemporary missionary work or that we can simply transfer the patterns from that time to our own.[20] Therefore, evangelistic praxis should not remain unmentioned. From the theological foundation which we have constructed, there are guidelines and helps for contemporary practical work, which ought to be sketched out for us, at least in outline. A theology of evangelism which does not include matters of praxis would be a contradiction in terms.

The Missionary Congregation

All missionary activity is related to the life of a missionary congregation. Alongside the fundamental proclamation of the apostles the existence of the congregation is the missionary event par excellence. Yet the missionary effectiveness of its simple existence does not derive from a simple accommodation to the society in which it finds itself (in biblical terms: "the world") but from a creative nonconformity which lets the alternative possibility for living which grows out of the gospel become visible to the outside world.[21] A missionary congregation will, therefore, have to find its way between an "opening" of the house of God which is so all-encompassing that neither contours nor functions of this house are still recognizable, because the protective roof and the walls which encompass it have been taken away for the sake of openness on the one side, and on the other there has been a shutting-out of the outside world so that the missionary activities appear more like short-term skirmishes outside the fortress under siege than like an invitation to enter through open doors.

Missionary existence is not something which needs to be added as a supplement to the essence of the New Testament community. It is a fundamental and inseparable part of such community. Due to the fact that this is not, in practice, universally the case, it becomes necessary to speak of developing a missionary attitude of church growth and congregational development.[22] Properly understood, this cannot be a new programmatic emphasis of or claim upon the church, but must be realized as a recollection of what the essence of Christian community really is.

The church of Jesus Christ lives in gathering and scattering, in being called together and in being sent forth. This dual motion is as necessary for her life as breathing in and breathing out is for human life. Wherever one or the other aspects atrophies, the local church becomes ill and dies away. To put it a bit bluntly: A congregation which lives only for its own in-gathering and self-nurture will die of spiritual arteriosclerosis; a congregation which pursues an unmitigated activism of missionary and service programs will succumb to consumption.[23]

For the elements involved in the *gathering*, Luke gives us the ideal image of Acts 2:42: "They devoted themselves to the apostles' teaching and fellowship, to the breaking of bread and the prayers." Listening to the word of Holy Scripture as the witness to the apostolic message of the salvific activity of God; the fellowship of sisters and brothers who are bound together by virtue of their being Christ's and who give one another sympathy and support; the celebration of the meal in which the crucified and risen Lord and his sacrificial life are present to us; and the prayer in which everything which touches the lives of those in the congregation is lifted up to God in thanksgiving and petition—these are the New Testament marks of the church.[24]

Complementary to this is the missionary *sending* of the congregation to carry forth the word of the gospel, to open her own fellowship as a space for others to experience grace, to proclaim in the sacred meal the death of the Lord (1 Cor. 11:26) while engaging itself in petition for the world, and to praise the mighty deeds of God.

This fundamental missionary sending based on the nature of the church manifests itself in divers vital signs of Christian witness and ministry in the world. These are essentially the same today as in New Testament times, although new possibilities have opened up in their practical execution. This is basic witness in the form of changed character and lifestyle of the Christian which becomes visible and tangible in the Christian's environment, together with a willingness to "make your defense to anyone who demands an accounting for the hope which is in you" (1 Pet 3:15).[25] Added to this is the proclamation in "public squares," which can look quite different according to the particular circumstances. The missionary sending is also reflected where the church finds "open doors" which gives opportunity to outsiders to get to know the fellowship of Christians.[26] Another essential part of the missionary sending is to be found in assisting people in need which lets God's love become concrete for them and—last but not least—the involvement in the public affairs of society by committing oneself to peace and justice issues.

I am personally convinced that the form which church membership takes should also make this fundamental structure of gathering and scattering visible. No one should be a member of a church who, after being baptized as an infant, has never said anything for or against church membership, but only those who have professed it to be their personal decision to be a member.[27] On the other hand, the church must find forms which signal to friends and guests that they, too, are welcome. This sort of "double-edged strategy" may well be an important characteristic of a missionary ecclesiology.

Basically, everything the congregation does in its basic functions of witness (*martyria*), fellowship (*koinonia*), and ministry (*diakonia*), carries in itself aspects of both gathering and scattering; at many points we find them inseparably bound in one another, at others they carry different weighting or have to be separated, practically seen.[28] This is equally true for the diverse charisms of the congregation which, according to their particular natures, are more strongly at play in the inner up-building of the congregation or in its missionary task; whatever the case, in some form or another they contribute both to the gathering and to the missionary scattering of the congregation.[29]

An evangelistic orientation in the narrower sense is present by our definition in the missionary and diaconal activity of the congregation, when the fundamental message of the gospel is named and the people addressed directly; when they are told: "This is intended for you!" and when they, perhaps, are invited, with the almost irrefusable urgency of an oriental host (cf. Luke 14:23), to accept this message for themselves. In this the evangelistic proclamation is one vital sign of the missionary congregation among others, yet, for the sake of the "clarity of the proclamation in the name of Jesus" the central vital sign.[30] Missionary proclamation is fed, carried, and accompanied by the strength of missionary living in the congregation. Proclamation may, of course, also be necessary before the missionary congregation can come into being or be newly revived in the first place. There is a fruitful mutuality involved.

Personal Evangelism

We established in our definition of evangelization that we do not want to understand evangelistic proclamation as only preaching by charismatically gifted speakers at special assemblies. Evangelistic proclamation which brings to peoples' attention that the love of God is also intended from them personally and which bids them to accept it for themselves occurs in personal conversation, too. So it is that the importance of "personal evangelization" has frequently been mentioned in recent times.[31] We have seen that this was the fundamental form of missionary activity in the early Christian period.

This is the most important and most difficult chapter of evangelistic practice. For talking unguardedly one-on-one about questions of faith is not easy. Even clergy who can speak easily about God and the world from the protection of their pulpit often have difficulty putting the spiritual dimensions of certain problems into words in personal conversation.

In his novella "Das verlorene Lachen" ("The Lost Smile"), Gottfried Keller describes the difficulties of such communication with the sharp eye of the critic. Justine, the main character of the tale, decides, in a personal crisis, to seek out two women she knows to discover "the secret of peace and faith." The visit ends in disappointment. She continues to be impressed by the honest human concern of the two women. But what they report about the foundations of their faith is not presented

> with the pleasantly human graciousness which was otherwise characteristic of everything they did or said, but with a hasty dryness, monotonous and colorless, as something they had learned by rote. At no point did the words become softer or milder, their eyes warmer or more lively, even the suffering and death of Jesus himself they treated like an object lesson and not as a matter of attitude or feelings. It was a world without essence for them about which they were speaking, and they themselves were in yet another world with their being. . . . thus Justine saw that the good ladies found their peace somewhere else than in the doctrines of the church and were incapable of giving their peace to her in conjunction with the doctrines.[32]

Without a doubt Keller, an atheist, is partisan. A successful conversation about faith would have had no place in the conception of his novella. But critics often see things especially clearly. Christians not only have the problem that often no deeds follow pious words. There is also the problem—and I think it occurs quite often—that we can find no words which make clear by what power the deeds of love are done which cause other people to take heed and ask about their motivation. Either we remain in embarrassed silence, or our sentences remain empty words which cannot transport the content of that which we have experienced and would gladly pass along. Is there a special "language of the gospel" which makes this possible? If so, how do we learn it?

In recent years increasing numbers of courses and seminars have been offered which purport to be such a "language school of faith." They can vary greatly in their effectiveness. Many offer nothing but a mediocre training for sales pitches. One learns how to respond to standard turn-offs and to recognize the right phrases to connect with to further one's own pitch.[33] The better of such courses are exceptional in their emphasis on attentive listening and responding to what the partner in conversation has said.[34] In general, however, it appears to me that such courses can only be a partial help for the problem. You learn languages by speaking them. We need places to practice spiritual speech. Such language schooling is available in house church groups, but also in every other small group where we succeed in providing sufficient openness that personal experiences and problems can be brought into the conversation with the promise and the claim of the gospel. Here we learn to speak openly about our trials and doubts, but also—and this seems to me to be by far the hardest part—to articulate the helpful, reassuring faith experiences which lead us forward. Here we can try to connect the big words of the traditional message with everyday events and feelings and to find the linguistic means to make this clear to outsiders.

It will become evident that the "language of the gospel" is always speech based on personal involvement, as "from faith to faith" (in a free articulation of the Pauline formulation in Rom 1:17) and precisely because of this it is at its heart evangelistic speech. We will learn that the "language of the gospel" has to be speech growing out of sympathetic understanding, because it is only in that way that we can do justice to the proper orientation of the gospel to the concrete situation and needs of people. And we will experience how God's spirit gives a "language of the gospel" to those who are open for it in a form of speech full of inviting images. Just as Jesus' parables make everyday events transparent for God's action and the "I am" passages in the Gospel of John make use of the profound aids to understanding of archetypal symbols, so we will notice how much of what we experience and observe with an observant heart can become a parable for that which we want to say about God. But it is at one and the same time vital—and a relief for the burden put on personal conversation—that we do not think that we must convince the other person down to the last detail through our skills of persuasion, but that we have sufficient trust to commit our partner in conversation to his or her own experience with Jesus and his message with the cordial invitation, "Come and see!"[35]

The Evangelistic Sermon

What is true of personal conversation is, of course, also true to a great degree for the evangelistic sermon.[36] Such a sermon is not limited to the occasion of special evangelistic services, but can and ought to have its place in the Sunday worship service, in occasional services of the church such as weddings, baptisms, or funerals, on the radio, or at other places.[37]

I would like to mention the following as characteristics of an evangelistic sermon: a clear presentation of the message of salvation of the gospel and the personal promise of this message to its hearers, the call to repentance and to faith, and the urgent plea gratefully to take the hand of God which is outstretched in reconciliation. From this point of departure we draw consequences for the language and content of the evangelistic sermon: It endeavors to provide *elementary talk* of God and his salvific action for humankind.[38] Without a false simplification of complex matters the basic lines of the message of the gospel are presented and drawn into the content of a person's life today. This does not have to become banal; rather I am absolutely convinced that there are basic expressions of faith which can be made understandable and exciting for college professors and assembly-line workers, young people and senior citizens at one and the same time.

Evangelistic preaching dares to make the claim to be *authorized talk* of God. I don't meditate in the presence of my hearers about what the "text" has to say to us (a process which is totally alien and outside the experience of their lives in any case), but I try to make it clear that God wants to speak to them in the gospel, and to articulate what is it is that God has to say to them and to me. This is the place for what Luther called the *assertio*—the assuring promise of the gospel.[39] Of course, this claim must be based on careful exegesis of the biblical word, through prayer and the direction of the Holy Spirit and through an openness to critical monitoring from the congregation.

And finally it is also true of evangelistic preaching that it must be *personal talk* of God. The words of warning of Paul, "For we do not proclaim ourselves; we proclaim Jesus Christ as Lord" (2 Cor 4:5), mark the principle boundary which can protect us from putting ourselves in the limelight and playing up our own experience in our proclamation. But because the evangelist, the apostle is, for the sake of Christ, the "servant" of his or her hearers, he cannot exclude his own person from his proclamation, but must stand at their disposal with the whole experience of his or her life.[40]

Characteristic of public evangelistic proclamation is that it always has to reckon with two different audiences—with those people for whom faith is totally foreign and who need to be invited to open themselves to the message of the gospel, and those who know the message and in principle affirm it, and who are then asked how serious their "yes" truly is. Yet, it is the same message which is to be offered to both groups of hearers (and, of course, to those who are between the two groups): namely, that God has said his "yes" to their lives and this means acceptance and salvation of their lives for time and eternity. This theological unity in the evangelistic message has been demonstrated impressively by our investigations.

I consider one type of evangelization very important—what has been called "teaching evangelization." In an age when many people have hardly any knowledge at all of the fundamental assertions of the Christian faith, basic information about the Christian faith can be offered in a series of sermons or lectures. The peculiarity of teaching evangelization is that it happens not in a purely descriptive way, but with a claim and a promise so that its assertions have fundamental significance for the life of its hearers. It is precisely for this purpose that it can be helpful to include evangelistic proclamation in types of events which have different possibilities for communication and service than an evening lecture might. Faith seminars, week-end retreats, and the like offer rich and successfully used alternatives.

The Call to Decision

The call to decision is among the most obvious and most controversial characteristics of "classical" evangelization, especially when this call is connected with the request to stand up or to come forward. For many, this is the core of evangelization by which the hearers receive that aid to decision which they need in order to make firm their commitment to God. For others, however, this is the most obvious symptom of the manipulative, forced, and short-circuited conversion sermon in many evangelizations.

Some of the representatives of this method are not blind to its dangers. S. Mung'oma, an evangelist who works closely with Billy Graham, gave an address at the Conference for Evangelization in Amsterdam in which he offered highly self-critical insights into manipulative forms of the challenge to come forward which he himself had used. Yet he holds fast to the principle: "Let the appeal be urgent, clear, and direct, but non-manipulative."[41] How do we respond to this?

Doubtless, the urgent, even forceful invitation to people to accept the message of God's reconciliation for themselves personally is biblically based. And it is important and legitimate that the hearers of the message are given opportunity to express their "yes" in a way perceptible to themselves and others. In the missionary situation of the New Testament, it was one of the functions of baptism to document this confession, and this is equally true today, of course, wherever our evangelization is taking place among the unbaptized. Where, however, it is aimed at the baptized—and this is true not only with an eye to those who were baptized as infants—we need other symbols and communicative aids.

One such aid can, at times, be that call forward, if it is clear what function this has: the possibility to confess the faith, but not the compulsion necessarily to have to do so just now. As our look at the biographical literature has shown us, the real "decisions" are made in solitude. Thus it seems important to me that possibilities to express one's decision to accept God's promises and to make it firm for oneself and in front of others, ought also to be offered time and again in the routine life of one's congregation. The suggestion to view the invitation to the Lord's Supper in this light can be one such aid, or also the offer of opportunity to silently agree in prayer with appropriately formulated prayer following the sermon in worship. Heribert Mühlen has prepared a "liturgy of conversion for baptized adults" whose basic elements are affirmation and laying on of hands; others have developed liturgies for the renewal of the baptismal covenant.[42]

In this regard it is important to note that there are people for whom it is important to speak in personally formulated words what they have received in faith, while others need the protection of their most intimate sphere which a "ritual" offers. "Ritualization" becomes dangerous, however, whenever there appears to be only one proper way and one proper expression of how coming to faith can occur. Here lurks the danger that the "ritual" no longer serves the interests of the recipient, but only of those who have planned the event.[43]

Pastoral Accompaniment

Pastoral care is written in big letters even in traditional evangelization. For mass evangelizations an army of spiritual workers are trained. Yet we must fear that precisely at this point there is to be found a weak point in this kind of evangelization. By fixing on a clearly defined goal for spiritual guidance, namely the commitment of one's life to Jesus, the spiritual worker is all too often prevented from truly hearing the needs of those who seek a spiritual conversation.[44] True spiritual guidance takes time; that is one of the reasons why evangelization can have meaning only when it is undertaken in a close relationship to local congregations and their pastoral workers or when it is undertaken directly by them. For those persons who have been spoken to by the message or who have very consciously accepted the same will need help to work through their pasts and to master their often complex contemporary problems. It is, after all, not necessarily the ambitious and hardworking who are the first to respond to the gospel, but more often those who are burdened psychologically, those whose lives are failures, or the down-and-out. In the task thus presented spiritual care groups and home church groups are immensely important aids.

Evangelistic spiritual guidance is not, however, only "follow-up" work for specific events or lecture series. It is an essential part of the spiritual task of the minister and the congregation in every case.[45] Precisely in the patient and long-term spiritual care of people in life's crises, of the ill or the specially challenged, of the doubters or those who struggle against their fate, the *kairos*—the opportune moment—will become evident when we can speak to people with the message and promise of the love of God and invite them to say their "yes" to it. Truly "accepting" pastoral care can make itself evident by seeking to make it clear to people how God provides them both a time and a place for such a "yes" and thus liberates them to say it in their own way.

The Question of Training

It is the almost unanimous opinion of those involved in evangelization that the missionary and evangelistic aspects of the training of pastors continue to receive insufficient emphasis. Yet to me it does not seem appropriate to overload the theological course of study with too many directly practice-oriented elements.[46] It seems more important that *all* theological work should have a stronger missionary accent.

We need exegesis in which the dynamism of the biblical message of God's gracious love to human beings can be sensed; we need dogmatics which help to recall for people today the essential parts of this message, homiletics which reckon with the fact that there are not only Christians in our audience and reflect upon how we might be able to speak to all people; and we need a pastoral theology which addresses the future situation of a minority church and therefore develops concepts of missionary church life in a secular environment. All these things exist, and I am convinced that precisely such a careful, scholarly theology committed to its task presents the best help for our present concern. But the fact that more work and more effective work could be done in this regard ought not to be something of concern only to the church situation today, but to the very central task of theology itself.[47]

Similarly, regarding the schooling of lay workers, it would seem to me to be less particular courses in preparation for specific evangelizations which would be of decisive help than ongoing work with the Bible, through which the basic thrusts of the Biblical message would be grasped, patient urging to express faith in one's own words could occur, and the long-term practice in methods of understanding pastoral conversation could take place.

The Risk for All

In my preparation of this book, I personally have been brought into a strange tension. The exegetical work often made me aware once more of the overwhelming depth of the gospel of Jesus Christ and its power to carry us along with it. This has painfully increased for me the problem that this message has practically no influence in our society outside the walls of the church. The question why I myself hardly see any possibility of passing on this message to my upper-middle-class neighbors or the homeless whom I meet in the subway stations makes me uncomfortable. Am I concerned that they will push me aside or have I (perhaps subconsciously) an even greater concern that they will take the message seriously and might get me involved in their problems in some way which would radically change my life? The slogan of a well-known evangelistic song, "Dare to with Jesus!" is, perhaps, not only for the hearer of the message, but just as much for those who deliver it. For whoever truly passes the message along in the authority of Jesus will have to reckon with the fact that not only his hearers will be changed, but that much may change for the preacher as well. Anyone who expects from evangelization only personal affirmation or an enrichment of the status quo will not receive much. To trust the gospel is a risk for all; but exactly therein lies the promise: to experience God's mercy and the power of his saving gospel.

Abbreviations

AB	Anchor Bible
AnBib	Analecta biblica
ATANT	Abhandlungen zur Theologie des Alten und Neuen Testaments
ATRSS	Anglican Theological Review Supplemental Series
BAGD	W. Bauer, W. F. Arndt, F. W. Gingrich, and F. W. Danker, *Greek-English Lexicon of the NT*
BBB	Bonner biblische Beiträge
BDR	F. Blass, A. Debrunner, and F. Rehkopf, *Grammatik des neutestamentlichen Griechisch*
BEvT	Beiträge zur evangelischen Theologie
BibS(N)	Biblische Studien (Neukirchen, 1951—)
BWANT	Beiträge zur Wissenschaft vom Alten und Neuen Testament
BZ	*Biblische Zeitschrift*
BZNW	Beihefte zur ZNW
CBQ	*Catholic Biblical Quarterly*
CTM	Calwer Theologische Monographien
EDNT	H. Balz and G. Schneider (eds.), *Exegetical Dictionary of the New Testament*
EHS	Europäische Hochschulschriften
EKKNT	Evangelisch-katholischer Kommentar zum Neuen Testament
EvT	*Evangelische Theologie*
FRLANT	Forschungen zur Religion und Literatur des Alten und Neuen Testaments
FS	Festschrift (name of honoree in brackets)
GTA	Göttinger theologische Arbeiten
HTKNT	Herders theologischer Kommentar zum Neuen Testament
HUT	Hermeneutische Untersuchungen zur Theologie

JBL	*Journal of Biblical Literature*
JETS	*Journal of the Evangelical Theological Society*
JSSR	*Journal for the Scientific Study of Religion*
MeyerK	H. A. W. Meyer, Kritisch-exegetischer Kommentar über das Neue Testament
MWF	Missionswissenschaftliche Forschungen
NIDNT	Ulrich Becker (ed.), *The New International Dictionary of New Testament Theology*
NIV	New International Version
NJB	H. Wansbrough (ed.), New Jerusalem Bible
NovTSup	Novum Testamentum, Supplements
NRSV	New Revised Standard Version
NTA	*New Testament Abstracts*
NTAbh	Neutestamentliche Abhandlungen
NTD	Das Neue Testament Deutsch
QD	Quaestiones disputatae
RelEd	*Religious Education*
RelS	*Religious Studies*
RevExp	*Review and Expositor*
RGG	*Religion in Geschichte und Gegenwart*, third edition
RNT	Regensburger Neues Testament
RSV	Revised Standard Version
SBM	Stuttgarter biblische Monographien
SBS	Stuttgarter Bibelstudien
SBT	Studies in Biblical Theology
SLA	Studien der Luther-Akademie
SNT	Studien zum Neuen Testament
SUNT	Studien zur Umwelt des Neuen Testaments
TBei	*Theologische Beiträge*
TBü	Theologische Bücherei
TDNT	G. Kittel and G. Friedrich (eds.), *Theological Dictionary of the New Testament*

TDOT	G. J. Botterweck and H. Ringgren (eds.), *Theological Dictionary of the Old Testament*
TEV	Today's English Version
THAT	Ernst Jenni (ed.), *Theologisches Handwörterbuch zum Alten Testament*
THKNT	Theologischer Handkommentar zum Neuen Testament
TLZ	*Theologische Literaturzeitung*
TRE	*Theologische Realenzyklopädie*
TZ	*Theologische Zeitschrift*
WMANT	Wissenschaftliche Monographien zum Alten und Neuen Testament
WUNT	Wissenschaftliche Untersuchungen zum Neuen Testament
ZMR	*Zeitschrift für Missionskunde und Religionswissenschaft*
ZNW	*Zeitschrift für die neutestamentliche Wissenschaft*
ZTK	*Zeitschrift für Theologie und Kirche*

Notes

Notes to Foreword

1. See Hans Jochen Margull, *Theologie der missionarischen Verkündigung. Evangelisation als ökumenisches Problem* (Stuttgart: Evangelisches Verlagswerk, 1959), 72.
2. Klaus Teschner, in Johannes Hansen and Christian Möller (eds.), *Evangelisation und Theologie. Texte einer Begegnung* (Neukirchen-Vluyn: Neukirchener Verlag, 1980), 5; cf. David L. Watson, "Christ All in All: The Recovery of the Gospel for North American Evangelism," *Missiology* 19 (1991), 443–59.
3. Teschner, 5.

Notes to Chapter 1

1. "Evangelisation und Volksmission," *RGG* 2:771. (This translation of the German original and of all other German-language texts cited in this book are by the translators unless otherwise indicated.)
2. David B. Barrett, *Evangelize! A Historical Survey of the Concept*, Global Evangelization Movement: The AD 2000 Series (Birmingham, Alabama: New Hope, 1987).
3. Cf. Jochen Margull, "Evangelism," *RGG* 2:795f. Both terms have only been in wide use since the nineteenth century; Wesley and Whitefield did not yet know them. Barrett, *Evangelize!, 24.*
4. Barrett, *Evangelize!* 51, 79.
5. See Margull, 795ff.; Emilio Castro and Gerhard Linn, "Evangelisation," *Evangelisches Kirchenlexikon*, third edition (Göttingen: Vandenhoeck & Ruprecht, 1986), 1:1194–98.
6. Paulus Scharpff, *Geschichte der Evangelisation* (Giessen: Brunnen Verlag, 1964), 1f.; a much broader understanding of "evangelism" is found in Milton L. Rudnick, *Speaking the Gospel Through the Ages: A History of Evangelism* (St. Louis: Concordia Publishing House, 1984).
7. Rendtorff, *RGG* 3:771.
8. Cf. Scharpff, 223f., 260ff.
9. Rendtorff, *RGG* 3:772.
10. Ibid., 773.
11. Cf. Johannes Christiaan Hoekendijk, *The Church Inside Out* (Philadelphia: Westminster Press, 1966); H. J. Margull, *Theologie*; Margull (ed.), *Mission als Strukturprinzip* (Geneva: WCC, 1967); Barrett, *Evangelize!*, 26–51.

12. Rendtorff, *RGG* 3:773ff.

13. David J. Bosch, "Mission and Evangelism: Clarifying the Concepts," *ZMR* 68 (1984), 161–94.

14. Cf. *Mission and Evangelism: An Ecumenical Affirmation* (Geneva: WCC, and New York: NCC, 1983), par. 34; cf. as well two volumes originating in the International Evangelical Conference on the Nature and Mission of the Church convened by the World Evangelical Fellowship held in Wheaton, Illinois, in 1983: David Allen Fraser (ed.), *The Church in New Frontiers for Missions* (Monrovia, CA: Missions Advanced Research and Communications Center, 1983); and Tom Sine (ed.), *The Church's Response to Human Need* (Monrovia, CA: Missions Advanced Research and Communications Center, 1983). See also Charles Sugden, "Evangelicals and Wholistic Evangelism," in Vinay Samuel and Arnold Hauser (eds.), *Proclaiming Christ's Way: Studies in Integral Evangelism* (Oxford: Regnum Books, 1989), 29–51. A fine summary of the relation of ecumenism and evangelism is given by Emilio Castro in his article on "Evangelism" in *Dictionary of the Ecumenical Movement*, ed. Nicholas Lossky, et al. (Geneva: WCC, and Grand Rapids: Wm. B. Eerdmans, 1991), 396–400.

15. A. Flannery (ed.), *Vatican Council II*, Volume 2: *More Post Conciliar Documents* (Dublin: Dominican Publications, 1982), 711–61.

16. Flannery, par. 16.

17. Barrett, *Evangelize!* 49f. The *Lexikon für Theologie und Kirche* only has the entry "Evangelisation, protestantische." But cf. David Bohr, *Evangelization in America: Proclamation, Way of Life and the Catholic Church in the United States* (New York: Paulist Press, 1977) and Kenneth Boyack (ed.), *The New Catholic Evangelization* (New York: Paulist Press, 1992).

18. *Puebla: La evangelización en el presente y en el futoro de América Latina* (San Salvador: UCA Editiores, 1979, 1983, 1985); Alvaro Barreiro, S.J., *Basic Ecclesial Communities: The Evangelization of the Poor* (Maryknoll, NY: Orbis Books, 1982); John Walsh, *Evangelization and Justice* (Maryknoll, NY: Orbis Books, 1982); Bruce J. Nicholls (ed.), *In Word and Deed: Evangelism and Social Responsibility* (Grand Rapids, MI: William B. Eerdmanns, 1986); Enoch H. Oglesby, "The Ethics of Communitas: Toward Social Evangelism in the Black Church," *Journal of the Academy for Evangelism in Theological Education* 4 (1989–1990), 4–16; William F. Warren, Jr., "Evangelism in the Context of Liberation Theology: Structural Sin and Structural Confession," *Journal of the Academy for Evangelism in Theological Education* 5 (1990–91), 5–31; Priscilla Pope-Levison, *Evangelization from a Liberation Perspective* (New York: Peter Lang, 1991). For the position of Orthodoxy, cf. Alexander Veronis, "Orthodox Concepts of Evangelism and Mission," *Greek Orthodox Theological Review* 27 (1982), 44–57; Ion Bria, *Go Forth in Peace: Orthodox Perspectives in Mission* (Geneva: WCC, 1986); David J. Bosch, *Transforming Mission* (Maryknoll, NY: Orbis Books, 1991), 205–9.

19. Gerhard Wahrig et al., *Deutsches Wörterbuch*, völlig überarbeitete Neuausgabe (Mosaik Verlag, 1982).

20. See below, pp. 19–21.

21. Karl Barth, *Church Dogmatics*, trans. G. T. Thompson, et al., 4 vols. in 14 (Edinburgh: T & T Clark, 1936–1977), IV.3.2:872f.

22. Barth, *Church Dogmatics*, IV.3.2:874.

23. Paul Tillich, *Systematic Theology*, 3 vols. in 1 (Chicago: University of Chicago Press, 1967), 3:194–96.

24. One finds absolutely nothing on the subject in Hermann Diem, *Theologie als kirchliche Wissenschaft, Volume III: Die Kirche und ihre Praxis* (Munich: Chr. Kaiser Verlag, 1963), similarly in Wolfgang Trillhaas, *Dogmatik* (Berlin: Alfred Töpelmann, 1962), cf. 528f. The following theologians are very hesitant to say anything about evangelism, if they do not reject it outright: Heinrich Ott, *Die Antwort des Glaubens* (Stuttgart: Kreuz-Verlag, 1972), Art. 37 and 43, and Hans-Georg Fritzsche, *Lehrbuch der Dogmatik IV* (Berlin: Evangelische Verlagsanstalt, 1988), 62. The following works treat evangelism briefly: Adolf Schlatter, *Christliche Dogmatik* (Stuttgart: Calwer Vereinsbuchhandlung, 1923), 212–14, 592; Paul Althaus, *Die christliche Wahrheit*, 2 vols. (Gütersloh: C. Bertelsmann, 1948), 2:312; Gerhard Ebeling, *Dogmatik des christlichen Glaubens*, 3 vols. (Tübingen: J. C. B. Mohr [Paul Siebeck], 1979), 2:133f., 137, 3:382f.; Wilfried Joest, *Dogmatik*, 2 vols., 3rd edition (Göttingen: Vandenhoeck & Ruprecht, 1989), 2:598f.; Thomas C. Oden, *Life in the Spirit: Systematic Theology, Volume 3* (San Fransico: Harper & Rowe, 1992), 338f. Evangelism receives a somewhat fuller discussion in Emil Brunner, *Dogmatics, Volume 1: The Christian Doctrine of God*, trans. Olive Wyon (Philadelphia: Westminster Press, 1950), 107–111; Otto Weber, *Foundations of Dogmatics*, trans. Darrell L. Guder, 2 vols. (Grand Rapids: William B. Eerdmanns, 1981), 1:47, 89, 2:533, 572, 619; and Edmund Schlink, *Ökumenische Dogmatik: Grundzüge* (Göttingen: Vandenhoeck & Ruprecht, 1983), 440–44, 569ff.

On the Roman Catholic side, Pietro Rossano has a long article on the theology of mission in Johannes Feiner and Magnus Lohrer (eds.), *Mysterium Salutis. Grundriß heilgeschichtlicher Dogmatik*, 7 vols. in 5 (Zürich: Benziger-Verlag, 1965–1972), 4.1:503–31. However the subject is mentioned only very briefly in other major works: Klaus Egger, *Christlicher Glaube in moderner Gesellschaft*, Vol. 28: *Christliche Glaubensrede im Raum personaler Begegnung* (Freiburg: Verlag Herder, 1982), 80–82; Karl Lehmann, *Christlicher Glaube in moderner Gesellschaft*, Vol. 29: *Sendung der Gemeinde* (Freiburg: Verlag Herder, 1982); and Peter Eicher (ed.), *Neue Summe Theologie*, Vol. 3: *Der Dienst der Gemeinde* (Freiburg: Verlag Herder, 1989), 71–74. Even Karl Rahner's *Foundations of Christian Faith*, trans. William V. Dyck (London: Darton, Longman & Todd, 1978), only offers on pages 400f. a short relevant section, "The uniqueness of the Christian offer of meaning in a pluralistic society."

25. Hans Küng, *The Church*, trans. Ray and Rosaleen Ockenden, (London: Burns & Oates Ltd., 1967), 438f., 487; Jürgen Moltmann, *The Church in the Power of the Spirit* (New York: Harper and Row, 1975), 81, 361, where the sending of the church into the world is a fundamental motif of the entire book; Wolfgang Huber, *Die Kirche* (Stuttgart: Kreuz-Verlag, 1979), 172f.; and Walter Kreck, *Grundfragen der Ekklesiologie* (Munich: Chr. Kaiser Verlag, 1981), 111.

26. Ulrich Kühn, *Die Kirche*, Handbuch der systematischen Theologie 10 (Gütersloh: Gütersloher Verlagshaus, 1981), 151–63, "Die Sendung der Kirche in die Welt."

27. Miguel María Garijo-Guembe, *Gemeinschaft der Heiligen. Grund, Wesen und Struktur der Kirche* (Düsseldorf: Patmos Verlag, 1988).

28. Friedrich Winter, *Handbuch der praktischen Theologie*, Volume 2: *Der Gottesdienst. Die kirchlichen Handlungen. Die Predigt* (Berlin: Evangelisches Verlagshaus, 1974), 279.

29. Reinhard Linder, "Evangelisation in der Volkskirche," and Theodor Lehmann, "Evangelisation in der atheistischen Gesellschaft," *Handbuch der praktischen Theologie*, Volume 4: *Praxisfeld: Gesellschaft und Öffentlichkeit*, Peter C. Bloth et al. (eds.), (Gütersloh: Gütersloher Verlagshaus, 1987), 79–88.

30. Lindner, 79; Lehmann, 88.

31. Rolf Zerfaß and Herbert Poensgen, "Predigt/Verkündigung" in *Gemeindepraxis in Grundbegriffen*, 354–68.

32. Zerfaß and Poensgen, 356.

33. Ibid., 356, 358.

34. *TDNT*, 2:707–37; *NIDNT*, 2:107–15; *EDNT*, 2:69–74; *TDOT*, 2:313–17; Barrett, *Evangelize!* 11–20.

35. Cf. Jeremiah 20:15; *TDOT* 2:314f. The LXX does not have *euangel-* in 1 Samuel 4:17!

36. *TDOT* 2:315.

37. *TDOT* 2:317.

38. Theodore H. Robinson, cited by Claus Westermann, *Isaiah 40–66*, Old Testament Library (London: SCM Press, 1969), 366.

39. Cf. "poverty" and "broken heart."

40. Cf. the birth narratives Luke 1:19, 2:10.

41. Cf. also Mark 1:14, 13:10, 14:9, and further 1 Thess 2:9, Col 1:23.

42. Cf., however, the peculiar expression in 10:36: "the word which he sent to Israel, preaching good news of peace by Jesus Christ" (RSV).

43. Cf. also Luke 20:1.

44. That is why the term could already be used in Luke 3:18 as a summary of the preaching of John the Baptist or in Luke 9:6 as a rendering of the Markan *ekēryxan hina metanoōsin* of Mark 6:2. Cf. Heinz Schürmann, *Das Lukasevangelium*, HTKNT III/1, fourth edition (Freiburg: Verlag Herder, 1984), 178f.

45. Ulrich Wilckens, *Der Brief an die Römer*, EKKNT VI/I, second edition (Neukirchen-Vlyun: Neukirchener Verlag, and Zürich: Benziger, 1987), who reviews the assorted hypotheses regarding this reference, is of the opinion that Paul does not want "to proselytize [the church] itself, rather pursue his mission to the Gentiles in its area" (80).

46. Walter Klaiber, *Rechtfertigung und Gemeinde*, FRLANT 127 (Göttingen: Vandenhoeck & Ruprecht, 1985), 195–203.

47. In opposition to Strecker, *EDNT* 2:70. Cf. in addition 1 Pet 1:12, 25; 4:6.

48. Apostolic commission: Gal 1:16; 1 Cor 9, 15:1-11; 2 Cor 10; Rom 15:14ff. Participation of the church: Phil 1:7, 27, 4:15.

49. John Stott, "The Biblical Basis of Evangelism," in *Let the Earth Hear His Voice*, J. D. Douglas (ed.), International Congress on World Evangelisation, Lausanne, Switzerland (Minneapolis: World Wide Publications, 1975), 65–78.

50. Ibid., 65f.

51. Ibid., 69; cf. Barrett, *Evangelize!* 51.

52. The ecumenical discussion in which the understanding of mission was developed mostly emphasizes the unity of mission and evangelism (cf. Margull, *Theologie der missionarischen Verkündigung*, 245–95, and Norman E. Thomas, "Ecumenical Directions in Evangelism: Melbourne to San Antonio," *The Journal of the Academy for Evangelism in Theological Education* 4 [1989–1990], 52–63). The distinction presented here can be found in Stott, 66ff., and David Bosch, "Mission," *ZMR* 68 (1984), 169ff.; cf. now from the same author, *Transforming Mission: Paradigm Shifts in Theology of Mission* (Maryknoll, NY: Orbis Books, 1991), 409–19.

53. This is a slight modification of the aspects of the evangelism (= mission) of the church named by Johannes Christiaan Hoekendijk ("The Call to Evangelism," in *The Church Inside Out*, 25ff.; cf. Margull, *Theologie*, 191ff.). Conceptually, my version coincides with that of Rolf Zerfaß and Herbert Poensgen, in *Gemeindepraxis in Grundbegriffen*, Christof Bäumler and Norbert Mette (eds.), (Munich: Chr. Kaiser Verlag, and Düsseldorf: Patmos Verlag, 1987), 363.

54. A multitude of comparable definitions can be found in Barrett, *Evangelize!*, particularly 42ff. Cf. Bosch, 170ff.

55. Bosch, 170.

56. Here I would like to name comparable investigations: David Lowes Watson, "Evangelism: A Disciplinary Approach," *International Bulletin of Missionary Research* 7:1 (1983), 6–9; Ben Campbell Johnson, *Rethinking Evangelism: A Theological Approach* (Philadelphia: The Westminster Press, 1987); Christopher C. Walker, *Connecting with the Spirit of Christ: Evangelism for a Secular Age* (Nashville: Discipleship Resources, 1988); Robert Kalb, *Speaking the Gospel Today: A Theology for Evangelism* (St. Louis: Concordia Publishing House, 1984); Arnold B. Lovell (ed.), *Evangelism in the Reformed Tradition* (Decatur, Georgia: Columbia Theological Seminary Press, 1990); Stephen S. Kim, "A Wesleyan Vision of Mission and Evangelism for the 21st Century," *Journal of the Academy for Evangelism in Theological Education* 5 (1990–91), 45–53; William J. Abraham, *The Logic of Evangelism* (Grand Rapids: William B. Eerdmans, 1989); Orlando E. Costas, *Liberating News: A Theology of Contextual Evangelization* (Grand Rapids: William B. Eerdmans, 1989); Roger E. Hedlund, *The Mission of the Church in the World: A Biblical Theology* (Grand Rapids, Michigan: Baker Book House, 1991); Walter Brueggemann, *Biblical Perspectives on Evangelism* (Nashville: Abingdon Press, 1993).

Notes to Chapter 2

1. In contrast to most works on evangelism and mission of the early church we do not orient ourselves so much on the history and execution of the mission, nor on the theological reflection on mission, but rather on the missionary message as such. Cf. on this point Walter Klaiber, "Die rettende Botschaft. Überlegungen zu den Inhalten evangelistischer Verkündigung," *TBei* 18 (1987), 65–80. However, I list here the works which I have looked at: Karl Georg Kuhn, "Das Problem der Mission in der Urchristenheit," *Evangelische Missionszei-*

tung 11 (1954), 161–68; Ferdinand Hahn, *Mission in the New Testament*, trans. Frank Clark, SBT 47 (Napierville, IL: Alec R. Allenson, and London: SCM Press, 1965); Michael Green, *Evangelism in the Early Church* (London: Hodder & Stoughton, 1970); Martin Hengel, "The Origins of Christian Mission," *Between Jesus and Paul* (London: SCM Press, 1983), 48–64; Lucian Legrand, J. Pathrapankal, M. V. Vellanickal, *Good News and Witness* (Bangalore, India: Theological Publications in India, 1973); Christoph Burchard, "Formen der Vermittlung des christlichen Glaubens im Neuen Testament," *EvT* 38 (1978), 313–40; Eugen Van Ness Goetchius, "The Concept of Evangelism in the New Testament," ATRSS (1979), 81–103; David E. Garland, "Evangelism in the New Testament," *RevExp* 77 (1980), 461–72; Karl Kertelge (ed.), *Mission im Neuen Testament*, QD 93 (Freiburg: Verlag Herder, 1983); Peter Stuhlmacher, "Weg, Stil, und Konsequenzen urchristlicher Mission," *TBei* 12 (1981), 107–35; E. Glenn Hinson, *The Evangelization of the Roman Empire* (Macon: Mercer University Press, 1981); William C. Weinrich, "Evangelism in the Early Church," *Concordia Theological Quarterly* 45 (1981), 61–76; Donald Senior and Carroll Stuhlmueller, *The Biblical Foundations for Mission* (Maryknoll, NY: Orbis Books, 1983); Gerhard Schneider, "First Evangelization—Its Circumstances and Theological Basis in the New Testament," *VERBUM SVD* 26 (1985), 18–30; Lucian Legrand, *Le Dieu qui vient: la mission dans la Bible* (Paris: Desdée, 1988); ET *Unity and Plurality: Mission in the Bible* (Maryknoll, NY: Orbis Books, 1990); Mortimer Arias and Alan Johnson, *The Great Commission: Biblical Models for Evangelism* (Nashville: Abingdon Press, 1992).

2. Instead of *kēryssōn to euangelion tēs basileias* (Matt 4:23) one reads *euangelizomenos tēn basileian tou theou*, a distinction which can scarcely be formulated in the English translation. In reference to the disciples one finds the expressions *kēryssein* (9:2) or respectively *diangellein tēn basileian* (9:60).

3. Cf. in addition to what the commentaries have to say about these passages, see Peter Stuhlmacher, *Das paulinische Evangelium I. Vorgeschichte*, FRLANT 95 (Göttingen: Vandenhoeck und Ruprecht, 1968), 218–44; Gerhard Dautzenberg, "Der Wandel der Reich-Gottes-Verkündigung in der urchristlichen Mission," *Zur Zeit des Urchristentums*, QD 27 (Freiburg: Verlag Herder, 1987), 11–32; Otto Betz, "Jesu Evangelium vom Gottesreich," in Peter Stuhlmacher (ed.), *Das Evangelium und die Evangelien*, WUNT 28 (Tübingen: J. C. B. Mohr [Paul Siebeck], 1983), 55–77; Peter Stuhlmacher, "Das paulinische Evangelium," in ibid., 157–82, 172ff.; Hubert Frankenmölle, "Jesus als deuterojesajanischer Freudenbote? Zur Rezeption von Jes 52,7 und 61,1 im Neuen Testament, durch Jesus und in den Targumim," in Hubert Frankenmölle und Karl Kertelge (eds.), *Vom Urchristentum zu Jesus: Für Joachim Gnilka* (Freiburg: Verlag Herder, 1989), 34–67.

4. Mark 1:15, Matt 4:17, Luke 10:9 = Matt 10:7. Cf. Helmut Merklein, "Jesu Botschaft von der Gottesherrschaft," *Stuttgarter Biblische Studien* 11 (Stuttgart: Katholisches Bibelwerk, 1983), 56ff.

5. Merklein, 63–66.

6. A standard work on these "contrast parables" is Joachim Jeremias, *The Parables of Jesus*, second revised edition, trans. S. H. Hooke (New York: Charles Scribner's Sons, 1963), 146ff.; cf. Merklein, 73ff.

7. Cf. Isa 29:18ff., 35:5ff., 42:7, 26:13, 61:1. Exorcisms are missing in the list; Merklein, 67.

8. Merklein, 67. It is disputed whether this is a post-resurrection summary of Jesus' works—thus Peter Stuhlmacher, *Das Paulinische Evangelium I*, 223ff.; Eduard Lohse, "Das Evangelium für die Armen," *ZNW* 72 (1981), 51–64, 59—or an authentic logion—thus Werner Kümmel, "Jesu Antwort an den Täufer. Ein Beispiel zum Methodenproblem in der Jesusforschung," in *Heils-geschehen und Geschichte II* (Marburg: N. G. Elwert, 1978), 177–200; Peter Stuhlmacher, "Das paulinische Evangelium," in *Das Evangelium und die Evangelien*, 174 n. 41; Otto Betz, "Jesu Evangelium vom Gottesreich," in *Das Evangelium und die Evangelien*, 62.

9. I assume for the time being that the tradition in Luke 6:20ff. is the more original version.

10. Cf. Jürgen Becker, *Das Heil Gottes*, SUNT 3 (Göttingen: Vandenhoeck und Ruprecht, 1964), 204ff., and Merklein, 46.

11. Frankemölle, 49, considers this reference to Isa 61:1 uncertain.

12. Robert Martin-Achard, " ành elend sein," *THAT* 2:349–50. Cf. Diethelm Michel, *TRE* 4:73–76.

13. Cf. Eduard Lohse, *ZNW* 72 (1981), 56. I consider the version with the direct address to be original. So does Josef Ernst, *Das Evangelium nach Lukas*, RNT (Regensburg: Friedrich Pustet, 1977), on this passage.

14. Julius Schniewind, *Das Evangelium nach Matthäus*, NTD 2, 9th edition (Göttingen: Vandenhoeck und Ruprecht, 1960), 41.

15. Luke 10:18, Mark 3:20-27, Matt 12:20-30, Luke 11:14, 23. Cf. Franz Annen, "Die Dämonenaustreibungen Jesu in den synoptischen Evangelien," *Theologische Berichte* 5 (1976), 107–46.

16. Mark 1:21-28, 5:1-20, 9:14-29.

17. Cf. Luke 4:39 with Mark 1:31. But see the distinction between healing and exorcism in the summary reports (Mark 1:32-34 and parallels, 3:7-12 and parallels). See also Wolfgang J. Bittner, *Heilung—Zeichen der Herrschaft Gottes*, 2nd edition (Neukirchen-Vluyn: Aussaat Verlag, 1988), 32f.

18. Cf. Merklein, 68–72, and Bittner, 37f.

19. Otto Betz, *EDNT* 3:571.

20. Ibid.

21. Cf. Mark 2:1-12, 5:25-34, Matt 8:5-10 and parallels, 15, 28. And see Joachim Jeremias, *New Testament Theology: Part One: The Proclamation of Jesus*, trans. John Bowden (London: SCM Press, 1971), 159–66.

22. So Hannah Wolff, *Jesus the Therapist* (Oak Park: Meyer-Stone Books, 1987), 26ff., referring to John 5:1-8.

23. Cf. Matt 11:6 in relation to 11:5.

24. Cf. Carsten Colpe, *"ho huos tou anthropou,"* *TDNT* 8:430–31.

25. Regarding the difficult tradition history of Mark 2:15-17 see Rudolf Pesch, *Das Markusevangelium*, HTKNT II,1 (Freiburg: Verlag Herder, 1976), 167ff., who considers 15, 16, 17b to be authentic, while Dietrich-Alex Koch in "Jesu Tischgemeinschaft mit Zöllnern und Sündern. Erwägungen zur Entste-hung von Mk 2:13-17," in Dietrich-Alex Koch (ed.), *Jesu Rede von Gott und ihre Nachgeschichte im frühen Christentum* [FS Willi Marxsen] (Gütersloh:

Gütersloher Verlag, 1989), 57–73, regards vv. 15*ab*, 16, and 17*a* as the basis of the Palestinian tradition which is rooted in the practice and attitude of Jesus (68). I consider v. 17 to be an authentic double logion of Jesus.

26. Cf. Joachim Jeremias, "Zöllner und Sünder," *ZNW* 30 (1931), 293–300, and ibid., *RGG* 6:1927f.; Otfried Hofius, *Jesu Tischgemeinschaft mit den Sündern* (Stuttgart: Calwer Verlag, 1967), 14–16.

27. Cf. Luke 7:37-39, Matt 21:31ff.

28. Cf. Otto Michel, *TDNT* 8:101ff.

29. So Jeremias and Hofius.

30. Fritz Herrenbrück, "Wer waren die 'Zöllner'?" *ZNW* 72 (1981), 178–94, esp. 194.

31. This is the tendency in Luise Schottroff and Wolfgang Stegemann, *Jesus and the Hope of the Poor* (Maryknoll: Orbis Books, 1984), 30.

32. Cf. Merklein, "Jesu Botschaft," 81, Michel, *TDNT* 8:105, n. 155. Zacchaeus fulfills the conditions mentioned above on his own de facto (Michel, 8:105, 107).

33. So Enrique Dussel, "Das Reich Gottes und die Armen," *Zeitschrift für Mission* 5 (1979), 154–72; quotation, 160: "In as far as the poor person is oppressed (and thus not a sinner, rather one of the righteous) and an active liberator (one of the people), he is a subject of the kingdom . . . (Lk 4,20)."

34. However, Jesus' action as such has a symbolism "in which the Gospel of God's saving love finds its sensible expression" (Jeremias, *RGG* 6:1928). See also Hofius, "Jesu Tischgemeinschaft," 16–20.

35. Cf. Rudolf Schnackenburg, *The Gospel According to St. John*, 3 vols. (New York: Crossroad, 1982–90), 2:167–8

36. Otfried Hofius, "Vergebungszuspruch und Vollmachtsfrage. Mk 2,1–12 und das Problem priesterlicher Absolution im antiken Judentum," in Hans-Georg Geyer, et al. (eds.), *"Wenn nicht jetzt, wann dann?"* [FS Hans-Joachim Kraus], 4th edition (Neukirchen-Vluyn: Neukirchner Verlag, 1983), 115–28.

37. Heinz Schürmann, *Das Lukasevangelium*, HTKNT III,1 (Freiburg: Verlag Herder, 1983), with reference to this passage.

38. Ernst Fuchs, "Das Zeitverständnis Jesu," in *Zur Frage nach dem historischen Jesus, Gesammelte Aufsätze II* (Tübingen: J. C. B. Mohr [Paul Siebeck], 1960), 353f. See also Hartwig Thyen, *Studien zur Sündenvergebung im Neuen Testament*, FRLANT 96 (Göttingen: Vandenhoeck und Ruprecht, 1970), 242 n.2, and cf. Peter Fiedler, *Jesus und die Sünder* (Frankfurt/Main: Peter Lang, 1966), 112.

39. That the father in the parable of the prodigal son "does not allow his son to finish speaking his confession" (Merklein, "Jesu Botschaft," 80) is valid only for the consequence ("treat me as one of your hired servants" v. 19*b*), but not for the confession of sin itself (v. 21=18, 19*a*).

40. To be sure, Luke 15:7 is often regarded as secondary (see Hans Weder, *Die Gleichnisse Jesu als Metaphern*, FRLANT 120, 2nd edition [Göttingen: Vandenhoeck und Ruprecht, 1980], 172, 175), but in my opinion the offensiveness of the verse speaks against this.

41. Cf. Fritz Rienecker, *Das Evangelium nach Lukas*, Wuppertaler Studienbibel, (Wuppertal: R. Brockhaus, 1953), on this passage. Karl Heinrich

Rengstorf, *Das Evangelium nach Lukas*, NTD 3, 10th edition (Göttingen: Vandenhoeck und Ruprecht, 1965), 183, argues against this position.

42. Cf. Mark 2:13-17 and parallels, Luke 7:36-50, 15:1ff.

43. Jeremias, *Parables*, 124, 37.

44. Cf. Eckhard Rau, *Reden in Vollmacht*, FRLANT 149 (Göttingen: Vandenhoeck und Ruprecht, 1990), 395ff. The thesis of Luise Schottroff in "Das Gleichnis vom verlorenen Sohn," *ZTK* 68 (1971), 27–52, that Luke 15:11-36 was composed by Luke to illustrate his theology of repentance can be regarded as refuted (cf. Hans Weder, *Gleichnisse*, 252–54).

45. But Weder, 189f., correctly points out that the point of the parable may not be reduced to the antithesis "Pharisee—tax collector."

46. Weder, 237, who, to be sure, sees the actual point in the call to discipleship.

47. Leonard Goppelt, *Theology of the New Testament: Volume One*, trans. John E. Alsup (Grand Rapids: William B. Eerdmanns, 1975), 188.

48. Cf. Peter Stuhlmacher, "Why Did Jesus Have to Die?" in *Jesus of Nazareth, Christ of Faith*, trans. Siegfried Schatzmann (Peabody, MA: Hendrickson Publishers, 1993), 39–57, and the authors he names in his notes. See further the methodogically very circumspect considerations of Joachim Gnilka, "Wie urteilte Jesus über seinen Tod?" and A. Vögtle, "Todesankündigungen und Todesverständnis Jesu," in Karl Kertelge (ed.), *Der Tod Jesu. Deutungen im Neuen Testament*, QD 74, 2nd edition (Freiburg: Verlag Herder, 1982), 13–113; Helmut Merklein, *Jesu Botschaft*, 131–44. On the basis of fundamental considerations Peter Fiedler rejects this position, *Jesus und die Sünder*, 277ff. See as a response Walter Klaiber, "Rechtfertigung und Kreuzesgeschehen," in Erich Lubahn and Otto Rodenberg (eds.), *Das Wort vom Kreuz* (Giessen: Brunnen Verlag, 1988), 109ff.

49. "The many" is to be understood inclusively as meaning "all" and points toward the world of many peoples. See Peter Stuhlmacher, "Vicariously Giving His Life for Many, Mark 10:45 (Matt. 20:28)," in *Reconciliation, Law, and Righteousness: Essays in Biblical Theology* (Philadelphia: Fortress Press, 1986), 16–29.

50. Cf. Hahn, *Mission*, 40–45; Hengel, "Origins," 61f.; Gerhard Schneider, "Der Missionsauftrag Jesu in der Darstellung der Evangelien," in *Mission im Neuen Testament*, 71–92.

51. Gerd Theißen, "Wanderradikalismus," *Studien zur Soziologie der Urchristentums*, 3rd edition (Tübingen: J. C. B. Mohr [Paul Siebeck], 1989), 79–108, and *Sociology of Early Palestinian Christianity*, trans. John Bowden (Philadelphia: Fortress Press, 1978); Schottroff and Stegemann, *Jesus and the Hope of the Poor*, 62–69; M. N. Ebertz, *Das Charisma des Gekreuzigten: Zur Soziologie der Jesusbewegung*, WUNT 45 (Tübingen: J. C. B. Mohr [Paul Siebeck], 1987); Theodor Schmeller, *Brechungen. Urchristliche Wandercharismatiker im Prisma soziologisch orientierter Exegese*, SBS 136 (Stuttgart: Katholisches Bibelwerk, 1989).

52. Bittner, *Heilung*, 24–38.

53. Matt 10:1 only names the authority to cast out demons and heal the sick.

54. Cf. John 13:20f., 20:21; 2 Cor 5:20. See also Alfons Weiser, "Wie mich

der Vater gesandt hat, so sende ich euch," in Heinrich Köster and Manfred Probst (eds.), *Wie mich der Vater gesandt hat, so sende ich euch* (Limburg: Lahn-Verlag, 1982), 26–32.

55. "Miraculous healing occupied the same place in the Jesus movement as terrorist actions in the resistance movement." Theißen, *Sociology*, 63.

56. Klemens Stock, "Theologie der Mission bei Markus," in *Mission im Neuen Testament*, 130–44, and Mortimer Arias and Alan Johnson, *The Great Commission*, 35–55.

57. Cf. Pesch, *Markus*, 2:544–56.

58. Walter Bauer, *Wörterbuch zum Neuen Testament*, sixth edition (Berlin/New York: Walter de Gruyter, 1988), 1250. For the relationship to the reports of Acts cf. Joachim Gnilka, *Das Evangelium nach Markus*, EKKNT II/2 (Neukirchen-Vluyn: Neukirchner Verlag, 1979), 356.

59. Dieter Georgi, *The Opponents of Paul in Second Corinthians* (Philadelphia: Fortress Press, 1986), 164ff., and Gerd Theißen, "Legimation and Subsistence: An Essay on the Sociology of Early Christian Movements," *The Social Setting of Pauline Christianity*, ed. and trans. John H. Schütz (Philadelphia: Fortress Press, 1982), 27–67.

60. Hahn, *Mission*, 101; Senior and Stuhlmueller, *Biblical Foundations*, 225ff.

61. Hubert Frankemölle, "Zur Theologie der Mission im Matthäusevangelium," in *Mission im Neuen Testament*, 93–129. Regarding Matt 28:16-20 see, besides the commentaries, the following: Günter Bornkamm, "The Risen Lord and the Earthly Jesus: Matthew 28:16-20," in J. M. Robinson (ed.), *The Future of Our Religions Past* (London: SCM Press, and Philadelpia: Fortress Press, 1971), 203–29; Ferdinand Hahn, "Der Sendungsauftrag des Auferstandenen. Matthäus 28,16-20," in *Fides pro mundi vita. Missionstheologie heute*, MWF 14 [FS Hans-Werner Gensichen] (Gütersloh: Gütersloher Verlag, 1980), 28–32; Gerhard Friedrich, "Die formale Struktur von Mt 28,18-20," *ZTK* 83 (1983), 137–83; Arias and Johnson, *The Great Commission*, 15–35; David Bosch, *Transforming Mission*, 56–83.

62. The Sermon on the Mount may be regarded as an outstanding example of Jesus' teaching as comfort and instruction simultaneously.

63. In John Wimber, *Power Evangelism* (London: Hodder and Stoughton, 1985), Matt 28:18-20 is—in contrast to Mark 16:14-20—not even considered (115), while Wolfgang Bittner is of the opinion that for the exegesis of Matt 28 "the contents of the commission in Matt 10 has to be considered" (*Heilung*, 43). Hahn, "Sendung," 33, rejects this: In Matthew "not without reason . . . the reference to the mighty deeds is deleted and is instead of this referred to the basic and unchangeable valid teaching of Jesus."

64. Paul Zingg, "Herr, sind es wenige, die gerettet werden? Impulse für eine missionarische Spiritualität im lukanischen Werk," in Horst Rzepkowski (ed.), *Allen alles werden* (Sankt Augustin: Steyler-Verlag, 1978), 30–52; Jakob Kremer, "Weltweites Zeugnis in der Kraft des Geistes. Zur lukanischen Sicht der Mission," in *Mission im Neuen Testament*, 145–63; David Bosch, "Mission in Jesus' Way: A Perspective from Luke's Gospel," *Missionalia* 17 (1989), 3–21, and *Transforming Mission*, 84–122; Arias and Johnson, *The Great Commission*, 56–77.

65. Gerhard Schneider, *Das Evangelium nach Lukas*, Ökumenische Taschen-

buchkommentar zum Neuen Testament 3/2 (Gütersloh: Gütersloher Verlag, 1977), 502.

66. See on this point Christoph Burchard, *Der dreizehnte Zeuge*, FRLANT 103 (Göttingen: Vandenhoeck und Ruprecht, 1970).

67. Ulrich Luz, *EDNT* 1:204. Cf. Martin Völkel, "Zur Deutung des 'Reiches Gottes' bei Lukas," *ZNW* 65 (1975), 57–70, esp. 66ff.

68. Luz, *EDNT* 1:490.

69. See above on Mark 16:15ff.

70. Cf. Gerd Theißen, *The Miracle Stories of the Early Christian Tradition* (Edinburgh: T & T Clark, 1983), 249ff.

71. "God's finger is not at our disposal," writes Christoph Burchard following Luke 11:20 in "Jesus für die Welt. Über das Verhältnis von Reich Gottes und Mission," in *Fides pro mundi vita*, 13–27, 17.

72. Raymond Fung speaks of those "sinned against." "Good News to the Poor—A Case for a Missionary Movement," in *Your Kingdom Come—Report on the World Conference on Mission and Evangelism, Melbourne, Australia, 1980* (Geneva: WCC, 1983), 840.

73. So Dussel, "Das Reich Gottes und die Armen," 33. For a different view see O. E. Costas, *Liberating News*, 22ff.

74. Regarding the relationship between Jesus' promise of salvation and his "social ministry" cf. Nikolaus Walter, "'Historischer Jesus' und Osterglaube," *TLZ* 101 (1976), 312–28, 333f.

75. Cf. Burchard, "Jesus für die Welt."

76. This is also maintained—if with varying clarity—by more recent works which propose a theology of missions in the perspective of the kingdom of God. Cf. Mortimer Arias, *Announcing the Reign of God: Evangelization and the Subversive Memory of Jesus* (Philadelphia: Fortress, 1984), Emilio Castro, *Freeedom in Mission: The Perspective of the Kingdom of God* (Geneva: WCC, 1985), William J. Abraham, *The Logic of Evangelism* (Grand Rapids: William B. Eerdmanns, 1989), which describes the task of evangelism as "initiation into the Kingdom of God" (95).

77. See on this point Helmut Flender, "Biblische Exegese und evangelistische Verkündigung," in Theodor Schober and Hans Thimme (eds.), *Gemeinde in diakonischer und missionarischer Verantwortung* (Stuttgart: Quell-Verlag, 1979), 46–53.

78. Cf. on the view of Mark Gnilka, *Markus*, 1:171, and on the relevant basis in Jesus' parabolic speech Rau, *Reden in Vollmacht*, 395ff.

79. Cf. Christian Blendinger and Dietrich Müller, "Disciple/Follow," *NIDNT* 1:480–90.

80. Cf. Klemens Stock, "Boten aus dem Mit-ihm-Sein. Das Verhältnis zwischen Jesus und den Zwölf nach Markus," AnBib 70 (1975).

81. Cf. Hans Weder, *Neutestamentliche Hermeneutik* (Zürich: Theologischer Verlag, 1986), 189ff.

82. It is interesting for our topic that, while Paul actually reminds the church of his earlier preaching, he uses the word *gnōrizō*, a word which does not mean "to remind" (in opposition to RSV, NRSV, NIV, NJB, and TEV); rather it is a term for a solemn and express announcement: "I make the message of salvation

known to you." Cf. BAGD under this entry. The reference to the first preaching, which grounded their faith, is more than a reminder!

83. Cf. Christian Wolff, *Der erste Brief des Paulus an die Korinther (Zweiter Teil)*, THKNT VII/2 (Berlin: Evangelische Verlagsanstalt, 1984), on this passage, who also names and discusses the many newer publications in an excursis (153–58); further Hans Conzelmann, *1 Corinthians*, Hermeneia (Philadelphia: Fortress Press, 1975), 251–58.

84. Cf. Rom 10:9, and see Werner Kramer, *Christ, Lord, Son of God*, SBT 50 (London: SCM Press, 1966), 26–28.

85. Cf. Wolff, 159, especially the bibliography.

86. This function of the witnesses to the resurrection is underlined by v. 6. This should be maintained in opposition to the diversely justified objections of Karl Barth in *Die Auferstehung der Toten* (Zürich: Theologischer Verlag, 1953), 83, and Rudolf Bultmann, *Faith and Understanding*, ed. Robert W. Funk (London: SCM Press, 1969), 66–94, 83ff. Cf. further Wolff, 167ff.

87. Cf. Ulrich Wilckens, *Der Brief an die Römer (1. Teilband Röm 1–5)*, EKKNT VI/1, (Neukirchen-Vluyn: Neukirchner Verlag, 1987), 56–61.

88. Cf. the continuation in v. 5.

89. Cf. Traugott Holz, *Der Erste Brief an die Thessalonicher*, EKKNT XIII (Neukirchen-Vluyn: Neukirchner Verlag, 1986), 54–62.

90. Holz, 62.

91. On anchoring this schema in the tradition of the deuteronomic sermon of judgment cf. O. H. Steck, *Israel und das gewaltsame Geschick der Propheten*, WMANT 23 (Neukirchen-Vluyn: Neukirchner Verlag, 1967), 167. On the missionary speeches in general see Ulrich Wilckens, *Die Missionsreden der Apostelgeschichte*, WMANT 5, 3rd edition (Neukirchen-Vluyn: Neukirchner Verlag, 1974), esp. 178ff., and Jürgen Roloff, *Die Apostelgeschichte*, NTD 5 (Göttingen: Vandenhoeck und Ruprecht, 1981), 49–51.

92. On this see Jürgen Becker, "Das Gottesbild Jesu und die älteste Auslegung von Ostern," in Georg Strecker (ed.), *Jesus Christus in Historie und Theologie* [FS Hans Conzelmann] (Tübingen: J. C. B. Mohr [Paul Siebeck], 1975), 105–26, 118ff.

93. It is not clear why Paul in this letter to the Romans selected the pairs of opposites Greeks and non-Greeks (literally barbarians), and wise and foolish to characterize the breadth of the address of the gospel. Is it the colorful mixture of different peoples in the capital of the empire that he refers to obliquely here (as Wilckens, *Römerbrief*, 1:83, believes)? In any event it shows that Paul knows not only the religious but also the cultural barriers which the gospel must and can overcome.

94. Cf. K. H. Schelkle, *EDNT* 3:327–29 and Werner Förster, *TDNT* 7:992–94.

95. Peter Stuhlmacher, *Gerechtigkeit Gottes bei Paulus*, FRLANT 87 (Göttingen: Vandenhoeck & Ruprecht, 1965), 78–84, and Klaiber, *Rechtfertigung und Gemeinde*, 77–80.

96. On this meaning of *ek pisteōs eis pistin* cf. Wilckens, *Römerbrief*, 1:88.

97. *Pephanerōtai* in 3:21 is a splendid example of the theological significance of a Greek perfect which unites "present and aorist in itself at the same

time . . . in that it expresses the *duration of that which has been completed*," thus BDR §340. Cf. further Wolfgang Schrage, "Römer 3,21–26 und die Bedeutung des Todes Jesu Christi bei Paulus," in Paul Rieger (ed.), *Das Kreuz Jesu* (Göttingen: Vandenhoeck und Ruprecht, 1965), 65–88, 72.

98. The present participles are future in meaning—so BDR §399, 2—or to be understood as timeless as types in dogmatic sentences—Johannes Weiß, *Der 1. Korintherbrief* (Göttingen: Vandenhoeck und Ruprecht, 1910), 25ff. On the entire discussion cf. Klaiber, *Rechtfertigung und Gemeinde*, 75–77.

99. Paul emphasizes that the force of the gospel can also lead to its rejection where the effectiveness of his preaching is challenged, 2 Cor 2:15f., 4:2f.

100. The aorist participles indicate a one-time event: Cf. Gal 1:15, 2 Cor 3:6, Phil 3:7ff. Cillies Breytenbach, *Versöhnung*, WMANT 60 (Neukirchen-Vluyn: Neukirchner Verlag, 1989), 132ff.

101. On the introductory formula and its construction see Breytenbach, 110f., and BAGD, 1192. The following translation seeks to take into account the different tenses of the participles: "As it is established that God is at work reconciling the world in Christ by not reckoning its sin and through appointing the word of reconciliation among us." My German translation is, "Wie es ja feststeht, daß Gott am Werk ist, die Welt in Christus zu versöhnen, indem er ihnen ihre Sünde nicht zurechnet und dadurch, daß er unter uns das Wort von der Versöhnung eingesetzt hat." Otfried Hofius makes another proposal for a German translation in "'Gott hat unter uns aufgerichtet das Wort von der Versöhnung' (2. Kor 5,19)," *ZNW* 71 (1980), 3–20, 6ff.

102. Cf. Eberhard Jüngel, "Die Autorität des bittenden Christus," in *Unterwegs zur Sache*, BEvT 61 (Munich: Chr. Kaiser Verlag, 1972), 179–88.

103. Breytenbach interprets the appeal to the church to reconciliation with God as an appeal to reconciliation with his envoy (136f., 178f). For a broader study see Jan Lambrecht, "The Favorable Time: A Study of 2 Cor 6,2a in its Context," in Hubert Frankenmölle und Karl Kertelge (eds.), *Vom Urchristentum zu Jesus. Für Joachim Gnilka*, (Freiburg: Verlag Herder, 1989), 377–90.

104. Breytenbach has shown this unequivocally (104, 220ff.).

105. Breytenbach, 140. Cf. further to 5:21 Stuhlmacher, *Gerechtigkeit Gottes*, 74–77; Karl Kertelge, *"Rechtfertigung" bei Paulus*, NTAbh NF 3 (Münster: Aschendorf, 1966), 99–107; Klaiber, *Rechtfertigung und Gemeinde*, 99f.; H. Giesen, "Jesu Tod als Zugang zur 'Gerechtigkeit Gottes'," *Theologie der Gegenwart (Bergen-Enkheim)* 26 (1983), 23–36.

106. Hans Joachim Iwand, *Rechtfertigung und Christusglaube* (Leipzig: I. C. E. Hinrichs, 1930; reprinted TBü 14 [Munich: Chr. Kaiser Verlag, 1966]), has vividly shown the constitutive connection of *sola fide* and *fides Christi* for Luther's beginnings.

107. Paul's struggle against "another gospel" in Gal 1 is a struggle for a message of salvation lived in mission.

108. On the terminology and the issue itself cf. Günther Bornkamm, "Sin, Law and Death (Romans 2)," *Early Christian Experience*, The New Tesament Library (London: SCM Press, 1969), 87–104, 90; Hans Hübner, *Law in Paul's Thought*, James C. G. Greig trans. (Edinburgh: T & T Clark, 1984), 72ff.; Gerd Theißen, *Psychological Aspects of Pauline Theology*, trans. John P. Galvin

(Edinburgh: T & T Clark, 1987), 179ff.; Walter Klaiber, *Rechenschaft über den Glauben. Bibelauslegung für die Praxis 21 (Römerbrief)* (Stuttgart: Katholisches Bibelwerk, 1989), 79.

109. Cf. my attempt to talk about justification in terms generally intelligible today in Walter Klaiber, *Wo Leben wieder Leben ist. Bekehrung, Wiedergeburt, Rechtfertigung, Heiligung: Dimensionen eines Lebens mit Gott* (Stuttgart: Christliches Verlagshaus, 1984), 45–63.

110. Cf. Klaiber, "Rechtfertigung und Kreuzesgeschehen," 116–18.

111. Johanna Herzog-Dürck, *Probleme menschlicher Reifung* (Stuttgart: Klett Verlag, 1969), 36ff.

112. It is very revealing how John Wimber, *Power Evangelism*, 60, emphasizes Paul's preaching in Corinth as an example of "Power Evangelism." He contrasts it with the unsuccessful sermon in Athens and describes it with the following, intentionally abbreviated quotation from 1 Cor 2:1, 4f: "When I came to you, brethren, I did not come with eloquence and persuasion or superior wisdom. . . . my message and my preaching were not with wise words, but with a demonstration of the Spirit's power." Wimber comments, "Paul changed his evangelistic methods: In Corinth he combined demonstration with proclamation." It is not possible to misunderstand Paul more thoroughly than this!

113. Cf. Erhard Güttgemanns, *Der leidende Apostel und sein Herr*, FRLANT 90 (Göttingen: Vandenhoeck & Ruprecht, 1966) and Klaiber, *Rechtfertigung und Gemeinde*, 130ff.

114. Cf. Ernst Käsemann, "Die Legitimität des Apostels," in K. H. Rengstorf (ed.), *Das Paulusbild in der neueren deutschen Forschung*, Wege der Forschung 24 (Darmstadt: Wissenschaftliche Buchgesellschaft, 1964), 475– 521.

115. On this circle of tradition see Ulrich B. Müller, *Die Menschwerdung des Gottessohnes. Frühchristliche Inkarnationsvorstellungen und die Anfänge des Doketismus*, SBS 140 (Stuttgart: Katholisches Bibelwerk, 1990).

116. Cf. the careful account and discussion of this question in Teresa Okure, *The Johannine Approach to Mission. A Contextual Study of John 4:1-42*, WUNT II,31 (Tübingen: J. C. B. Mohr [Paul Siebeck], 1988), 1–35, and further Hahn, *Mission*, 135–45; Legrand, Pathrapankal and Vallanickal, *Good News*, 124–64; Rudolf Schnackenburg, "Der Missionsgedanke des Johannesevangeliums im heutigen Horizont," in *Das Johannesevangelium IV*, HTKNT IV/4 (Freiburg: Verlag Herder, 1984), 58–72.

117. Cf. Schnackenburg, *The Gospel According to St. John*, 3:338, and Okure, 39–49.

118. On "God's mission (which is to be understood in trinitarian terms)" as the foundation of a theology of mission cf. Margull, "Mission. III. Christliche Mission," in *RGG* 4:973–80, and further G. F. Vicedom, *Missio Dei* (Munich: Chr. Kaiser Verlag, 1958), 39. On the Johannine "Sendungstheologie" cf. Jan Adolf Bühner, *Der Gesandte und sein Weg im 4. Evangelium*, WUNT II,2 (Tübingen: J. C. B. Mohr [Paul Siebeck], 1977); José P. Miranda, *Der Vater, der mich gesandt hat*, EHS 7 (Frankfurt/Main: Verlag Peter Lang, 1972) and *Die Sendung Jesu im 4. Evangelium*, SBS 87 (Stuttgart: Katholisches Bibelwerk, 1977), and Schnackenburg, "Missionsgedanke," 60ff.

119. On the reasons for the following interpretation against the background

of the exegetical discussion cf. Walter Klaiber, "Die Aufgabe einer theologischen Interpretation des 4. Evangeliums," *ZTK* 82 (1985), 300–24, 307ff.

120. In 1:7 the aorist subjunctive is uniformly witnessed in the textual tradition!

121. This is how Hartmut Gese translates *charis kai alētheia* (German: *unverbrüchlich währende Wahrheit*) in "Der Johannesprolog," in *Zur biblischen Theologie*, BEvT 78 (Munich: Chr. Kaiser Verlag, 1977), 152–201, 186ff.

122. Cf. Ferdinand Hahn, "Die Jüngerberufung Joh 1,35-51," in Joachim Gnilka (ed.), *Neues Testament und Kirche* [FS Rudolf Schnackenburg] (Freiburg: Verlag Herder, 1974), 172–90.

123. Cf. Walter Klaiber, "Der irdische and der himmlische Zeuge. Eine Auslegung von Joh 3,22-36," *NTS* 36 (1990), 205–33.

124. Besides Okure cf. Hubert Ritt, "Die Frau als Glaubensbotin. Zum Verständnis der Samariterin von Joh 4,1-42," in *Vom Urchristentum zu Jesus: Für Joachim Gnilka*, 287–306.

125. Okure, 140–64.

126. Here as well the present subjunctive in contrast to the aorist subjunctive is the better attested reading; nonetheless, the meaning is unequivocally missional. Cf. Schnackenburg, *The Gospel According to St. John*, on this passage.

127. Rudolf Bultmann, *Theology of the New Testament*, trans. Kendrick Grobel, 2 volumes in 1, (New York: Charles Scribner's Sons, 1951 and 1955), 2:66.

128. Schnackenburg, *The Gospel According to St. John*, 2:200.

129. In opposition to Bultmann, *Theology*, 2:66.

130. Klaiber, "Aufgabe," 317.

131. In the face of the Johannine dualism it is very controversial whether the "offer of salvation to the world" in the context of the Gospel really has positive meaning or not. Luise Schottroff, *Der Glaubende und die feindliche Welt*, WMANT 37 (Neukirchen-Vluyn: Neukirchner Verlag, 1970), 284ff., denies this. See in opposition Karl Wolfgang Tröger, "Ja oder Nein zur Welt," *Theologische Versuche* 7 (1976), 61–80, 37, and Takashi Onuki, *Gemeinde und Welt im Johannesevangelium*, WMANT 56 (Neukirchen-Vluyn: Neukirchner Verlag, 1983), 52ff.

132. Schnackenburg, *The Gospel According to St. John*, 3:65.

133. Werner Kramer, *Christ, Lord, Son of God*, SBT 50 (London: SCM Press, 1966), 111–19.

134. Kramer, 115–19.

135. But also cf. Eph 5:2, Gal 1:4 and Rom 4:25, and on these passages, Kramer, 118ff., and Wiard Popkes, *Christus Traditus*, ATANT 49, (Zürich: Theologischer Verlag, 1967), 274ff., 286ff.

136. Cf. Wilfried Haubeck, *Loskauf durch Christus* (Gießen/Basel/Vienna: Brunner-Verlag/Bundes-Verlag, 1985), 149–61, 312ff.

137. Wilckens, *Römerbrief*, 2:172f.

138. Friedrich Lang, *Die Briefe an die Korinther*, NTD 7 (Göttingen: Vandenhoeck und Ruprecht, 1986), 319. On the tradition critical (traditionsgeschichtlich) background see Victor Paul Furnish, *II Corinthians*, AB 32A (New York: Doubleday & Co., 1980), 417.

139. Cf. Ernst Käsemann, "Kritische Analyse von Phil 2,5-11," *Exegetische Versuche und Besinnungen I* (Tübingen: J. C. B. Mohr [Paul Siebeck], 1970), 51–95.

140. Ernst Käsemann, *Commentary on Romans* (Grand Rapids: William B. Eerdmanns, 1980), 157–58..

141. Cf. William R. Loader, *Sohn und Hohepriester*, WMANT 53 (Neukirchen-Vluyn: Neukirchner Verlag, 1981).

142. August Strobel, *Der Brief an die Hebräer*, NTD 9 (Göttingen: Vandenhoeck & Ruprecht, 1975), 104.

143. Strobel, 105.

144. Strobel, 129, paraphrases, "had to learn." "There is true Sonship only through obedience."

145. Heb 5:9 (like Phil 2:6-11) depicts Jesus' way as the basis of salvation as well as an example for his disciples. Cf. Strobel and, on the relationship between Hebrews and Philippians 2 generally, Otfried Hofius, *Der Christushymnus Philipper 2,6–11*, WUNT 17 (Tübingen: J. C. B. Mohr [Paul Siebeck], 1976).

146. Cf. Loader, 109f., on the Gethsemane tradition, and Otto Michel, *Der Brief an die Hebräer*, MeyerK 13, (Göttingen: Vandenhoeck und Ruprecht, 1984), 211ff., on the temptation.

147. Cf. Horst Balz, *EDNT* 2:78ff.; the closest term (etymologically as well) is *stenochoria*, "(literally) narrowness; anxiety": Rom 2:5, 8:35, 2 Cor 6:4, 12:10.

148. Martin Heidegger, *Being and Time* (London: SCM Press, 1962), §40.

149. Søren Kierkegaard, *The Concept of Dread*, trans. Walter Lowrie, 2nd edition (Princeton: Princeton University Press, 1957), 55.

150. Eugen Drewermann, in his first work, *Strukturen des Bösen* (Munich: Verlag Friedrich Schöningh, 1989), and especially in Volume 3 (*Die jahwistische Urgeschichte in philosophischer Sicht*) on the basis of Gen 2–11 (J) and in critical discussion with psychoanalysis (XIVff.; 564ff.), has clearly shown the connection between anxiety and sin. In further works he has exclusively pursued anxiety as the "point of connection" for God's message; see *Tiefenpsychologie und Exegese II* (Olten: Walter Verlag, 1989), 34, 621ff., and the index. In spite of all necessary criticism, especially in regard to Drewermann's understanding of revelation and the gospel, we must pay attention to his analysis of the needs of contemporary men and women! See also Gian Condrau, *Angst und Schuld als Grundproblem der Psychotherapie* (Frankfurt: Suhrkamp-Verlag, 1976).

151. Käsemann, *Romans*, 228.

152. Cf. Horst Eberhard Richter, *All Mighty: A Study of the The God Complex in Western Man*, trans. Jan van Heurck (San Bernadino, CA: Borgo Press, 1986)].

153. Cf. Klaiber, *Wo Leben wieder Leben ist*, 26–44.

154. Hans Weder, "Die Menschwerdung Gottes," *ZTK* 82 (1985), 324–60, 359.

155. Weder, 358.

156. Jan Adolf Bühner, "Denkstrukturen im Johannesevangelium," *TBei* 13 (1982), 224–31, 231.

157. Cf. 8, 15ff., 26.

158. Cf. the temporal and material priority of the proclamation of faith before the reception of the Spirit according to Gal 3:2, 5. See on this point Joachim Rohde, *Der Brief des Paulus an die Galater*, THKNT 9 (Berlin: Evangelische Verlagsanstalt, 1988), 131ff.

159. Cf. Otfried Hofius, "Gesetz und Evangelium nach 2. Kor 3," *Jahrbuch für Biblische Theologie* 4 (1989), 105–50, 115.

160. Hofius, 148: It is "this spirit through which Christ redemptively discloses himself in the Gospel."

161. Takashi Onuki, *Gemeinde und Welt im Johannesevangelium*, 148: That "the already consummated judgment of the world is 'disclosed'" is the foundation of the call to faith and to salvation.

162. On the understanding of the Paraclete cf. Felix Porsch, *EDNT* 3:28–29, who calls attention to the connection of John 15:27 and Mark 13:9-13.

163. Onuki, *Gemeinde und Welt im Johannesevangelium*, 111–15, 213–18, has demonstrated this "function of Johannine 'dualisn'" very clearly.

Notes to Chapter 3

1. Donald Senior, "The Struggle to be Universal," *CBQ* 44 (1984), 63–81, 65ff.

2. Egon Brandenburger, "Pistis und Soteria zum Verstehenshorizont von Glaube im Urchristentum," *ZTK* 85 (1988), 165–98, 196.

3. Cf. especially 3:36. And see on this point Brandenburger, 191 and Klaiber, "Der irdische und der himmlische Zeuge," 218–30.

4. On the missional dimension of the existence of Israel see, however, Carroll Stuhlmueller, "The Foundations for Mission in the Old Testament," in Donald Senior and Carroll Stuhlmueller (eds.), *Biblical Foundations for Mission*, 9–138, and Legrand, *Unity and Plurality*, 21–58.

5. Karl Dietrich Schmidt, *Grundriß der Kirchengeschichte*, third edition (Göttingen: Vandenhoeck & Ruprecht, 1960), 105.

6. Athanasius, *On the Incarnation,* §54.3.

7. For an example of a traditio-critical approach cf. Peter Stuhlmacher, "Das Evangelium von der Versöhnung in Christus," in Peter Stuhlmacher and Helmut Claß (eds.), *Das Evangelium von der Versöhnung in Christus* (Stuttgart: Calwer Verlag, 1979), 13–53, and further James D. G. Dunn, *Unity and Diversity in the New Testament*, 2nd edition (London: SCM Press/Philadelphia: Trinity Press International, 1977, 1990).

8. Hartwig Thyen, *TRE* 17:218ff.

9. Cf. Erich Lubahn, *Heilgeschichtliche Theologie und Verkündigung* (Stuttgart: Christliches Verlagshaus, 1988) and Helge Stadelmann (ed.), *Glaube und Geschichte: Heilsgeschichte als Thema der Theologie* (Giessen/Basel: Brunnen Verlag, and Wuppertal: R. Brockhaus Verlag, 1986).

10. But see Wolfgang Bittner, "Geschichte und Eschatologie im Johannesevangelium" in Stadelmann, 154–80.

11. Ernst Ferdinand Ströter, *Der Fürst des Lebens muß einst alles erben* (Heilbronn: Paulus Verlag, 1966), 171.

12. Schottroff and Stegemann, *Jesus and the Hope of the Poor*, passim.

13. Luise Schottroff, "Die Schreckensherrschaft der Sünde und die Befreiung durch Christus nach dem Römerbrief des Paulus," *EvT* 39 (1979), 497–509.

14. Cf. regarding parallel phenomena in gnosticism, see Kurt Rudolph, "Das Problem einer Soziologie und 'sozialen Verortung' der Gnosis," *Kairos* 19 (1977), 35–44.

15. Klaus Wengst, *Bedrängte Gemeinde und verherrlichter Christus: Der historische Ort des Johannesevangeliums als Schlüsssel zu seiner Interpretation*, BibS(N) 5 (Neukirchen-Vluyn: Neukirchner Verlag, 1981).

16. Jürgen Moltmann, *The Crucified God*, trans. by R. A. Wilson and John Bowden (London: SCM Press, 1974), 7ff.

17. Peter Stuhlmacher, *Das paulinische Evangelium*, FRLANT 95 Göttingen: Vandenhoeck und Ruprecht, 1968), 97.

18. One should nonetheless observe that Paul himself does not address his accusation to different groups, but rather speaks of the general human state of affairs (1:18, 2:1)! He does not speak to "the Jews" until 2:17!

19. Walter Schmithals, *Der Römerbrief als historisches Problem*, SNT 9 (Gütersloh: Gütersloher Verlag, 1975), 69–90, and Klaus Haacker, "Urchristliche Mission und kulturelle Identität," *TBei* 19, (1988), 61–72.

20. Cf. Georg Eichholz, "Der missionarische Kanon des Paulus (1. Kor 9,19–23), in *Tradition und Interpretation*, TBü 29, (Munich: Chr. Kaiser Verlag, 1965), 114–20, and Günther Bornkamm, "The Missionary Stance of Paul in 1 Corinthians 9 and Acts," in Leander E. Keck and J. L. Martyn (eds.), *Studies in Luke-Acts* (Nashville: Abingdon Press, 1966), 194–207.

21. Georg Eichholz, *Die Theologie des Paulus im Umriß* (Neukirchen-Vluyn: Neukirchner Verlag, 1988), 41.

22. Christian Wolff, *1. Korinther*, THKNT 7/11, 31.

23. Bornkamm, "Missionary Stance," 196.

24. Cf. Peter Richardson, "Pauline Inconsistency: 1 Corinthians 9:19-23 and Galatians 2:11-14," *NTS* 29 (1980), 347–62, and Klaiber, *Rechtfertigung und Gemeinde*, 146ff., 253ff.

25. Cf. Klaus Haacker, "Die Berufung des Verfolgers und die Rechtfertigung des Gottlosen," *TBei* 6 (1975), 1–19; Christian Dietzfelbinger, *Die Berufung des Paulus als Ursprung seiner Theologie*, WMANT 58 (Neukirchen-Vluyn: Neukirchner Verlag, 1985); and Seyoon Kim, *The Origin of Paul's Gospel*, WUNT II,4 (Tübingen: J. C. B. Mohr [Paul Siebeck], 1984).

26. See pp. 83–86 below on Acts 17:22ff.

27. Walter Hollenweger, *Evangelisation gestern und heute* (Stuttgart: J. F. Steinkopf, 1973), 9–24; *Erfahrungen der Leiblichkeit*, Interkulturelle Theologie 1 (Munich: Chr. Kaiser Verlag, 1979), 127ff.; *TRE* 10:640.

28. Hollenweger, *Evangelisation*, 10.

29. Hollenweger, 16.

30. We can see how difficult this is in practice in Paul's wrestling with the Corinthians about the message of the resurrection. Here he tries to distinguish concepts he brought from Judaism (cf. 1 Cor 15:50) from the essence of the message.

31. Martin Dibelius, "Paulus auf dem Areopag," in *Aufsätze zur Apostelgeschichte*, FRLANT 60, (Göttingen: Vandenhoeck und Ruprecht, 1961), 29–70, esp. 70.

32. So Theodor Zahn, *Apostelgeschichte*, Kommentar zum Neuen Testament V,2 (Leipzig: A. Deichertsche Verlagsbuchhandlung, 1921) and John Wimber, *Power Evangelism*, 60.

33. On the history of interpretation see Rudolf Pesch, *Die Apostelgeschichte*, EKKNT V/2 (Neukirchen-Vluyn: Neukirchner Verlag, 1986), 142– 44.

34. Pesch, 142, and C. K. Barrett, "Paulus als Missionar und Theologe," *ZTK* 86 (1989), 18–32, 27f.

35. Jürgen Roloff, *Die Apostelgeschichte*, NTD 5 (Göttingen: Vandenhoeck und Ruprecht, 1981), 260.

36. See Roloff and Pesch on this passage, and cf. below on Rom 1:19ff.

37. See pages 102ff. below.

38. A basic work on this topic is Günther Bornkamm, *The Revelation of God's Work (Romans 1–3): Early Christian Experience* (London: SCM Press, 1969), 47–70. Cf. Käsemann, *Romans,* and Wilckens, *Römerbrief*, on this passage as well.

39. Wolfhart Pannenberg, *Systematic Theology*, trans. Geoffrey W. Bromiley, 2 vols. (Edinburgh: T & T Clark, 1991, 1994), 1:183–84, describes this as the danger of every "natural theology." What "ought" to have been and to have been able to be "natural" knowledge of God is described neither in Acts 17 nor in Rom 1:19-22 as a "natural" human capacity. Rather, in both cases the revelatory activity is ascribed to God: "God has shown it to them" (Rom 1:19) and "He [God] has made . . . and has determined. . . . that they should seek the Lord" (Acts 17.26ff.).

40. Verse 12 is also to be understood thus. Cf. Otfried Hofius, "Struktur und Gedankengang des Logos-Hymnus in Joh 1,1-18," *ZNW* 78 (1978), 1–25, 21ff.

41. "Die andere Aufgabe der Theologie*," Zwischen den Zeiten* 7 (1929), 255–76 and "Die Frage nach dem 'Anknüpfungspunkt' als Problem der Theologie," *Zwischen den Zeiten* 10 (1932), 505–32.

42. "Nature and Grace: A Contribution to the Discussion with Karl Barth" (1934), in *Natural Theology*, trans. Peter Framkel (London: The Centenary Press, 1946), 15–64, 58.

43. Heinrich Leopold, "Anknüpfung I," *TRE* 2:744ff.

44. Barth, *Church Dogmatics*, I.1:29; "No! Answer to Emil Brunner!" in *Natural Theology*, 127.

45. Barth, "No!" in *Natural Theology*, 127. In retrospect one can say that Barth was basically right, but in many respects did not understand Brunner's concern.

46. *God Transcendent: Foundation for a Christian Metaphysic*, trans. Edgar P. Dickie (London: Nisbel and Co., 1935), is based on the third German edition, which is *de facto* a new book.

47. Cited according to the first edition of *Glaube und Denken. Philosophische Grundlegung einer christlichen Lebensanschauung* (Berlin: Furche Verlag, 1931), 433f. This passage does not appear in the third German edition and is thus not in the English translation.

48. *Glaube und Denken*, 433f.

49. Adolf Schlatter, "Idealismus oder Theologie?" *Monatsschrift für Pastoraltheologie* 27 (1931), 356–71, 358f. We find a similar concern in Dietrich

Bonhoeffer's letter of June 8, 1944, from Tegel Prison to Eberhard Bethge in *Letters and Papers from Prison*, enlarged edition, ed. Eberhard Bethge, trans. Reginald W. Fuller (London: SCM Press, 1971), 177–82.

50. Reinhard Slenczka, "Glaube VI," *TRE* 13:358.

51. Zdenek Kučera, "Karl Heim," *TRE* 14:776.

52. Bultmann, *Faith and Understanding*, 313–30, 322ff.

53. Ibid., 322. The English translation concludes this passage with the words "it *banishes* 'natural theology.'" That is a misleading mistake in the translation.

54. Ibid., 327.

55. Ibid., 328.

56. Ibid, 330. This translation differs from the published text of the English edition.

57. Bultmann, *Essays: Philosophical and Theological*, trans. James C. G. Greig (London: SCM Press, 1955), 90–118, italics added.

58. Ibid., 133–50; quotations, 136–38.

59. Tillich, *Systematic Theology*, 1:61–62.

60. Ibid., 1:66.

61. Ibid., 1:64.

62. C. Rhein, "Tillich, Paul," *RGG* 6:900ff. Cf. also Bonhoeffer's position on these attempts—insofar as he put them on paper up to 1944—in *Letters and Papers from Prison*. I have decided against sketching Bonhoeffer's own concept of "non-religious interpretation" of religion because it is too fragmentary.

63. Pannenberg, *Systematic Theology*, 1:116.

64. Rahner, *Foundations of Christian Faith*, 225.

65. Ibid., 20.

66. Ibid., 21.

67. Ibid., 123.

68. Ibid.

69. Ibid., 173.

70. Ibid., 174.

71. Pannenberg, *Systematic Theology*, 1:116.

72. Ibid., 1:156ff.

73. Ibid., 1:184.

74. Ibid., 1:187.

75. Eberhard Jüngel, "*Extra Christum nulla salus*—a Principle of Natural Theology? Protestant Reflections on the 'anonymity' of the Christian," in *Theological Essays*, trans. D. B. Webster (Edinburgh: T & T Clark, 1989), 173–88, and "Das Dilemma der natürlichen Theologie und die Wahrheit ihres Problems. Überlegungen für ein Gespräch mit Wolfhart Pannenberg," in *Entsprechungen*, BEvT 88 (Munich: Chr. Kaiser Verlag, 1980), 158–77.

76. Jüngel, "Dilemma," 174ff.

77. Barth, "No!" in *Natural Theology*, 86ff.

78. Richter, *All Mighty*, 192.

79. Cf. the critical remarks of Hans Weder, *Neutestamentliche Hermeneutik* (Zürich: Theologischer Verlag, 1986), 140ff., on "making contact" using the problem of God.

80. Let me refer to my practical attempt to make such "contact" in Walter Klaiber, *Das kannst du glauben. Fünf Versuche, auf Grundfragen menschlichen Lebens zu antworten* (Stuttgart: Christliches Verlagshaus, 1988). Eugen Drewermann's proposal to make contact with the images anchored in the "collective unconsciousness of the human psyche" (*Tiefenpsychologie und Exegese*, 2:591, 777)—as fascinating as it may be—requires a thorough analysis in biblical perspective.

81. *TRE* 2:746.

82. Cf. the following essays in Walter Arnold (ed.), *Evangelisation im ökumenischen Gespräch* (Erlangen, Germany: Verlag der Evangelisch-lutherischen Mission, 1974); Halina Bortnowa, "Der hermeneutische Prozeß in der Evangelisation," 12–29; Michael Cassidy, "Der dritte Weg," 30–48; Orlando E. Costas, "Evangelisation—Zeugnis vom Heil der Welt," 49–62, as well as Christopher Sugden, "Evangelicals and Wholistic Evangelism," in Vinay Samuel and Albrecht Hauser (eds.), *Proclaiming Christ in Christ's Way: Studies in Integral Evangelism* [FS Walter Arnold] (Oxford: Regnum Books, 1989), 29–51.

83. Here I must draw attention to 1 Peter with its conception of suffering in the "footsteps of Christ" as bearing witness to the world (2:19-24, 3:14-17, 4:12-14). The impulse which lies in Christians' nonconformity is simultaneously an occasion for suffering and an occasion for questions about the foundations of their lives; cf. Peter Lippert, *Leben als Zeugnis*, SBM 4 (Stuttgart: Katholisches Bibelwerk, 1968) and Norbert Brox, "Situation und Sprache der Minderheit im 1. Petrusbrief," *Kairos* 19 (1977), 1–13.

84. Evelyn Albrecht, *Zeugnis durch Wort und Verhalten*, Theologische Dissertationen 13 (Basel: Emil Reinhardt, 1977), 216; Karl Müller, "Meaning and Priority of First Evangelisation in Today's Missiological Discussion," *VERBUM SVD* 26 (1985), 3–17; Heinrich Döring, "First Evangelism as Self-Actualization of the Church," *VERBUM SVD* 26 (1985), 31–64.

85. Orthodox theologians were the first to relate incarnation and evangelism: Mundurcl V. George, "Die Botschaft von der Menschwerdung in liturgischer Verkündigung," in *Evangelisation im ökumenischen Gespräch*, 63–75. But cf. also Timothy Gorringe, "Evangelism and Incarnation," *Indian Journal of Theology* 30 (1981), 69–77, and John Stott, "Christus und Mission—die Herausforderung der Gegenwart," *TBei* 21 (1990), 151ff.

86. These facts are a great challenge for evangelistic preaching for large groups of hearers.

87. Helmut Gollwitzer, *Krummes Holz—aufrechter Gang. Zur Frage nach dem Sinn des Lebens* (Munich: Chr. Kaiser Verlag, 1970).

88. Cf. Eberhard Jüngel, *Geistesgegenwart: Predigten* (Munich: Chr. Kaiser Verlag, 1974).

89. Jüngel, "Dilemma," 175.

90. Cf. pages 59ff. above.

91. Cf. pages 72ff. above.

92. Walter Klaiber, *Embraced by the Spirit*, trans. James A. Dwyer (Nashville: Abingdon Press, 1993), 61–65.

93. Cf. George W. Peters, *A Biblical Theology of Missions* (Chicago: The Moody Bible Institute of Chicago, 1972), chapter 7.

94. Cf. how soberly Georg Strecker, *EDNT* 2:70, takes stock of Michael Green's extensive discussion in *Evangelism*, 166–93.

95. Walter Rebell, "Gemeinde als Missionsfaktor im Urchristentum. I Kor 14.24f als Schlüsselsituation," *TZ* 44 (1988), 117–34.

96. Leslie William Barnard, "Apologetik I," *TRE* 3:408.

97. Karl Barth, *Church Dogmatics*, IV.3.1:109. Cf. Karl Gerhard Steck, "Apologetik II," *TRE* 3:411–24.

98. *Mission and Secularization*, CEC Study Document 18 (Geneva: Conference of European Churches, 1989), 77.

99. Brandenburger, "Pistis und Soteria," 193.

100. Albrecht Oepke, *Die Missionspredigt des Apostel Paulus*, Missionswissenschaftliche Forschungen 2 (Leipzig, 1920), 100ff., and *TDNT* 3:586 n.49; Claus Bussmann, *Themen der paulinischen Missionspredigt auf dem Hintergrund der spätjüdisch-hellenistischen Missionsliteratur*, Europäische Hochschulschriften: Theologie 23 (Frankfurt/Main: Verlag Peter Lang, 1975), 108–22.

101. Otto Michel, *Der Brief an die Römer*, fifth edition, MeyerK VI/1 (Göttingen: Vandenhoeck und Ruprecht, 1987), 97; Ulrich Wilckens, *Römer*, 101–103; Helmut Merklein, "Gericht und Heil. Zur hermeneutischen Funktion des Gerichtes bei Johannes dem Täufer," *Jahrbuch für Biblische Theologie 5* (Neukirchen-Vluyn: Neukirchner Verlag, 1990), 71–92, esp. 84.

102. Hans-Joachim Eckstein, "'Denn Gottes Zorn wird vom Himmel her offenbar werde'. Exegetische Erwägungen zu Röm 1,18," *ZNW* 78 (1987), 74–89.

103. Adolf Schlatter, *Gottes Gerechtigkeit (Römerbrief)* (Stuttgart: Calwer Verlag, 1991), 46–48; Bornkamm, *The Revelation of God's Work*, 47–70.

104. Bornkamm, 62f.; Käsemann, *Romans*, 31f.; Egon Brandenburger, "Gericht Gottes III," *TRE* 12:476, 50.

105. Brandenburger, "Pistis und Soteria," 193.

106. The following exegetes, whom we have already cited, answer this question affirmatively: Oepke, *Missionspredigt*, 100f., and *TDNT* 3:586, n. 49; Bussmann, 108–22; Michel, *Römer*, 96; Brandenburger, "Pistis und Soteria," 189f., and "Gericht," *TRE* 12:476. Käsemann, *Romans*, 31, is skeptical.

107. Klaus Seybold, "Gericht Gottes I," *TRE* 12:401, and Gerhard Liedke, "*špt / richten*," *THAT* 2:1008.

108. German: "Tun-Ergehen-Zusammenhang." Seybold, *TRE* 12:460.

109. Basic works here are Hans Walter Wolff, "Das Thema 'Umkehr' in der alttestamentlichen Prophetie," *Gesammelte Studien zum Alten Testament*, TBü 22 (Munich: Chr. Kaiser Verlag, 1964), 130–50, and Werner H. Schmidt, *Zukunftsgewißheit und Gegenwartskritik. Grundzüge prophetischer Verkündigung*, BibS(N) 64 (Neukirchen-Vluyn: Neukirchner Verlag, 1973). Cf. pp. 137–60 below for the discussion.

110. Claus Westermann, "Boten des Zornes Gottes. Der Begriff des Zornes Gottes in der Prophetie," in Jörg Jeremias and Lothar Perlitt eds., *Die Botschaft und die Boten* [FS Hans Walter Wolff] (Neukirchen-Vluyn: Neukirchner Verlag, 1981), 157–68.

111. Seybold, *TRE* 12:462.

112. Hans W. Wolff, "Die eigentliche Botschaft der klassischen Propheten," in Herbert Donner et al. (eds.), *Beiträge zur alttestamentlichen Prophetie* [FS Walter Zimmerli] (Göttingen: Vandenhoeck und Ruprecht, 1977), 547–57, esp. 555.

113. Wolff, "Botschaft," 553.

114. Wolff, 556.

115. Cf. Henning Graf Reventlow, *Rechtfertigung im Horizont des Alten Testaments*, BEvT 58, (Munich: Chr. Kaiser Verlag, 1971). 60ff., and Werner H. Schmidt, "'Rechtfertigung der Gottlosen' in der Botschaft der Propheten," in *Die Botschaft und die Boten*, 157–68.

116. Cf. on this issue Jer 31:29f.

117. Dan 7:10.27; *Pss.Sol.* 3:11f.; 1 Enoch 51:1-3. On apocalyptic Judaism see further Roger David Aus, "Gericht Gottes II," *TRE* 12:466–68, and on the relationship between the apocalyptic, the Old Testament and New Testament message of judgment see Egon Brandenburger, *Gerichtskonzeptionen im Urchristentum und ihre Voraussetzungen*, Studien zum Neuen Testament und seiner Umwelt 16 (Linz, 1991), 5–54.

118. Cf. Jürgen Becker, *Johannes der Täufer und Jesus von Nazareth*, BibS(N) 63 (Neukirchen-Vluyn: Neukirchner Verlag, 1972), 27ff.; Josef Ernst, *Johannes der Täufer*, BZNW 53 (Berlin: Walter DeGruyter, 1989), 300ff.; and Stephanie von Dobbeler, *Das Gericht und das Erbarmen Gottes. Die Botschaft Johannes' des Täufers und ihre Rezeption bei den Johannesjüngern im Rahmen der Theologiegeschichte des Frühjudentums*, BBB 70 (Frankfurt/Main: Verlag Peter Lang, 1988)

119. Becker, 27–33, and Merklein, *Jesu Botschaft*, 30.

120. In opposition to Otto Böcher, "Johannnes der Täufer," *TRE* 17:176ff., 44ff.

121. This is a controversial interpretation (Becker, 39f.). I owe this interpretation to a seminar of Ferdinand Hahn. He adopted observations from Günther Bornkamm, *Jesus of Nazareth*, third edition (London: Hodder and Stoughton, 1969), 47, and Erich Dinkler, "Taufe II. Im Urchristentum," *RGG* 6:628f., and linked the eschatological seal of Ezek 9:4 (cf. Mark 8:34) with the motif of flood as an act of judgment (Job 9:31, 1 Pet 3:20f.; cf. Mark 10:38).

122. Cf. Ernst Haenchen, *Der Weg Jesu* (Berlin: Verlag Alfred Töpelmann, 1966), 59, and Hannah Wolf, *Neuer Wein—Alte Schläuche*, third edition (Stuttgart: Radius Verlag, 1985), 43ff.

123. Cf. Brandenburger, "Gericht Gottes III," *TRE* 12:470.

124. Regarding the authenticity of the parable cf. Merklein, *Jesu Botschaft*, 158–64.

125. For the Old Testament background cf. Neh 9:26ff., and Odil H. Steck, *Israel und das gewaltsame Geschick der Propheten*, WMANT 23 (Neukirchen-Vluyn: Neukirchner Verlag, 1967), 269–73. Rudolf Pesch, *Markus*, 2:221, regards the parable as an authentic parable of Jesus; Joachim Gnilka, *Markus*, 2:144, 148ff., maintains the parable is secondary.

126. Matt 21:43, 22:7, 27:25 (cf. Isa 5:1-7).

127. Cf. on the theme of judgment, Martin Reiser, *Die Gerichtspredigt Jesu. Eine Untersuchung zur eschatologischen Verkündigung Jesu und ihrem frühjüdischen Hintergrund*, NTA 23 (Münster: Aschendorf, 1990) and further

on the substance of the parables, Hans Weder, *Gleichnisse*, whose literary or interpretive exclusion of the concept of judgment from the "Jesus-level" has its origin in a circular argument (cf. 125, 144, 206, 212ff.). On Matt 25:31-46 cf. Johannes Friedrich, *Gott im Bruder?*, CTM 7 (Stuttgart: Calwer Verlag, 1977); Ulrich Wilckens, "Gottes geringste Brüder," in Earle E. Ellis and Erich Grösser (eds.), *Jesus und Paulus* [FS Werner Georg Kümmel] (Göttingen: Vandenhoeck und Ruprecht, 1975), 363–83; and Egon Brandenburger, *Das Recht des Weltenrichters*, SBS 99 (Stuttgart: Katholisches Bibelwerk, 1980). Matthew underlines the judgment motif. See on this subject Günther Bornkamm, "End Expectation and Church in the Gospel of Matthew," in G. Bornkamm, G. Barth, and H. J. Held (eds.), *Tradition and Interpretation in Matthew*, 2nd edition (London: SCM Press, and Philadelphia: Fortress Press, 1983), 15–51; and Hans Conzelmann, *An Outline of the Theology of the New Testament*, trans. John Bowden, (London: SCM Press, 1969), 187.

128. Cf. Lieselotte Mattern, *Das Verständnis des Gerichts bei Paulus*, ATANT 47 (Zürich: Theologischer Verlag, 1966); Ernst Synofzik, *Die Gerichts- und Vergeltungsaussagen bei Paulus*, GTA 8 (Göttingen: Vandenhoeck und Ruprecht, 1977), and Karl Paul Donfried, "Justification and Last Judgment in Paul," *ZNW* 67 (1976), 90–110.

129. Brandenburger, "Gericht Gottes III," *TRE* 12:473, 475.

130. Hans Conzelmann, "Zorn Gottes. III. Im Judentum und NT," *RGG* 6:1932. See above pp. 102ff.

131. Cf. on Gal 5:21 Franz Mußner, *Galaterbrief*, HTKNT 9 (Freiburg: Verlag Herder, 1974), 383; on Rom 1:19f. see note 100.

132. Cf. W. Pesch, *EDNT* 2:529–30.

133. The cross is judgment of human wisdom and strength, 1 Cor 1:18-19.

134. 2 Thess 1:6-10 sounds deuteropauline in this regard.

135. Brandenburger, "Gericht Gottes," 478, 25f.

136. Ibid., 477.

137. Cf. Luke 18:9-14 and Rom 11:17-24. 1 Cor 3:15 and 5:5 appear to describe a salvation that passes through judgment. See Walter Klaiber, *Rechtfertigung und Gemeinde*, 246ff.

138. Brandenburger, "Gericht Gottes," 481f.

139. Ulrich B. Müller, *Prophetie und Predigt im Neuen Testament*, SNT 10 (Gütersloh: Gütersloher Verlagshaus, 1975), 76.

140. On the connection with prophecy in early churches see Müller, 236. On the function of the letter see Wiard Popkes, "Die Funktion der Sendschreiben in der Johannesapokalyse," *ZNW* 74 (1983), 90–107, and David Edward Aune, "The Form and Function of the Proclamation to the Seven Churches," *NTS* 36 (1990), 182–204.

141. Müller, 101f.

142. Cf. Dan 7:26f. on the connection between judging and the assumption of power.

143. Isa 65:6; Dan 7:10; 4 Ezra 6:19f.; 1 Enoch 61:2, 4; 89:62, 70f., 76. Cf. Horst Balz, *EDNT* 1:212.

144. See Martin Noth, *Exodus*, Old Testament Library (London: SCM Press, 1962), 251.

145. Cf. Isa 4:3 and see Hans Wildberger, *Jesaja*, BKAT X/1, second edition (Neukirchen-Vluyn: Neukirchner Verlag, 1980), 157. Cf. further Mal 3:16; 1 Enoch 47:3; Luke 10:12; Phil 4:3; Rev 3:5; 13:8; 17:8; 20:12*c*, 15; 21:17.

146. A technical term in reformed (Calvinist) theology for the coincidence of divine election and earthly behavior and fortune.

147. Thus Balz, *EDNT* 1:212.

148. Thus Adolf Pohl, *Die Offenbarung des Johannes, Zweiter Teil* (Wuppertal: R. Brockhaus, 1974), 295.

149. In the missionary sermon of the second century this motif appears to have been popular. See Ramsay Macmullen, "Two Types of Conversion to Early Christianity," *VC* 37 (1983), 174–92, 181.

150. Konrad Stock, "Gott der Richter. Der Gerichtsgedanke als Horizont der Rechtfertigungslehre," *EvT* 40 (1980), 240–57.

151. Paul Althaus, *Die letzten Dinge. Lehrbuch der Eschatologie*, fifth revised edition (Gütersloh: C. Bertelsmann Verlag, 1949), 187–88.

152. Ibid., 195–96. Cf. Paul Althaus, *Die christliche Wahrheit*, 2:489–90.

153. Barth, *Church Dogmatics*, II.2:417.

154. Emil Brunner, *The Christian Doctrine of God* (London: Lutterworth Press, 1949), 346ff.

155. Emil Brunner, *The Christian Doctrine of the Church, Faith, and the Consummation* (London: Lutherworth Press, 1962), 415–24, quotation 424.

156. Helmut Thielicke, *Theologische Ethik II/I*, fifth edition (Tübingen: J. C. B. Mohr, 1986), 578–621. This passage is not included in the published English translation.

157. Ibid., 620.

158. Thielicke, *The Evangelical Faith*, trans. and ed. Geoffrey W. Bromiley (Grand Rapids: William B. Eerdmans, 1982), 447.

159, Tillich, *Systematic Theology*, 3:398–99.

160. Ibid., 3:407–8.

161. Ibid., 3:409.

162. Ebeling, *Dogmatik*, 3:469.

163. Ibid., 3:469f.

164. Stock, 251–53, 255f. On this issue see Gisbert Greshake, "Heil *und* Unheil? Zu Bedeutung und Stellenwert von Strafe und Sühne, Gericht und Hölle in der Heilsverkündigung," *Theologisches Jahrbuch* (Leipzig: St. Benno-Verlag, 1986), 48–75.

165. 5:6, 8, 12; 13:8.

166. "The Law Established by Faith, I," §1.1–3, *The Works of John Wesley*, Volume 2: *Sermons II, 34–70*, ed. Albert C. Outler (Nashville: Abingdon Press, 1985), 22f.

167. *The Works of John Wesley*, Volume 26: *Letters II, 1740–1755*, ed. Frank Baker (Oxford: Clarendon Press, 1982), 482–84.

168. Oddly enough, hardly any of Wesley's published sermons correspond to this schema.

169. Friedrich Wilhelm Graf, "Gesetz VI," *TRE* 13:101.

170. Hans-Martin Barth, "Gesetz und Evangelium I," *TRE* 13:128.

171. Rudolf Mau, "Gesetz V," *TRE* 13:82.

172. Cf. Ferdinand Hahn, "Das Gesetzesverständnis im Römer- und Galaterbrief," *ZNW* 67 (1976), 29–63, 58.

173. "Gesetz und Evangelium nach 2. Korinther 3," *Jahrbuch für Biblische Theologie* 4 (1989), 105–49.

174. Hofius, 112f.

175. Ibid., 115.

176. Ibid., 148.

177. Ebeling, *Dogmatik*, 3:268ff. Cf. to that the demand of Francis A. Schaeffer, *The God Who Is There* (London: Hodder and Stoughton, 1968), 144.

178. Ebeling, *Dogmatik*, 3:284.

179. Ibid., 273.

180. Cf. the fatal identification of law with the "Volksnomos" in the works of Friedrich Gogarten and Wilhelm Stapel. See Friedrich Wilhelm Graf, "Gesetz VI," *TRE*, 13:124, and Hans-Martin Barth, "Gesetz und Evangelium I," *TRE* 13:132–33.

181. "Gesetz und Evangelium I," *TRE* 13:139f. Cf. Albrecht Peters, *Gesetz und Evangelium*, Handbuch der systematischer Theologie 2 (Gütersloh: Gütersloher Verlagshaus, 1981), 332–33.

182. Cf. Ebeling's provocative thesis in *Dogmatik* 3:295: "There are situations in which one must preach the law as if there were no gospel, and situations in which one must offer the comfort of the gospel as if the law had ceased to be an issue."

183. Cf. The Lausanne Covenant, 3; The Manila Manifesto I,7; Ulrich Parzany, "Die Einzigartigkeit Jesu Christi," in Horst Marquardt and Ulrich Parzany (eds.), *Evangelisation mit Leidenschaft* (Neukirchen-Vluyn: Aussaat-Verlag, 1990), 86–93.

184. Karl Rahner, "Christianity and the Non-Christian Religions," *Theological Investigations*, Volume 5 (London: Darton, Longman and Todd, 1966), 115–34; quotation, 123.

185. "Observations on the Problem of the 'Anonymous Christians,'" *Theological Investigations*, Volume 14 (London:Darton, Longman and Todd, 1966), 280–94; *Foundations*, 306. Cf. the bibliography in Julian Bednarz, *Chrétiens Anonymes et Évangelisation* (Katowice: n.p., 1986), 43–49. For the discussion on this issue cf. Elmar Klinger (ed.), *Christentum innerhalb und außerhalb der Kirche*, QD 73 (Freiburg: Verlag Herder, 1976)—here see especially Eberhard Jüngel, "*Extra Christum nulla salus*," 122–38.

186. See most recently Paul F. Knitter, *No Other Name? A Critical Survey of Christian Attitudes toward World Religions* (London: SCM Press, 1985); John Hick and Paul F. Knitter (eds.), *The Myth of Christian Uniqueness: Toward a Pluralistic Theology of Religions* (Maryknoll, NY: Orbis Books, 1987); and Paul F. Knitter, "Nochmals die Absolutheitsfrage," *EvT* 49 (1989), 505–16.

187. Knitter, "Nochmals," 515. See also Reinhold Bernhardt, "Ein neuer Lessing?," *EvT* 49 (1989), 516–28, and Jürgen Moltmann, "Dient die 'pluralistische Theologie' dem Dialog der Weltreligionen?" *EvT* 49 (1989), 528–36.

188. Christian Maurer, "Der Exklusivitätsanspruch des Christus nach dem Johannesevangelium," in *Studies in John*, NovTSup 24 [FS J. N. Sevenster] (Leiden: E. J. Brill, 1970), 143–54, 153. Cf. Ebeling, *Dogmatik*, 1:137.

189. Maurer, 153.

190. Alexandre Ganoczy, "The Absolute Claim of Christianity: The Justification of Evangelization or an Obstacle to It?" in N. Greinacher and A. Mueller (eds.), *Evangelization in the World Today*, Concilium 114 (New York: Crossroad, 1979), 19–29: The exclusive claim places a demand on the preacher him-or herself. Cf. F. R. Wilson (ed.), *The San Antonio Report* (Geneva: WCC, 1990), §I, 26. Further see Carl E. Braaten, *No Other Gospel? Christianity Among the World's Religions* (Philadelphia: Fortress Press, 1992); Peter Donovan, "The Intolerance of Religious Pluralism," *RelS* 29 (1993), 217–30; Michael von Brück and Jürgen Werbick (eds.), *Der einzige Weg zum Heil? Die Herausforderung der christlichen Absolutheitsanspruch durch pluralistische Religionstheologien*, QD 143 (Freiburg: Verlag Herder, 1993).

191. Evangelical circles are also aware of this problematic issue. See for example E. D. Osburn, "Those Who Have Never Heard: Have They No Hope?" *JETS* 32:3 (1989), 367–72.

192. Schaeffer, *The God Who is There*, 141.

193. Quoted as found in Wimber, *Power Evangelism*, 65. See also the four points in Schaeffer, 141.

194. Quoted as found in Walter Mostert, "Ist die Frage nach der Existenz Gottes wirklich radikaler als die Frage nach dem gnädigen Gott?" *ZTK* 74 (1977), 86.

195. Thus Wilckens, *Missionsreden*, 81ff., 190ff.; Bultmann, *Theology* 1:67–68; Gerhard Schneider, "Urchristliche Gottesverkündigung," *BZ* NF 13 (1969), 59–75, and Haacker, "Urchristliche Mission," 71. Stuhlmacher, *Das paulinische Evangelium*, 261, regards the matter as more complex.

196. Holtz, 62. Cf also C. K. Barrett, "Paulus als Missionar und Theologe," 26ff.

197. Wolfgang Schrage, "Theologie und Christologie bei Paulus auf dem Hintergrund der modernen Gottesfrage," *EvT* 36 (1976), 121–54, 123.

198. Ibid., 126.

199. See Mostert, 86–122, on this.

200. One cannot forget that Gen 1:1 and John 1:1 do not have "In the beginning was God"!

201. A basic work here is Eberhard Jüngel, *God as the Mystery of the World*, trans. Darell L. Gardner (Grand Rapids: William B. Eerdmanns, 1983).

202. Ingolf U. Dalferth, *Religiöse Rede von Gott*, BEvT 87 (Munich: Chr. Kaiser Verlag, 1981), 598, and Dalferth, *Existenz Gottes und christlicher Glaube*, BEvT 93 (Munich: Chr. Kaiser Verlag, 1984), 185. Jüngel and Dalferth, however, do not consider God's revelation in the Old Testament in their works.

203. This remains a question for the extraordinarily instructive book by Hans Küng, *Does God Exist? An Answer for Today*, trans. Edward Quinn, (New York: Doubleday & Co., 1978).

204. Amos E. Wilder-Smith, *Die Zuverlässigkeit der Bibel und christliche Vollmacht*, second edition (Stuttgart: Hänssler, 1979), and Helge Stadelmann, *Grundlinien eines bibeltreuen Schriftverständnisses* (Wuppertal: R. Brockhaus, 1985), 9ff.

205. Nonetheless consider Acts 26:27 (an exception).

206. Cf. 1 Cor 15:3f.; Acts 2:25f., 3:18, 10:43 (before the God-fearers), 13:17ff., 17:11, but not 14:15-17 or 17:22-31!

207. See Schmithals, 69–90, and Haacker, "Urchristliche Mission," 61–72.

208. According to Hans von Campenhausen, *The Formation of the Christian Bible*, trans. John Austin Baker, (London: Adam and Charles Black, 1972), 88, the Apologists were the first to use a doctrine of the formal authority of Scripture to try to give Christian preaching a secure foundation. On the role of the Bible in the mission of the early church cf. Adolf von Harnack, *The Mission and Expansion of Christianity in the First Three Centuries* (Harper & Brothers, 1962), 279–89, and Hinson, 193ff.

209. See on this issue, however, Article XIX of the Chicago Statement on Biblical Inerrancy which rejects the assertion that confessing the Bible to be infallible and without error "is necessary for salvation." Quoted from Ronald Youngblood (ed.), *Evangelicals and Inerrancy* (Nashville: Thomas Nelson Publisher, 1984), 235.

210. Schaeffer, *The God Who Is There*, 141. Cf. Schaeffer, *He Is There and He Is Not Silent* (Wheaton: Tyndale House Publishers, 1972), and the following books by Amos E. Wilder-Smith, *God: To Be or Not To Be? A Critical Analysis of Monod's Scientific Materialism* (Stuttgart: Hänssler, 1975); *Man's Origin, Man's Destiny* (Stuttgart: Hänssler, 1974); and *Wer denkt, muß glauben* (Stuttgart: Hänssler, 1983). See further Lutz von Padberg, "Evangelikale Apologetik," *Materialdienst der Evangelischen Zentralstelle für Weltanschauungsfragen* 53 (1990), 177–89.

211. Cf. above all volume 4, *Der christliche Gottesglaube und die Naturwissenschaften*, second edition (Hamburg: Furche-Verlag, 1953) and volume 5, *Die Wandlung im naturwissenschaftlichen Weltbild*, third edition (Hamburg: Furche-Verlag, 1954).

212. Lesslie Newbigin, *Foolishness to the Greeks* (Grand Rapids: William B. Eerdmanns, 1986), as well as two other books by Newbigin, *The Other Side of 1984—Questions for the Churches*, Risk Book Series 18, (Geneva: WCC, 1983); and *The Gospel in a Pluralistic Society* (Grand Rapids: William B. Eerdmans, 1989). Cf. Meredith B. Handspicker, "Toward a Postliberal Apologetics," *Journal of the Academy for Evangelism in Theological Education* 6 (1991–92), 72–81.

213. Newbigin, *The Other Side*, 18ff.

214. Barth, *Church Dogmatics*, IV.3.1:139.

215. *Die Welt als Gleichnis*, BEvT 73 (Munich: Chr. Kaiser Verlag, 1976), 249.

216. Gerhard von Rad, *Old Testament Theology*, trans. D. M. C. Stalker, 2 vols. (New York: Harper & Row, 1962), 1:148.

217. Cf. Günter Altner, *Grammatik der Schöpfung. Theologische Inhalte der Biologie* (Stuttgart: Kreuz Verlag, 1971), and Jürgen Moltmann, *God in Creation* (London: SCM Press, 1985).

218. See Küng, *God*, 1–166, 628–30, on this issue. Cf. the way theological essays and essays in the natural sciences stand practically unmediated next to one another in the anthologies Wolfgang Böhme (ed.), *Evolution und Gottesglaube* (Göttingen: Vandenhoeck & Ruprecht, 1988) and Jürgen Audretsch and

Klaus Mainzer (eds.), *Vom Anfang der Welt*, Second Printing, (Munich: C. H. Beck, 1990).

219. Alfons Deissler, "Biblische Schöpfungsgeschichte und physikalische Kosmogonie," in Audretsch and Mainzer, 176–87, 186.

220. Schaeffer, *The God Who Is There*, 50.

221. H. J. Margull (ed.), *Mission als Strukturprinzip*.

222. Of all New Testament texts that fundamentally address mission Matt 28:19 has the most pronounced ecclesiological accent. But "to make disciples" means primarily to call someone to follow Jesus!

223. Cf. Klaiber, *Rechtfertigung und Gemeinde*, 257, 101–4, 121f.

224. Cf. Klaiber, "Rechtfertigung und Kreuzesgeschehen," 116f.

225. On this issue see Heribert Mühlen, *Neu mit Gott. Einübung in christliches Zeugnis und Leben* (Freiburg: Verlag Herder, 1990), 90–120.

226. On Rom 1:20ff. and Gal 5:22, see above.

227. Cf. Rom 5:5, 6:4, 8:13; 1 Cor 6:9-11; Gal 5:22 and Wolfgang Schrage, *The Ethics of the New Testament*, trans. David E. Green (Philadelphia: Fortress Press, 1988), 167ff.

228. Cf. Harnack, 199–218, and Hinson, 233ff.

229. Schrage, *Ethics of the New Testament*, 11.

230. In the history of evangelism it was above all John Wesley who emphasized the content of the gospel message as the power of God's love that fulfills and forms life. "Holiness and Happiness," acting in accord with the will of God and with one's self, were important aspects of present salvation for Wesley. Cf. the critical evaluation in Albert C. Outler, *Evangelism in the Wesleyan Spirit* (Nashville: Tidings, 1971).

231. Cf. Klaiber, *Das kannst du glauben*, 81ff.

232. Cf. Jürgen Moltmann, *Theology of Hope*, trans. James Leitch, New York: Harper & Row, 1967), and Klaiber, *Embraced by the Spirit*, 71ff.

233. Hermann Obendiek, "Die Kirche in der Missionssituation, in *Pietismus und Theologie*, ed. Otto Schmitz (Neukirchen/Moers: Verlag der Buchhandlung des Erziehungsvereins, 1956), 9–30, 21.

Notes to Chapter 4

1. Werner H. Schmidt, "Werk Gottes und Tun des Menschen. Ansätze zur Unterscheidung von 'Gesetz und Evangelium' im Alten Testament," *Jahrbuch für biblische Theologie* 4 (1980), 11–28.

2. In Abraham's "faith it becomes clear that his position before God is 'in order'" (Hans Wildberger, *THAT* 1:191). The Hebrew text, in contradistinction to the Septuagint, has no "ingressive" significance, cf. Klaus Haacker, "Glaube II/2," *TRE* 13:283ff.

3. Walther Zimmerli, "'Leben' und 'Tod' im Buch des Propheten Ezechiels" in *Gottes Offenbarung*, second edition, TBü 19 (Munich: Chr. Kaiser Verlag, 1963), 178–91, 185. Regarding the controversial translation with "faith" or "fidelity" ("Glauben oder Treue") cf. Haacker, 287f.

4. Since Bernhard Duhm's work this passage is viewed as the "'hour of

birth' of faith" in the Old Testament; cf. Haacker 280f. Cf. further Isa 28:16 (and, as its after effect, 2 Chr 20:20).

5. Cf. Wildberger, "Jesaja," *Biblischer Kommentar* X/3 (Neukirchen-Vluyn: Neukirchner Verlag, 1983), 1193ff.

6. Brandenburger, "Pistis und Soteria," 173ff., 183ff.

7. For a treatment of faith as "recognition of the messenger of God" cf. Exod 4:1, 5, 8, 9 and 31; 14:31; 19:9 (neg. Pss 78:22, 32; 106:24); cf. Haacker, 284f.

8. Brandenburger, "Pistis und Soteria," 184.

9. Hans Walter Wolff, "Dodekapropheton 3 Jona," *Biblischer Kommentar* XIV/3 (Neukirchen-Vluyn: Neukirchner Verlag, 1977).

10. Cf. also Weish 12, 2(9) and in response Brandenburger, "Pistis und Soteria," 178–86.

11. Wildberger, *THAT* 1:189. Martin Buber's thesis of a coexistence of an Old Testament-Jewish and a Christian-Hellenistic way of faith in the New Testament is open to theological challenge; see *Two Types of Faith* (London: Routledge and Paul, 1951). Cf. Haacker, 280.

12. Hans Walter Wolff, "Das Thema 'Umkehr' in der alttestamentlichen Prophetie" in *Gesammelte Studien zum Alten Testament*, second edition, TBü (Munich: Chr. Kaiser Verlag, 1973), 130–50, 138.

13. Martin Buber, *The Prophetic Faith* (New York: Macmillan Co., 1949), 103. Georg Fohrer in particular continues to represent this point of view; cf. *Studien zur alttestamentlichen Prophetie* (1967), 231f., 240; in response Ludwig Markert and Gunther Wanke, "Die Propheteninterpretation," *Kerygma und Dogma* 22 (1976), 191–220.

14. "Scheltwort": Amos 4:6-11; Isa 30:15; Hos 5:4; 7:10; 11:5; Jer 3:1-10; 8:4-7; "Heilsspruch": Hos 2:8f.; 3:5; 14:2ff.; Jer 3:21-25; 31:15-20 (Wolff, "Umkehr," 138–45.

15. Wolff, "Umkehr," 143; cf. Georg Fohrer, "Umkehr und Erlösung beim Propheten Hosea, *Studien zur alttestamentlichen Prophetie* (1967), 227–41. Re: Jeremiah: Rudolf Mosis, "Umkehr und Vergebung—eine Auslegung von Jer 3:21–4:2," *Trierer Theologische Zeitschrift* 98 (1989), 39–60.

16. "Amos," *TRE* 2:478. The discussion is made more difficult by the question of the authenticity of certain sayings, in which it is easy to engage in circular argumentation. Re: Amos: cf. Rudolf Smend, "Das Nein des Amos," *Evangelische Theologie* 29 (1969), 404–23; re: Isaiah: Georg Fohrer, "Jesaja 1 als Zusammenfassung der Verkündigung Jesajas," *Studien zur alttestamentlichen Prophetie*, 148–66; Georg Sauer, "Die Umkehrforderung in der Verkündigung Jesajas," in *Wort-Gebot-Glaube* [FS Walter Eichrodt] (Zürich, 1980), 277–95. On this whole matter, see Werner H. Schmidt, "Zukunftsgewißheit," and a response by Hans Walter Wolff, "Die eigentliche Botschaft," discussed on pp. 104ff. above.

17. Cf. Hans Walter Wolff, *Hosea*, translated by Gary Stansche, Hermeneia (Philadelphia: Fortress Press, 1974), 196f., 203f.

18. In this regard, Walter Zimmerli, "'Leben' und 'Tod'"; 33:10-20 is "Trostrede an die Verzagten" ["Consolation for the Despairing"], 18; "Auseinandersetzung mit der frechen Aufsässigkeit im Volke" ["Confrontation with the Smart-aleck Attitude among the People"], 182.

19. Walter Zimmerli, *Ezekiel 2,* Hermeneia (Philadelphia: Fortress Press, 1983), 190.

20. Zimmerli, "'Leben' und 'Tod'," 191.

21. Op. cit.

22. 40:1-11; 43:1-7; 44:1-5; 49:8-12, 18-21; 51:1-10; 54:1-17.

23. 40:27-31; 50:1-3 (concerning the disputational saying cf. Karl Elliger, "Deuterojesaja," second edition, *Biblischer Kommentar* XI/1 [Neukirchen-Vluyn: Neukirchner Verlag, 1989], 44): further 43:8-13, 22-28; 49:14-17.

24. Wolff, "Umkehr," 145; Elliger, op. cit., 447. Cf. 45:22: the "invitation to those from among the nations who survived the avalanche to participate in salvation!" (Claus Westermann, *Isaiah 40–66*; 175f.).

25. Cf. in this regard Wolff, "Das Kerygma des Deuteronomistischen Geschichtswerkes," *Gesammelte Studien zum Alten Testament* (Munich: Chr. Kaiser Verlag, 1973), 308–24, 318ff.

26. In this regard, Hans Wildberger, *THAT* 1:299

27. Horst Seebaß, *TDOT* 2:84.

28. Wolff, "Das Kerygma," 322f.

29. Cf. Ab 2:10; bSchab 153a (Paul Billerbeck, *Kommentar zum Neuen Testament*, ninth edition [Munich: Verlag C. H. Beck, 1986], 1:165).

30. Cf. Everett Ferguson, *Backgrounds of Early Christianity* (Grand Rapids: William B. Eerdmans, 1987, 459.

31. Helmut Merklein, "Die Umkehrpredigt bei Johannes dem Täufer und Jesus von Nazaret," *BZ* 25 (1981), 29–46, 35. Cf. Matt 3:9.

33. Ibid, 36.

34. Ibid., 37.

35. Julius Schniewind, "Was verstand Jesus unter Umkehr?" in *Die Freude der Buße*, Kleine Vandenhoeck Reihe 32 (Göttingen: Vandenhoeck & Ruprecht, 1956), 19–33, 24.

36. Wolfgang Trilling, "Metanoia als Grundforderung der neutestamentlichen Lebenslehre" in *Einübung des Glauben. Klemens Tillmann zum 60.*, ed. Gunter Stackel and Alois Zenner (Würzburg: Echter-Verlag, 1965), 178–90, 180.

37. Cf. Hans Conzelmann, *The Theology of Luke* (New York: Harper); Merklein, "Umkehrpredigt," 40.

38. Cf. Meinard Limbeck, "Jesu Verkündigung und der Ruf zur Umkehr," in *Das Evangelium auf dem Weg zum Menschen* [FS H. Kahlefeld], ed. Otto Knecht, Felix Messerschmid, and Alois Zenner (Frankfurt/Main: J. Knecht, 1973), 34–42; Merklein, "Umkehrpredigt," 39–41; Ilija Čabraja, *Der Gedanke der Umkehr bei den Synoptikern* (Sankt Ottilian: EOS-Verlag, 1985). In my opinion *metanoein* is the equivalent of the Hebrew *shub* (according to the linguistic usage in the OT Pseudepigrapha, which differs from the LXX); cf. Johannes Behm, *TDNT* 4:991f., against Čabraja, 24.

39. For use of the phrase *pisteuete en tō euangeliō* concerning the background in light of the history of tradition, cf. Čabraja 62–89; Gnilka, *Markus*, 1:64f. Among those considering 1:15 to be a tradition going back to Jesus himself are Pesch, *Markus*, 1:103, and Stuhlmacher, *Das Evangelium und die Evangelien*, 21 (as opposed to *Das paulinische Evangelium*, 237f.).

40. Čabraja 107–13; Ulrich Luz, *Matthew 1–7* (Edinburgh: T & T Clark, 1989), 132ff.

41. Cf. Schottroff, "Gleichnis vom verlorenen Sohn," 32f.; Merklein, "Umkehrpredigt," 40; Weder (with a clear criticism of the content) considers vv. 7 and 10 to be secondary, but pre-Lukan ("Gleichnisse," 170, 174f.)

42. Johannes Becker, "Johannes," 87f.; Merklein, "Umkehrpredigt," 41f.

43. Becker, "Johannes," 98f.

44. Merklein, "Umkehrpredigt," 42; cf. also Luke 12:8f (Becker, "Johannes," 100–103).

45. Cf. the excellent exegesis of Johannes Schniewind, "Das Gleichnis vom verlorenen Sohn" in *Die Freude der Buße*, 34–87.

46. Joachim Jeremias, *The Parables of Jesus*, 3rd rev. ed. (London: SCM Press, 1972), 131f.; 135f.

47. Merklein, "Umkehrpredigt," 43.

48. Wolfgang Harnisch, *Die Gleichniserzählungen Jesu*, Uni Taschenbücher 1343 (Göttingen: Vandenhoeck & Ruprecht, 1985), 227f.: It remains an open question "whether, in the light of what has already been said, penance would be understood as a turning in which the finding of that which was lost takes place."

49. Merklein, "Umkehrpredigt," 44, refers to Jeremias, *New Testament Theology*, 158; cf. Limbeck, "Jesu Verkündigung," 40: "Jesus' call to repentance found its primary expression as a committed and moving actualization of the mercy and goodness of God."

50. Cf. Eduard Schweizer, *The Good News According to Mark*, trans. Donald Madrig (Richmond: John Knox Press, 1970), 205–208; Pesch, *Markus*, 2:133; in contradistinction, Gnilka, *Markus*, 2:80, considers Matthew 18:3 to be the old form of the Logion.

51. Pesch, *Markus*, 2:134.

52. With this exposition I am modifying the interpretation of Ernst Fuchs, "Das Zeitverständnis Jesu," in *Zur Frage nach dem historischen Jesus. Gesammelte Aufsätze* II (Tübingen: J. C. B. Mohr [Paul Siebeck] 1960), 334ff.: Eberhard Jüngel, "Paulus und Jesus," second edition, HUT 2 (Tübingen: J. C. B. Mohr [Paul Siebeck], 1986), 142–45, and Weder, "Gleichnisse," 140ff.: "der eigentliche Aktant" is exclusively "der Fund"!

53. Eduard Schweizer, *The Good News According to Matthew*, translated by David E. Green (Atlanta: John Knox Press, 1975), 312.

54. Cf. Ulrich Busse, "Nachfolge auf dem Weg Jesu" in Frankemölle and Kertelge (eds.), *Vom Urchristentum zu Jesus*, 68–81, 69–75.

55. Cf. Martin Hengel, *The Charismatic Leader and his Followers*, trans. James C. G. Greig (Edinburgh: T & T Clark, 1981).

56. Schweizer, *Mark*, 215: "It is a general principle that the gift of discipleship is absolutely miraculous."

57. Regarding the many-layered mutual cause and effect between Jesus' ministry and the faith of individuals, cf. Haacker's article on faith "Glaube II/3" *TRE* 13:293f.

58. Regarding the following, cf. Charles Kingsley Barrett, "Proclamation and Response" in *Tradition and Interpretation in the New Testament* [FS Earle

E. Ellis] (Tübingen: J. C. B. Mohr [Paul Siebeck], 1987), 3–15. Cf. Wilckens, *Missionsreden*, 54.

59. *metanoein*: 2:38; 3:19; 5:37; 17:30; 26:20.

60. *apo- / epistrephein*: 3:19, 26; 14:15; 26:18, 20.

61. Only 2:38; 22:16!

62. 10:43; 11:38; 15:7; 16:31; 19:4.

63. 2:38; 3:19, 26; 5:31; 10:41; 11:31; 22:16; 26:18; alongside "to be saved" 2:40, 47; 4:12; 11:14; 15:1, 11; 16:30.

64. Faith: 4:4; 8:12f.; 11:21; 13:12, 48; 14:1, 23, 27; 17:12, 34; 18:8; baptism: 2:41; 8:12f.; 9:18; 10:48; 16:15, 33; 18:8; 19:5; both: 8:12f.; 16:33ff.; 18:8.

65. Be converted only 11:21; 15:19; receive the word and similarly: 2:41; 16:14.

66. Cf. Jens W. Taeger, *Der Mensch und sein Heil. Studien zum Bild des Menschen und zur Sicht der Bekehrung bei Lukas*, SNT 14 (Göttingen: Vandenhoeck & Ruprecht, 1982), 105ff.; Brandenburger, "Pistis und Soteria," 190ff.

67. 11:21; 14:15; 15:19; 26:18, 20 (cf. 15:3).

68. Cf. Taeger, 139f., Georg Bertram, *TDNT* 7:727.

69. It therefore shares the "Fundamental Message" of the "Jerusalem-Hellenists-Antioch" circle of tradition (Brandburger, "Pistis und Sophia," 196); see above, p. 75.

70. Cf. also 14:27: God has "opened the door of faith for the heathens," i.e., he opens to them "the possibility of entering into the room of faith" (Jürgen Roloff, *Die Apostelgeschichte*, NTD5, seventh edition [Göttingen: Vandenhoeck & Ruprecht, 1981], 220). Cf. Roloff also on 17:31: *pistin paraschon* has the double meaning: *certifiying* and *offering* faith!

71. Conzelmann, *The Theology of Luke*, 211; cf. also the phrase with its predestinarian ring in 13:48.

72. Taeger, 222.

73. The Greek *apostrephein* is intransitive (BDR 308, #3), as is almost universally attested in German-language translations and commentaries. The English-language tradition of translation (e.g., RSV, NRSV, NIV, NEB, NJB) prefers the transitive meaning " by turning each of you." Cf. Gerhard Schneider, *Die Apostelgeschichte*, HTKNT V/2 (Freiburg im Breisgau: Verlag Herder, 1982), 329 n.124.

74. Cf. Taeger, 188ff.; Beverly Roberts Gaventa, *From Darkness to Light—Aspects of Conversion in the New Testament* (Philadelphia: Fortress Press, 1986), 96ff.

75. Roloff, 152: Paul comes "into the picture only as [an] object of that event which proceeds from the exalted Lord."

76. The Jewish Christians are supposed to recognize that: "It is God himself who is at work here" (Roloff, 174).

77. It is significant that the textual tradition finds it necessary to add verse 37!

78. *me pistēn . . . einai* describes the condition of faith (cf. Schneider, *Die Apostelgeschichte*, 214).

79. "Even the perfect tense form of *pisteuō* points back to the unique,

one-time act of entrance into the Christian faith." Haacker, *TRE* 13:297, but also emphasizes the result at the same time (cf. 15:5; 18:27 inter al.)

80. Cf. also 13:7-12; negative 17:2-4; 28:28f.

81. Cf. also the sermon in Luke 19:5-9; 23:43.

82. Cf. besides 16:15, 31, 33f.; also 18:8, the conversion of Crispus and Luke 19:9. In this regard Alfons Weiser, "Evangelisierung im antiken 'Haus'" in Wolfgang Hering (ed.), *Aspekte der Evangelisierung* (Limburg: Lahn-Verlag, 1989), 35–65.

83. Bultmann, *TDNT* 6:208ff.; Gerhard Barth, *EDNT* 3:93–94; Haacker, *TRE* 12:297.

84. Bultmann saw in this a "catchword in those religions which engaged in propaganda" (*TDNT* 6:181; *Theology of the New Testament*, 89: "The Missionary Activity of Judaism and of Gentile Religion"). Dieter Lührmann, "Pistis im Judentum," *ZNW* 64 (1973), 19–38, contradicts this—and correctly so for the Hellenistic religions (Brandenburger, "Pistis und Soteria," 166).

85. Brandenburger, "Pistis und Soteria," 178–86.

86. Ibid., 195.

87. Hans Conzelmann, "Was glaubte die frühe Christenheit?" in *Theologie als Schriftauslegung*, BEvT 65 (Munich: Chr. Kaiser Verlag, 1974), 106–20; Kramer, *Christ, Lord, Son of God*, §§3, 15; cf. Käsemann and Wilckens on this passage.

88. Heinrich Schlier, "Das Hauptanliegen des 1. Korintherbriefes" in *Die Zeit der Kirche*, fourth edition (Freiburg im Breisgau: Verlag Herder, 1966), 147–59, 152. On faith as a "pre-condition" cf. further Acts 16:31 and the passages cited in Gerhard Friedrich, "Glaube und Verkündigung in Paulus," in Ferdinand Hahn and Hans Klein (eds.), *Glauben im Neuen Testament*, Biblisch-theologische Studien 7 (Neukirchen-Vluyn: Neukirchner Verlag, 1968), 93–113, esp. 109 nn.59–64

89. 1 Thess 1:7; 2:10, 13; 1 Cor 14:22.

90. Walter Klaiber, *Rechtfertigung und Gemeinde*, 175.

91. Universality is emphasized; the durative present tense shows that it is not the "one-time faith-act of conversion" which is done, but the abiding holding fast to the foundation of the relationship with God (Haacker, *TRE* 13:298. Cf. Axel von Dobbeler, *Glaube als Teilhabe*, WUNT II, 22 (Tübingen: J. C. B. Mohr [Paul Siebeck], 1987), 275f.

92. According to Galatians 3:10-12 with Josef Blank, "Warum sagt Paulus: 'Aus Werken des Gesetzes wird niemand gerecht'?" EKKNT 1 (Neukirchen-Vluyn: Neukirchner Verlag, 1969), 79–95, in opposition to Ulrich Wilckens, "Was heißt bei Paulus 'Aus Werken des Gesetzes wird kein Menschen gerecht'?" op. cit., 51–57 (= *Rechtfertigung als Freiheit* [Neukirchen-Vluyn: Neukirchner Verlag, 1974], 77–109).

93. Käsemann, *Romans*, 105f.

94. Cf. Heinrich Schlier, *Der Brief an die Galater*, Kritisch-exegetischer Kommentar VII, fifteenth edition (Tübingen: J. C. B. Mohr [Paul Siebeck], 1983), 92f., Ernst Käsemann, "The Faith of Abraham in Romans 4," in *Perspectives on Paul*, trans. by Margarete Kohl (London: SCM Press, 1971), 79–101, 93. For a discussion of the genitive declension cf. Wolfgang Schenk, "Die

Gerechtigkeit Gottes und der Glaube Christi," *TLZ* 97 (1972), 161–74; Dieter Lührmann, *Glaube im frühen Christentum* (Gütersloh: Gütersloher Verlagshaus, 1976), 58f.

95. Schrage, "Römer 3:21-26," 76f.

96. Yet we should not make this passage the hinge of our understanding of faith as Herrmann Binder does in *Der Glaube bei Paulus* (Berlin: Evangelische Verlagsanstalt, 1968), 43. Cf. Käsemann, "The Faith of Abraham," 100; Lührmann, *Glaube im frühen Christentum*, 58f.; Friedrich, "Glaube," 95–99.

97. Klaiber, *Rechenschaft über den Glauben*, 107.

98. Eduard Lohse, "Taufe und Rechtfertigung bei Paulus," in *Die Einheit des Neuen Testaments* (Göttingen: Vandenhoeck & Ruprecht, 1973), 228–44; Klaiber, *Rechtfertigung und Gemeinde*, 182ff.

99. Cf. Ferdinand Hahn, "Taufe und Rechtfertigung," in Johannes Friedrich, Wolfgang Pöhlmann, and Peter Stuhlmacher (eds.), *Rechtfertigung* [FS Ernst Käsemann] (Göttingen: Vandenhoeck & Ruprecht; Tübingen: J. C. B. Mohr [Paul Siebeck], 1976), 95–124, 120.

100. Cf. Hubert Frankemölle, "Das Taufverständnis des Paulus," SBS 47 (Stuttgart: Katholisches Bibelwerk, 1979), 14; G. R. Beasley-Murray, *Baptism in the New Testament* (Exeter: Paternoster Press, 1962), 272f.; Lohse, 242ff.; Kertelge, *"Rechtfertigung" bei Paulus*, 246.

101. 1 Cor 15:1ff. recalls the fundamental proclamation; Gal 3:2, 5, recalls the reception of the Holy Spirit through the proclamation of faith!

102. Dietzfelbinger, Berufung des Paulus, especially 102–6.

103. The perfect tense *hēgēmai* (3:7) points to the proper decision, the double present tense *hēgoumai* (3:8) to the current and present attitude (cf. Joachim Gnilka, *Der Philipperbrief*, HTKNT X/3, fourth edition [Freiburg im Breisgau: Verlag Herder, 1987], 191f.); cf. Bultmann, *Theology of the New Testament*, 180ff.

104. Cf. Dietzfelbinger, *Berufung des Paulus*, 29ff.; Kim, *The Origin of Paul's Gospel*, 47; Klaiber, "Rechtfertigung und Kreuzesgeschehen," 95ff.; of another opinion is Gaventa, *From Darkness to Light*, 39.

105. Cf. v. 7: *dia ton Christon*; further v. 8f.!

186. Friedrich, "Glaube," 109; Fritz Neugebauer, *In Christus* (Göttingen: Vandenhoeck & Ruprecht, 1961), 165.

107. Käsemann, *Romans*, 276ff.

108. This is the tendency in Egon Brandenburger, *Adam und Christus*, WMANT 7 (Neukirchen-Vluyn: Neukirchner Verlag, 1962), 230: Life "must be grasped by the individual"; similarly Bultmann, *Theology of the New Testament*, 302: After Christ "a decision must be made." On the other side, Eberhard Jüngel, "Das Gesetz zwischen Adam und Christus," in *Unterwegs zur Sache*, 145–72, esp. 167: "On the 'Christ-side of things' people are essentially recipients."

109. Friedrich, "Glaube," 112. Cf. Wolfgang Vorländer, *Christus erkennen* (Neukirchen-Vluyn: Edition Aussaat, 1986), 64: "Faith is passive receptivity, unfaith is an active throwing away."

110. Otfried Hofius' "Erwägungen zur Gestalt und Herkunft des paulinischen Versöhnunggedanken," *ZTK* 77 (1980), 186–99, emphasizes that this

imperative, as that in Second Isaiah, is anchored in the promise of salvation. The call to reconciliation is "the salvation-bringing Word of God . . . , which invites and liberates the reconciled to have faith in the reconciliation already completed" (198).

111. Cf. Victor Paul Furnish, *II Corinthians*, AB 32A (Garden City, NY: Doubleday, 1984), 350: "The concept of reconciliation employed here [2 Cor. 5:20] expresses particularly well the radical priority of God's grace to which faith is a response."

112. *TRE* 13:295; cf. Bultmann, *TDNT* 6:222–29; Lührmann, *Glaube im frühen Christentum*, 60–69; Ferdinand Hahn, "Das Glaubensverständnis im Johannesevangelium" in Erich Grässer and Otto Merk (eds.), *Glaube und Eschatologie* [FS W.G. Kümmel] (Tübingen: J. C. B. Mohr [Paul Siebeck], 1985), 51–70; Jean Zumstein, "L'évangile johannique: une strategie du croire," *Recherches de science religieuse* 77 (1988), 217–32.

113. Ferdinand Hahn, "Sehen und Glauben im Johannesevangelium" in Heinrich Baltensweiler and Bo Reicke (eds.), *Neues Testament und Geschichte* [FS Oscar Cullmann] (Tübingen: J. C. B. Mohr [Paul Siebeck], 1972), 125–42; Wolfgang Bittner, "Jesu Zeichen im Johannesevangelium,' WUNT II, 26 (Tübingen: J. C. B. Mohr [Paul Siebeck], 1987), 134, 195f.; Johannes Beutler, "Martyria," Frankfurter theologische Studien 10 (Frankfurt/Main: J. Knecht, 1972), 237ff.

114. Schnackenburg, *The Gospel According to St. John*, 3:71; Christian Dietzfelbinger, "Die größeren Werke (Joh 14,12f)," *New Testament Studies* 35 (1989), 27–47.

115. Cf. 12:48 and in this regard pages 110–12 above.

116. Josef Blank, *Krisis* (Freiburg im Breisgau: Lambertus Verlag, 1964), 342; the following quotation is also from this work.

117. Thus also with emphasis Helmut Gollwitzer, "Außer Christus kein Heil? (Joh 14,6)" in Willehad Paul Eckert, et al. (eds.), *Antijudaismus im Neuen Testament?* (Munich: Chr. Kaiser Verlag, 1967), 171–94, 188: "Faith is . . . not a precondition, but . . . identical with having eternal life itself."

118. Schnackenburg, *Missionsgedanke,* 71.

119. So it appears according to 6:64; 10:16, 26; 11:52.

120. Cf. in this regard Bultmann, *Theology of the New Testament*, 2:21ff.; Schottroff, *Der Glaubende*, 282ff.; Roland Bergmeier, "Glaube als Gabe nach Johannes," BWANT 112 (Stuttgart: W. Kohlhammer, 1980), 200ff.

121. Blank, *Krisis*, 342.

122. Conzelmann, *Outline*, 354.

123. This is also true if the *idioi* refers to Israel (see Raymond Brown, *The Gospel According to John*, 2 vols., AB 29A & 29B [Garden City, NY: Doubleday, 1975], 1:30; in opposition, Otfried Hofius, "Struktur des Gedankengangs des Logos-Hymnus in Joh 1,1–18," *ZNW* 78 (1987), 1–25, 21.

124. "That there are persons who 'receive' the Logos at all is solely the work and the deed of the Logos itself." Hofius, "Struktur," 22f., with reference to Karl Barth, *Erklärung des Johannesevangeliums. Gesamtausgabe II, 9* (Zürich: Theologischer Verlag, 1976), 91: "The 'Word' finds its own audience."

125. Klaiber, "Der irdische und der himmlische Zeuge," 227.

126. Schnackenburg, *The Gospel According to St. John*, 2:19.

127. Johannes Riedl, *Das Heilswerk Jesu nach Johannes*, Freiburger Theologische Studien 93 (Freiburg im Breisgau: Verlag Herder, 1973), 319ff., 425.

128. Eduard Lohse, *Grundriß der neutestamentlichen Theologie*, Theologische Wissenschaft 5, second edition (Stuttgart: W. Kohlhammer, 1979), 1:137; cf. also 3:11.

129. Cf. Schnackenburg, *The Gospel According to St. John*, 2:105–6.

130. Cf. also 6:35, 8:12 and note the present tense form of the participles.

131. Cf. Riedl, 425ff.; also Conzelmann, *Outline*, 384.

132. Cf. Hosea, Jeremiah, Ezekiel.

133. *Metanoein* is in the aorist mood (2:5, 16, 21; 3:9)!

134. Thus also now Rau, *Reden in Vollmacht*, 403f.

135. The problem lies in the fact that the sources not only do not make any clear statement about infant baptism, but that there is also nothing reported about the "evangelisation" of those growing up in the community. Cf. Kurt Aland, *Die Stellung der Kinder in den frühen Christlichen Gemeinden—und ihre Taufe*, Theologische Existenz heute 138 (Munich: Chr. Kaiser Verlag, 1967); Rainer Lachmann, "Kind," *TRE* 18:158ff.; Ferdinand Hahn, "Kindersegnung und Kindertaufe im ältesten Christentum," in Frankemölle and Kertelge (eds.), *Vom Urchristentum zu Jesus*, 497–507.

Notes to Chapter 5

1. J. R. W. Stott, *The Lausanne Covenant: An Exposition and Commentary* (Minneapolis: World Wide, 1975).

2. Charles G. Finney, "What a Revival of Religion Is," in *Revivals of Religion* (Virginia Beach, VA: CBN University Press, 1978), 9–23.

3. Finney, "False Comforts for Sinners, in *Revivals*, 333–60. Cf. Edward Rommen, "Die Notwendigkeit der Umkehr," *Missionsstrategie und Gemeindeaufbau in der Sicht evangelikaler Missionswissenschaftler* (Giessen: Brunnen Verlag, 1987), 163f.

4. E.g., in Ralph Bell, "Extending the Evangelistic Invitation," in J. D. Douglas (ed.), *The Calling of an Evangelist* (Minneapolis: World Wide Publications, 1987), 189. On the same subject: Stephen Mung'oma, "The Evangelist's Message: The Response of Faith," ibid., 163–70; Billy Graham, "The Evangelist's Appeal for Decision," ibid., 171–74.

5. Alfred Kuen, *Ihr müßt von neuem geboren werden* (Wuppertal: Brockhaus, 1969), 31f. Cf. also Blank, *Krisis*, 342 (see above, 158f.).

6. Cf. Erasmus, *On the Freedom of the Will*, in *Luther and Erasmus: Free Will and Salvation*, tr. and ed. E. Gordon Rupp and Philip S. Watson, Library of Christian Classics 17 (Philadelphia: Westminster Press, 1969), 33–92, esp. 59–63.

7. Thus in John Stott and Basil Meeking (eds.), *The Evangelical-Roman Catholic Dialogue on Mission, 1977–1984: A Report* (Grand Rapids: Wm. B. Eerdmanns, 1986), 40, from an evangelical point of view.

8. Thus the question of Christian Möller in Johannes Hansen and Christian

Möller, *Evangelisation und Theologie* (Neukirchen-Vluyn: Neukirchner Verlag, 1980), 14ff.

9. Eilert Herms, "Entscheidung," *TRE* 9:695.

10. Ibid., 6:697; here also the following quotations.

11. Rudolf Bultmann, *Jesus and the Word* (New York: Scribner's, 1958), 112.

12. "Sola fide" in *Wagnis des Glaubens* (Neukirchen-Vluyn: Neukirchner Verlag, 1979), 260–67, 265.

13. *The Courage to Be* (New Haven: Yale University Press, 1952), 176ff.; on the further development cf. Herms, 6:698.

14. The question was also raised by Heinrich Schlier, *Zeit der Kirche*, 157, 215ff.

15. Cf. his translation of Romans 1:16: "Die Möglichkeit zum Heil ist das Evangelium" [in English: "The possibility of salvation is the good news"; cf. RSV, NRSV, etc.], in "DIKAIOSYNE THEOU," *Exegetica* (1967), 470–75, 473 n.6, and Ernst Käsemann's reply, "'The Righteousness of God' in Paul," in *New Testament Questions of Today*, The New Testament Library (London: SCM Press, 1964), 169–82, 173 n.4; cf. also Bultmann, *Theology of the New Testament*, 302.

16. Cf. Christian Andresen, "Wiederbringung Aller I," *RGG* 6:1693f.

17. The Biblical basis for this was Romans 9; cf. Ernst Kähler, "Prädestination II," *RGG* 5:483–87.

18. Richard Slenczka, "Glaube VI," *TRE* 13:322f.

19. *Solida Declaratio*, Article II, "Free Will or Human Powers," in *The Book of Concord: The Confessions of the Evangelical Lutheran Church*, tr. and ed. Theodore G. Trappert (Philadelphia: Fortress Press, 1959), 525.

20. Kähler, *RGG* 5:486; similarly the Dordrecht Synod (ibid., 487).

21. Barth, *Church Dogmatics*, IV.2:580 ("The Awakening to Conversion").

22. Ibid., IV.1:744.

23. Ibid., IV.1:747; cf. Vorländer, *Christus erkennen*, 62ff.

24. Hans Weder, *Neutestamentliche Hermeneutik* (Zürich: Theologischer Verlag, 1986), 151ff.

25. Dalferth, *Existenz Gottes*, 243. Dalferth thus radicalizes the Lutheran "merely passive" side of conversion (cf. *The Book of Concord*, 533, 538).

26. *Christsein gestalten. Eine Studie zum Weg der Kirche* (Gütersloh: Gütersloher Verlagshaus, 1986), 46.

27. Ibid., 177.

28. Cf. Bultmann, *TDNT* 6:219f.; von Dobbeler, *Glaube als Teilhabe*, 54–73.

29. The assertion of Eberhard Jüngel ("'Theologische Wissenschaft und Glaube' im Blick auf dem Armut Christi," *Unterwegs zur Sache*, 11–33) that "faith is not an achievement of the human agent, but something which happens to him" (p. 23) is an unacceptable generalization of the meaning of Galatians 3:23, 25. It is quite a different matter in Karl Barth's writing (*Church Dogmatics*, IV.1:757–79).

30. Cf. also Karl Rahner's attempt to combine "Anonymous Christianity and the Missionary Task of the Church," *Theological Investigations* 12 (1974), 161–80. Cf. Julian Bednarz, *Chrétiens Anonymes et Évangelisation*.

31. *The Works of John Wesley*, Volume 3: *Sermons III: 71–114*, ed. Albert C. Outler (Nashville: Abingdon Press, 1986), Sermon 110 (pp. 542–46); cf. also "Predestination Calmly Considered" (1752), in Albert C. Outler (ed.), *John Wesley* (New York: Oxford University Press, 1964), 427ff.

32. On December 24, 1740 (see *The Works of the Rev. George Whitefield, M.A.*, 6 vols. [London: Printed for Edward and Charles Dilley, 1771–1772], 4:53–73). Concerning this conflict, cf. Timothy L. Smith, *Whitefield and Wesley on the New Birth* (Grand Rapids: Francis Asbury Press, 1986), and Antoine Schluchter, "Whitefield et Wesley, une controverse sur l'evangelisation," *Revue Reformé* 37 (1986), 177–82.

33. Whitefield, *Works* 4:71.

34. Wesley, "Predestination Calmly Considered," §XLVI, in Outler, *John Wesley*, 447; Sermon 85, "On Working Out Our Own Salvation," §III.4, *Works* 3:201–2.

35. Wesley emphasizes very strongly that faith is God's gift and God's doing: see Sermon 5, "Justification by Faith," §IV.5, *Works* 1:196; "An Earnest Appeal to Men of Reason and Religion," *The Works of John Wesley*, Vol. 11: *The Appeals to Men of Reason and Religion and Certain Related Open Letters*, ed. Gerald R. Cragg (Oxford: Oxford University Press, 1975), §11, pp. 48–9; cf. *A Farther Appeal to Men of Reason and Religion*, Part I, ibid., §I.6, pp. 107–8). People can, however, prepare themself for God's giving through the use of the means of grace ordained by God; cf. Sermons 85 "On Working Out Our Own Salvation" [on Phil 2:12-13], §II.4, *Works* 3:205–6.

36. Regarding this development cf. Michel Weyer, "Die Bedeutung von 'Aldersgate' in Wesleys Leben und Denken," in Michel Weyer, et al., *Im glauben gewiss*, Beiträge zur Geschichte der evangelisch-methodistischen Kirche 32 (1988), 7–39, 36f.

37. Wesley seldom uses the word "conversion"; cf. "A Letter to the Author of the Enthusiasm of Methodists and Papists Compared," *Works* 11:368ff.

38. Wesley not only taught justification by faith, but also sanctification by faith; cf. Sermon 43, "The Scripture Way of Salvation," §III.3, *Works* 2:163–64.

39. Dietrich Stollberg, *Predigt praktisch* (Göttingen, Vandenhoeck & Ruprecht, 1979), 15.

40. Notice the almost painful tension in Article IV of the "Declaration of the Second International Congress for Itinerant Evangelists in Amsterdam," in Douglas (ed.), *The Calling of the Evangelist*, 429: "God loves every human being who, apart from faith in Christ, is under God's judgement and destined to hell."

41. Thus Karl Barth, Konrad Stock, et al.; see pages 113–17 above.

42. Weder, *Neutestamentliche Hermeneutik*, 152; cf. Blank, *Krisis*, 342ff.

43. H, Burkhardt, *Die biblische Lehre von der Bekehrung* (1987), 79.

44. Ibid., 80.

45. Cf. Julius Schniewind, "Das biblische Wort von der Bekehrung", in Otto Schmitz (ed.), *Pietismus und Theologie* (Neukirchen: Verlag des Erziehungsvereins, 1956), 48–61, 57; cf. also Billy Graham, *Peace with God* (Kingswood: Tadsworth, Surrey: The World's Work, 1954), 115: "Are we actually saved by faith? No, we're saved by grace through faith."

46. Dalferth, *Existenz Gottes*, 243.

47. Wolfhart Schlichting, "Was ist Bekehrung?" in Matthias Dannenmann (ed.), *Bekehrung* (Wuppertal: Aussaat-Verlag, 1977), 17–31, indicates the foundation of the Lutheran view that only God is active in conversion in Jeremiah 31:18 (LXX); 1 Peter 2:15 and context; but these passages cannot take away the significance of the many examples of the Act. Imp.; cf. Adolf Schlatter, "Die passive Bekehrung," in Schmitz (ed.), *Pietismus und Theologie*, 87–98, esp. 95ff. Emil Brunner's view is particularly helpful, *Dogmatics*, Vol. II ("We must repent; God alone creates that which is new in us") as is Falk Wagner, "Bekehrung III," *TRE* 5:472!

48. Augustine, Sermon 169 (on Philippians 3:3-16), §XI.13; followed by Wesley, Sermon 63, "The General Spread of the Gospel," §12, *Works* 2:490; cf. Sermon 85, "On Working Out Our Own Salvation," §III.7, *Works* 3:208.

49. Paul Althaus, *Die christliche Wahrheit*, 2:452.

50. Otto Weber, "Not und Verheissung unserer Predigt," in *Wort und Antwort* (Neukirchen: Verlag des Erziehungsvereins, 1966), 17.

51. Hans Weder, "Die Entdeckung des Glaubens im Neuen Testament" in *Glauben heute. Christ werden—Christ bleiben* (Gütersloh, Gütersloher Verlaghaus, 1988), 52–63, 58.

52. Ibid.; cf. Johannes Hansen, in Hansen and Möller (eds.), *Evangelisation und Theologie*, 50.

53. Eberhard Jüngel, "The World as Possibility and Actuality—The Ontology of the Doctrine of Justification," in *Theological Essays*, trans. J. B. Webster (Edinburgh: T & T Clark, 1989), 95–123.

54. Ibid., 230.

55. Cf. the excellent essay by Wolf Krötke, "Gott auf der Suche nach dem Menschen," *ZTK* 86 (1989), 517–32: "The lost state of the human person is not a divine prejudice, but the reality in which God encounters the human person. It is no indication, therefore, of 'openness' for this reality if the lostness of the human person is not even a topic to be discussed" (532). "God's searching for the lost . . . corresponds to God's essential nature . . ." (527).

56. Joachim Heubach characterizes evangelistic proclamation by means of another image in Gerhard Maier and Gerhard Rost (eds.), *Taufe—Wiedergeburt—Bekehrung in evangelistischer Perspektive* (Lahr-Dinglingen: Verlag des St. Johannis-Druckerei, 1980), 71–86: As a mother kneels before her child when it is to learn to walk and calls, urging, "Come, my child, come!", so evangelistic proclamation "urges" its hearer "to make the step of faith" (75).

57. Thus also Jüngel, "*Extra Christum nulla salus*," *Theological Essays*, 186: "In view of the justification of all which has already taken place, faith is that human attitude in which we affirm that we are justified and thereby also affirm that we need add nothing to our salvation and have nothing to add apart from this affirmation."

58. Letter to "John Smith" (December 30, 1745), Wesley, *Works* 26:182.

59. Ibid., 2:176ff.

60. In opposition to Schlier, *Zeit der Kirche*, 215ff.

61. Cf. the instructive examples of Hans Kasdorf, *Christian Conversion in Context* (Scottsdale: Herald Press, 1980), 65ff.

62. Cf. the reflections of the Mennonite Kasdorf concerning "conversion in the passing of generations," ibid.

63. Ibid., 172, 178.

64. Theo Sorg, "Kindertaufe und Gemeindeaufbau," in *Christus vertrauen— Gemeinde erneuern* (Stuttgart: Calwer-Verlag, 1987), 84–106.

65. Nevertheless, the "Old Baptist" view is of baptism as the dutiful confessional action of the human person (as also for Kasdorf, op. cit.).

66. In opposition to Ch. Möller, in Hansen and Möller, *Evangelisation und Theologie*, 16, 36 (cf. Hansen, ibid., 26ff).

67. Thus Paul Althaus, "Die Bekehrung in reformatorischer und pietistischer Sicht," in *Um die Wahrheit des Evangeliums. Aufsatze und Vortrage von Paul Althaus* (Stuttgart: Calver Verlag, 1962), 242: "The New Testament pattern is valid only in a 'missionary situation,' not in the 'internal ecclesial situation'"; cf. Wilfried Joest, *Dogmatik*, 2:481ff.; Falk Wagner, "Bekehrung II/III," *TRE* 5:459–80, esp. 474–77.

68. Althaus, "Die Bekehrung," 243.

69. Ebeling, *Dogmatik*, 3:44

70. Ibid. 153

71. Klaiber, *Wo Leben wieder Leben ist*, 24ff.

72. In this regard, cf. Paul Althaus, "Paulus und Luther über den Menschen," Studien der Luther-Akademie 14, 3rd edition (Gütersloh: C. Bertelsmann Verlag, 1958); Wilfried Joest, "Paulus und das Luthersche Simul Justus et Peccator," *Kerygma und Dogma* 1 (1955), 263–320.

73. Cf. Gal 3:27; Col 3:9f. with Rom 13:14; Eph 4:22-24.

74. That is the biblical meaning of the old idea of the "immortal soul."

75. Cf. Klaiber, *Rechtfertigung und Gemeinde*, 101ff., 214ff., 249ff.

76. Cf. Bernard Lonergan, in Walter E. Conn (ed.), *Conversion: Perspectives on Personal and Social Transformation* (New York: Alban House, 1978), 13.

77. Cf. Michael Trowitzsch, *Gott als "Gott für dich." Eine Verabschiedung des Heilsegoismus*, BEvTh 92 (Munich: Chr. Kaiser Verlag, 1983).

78. Emilio Castro, "Conversion and Social Transformation," in J. C. Bennett (ed.), *Christian Social Ethics in a Changing World: An Ecumenical Theological Inquiry* (New York: Association Press, 1966), 348–66; Jim Wallis, *The Call to Conversion* (San Francisco: Harper & Row, 1981); O. E. Costas, *Liberating News*, 112ff.; Chris Sugden, "Evangelicals and Wholistic Evangelism"; further: Edward P. Wimberly, *Liberation and Human Wholeness: The Conversion Experiences of Black People in Slavery and Freedom* (Nashville: Abingdon Press, 1986); William F. Warren, Jr., "Evangelism in the Context of Liberation Theology: structural sins and structural conversions," *Journal of the Academy for Evangelism in Theological Education* 6 (1990–91), 5–31. Regarding the integration of the various "conversion perspectives," see Donald Evans, "Conflicting Paradigms of Conversion," in Alastair Kee and Eugene T. Long (eds.), *Being and Truth: Essays in Honor of John Macquarrie* (London: SCM Press, 1986), 136–54. See also the following thematic materials: *Ecumenical Review* 19 (1967), 252ff., and 44 (1992), "Bekehrung" by J. Fichtner, K. H. Rengstorf, G. Friedrich, W. Joest, and W. Freytag, *RGG* 1:976–84; Gabriel

Fackre, "Conversion," *Andover-Newton Quarterly* 14 (1974), 171–89; José Míguez Bonino, "Conversion, New Creature and Commitment," *International Review of Mission* 72 (1983), 324–32; Park Hyung Kyn, "Conversion as Pilgrimage to Liberation," ibid., 380–87; the collection edited by Walter E. Conn, *Conversion*; Hugh T. Kerr and John Mulder (eds.), *Conversion: The Christian Experience* (Grand Rapids: William B. Eerdmans, 1983); Charles R. Taber, "God vs. Idols: A Model of Conversion," *Journal of the Academy for Evangelism in Theological Education* 3 (1977–78), 20–32; David F. Wells, *Turning to God: Biblical Conversion in the Modern World* (Grand Rapids: Baker Book House, 1985); V. Bailey Gillespie, *The Dynamics of Religious Conversion: Identity and Transformation* (Birmingham: Religious Education Press, 1991); Tony Baker, "What is Conversion?" *Churchman* 105 (1991), 6–17; and the bibliography by Lewis Rambo, *Current Research on Religious Conversion* 8 (1982), 146–59, with 432 titles!

Notes to Chapter 6

1. See the definition of William James in *Varieties of Religious Experience* (New York: Longmans, Green, 1902; reprint 1952), 186: "the process, gradual or sudden, by which a self hitherto divided, and consciously wrong, inferior, and unhappy, becomes unified and consciously right, superior, and happy, in consequence of its firmer hold upon religious realities"; that of Richard Travisano, quoted in John Loftland and Norman Skonovd, "Conversion Motifs," *JSSR* 20 (1981), 373–85, 375: "a radical reorganization of identity, meaning, life"; or that of Lewis R. Rambo: "a significant, sudden transformation of a person's loyalties, pattern of life, and focus of energy" ("Psychological Perspectives on Conversion," *Pacific Theological Review* 13 [1980], 21–26, 22), which James W. Fowler has expanded in *Stages of Faith: The Psychology of Human Development and the Quest for Meaning* (San Francisco: Harper & Row, 1981): "Conversion is a significant recentering of one's previous conscious or unconscious images of value and power, and the conscious adoption of a new set of master stories in the commitment to reshape one's life in a new community of interpretation and action" (281f.). The available literature about such research can hardly be comprehended; my personal bibliography includes more than 250 titles.

2. Arthur Darby Nock, *Conversion: The Old and the New in Religions from Alexander the Great to Augustine of Hippo* (Oxford: Clarendon Press, 1933; reprint 1969), 7. Nock has sought to distill the most singular aspects of the Christian understanding of conversion in the ancient world; cf. in this regard Ramsey Macmullen, "Two Types of Conversion to Early Christianity," *Vigiliae Christianae* 37 (1983), 174–92; Macmullen, "Conversion: An Historian's View," *The Second Century* 5:2 (1985–1986), 67–96; further, Eugene V. Gallagher, "Conversion and Community in Late Antiquity," *Journal of Religion* 73 (1993), 1–15.

3. Richard Travisiano, "Alternation and Conversion as Qualitatively Different Transformations," in G. P. Stone and M. Garverman (eds.), *Social*

Psychology Through Symbolic Interaction (1970), 594–606, cited in James T. Richardson, "Types of Conversion and 'Conversion Careers' in New Religious Movements," Paper for the American Association for the Advancement of Science Annual Meeting (1977), 14ff.

4. Cf. the remark of Romano Guardini, *Die Bekehrung des Hl. Aurelius Augustinus*, third edition (1959), 167f., that Augustine "did not become a Christian by virtue of that conversion, for the simple reason that he had never been a heathen. In the deepest depths of his thinking he had always been a Christian—in as much as it is possible to be a Christian without decision."

5. In regard to Paul, Augustine, and Wesley, Eric Routley speaks of "archetypal conversion experiences" (*The Gift of Conversion* [London: Lutterworth Press, 1952], 26); cf. Paul B. Maves, "Conversion: A Behavioral Category," *Review of Religious Research* 5 [1963], 41–48); cf. Hans Jürgen Baden, *Literatur und Bekehrung* (Stuttgart: Ernst Klett Verlag, 1968); Christian Gremmels, "Bekehrung und Lebensgeschichte," *Wissenschaft und Praxis in Kirche und Gesellschaft* 66 (1977), 488–505.

6. One might have mentioned Ignatius Loyola, George Whitefield, or C. S. Lewis just as well; on the other hand, virtually no one today speaks of Luther's "conversion," cf. Martin Brecht, *Martin Luther. Sein Weg zur Reformation, 1483–1521*, third edition (Stuttgart: Calwer-Verlag, 1989), 215ff.

7. Cf. Augustine, *Confessions* VIII.11, 25f.; Guardini, op. cit.; Alfred Schindler, *TRE* 4:649ff.

8. Cf. *Werke in Auswahl*, ed. Erhard Peschke (1969), 4–29; Kurt Aland, "Bemerkungen zu A. H. Francke und seinem Bekehrungserlebnis," in *Kirchgeschichtliche Entwürfe* (1960), 543f.; Friedrich de Boor, *TRE* 11:313.

9. Cf. *The Works of John Wesley*, Volume 18: *Journal and Diaries I (1735–1738)*, ed. W. Reginald Ward and Richard P. Heitzenrater (Nashville: Abingdon Press, 1988), 206ff., 242ff. (re: May 24, 1738; Martin Schmidt, *John Wesley: A Theological Biography*, Volume 1, trans. Norman P. Goldhawk (Nashville: Abingdon Press, [1962]), 213–309; Weyer, "Die Bedeutung von 'Aldersgate,'" bibliography.

10. Cf. Paul Claudel, *Gesammelte Werke VI: Religion* (Heidelberg/Einsiedeln: Benziger, 1962), 10ff.; Baden, *Literatur und Bekehrung*, 76–79.

11. This is true, interestingly enough, for most of the conversions which have found literary form; cf., e.g., Max Dauthendey, "Letzte Reise," *Gesammelte Werke 2*, cited in Hjalmar Sundén, *Religion und die Rollen. Eine psychologische Untersuchung der Frömmigkeit* (Berlin: Töpelmann, 1966), 21ff.; Keith Miller, *The Taste of New Wine* (Waco, TX: Word Books, 1965). An investigation of the bibliographical material from early Methodism has demonstrated that the direct influence of the large revival meetings on conversion and rebirth is also less evident than is often assumed; see Thomas R. Albin, "An Empirical Study of Early Methodist Spirituality," in Theodore Runyon (ed.), *Wesleyan Theology Today* (Nashville: Kingswood Books, 1985), 275–90.

12. This was especially true of Wesley; cf. Karl Heinz Voigt, *Hat John Wesley sich am 24. Mai 1738 "bekehrt"?* EmK heute 57 (Stuttgart: Christliches Verlagshaus, 1988); Richard P. Heitzenrater, "Great Expectations: Aldersgate and the Evidence of Genuine Christianity," in Randy L. Maddox (ed.), *Alders-*

gate Reconsidered (Nashville: Kingswood Books, 1990), 48–91. Cf., as well, the provocative title of the book by Routley, *The Gift of Conversion*.

13. Additionally Gremmels, especially, "Bekehrung und Lebensgeschichte," 197ff. Of interest is the later partial retraction of this judgment by Wesley in the errata of the 1774 edition of his works (cf. *Works* 18:214f.; Weyer, 36f.).

14. "Francke emphasized that conversion was an extraordinary, supranatural phenomenon, a 'work above all nature.'" Erhard Peschke, *Studien zur Theologie A. H. Franckes*, 2 vols. (Berlin: Evangelische Verlaganstalt, 1964–1966), 1:45.

15. Wesley and Whitefield did not preach the necessity of conversion, but of new birth; cf. Timothy L. Smith, *Whitefield and Wesley on the New Birth* (Grand Rapids: Francis Asbury Press, 1986); Voigt, *Hat John Wesley sich am 24. Mai 1738 "bekehrt"?* Cf. also Wesley, "A Letter to the Author of the Enthusiasm of Methodists and Papists Compared," *Works* 11:368f. The possibility and necessity of a faith in assurance of salvation is the central message of Wesley's sermons after Aldersgate; regarding his careful retraction in old age in Sermon 106, "On Faith," *Works*, 3:491ff.; cf. Weyer, 37.

16. See also Jean-Pierre Belche, "Die Bekehrung zum Christentum nach Augustins Büchlein De Catechizandis Rudibus," *Augustiniana* [Louvain] 27 (1977), 26–69, 333–63; 28 (1968), 255–87; 29 (1979), 247–79; 32 (1982), 42–87, 282–11; and Elisabeth Fink-Dendorfer, *Conversio: Motive und Motivierung zur Bekehrung in der Alten Kirche* (Frankfurt/Main: Verlag Peter Lang, 1986), 134–232, who clearly draws out the differences between reports of conversions and catechetics in the early church (341–45).

17. Cf. Baden, *Literatur und Bekehrung*, 198ff. Ignatius Loyola must also be mentioned in this context; cf. Brendan Byrne, "Ignatius Loyala and John Wesley: Experience and Strategies of Conversion," *Colloquium [Sidney] 19* (1986), 54–66.

18. Maves, "Conversion," 47.

19. Hans Leitner, *Psychologie jugendlicher Religioosität innerhalb des deutschen Methodismus* (München: Beck, 1930); cf. Werner Gruehn, *Die Frömmigkiet der Gegenwart*, second edition (Konstanz: Friedrich Bahn Verlag, 1960), 50ff. (re: Starbuck), 67ff. (re: Leitner).

20. Ronald C. Wimberley, Thomas C. Hood, C. M. Lipsey, Donald Clelland, and Marguerite Hay, "Conversion in a Billy Graham Crusade: Spontaneous Event or Ritual Perfomance?" *Sociological Quarterly* 16 (1975), 162–70, 166, cf. also Frederick L. Whitam, "Revivalism as Institutionalized Behavior: An Analysis of the Social Base of a Billy Graham Crusade," *Social Science Quarterly* 49 (1968), 115–27; W. E. Oates, "Conversion: Sacred and Secular," in Conn, *Conversion*, 149–69, 164; John G. Stackhouse, Jr., "Billy Graham and the Nature of Conversion: A Paradigm Case," *Studies in Religion* 21 (1992), 337ff.

21. Erik Erikson, *Childhood and Society*, second edition (New York: W. W. Norton & Co., 1963; Fowler, *Stages of Faith*, 151ff.

22. John Westerhoff III, "A Necessary Paradox, Catechesis and Evangelism, Nurture and Conversion," *RelEd* 73 (1978), 409–16, 414.

23. James initially distinguishes, as does Starbuck, between the "volitional" conversion (202) and conversion by "self-surrender"; in the latter "the subconscious effects are more abundant and often startling" (204). Then there are "those striking instantaneous instances . . . in which, often amid tremendous emotional excitement or perturbation of three senses, a complete division is established in the twinkling of an eye between the old life and the new" (213).

24. Sigmund Freud, "Eine religiöse Erfahrung" (1928), in *Gesammelte Werke*, fifth edition (Frankfurt: S. Fischer, 1976), 14:391–96. In the thought of C. G. Jung, experiences of conversion are obviously integrated in the process of individuation; Seward Hiltner, "Toward a Theology of Conversion in the Light of Psychology," in Conn, *Conversion*, 179–90.

25. Erik Erikson, *Young Man Luther: A Study in Psychoanalysis and History* (New York: W. W. Norton & Co., 1958).

26. Cf. re: Augustine: James E. Dittes, "Continuities Between the Life and Thought of Augustine," *JSSR* 5 (1965), 130–43; "[He] abandoned the effort to be a father. Instead he became an obedient son" (137). Cf. also Lawrence J. Daly, "Psychohistory and St. Augustine's Conversion Process: An Historiographical Critique," *Augustiniana* [Louvain] 28 (1978), 231–54. Re: Wesley, see Grace Elizabeth Harrison, *Son to Susannah* (Nashville: Cokesbury Press, 1938); Robert L. Moore, *John Wesley and Authority: A Psychological Perspective*, AAR Dissertation Series 29 (Missoula, Montana: Scholars Press, 1979), which works with Sundén's role theory.

27. Joel Allison. "Religious Conversion: Regression and Progression in an Adolescent Experience," *JSSR* 8 (1969), 23–38.

28. Cf. Michael Balint, *The Basic Fault: Therapeutic Aspects of Regression* (London: Tavistock, 1968), chapter 22; a critical response is found in Klaus Winkler, *Werden wie die Kinder? Christlicher Glaube und Regression* (Mainz: Grünewald, 1992).

29. Sundén, *Religion und die Rollen*, 363–96; cf. Albert H. Zetterberg, "The Religious Conversion as a Change of Social Roles," *Sociology and Social Research* 36 (1952), 159–66.

30. Let me mention but a few works: John Lofland and Rodney Stark, "Becoming a World-Saver: A Theory of Conversion to a Deviant Perspective," *American Sociological Review* 30 (1965), 862–75; John Lofland, "'Becoming a World-Saver' Revisited," *American Behavioral Scientist* 20 (1977), 805–18; James T. Richardson and Mary Stewart, "Conversion Models and the Jesus Movement," ibid., 819–38; Max Heirich, "Change of Heart: A Test of Some Widely Held Theories about Religious Conversion," *American Journal of Sociology* 83 (1977), 653–80; Theodore Long and Jefrey K. Hadden, "Religious Conversion: Integrating the Brainwashing and Drift Models," *JSSR* 22 (1983), 1–14; Willem Kox, Wim Meens, and Harm 'tHart, "Religious Conversion of Adolescents: Testing the Lofland and Stark Model of Religious Conversion," *Sociological Analysis* 52:3 (1991), 227–40; an overview and discussion of more recent literature can be found in Larry D. Shinn, "Who Gets to Define Religion? The Conversion/Brainwashing Controversy," *Religious Studies Review* 13 (1993), 195–202.

31. Cf. Richardson, "Types of Conversion."

32. James A. Beckford, "Accounting for Conversion," *British Journal of*

Sociology 29 (1978), 249–62; concerning the connection between the reporting and the experience of conversion cf. also Gremmels, *Bekehrung*, 496: "Conversion has occurred to a certain extent according to the way in which it has been described."

33. John Lofland and Norman Skonovd, "Conversion Motifs," *JSSR* 20 (1981), 373–85.

34. Brock Kilbourne and James T. Richardson, "Paradigm Conflict, Types of Conversion and Conversion Theories," *Sociological Analysis* 50 (1988), 1–21.

35. Ibid., 15.

36. Ibid., 14.

37. William Sargant, *Battle for the Mind* (London: William Heinemann, 1957); concerning the historical, psychological, and theological debate with Sargant, cf. Ian Ramage, *The Battle for the Free Mind* (London: George Allen and Unwin, 1967).

38. Kilbourne and Richardson, 13.

39. Fowler, *Stages of Faith*, 269–91; additionally there is the impressive report of "Mary's Pilgrimage" (217–68); cf. also James Fowler, "John Wesley's Development in Faith," in M. Douglas Meeks (ed.), *The Future of Methodist Theological Traditions* (Nashville: Abingdon Press, 1985), 172–92.

40. Regarding the debate with Fowler, see Stephen Happel and James J. Walker, *Conversion and Discipleship: A Christian Foundation for Ethics and Doctrine* (Philadelphia: Fortress Press, 1986).

41. Max Frisch, *Stiller* (Frankfurt/Main: Fischer Verlag, 1965), 244.

42. In Joachim Scharfenberg, et al., "Religion-Selbstbewußtsein-Identität," *Theologische Existenz heute* 182 (Munich: Chr. Kaiser Verlag, 1974), 44–57.

43. Ibid., 55; cf. Gremmels, *Bekehrung*, 501: "Conversion is acceptance of the past carried out through [its] radical reformulation in the light of the new."

44. Cf. Gerd Theißen, *Psychological Aspects of Pauline Theology*, trans. John P. Calvin (Philadelphia: Fortress Press, 1986), 222–48.

45. Dietrich Stollberg and Dieter Lührmann, "Tiefenpsychologische oder historisch-kritische Exegese? Identität und der Tod des Ichs (Gal 2,19-20)," in Yorick Spiegel (ed.), *Doppeldeutlich. Tiefendimensionen biblischer Texte* (Munich: Chr. Kaiser Verlag, 1978), 215–36. Cf. the critique by Michael Klessmann, "Zum Problem der Identität des Paulus," *Wege zum Menschen* 41 (1989), 156–72.

46. Fritz Riemann, *Grundformen der Angst* (Munich and Basel: Ernst Reinhardt Verlag, 1976), 11.

47. Cf. Rambo, "Psychological Perspectives," 22: "A strong view of the incarnation leads me to believe that God works through the so-called natural world to fulfill God's purposes." To recognize the "psychic mechanisms" which may have effected a conversion by no means implies a judgment as to its spiritual significance!

48. Thus it was even for Paul, in 1 Tim. 1:15ff.

49. This is portrayed most effectively in James, where former drinkers tell of their conversions while the reporter, also an alcoholic, raises the question, "I wonder if God can save *me*?" (198–99)

50. Maves, "Conversion," 46, quotes DeSanctis who talks of "adaptation for defense."

Notes to Chapter 7

1. For a series of addresses on this theme by John Paul II, cf. the Angelus address in St. Peter's on 14 January 1990; for the Lausanne Movement cf. the Manila Document II, p. 11; the Lambeth Conference of 1988 called for a "Decade of Evangelism" (Resolution. Pp. 43f.); regarding The United Methodist Church, cf. the mission declaration of the 1988 General Conference, "Grace Upon Grace—God's Mission and Our Task" and also the program "Vision 2000."

2. Cf. Hans-Werner Gensichen, *Glauben für die Welt. Theologische Aspekte der Mission* (Gütersloh: Gütersloher Verlagshaus, 1971), 49; Ferdinand Hahn, "Der Sendungsauftrag des Auferstandenen," 28.

3. Gerhard Schneider, "Der Missionsauftrag," 72, 75f. Regarding the Acts of the Apostles this is contested by Christoph Burchard, *Der dreizehnte Zeuge*, 177ff., but in my opinion Burchard is not correct.

4. Cf. Jürgen Roloff, *TRE* 3:435f.; in contrast Philip is, strangely enough, not called an "evangelist" until he has settled in Caesarea (Acts 21:9). Is that which is intended "here as in 2 Tim 4:5 the function of the congregational leader" (Roloff, *Apostelgeschichte*, 310)? In contrast Gerhard Schneider, *Apostelgeschichte*, 304 n.25, would rather interpret the designation "in connection with 8:4f., 35, 40, with the meaning 'preacher of the gospel.'"

5. Further, at length, Norbert Brox, "Zur christlichen Mission in der Spätantike," in Kertelge (ed.), *Mission im Neuen Testament*, 190–237, 194ff.

6. Cf. Jim Petersen, *Evangelism as a Lifestyle* (Colorado Springs, CO.: NavPress, 1980).

7. Regarding the exegetical questions, cf. Luz, *Matthew 1–7*, 246–55.

8. Hahn, "Der Sendungsauftrag des Auferstandenen": "Whoever belongs to Jesus has taken on the missionary task, independent of how such a person makes his or her contribution, case by case" (38). "It is not because of any character as a command which these word of the Resurrected may have which make them binding upon us, but because their witnesses are bound to the self-revelation of Jesus, who passes his assignment from the father, and involves all who become his disciples in his ministry and service" (39).

9. Cf. the wonderful interpretation of this passage in Ernst Käsemann, "A Pauline Version of the 'Amor Fati'," in *New Testament Questions of Today*, 217–35, esp. 233f.

10. This is especially pronounced in Oswald Sanders, *The Divine Art of Soul-Winning* (London: Pickering & Inglis Ltd., 1977); cf. the discussion of this topic in Eduard Rommen, *Die Notwendigkeit der Umkehr. Missionsstrategie und Gemeindeaufbau in der Sicht evangelikaler Missionswissenschaftler Nordamerikas* (Giessen-Basel: Brunnen Verlag 1987), 160ff.

11. That this does happen in Evangelical circles is shown in E. D. Osburn, "Those Who Have Never Heard: Have They No Hope?" *Journal of the Evangelical Theological Society* 32:3 (1989), 367–72.

12. This has been emphasized by reference to Mark 13:10 that the proclamation among the nations is the precondition for the Second Coming of Christ.

13. It is not possible within the framework of this study to introduce and

discuss the vast amount of relevant literature. Fundamental is David McGavran, *Understanding Church Growth*, third edition, revised and edited by Peter Wagner (Grand Rapids: William B. Eerdmans, 1990); cf. the summary of his life's work in *Effective Evangelism: A Theological Mandate* (Phillipsburg, NJ: Presbyterian and Reformed Publishing House, 1988). Additionally, the critical discussion of the literature in Rommen, *Die Notwendigkeit der Umkehr*, 66ff.; Michael Herbst, *Missionarischer Gemeindeaufbau in der Volkskirche* (Stuttgart: Calwer-Verlag, 1987), 253ff.; William J. Abraham, "Church Growth Theory and the Future of Evangelism," *Journal of the Academy for Evangelism in Theological Education* 2 (1986–87), 20–30. Ecclesial interests also provide motivation for evangelism when concern about the substance of the church calls for it; cf. e.g., Fritz and Christian Schwarz, *Theologie des Gemeindeaufbaus* (Neukirchen-Vluyn: Aussaat- und Schriftenmissions-Verlag. 1984), 85ff.

14. The passive formulations are characteristic of the action of God! George W. Peters, *A Theology of Church Growth* (Grand Rapids: Zondervan, 1981), on the other hand, would like to derive principles of church growth from the Acts of the Apostles (cf. 231ff.)

15. George G. Hunter III, *To Spread the Power: Church Growth in the Wesleyan Spirit* (Nashville: Abingdon Press, 1987), speaks about the "marketing approach" (138) and a "marketing strategy" (142)!

16. Cf. Rommen, *Die Notwendigkeit der Umkehr*, 74ff.; Herbst, *Missionarischer Gemeindeaufbau*, 259ff.; Hunter, *To Spread the Power*, 173ff.

17. Cf. the differentiated presentation in Gensichen, *Glaube für die Welt*. Cf. also the well-known dictum of Wesley's: "Preaching like an apostle, without joining together those that are awakened, and training them up in the ways of God, is only begetting children for the murderer"; *The Works of John Wesley*, Volume 21: *Journal and Diaries IV (1755–1765)*, ed. W. Reginald Ward and Richard P. Heitzenrater (Nashville: Abingdon Press, 1992), 424 (25 August 1763).

18. Thus Christian Wolff, *1. Korintherbrief*, 33.

19. I recall once again the book by Michael Trowitzsch, *Gott als "Gott für dich"*, BEvT 92 (Munich: Chr. Kaiser Verlag, 1983), with its provocative subtitle, "A Farewell to Salvation Egotism."

20. Thus many evangelical authors, and thus also the much-used volume by Robert E. Coleman, *The Master Plan of Evangelism* (Grand Rapids: Fleming H. Revell Co., 1963), which had its 63rd printing 1993!.

21. Cf. Romans 12:1f. and especially the message of 1 Peter; in this regard see above, chapter 2, note 82.

22. I will mention only the most important literature: Fritz Schwarz and Christian A. Schwarz, *Theologie des Gemeindeaufbaus* (Neukirchen-Vluyn: Aussaat- und Schriftenmissions-Verlag, 1984); Rudolf Weth (ed.), *Diskussion zur Theologie des Gemeindeaufbaus* (Neukirchen-Vluyn: Aussaat-und Schriftenmissions-Verlag, 1986); Manfred Seitz, *Erneuerung der Gemeinde: Gemeindeaufbau und Spiritualität* (Göttingen: Vandenhoeck & Ruprecht, 1985); Michael Herbst, *Missionarischer Gemeindeaufbau in der Volkskirche* (Stuttgart: Calwer Verlag, 1987); see esp. the bibliography; Christian Möller, *Lehre vom Gemeindeaufbau*, 2 vols. (Göttingen: Vandenhoeck & Ruprecht, 1982, 1990); Theo

Sorg, *Christus vertrauen—Gemeinde erneuern. Beiträge zum missionarischen Gemeindeaufbau in der Volkskirche,* second edition (Stuttgart: Calwer-Verlag, 1988); Loren B. Mead, *The Once and Future Church: Reinventing the Congregation for a New Mission Frontier* (New York: Alban Institute, 1991); Maxie D. Dunnam, *Congregational Evangelism: A Pastor's View* (Nashville: Discipleship Resources, 1991).

23. For this reason as well, I consider a program of "total evangelism" to be unbiblical (as opposed to George W. Peters, *Saturation Evangelism* [Grand Rapids: Zondervan, 1970]), even if the greater of the two dangers today certainly remains "congregational centripetalism" instead of "congregational centrifugalism" (43).

24. In the overall biblical picture, diaconal endeavor would have to be more strongly emphasized. In any case, the definition of the Augsburg Confession, Article VII, proves to be too narrow for a total description of the essence and nature of the church

25. Cf. the connection between intercession for the rulers and the fundamental soteriological declaration in 1 Tim 2:1-6.

26. Cf. John 13:35 and additionally the exceptionally fortunate expression of evangelistic "body language" of the congregation as the Body of Christ in Vernard Eller, *Proclaiming Good Tidings—Evangelism for the Faith Community* (Elgin, Illinois: Brethren Press, 1987), 29ff.

27. I hope that in The United Methodist Church the theological difference between "baptised membership" and "professing membership" will not be levelled out in this respect. The study document *By Water and the Spirit* (Nashville: The United Methodist Publishing House, 1996) is not sufficiently clear on this matter. Cf. the excellent presentation of the German United Methodist position by Rudolf Weth in Christine Lienemann-Perrin (ed.), *Taufe und Kirchenzugehörigkeit* (Munich: Chr. Kaiser Verlag, 1983), 358ff.

28. Cf. Norbert Mette, "Evangelisierung in einer religiös indifferenten Gesellschaft," *Werkstatt Gemeinde* 7 (1989), 151–70.

29. Cf. Walter Klaiber, *Embraced by the Spirit*, 52ff.; Herbst, *Missionarischer Gemeindeaufbau*, 277ff., 359ff.

30. S. Christian Möller, "Von der Eindeutigkeit der Verkündigung im Namen Jesu: Zur evangelistischen Dimension kirchlichen Handelns," *TBei* 13 (1982), 158–77; Manfred Seitz, "Elementare Verkündigung und veränderte Gemeinde," in *Erneuerung der Gemeinde*, 29–37.

31. Jim Petersen, *Evangelism as a Lifestyle* (Colorado Springs, CO.: NavPress, 1980).

32. Gottfried Keller, "Die Leute von Seldwyla," in *Gesammelte Werke*, ed. H. Schumacher (Zürich: Büchergilde Gutenberg, 1960), 1:901ff.

33. Very problematic is, for example, D. James Kennedy, *Evangelism Explosion,* second edition (Wheaton: Tyndale, 1976).

34. Thus, for example, the course by William J. Abraham, *Basic Christianity* (Uvalde, TX: First United Methodist Church, 1989).

35. See above, 99–101.

36. As we saw in chapter one, there is little homilectical literature on the question. Besides the handbooks mentioned on p. 20ff. above, cf. Andreas

Husar, *Missionarische Predigt im Gottesdienst* (Berlin: Evangelische Verlagsanstalt, 1987), bibliography; Gerhard Röckle, "Homiletische Überlegungen zur evangelistischen Predigt," *TBei 17* (1986), 137–44; Alan Walker, *Evangelistic Preaching* (Grand Rapids: Francis Asbury Press, 1988).

37. In principle the distinction should be made, as do Fritz and Christian Schwarz, between "congregational sermon and evangelistic speech" (87ff.). Practically, and regarding the locus, such a separation is not appropriate. Cf. the discussion on this matter in Johann Hansen and Christian Möller, *Evangelistaion und Theologie,* 31f., 39ff. and the continuation in Christian Möller, "Von der Eindeutigkeit," 160ff.

38. Werner Jetter, "Elementare Predigt," *ZTK* 59 (1962), 346–88, esp. 382ff.; Johannes Hempel, "Elementare Verkündigung," *Deutsches Pfarrerblatt* 30 (1970), 297–300; Rolf Heue, "Elementare Verkündigung," *Das missionarische Wort* 29 (1976), 17–23; cf. the animated discussion in this regard between Fritz and Christian Schwarz (93ff.) and Friedrich Winter, *Handbuch der praktischen Theologie, II. Der Gottesdienst. Die Kirchlichen Handlungen. Die Predigt* (Berlin: Evangelische Verhagsanstalt, 1974), 279–82.

39. Cf. Luther, *On the Bondage of the Will,* Part V, in *Luther and Erasmus: Free Will and Salvation,* tr. and ed. E. Gordon Rupp and Philip S. Watson, Library of Christian Classics 17 (Philadelphia: Westminster Press, 1969), 263ff.

40. Hans-Hermann Ulrich, "Kommunikative Evangelisation," *Das missionarische Wort* 29 (1976), 9–16.

41. Stephen Mung'oma, "The Evangelist's Message: The Response of Faith" in J. D. Douglas (ed.), *The Calling of an Evangelist* (Minneapolis: World Wide Publications, 1987), 163–70, 167; on the same matter, see Billy Graham, "The Evangelist's Appeal for Decision," ibid., 171–77; Ralph Bell, "Extending the Evangelistic Invitation," ibid., 183–89; Lloyd Merle Perry, "Preaching for Decision," in Robert E. Coleman, *Evangelism on the Cutting Edge* (Old Tappan, N.J.: Fleming H. Revell, 1986), 15–126; Alan Walker, *Evangelistic Preaching,* 1988, 74ff. ("How to Call for Commitment"); William Abraham, *The Logic of Evangelism,* 131 (bibliography).

42. Heribert Mühlen, *Die Grundentscheidung,* 141ff.

43. Cf. the studies—however problematic their methods may be—of David L. Altheide and John M. Johnson, "Counting Souls. A Study of Counseling at Evangelical Crusade, *Pacific Sociological Review* 20 (1977), 323–48, which demonstrates how the inner (and outward) pressure for success and the fixation on a specific course of a "decision for Christ" prevents the counseling assistants from being sensitive to the person with whom they are speaking. I find similar observations in Larry C. Ingram, "Evangelism as Frame Intrusion: Observations on Witnessing in Public Places," *JSSR* 28 (1988), 17–26.

44. See above, note 23.

45. Christian Möller, Von der Eindeutigkeit der Verkündigung, 171ff., with explicit reference to Helmut Tacke, *Glaubenshilfe als Lebenshilfe* (Göttingen: Vandenhoeck & Ruprecht, 1975).

46. Cf. Jim L. Webb, "Evangelism and the Theological Curriculum," *Journal of the Academy for Evangelism in Theological Education* 3 (1987–88), 40–45; William J. Abraham, "Athens, Aldersgate, and SMU: Reflections on the

Place of Evangelism in the Theological Encyclopedia," *Journal of the Academy for Evangelism in Theological Education* 5 (1989–90), 64–75.

47. As encouraging examples of growing efforts in this direction I want to mention James C. Logan (ed.), *Theology and Evangelism in the Wesleyan Heritage* (Nashville: Kingswood Books, 1994), and Logan (ed.), *Christ for the World: United Methodist Bishops Speak on Evangelism* (Nashville: Kingswood Books, 1996).

Index of Biblical Texts

Index of Authors